RIDGEWELL'S FLYING FORTRESSES

RIDGEWELL'S FLYING FORTRESSES

The 381st Bombardment Group (H) in World War II

Ron Mackay

Schiffer Military History
Atglen, PA

Acknowledgements

I would like to express my gratitude to the members of the 381BGMA and their families.
Over 22 years they have shown un-stinted friendship. The bulk of this book"s content derives from numerous personal files, and specific names coming to mind are; Ray Ater, Bill Blackmon, Turner Brashear, Maurice Calderon, Percy Casey, Darrell DeBolt, Joe Doerfler, Phil Dreisun, John Howland, Ed Klien, Herb Kwart, "Pete" Lear, George Mackintosh, Dave Morgan (who introduced me to the Group in 1976), Bob Nelson, Ernie Neves, George Porter, Jack Prillaman, John Silvernale, Frank Slomczenski, Len Spivey Ken Stone, Bob Van Buskirk, and Bob Weniger.
Special thanks goes to my close friend and 8USAAF "super-enthusiast" Mark Copeland, without whose assistance this book might well not have come to fruition. Finally, thanks goes to Bill Adams and Paul Andrews whose Roll of Honor and 381BG aircraft records formed the basis for the relative Appendices contained within the book.

Ron Mackay

Dedication

This book is dedicated to Capt. Edwin R Manchester, KIA over Bremen on 8 October 1943. His, and his colleagues, sacrifice has ensured a life free from oppression for my generation. Also included here is T/Sgt Tom LaMore who "fought the good fight" both in War and Peace before passing away in 1997, and whom I miss so very much.

Dust jacket artwork by Steve Ferguson.

Book Design by Ian Robertson.

Library of Congress Catalog Number: 99-68116.

Printed in China.
ISBN: 0-7643-1063-1

We are interested in hearing from authors with book ideas on military topics.

Published by Schiffer Publishing Ltd.
4880 Lower Valley Road
Atglen, PA 19310 USA
Phone: (610) 593-1777
FAX: (610) 593-2002
E-mail: Schifferbk@aol.com.
Visit our web site at: www.schifferbooks.com
Please write for a free catalog.
This book may be purchased from the publisher.
Please include $3.95 postage.
Try your bookstore first.

In Europe, Schiffer books are distributed by:
Bushwood Books
6 Marksbury Ave.
Kew Gardens
Surrey TW9 4JF
England
Phone: 44 (0)208 392-8585
FAX: 44 (0)208 392-9876
E-mail: Bushwd@aol.com.
Free postage in the UK. Europe: air mail at cost.
Try your bookstore first.

CONTENTS

1

TRAINING - PYOTE TO RIDGEWELL

By June 1943 the Daylight Bombing Offensive had passed through nine months of experimentation and was on the point of reaching fruition. During the initial stages of the Offensive target choice had been mainly limited to locations within France and the Low Countries, with occasional thrusts at targets positioned on or close within Germany's Western borders.

The current lack of long-range fighter escorts had been one factor in restricting the overall range of operations, although the proponents of the "self-defending bomber" principle – in which the heavy armament borne by the B-17s and B-24s was regarded as more than sufficient to gain access to targets with an acceptable loss-ratio – were still soberly confident of success. However, their enthusiasm must already have been tempered by the 17 April mission when 16 of the 115 bombers assaulting Bremen were MIA. In any event, only a sustained period of deep-penetration operations bereft of fighter escorts would settle the issue for better or worse.

The Winter of 1942/43 was a fast receding memory for the four operational B-17 Groups and two B-24 Groups which had pioneered the bombing policy against a background of steady losses that were barely balanced by adequate material or personnel replacements. April and May did, however, witness the arrival of six more Bomb Groups. Three of these formed the basis for the 4th Bomb wing, and the other three were assigned to the 1st Bomb Wing. A further addition to the 8USAAF's operational strength was the return from training to operational status for the 92BG.

One of the new arrivals within 1st Wing was the 381BG. Behind its arrival in Britain at the end of May and beginning of June lay five months of very hard endeavour on the part of all ranks, from Colonel to PFC, from airplane commander to clerk. Working up in the cold, arid Texas plains around Pyote with its minimal habitation and attendant comforts inevitably created both physical and material strains; the latter stages of training at Pueblo in Colorado were equally strenuous, although the living conditions were noticeably improved. Under the driving energy of the Senior Officer cadre – headed by Lt Col. Joseph J Nazzaro (Group CO), Lt Col. Leland Fiegel (Deputy Group CO), and Maj. Conway S Hall (GP Operations) – the personnel were to achieve a high standard of efficiency, both in the air and on the ground, losing no aircraft and incurring just a single fatal ground crew casualty in the process.

Col. Nazzaro's appointment as the embryonic unit's CO was confirmed by orders dated 1 Dec. 42 and effective from 1 Jan. A graduate of West Point, the 29 year old Nazzaro was a firm if somewhat self-effacing man with a reputation for an equally fair application of discipline coupled with a penchant for hard sustained work; in short, he asked no more from his men than from himself. His arrival at Pyote with Capts Linn S Kidd (S2), John T Goodrum (S4), and Dave Kunkel on 3 Jan. was to be closely followed by a further (and also hand-picked) cadre of senior M/Sgts and Enlisted Men. However, such was the overall state of readiness among these staff that the Colonel could more truthfully have been seen as selecting the least ill-prepared personnel!

Blankets and bedding were at a premium, as the Advance Parties for three of the four Sqdns quickly discovered upon their arrival. Even more disconcerting was the functioning of the heating system which operated off natural gas – as M/Sgt Cota found out to his cost when lighting up the first stove. The act of ignition led to the stove doors blowing off, while the Sgt was blown bodily backwards, thankfully escaping serious injury. A more minor annoyance involved the accidental cross-linking of the hot water and latrine pipe systems; this was perhaps not so minor for the two G.I.s who were also blown off their "thrones" by the steam jets gushing into the toilet bowls when these were flushed!

Each party possessed its CO, Sqdn Operations, Engineering, and Communications Officers and Adjutant, as well as a single "model" combat crew. In charge of the 533BS was the tall, smiling Capt Landon C Hendricks. In the case of the 534BS, its command soon passed from the original holder Capt Don Appert to Dave Kunkel. The 535BS was headed by Capt William H Ingenhutt, who soon developed into a Base terror. To sight him approaching with his short, stocky build and cap thrust back upon his head was to expect a blistering verbal attack expressed in language more suited to the lumber camp in which he had spent some years, rather than the Minnesota University of which he was a graduate! The basic Group structure was finalised on 13 Jan. when the 532BS party arrived; once again, the original Co, in this case Capt Wybell, was displaced four days later by Capt Robert B Post, who had been transferred-in from the 302BG. Accompanying him was Capt George G Shackley, who was to go on to establish himself as a prominent figure within the 381BG by commanding two of its Sqdns at various stages and finish up as Group Air Executive.

The majority of the four Sqdn personnel were now dispatched over to the 2nd Bomber Command School at El Paso where they attended tactical study courses. Those who remained behind at Pyote were left with the Herculean task of cleaning up the airfield. Their endeavours were not spurred on by the reputed presence of rattlesnakes in the sage brush. The absence of both aircraft and equipment led to approaches being made to the San Antonio Air Depot and Gen. Walter Frank, in charge of the Air Service Command down at Paterson Field. The dismaying response to such enquiries was to the effect that no O.E.L. equipment would be made available until the third training Phase. However, the presence of the 19BG and 96BG at Pyote, when coupled with the piles of material laying around and intended for structures, such as the Base Theater, was an open invitation for Group personnel to indulge in what was to be termed "compulsory appropriation" – in other words, simple theft! The 96BG were to suffer from these depredations particularly in regard to its bomb-laden trailers; these were regularly borrowed to supplement the 381BG's insatiable demand for ordnance, such was the rate of usage under Nazzaro's flying programme.

The amenities offered by downtown Pyote during the Group's initial training-up period were very sparse. This is the main – and single – street existing in the town!

Maj Hall was a 5 ft 5 in., sandy-haired martinet who arrived on 15 Jan and was appointed Group Operations Officer. Next day saw Col Fiegel's arrival; he initially took up the post of Air Executive. This officer's previous duties had included the piloting of the "Mission to Moscow" aircraft. In concert with Nazzaro, this triumverate would ever be regarded as the bedrock upon which the Group's success was founded. Nazzaro was treated as the tactician with his training experience, while Fiegel's flying experience and Hall's spell of combat operations in North Africa added valuable support.

Four B-17s were assigned around 9 Jan., but little flying was carried out even with the "model" crews on hand, concentration on ground training taking priority. Long hours were being worked in the face of crowded and dusty living quarters, ice-cold water systems, and frequent failures of the heating system. Outside conditions were even less pleasant. The high winds were so frequent that un-shackled buildings were liable to face prompt destruction. Sand was a constant menace to both living and maintenance conditions.

Joe Hudrick, a T/Sgt of some years service who had been present at Pearl Harbor on 7 Dec 1941, was to recall how the bombers were readied at Pyote for flights between 1200 and 1600 hours. During this period of time the dust storms tended to make their presence felt, with gusts of up to 40 mph throwing a screen as high as 2000 ft before waning as quickly as they had waxed. Sending the B-17s aloft had the beneficial effect of allaying the worst effects of sandblasting wear upon the sensitive Wright Cyclone engines. Rain, by contrast, was so rare that the local joke concerned a citizen who was struck by a raindrop and had to be revived by having a bucket of sand thrown over him! Every morning prior to flying operations the ground crew would mount up on Jeeps and herd the local cattle off the runways. The beasts were attracted by the green weed patches on the runway verges, which in turn were created and nurtured by the water sprays used to wash down the runway surfaces. A particular servicing irritation concerned the regular malfunction of top-turret micro-switches. Their failure when the guns were being fired across the line of the vertical stabilisers added to the workload of the already hard pressed groundcrew; neither were the combat crews greatly impressed by the resultant damage to their aircraft.

Although radios were available, Joe remembered that these were of marginal value because the sole radio station capable of being picked up tended to play what the Northern Boys caustically referred to as "Hill Billy music." There was an alternate source of night serenading, but from a totally different direction, the desert being home to coyotes who kept up a keening chorus all night!

His assigned B-17 was 42-30013, whose uncertain take-off characteristic did not endear itself to those pilots flying the bomber, since it tended to utilise the full length of the runway before teetering off the end. Finally taken in charge by Lt Moore, this pilot employed a "bouncing" technique halfway down the runway, which got the aircraft airborne. One day another crew took off with Joe on board. His initial enthusiasm started to wane rapidly as the runway-end loomed up with the B-17 still firmly anchored to the surface. He called out for the pilots to "bounce" the bomber, but instead they employed the standard method of pulling back on the controls – and to his amazement (and definite relief) the aircraft responded perfectly!

The initial absence of an Officers Club, PX, or Theater forced the personnel to seek out the limited facilities of Pyote, once an oil-boom town of 18000 people, but now reduced to a mere 75 residents; however, it did possess a couple of steak-houses. As passes became more regularly available the men ventured further afield to Monoghans or Odessa. More leisure time for inter-Sqdn sport was fulfilled when the gymnasium was erected, and the officers' leisure circumstances were similarly enhanced with the opening of their Club. A "fly in the ointment" situation tended to occur with the personally allocated bottles of spirits which were held behind the Club bar. These were assigned on a number basis, and this arrangement worked fine, just so long as one's fellow officer did not do the dirty by quoting a number belonging to a colleague and purloining the contents!

Adequate lounge facilities permitted wives to be invited along, but such was the rush of potential attendees that the CO was forced to ration individual visits to twice a week. A more contentious note was struck by the presence of a trailer colony that housed either Base civilians or what were termed "a number of attractive women." The regular sight of Group vehicles outside the latter set of trailers soon brought Nazzaro's wrath down upon the men involved, although no disciplinary action followed.

The arid Texan plain is the background for 42-29978 "Hells Angels" of the 534BS. This B-17F was flown by Lt. Reinhard King's crew, and both were fated to go down on 17 August 1943 during the first Schweinfurt mission; happily, all ten crewmen baled out safely.

Tuesday was gas-mask day. Even with this forewarning, which was backed up by regular snap-checks, the overall state of individual preparedness was poor. This situation was primarily due to the containers being utilised for storing items, but there were instances where it was found that the mask face-pieces were still wrapped up in their covers. Bill Fullick, who had been appointed Group Bombardier on 30 Jan., firmly regarded himself as a gas mask "conscientious objector." His stance was not lost upon the team assigned to the tear-gas Jeep, who naturally singled him out for special attention. One chase extending over a quarter of a mile resulted in a purple-faced Fullick making it safely to the Mess Hall, but on other occasions he was not so lucky!

The caption to this picture of several members from Lt. King's crew (King is on the right) sardonically states; "Hard at work!" In fact, the opportunity for relaxation on the flight-line was minimal, since Col. Nazzaro and his senior combat staff worked the crews extremely hard.

In late January the initial flying training culminated in the full Group strength of five B-17s providing an element of a sea-search mission which was flown out of Muroc Lake, CA. Nazzaro, Fiegel, Hall, and the Sqdn COs shared the briefing with the "model" crews, while Capt Kidd led a party providing intelligence and briefing facilities. Thick clouds over the Sierras raised the unpleasant specter of an instrument descent into the staging field at March, but a diversion order direct to Muroc was received in time. The exercise was completed next day, but little was learnt about de-briefing techniques. There was one talking point regarding an anonymous gunner who allegedly tested his weapon near to a Naval vessel, but with nobody owning up to the incident! Return to Pyote coincided with a notable uplift in aircraft establishment, as well as personnel. The total of 20 aircraft were shared out equally between the Sqdns, and now the Group leaders could begin to instill the principles of large-scale close formation flying into their charges. It is a matter of conjecture whether or not Col. Nazzaro was aware even at this early stage of preparation that his Group would be assigned to the 8USAAF where such tactics were an absolute pre-requisite for both individual and corporate survival. The available operational strength in Europe involved a majority of B-17 units compared to the B-24. The Pacific Theater of Operations as yet displayed little tendency towards a predominant use of the B-24, whose greater endurance coupled with the ability to fly looser formations in the face of the much more limited aerial opposition would see the Consolidated bomber steadily supersede its Boeing stable-mate. Whatever the facts, the benefits derived from such precise training were to prove invaluable in the months ahead.

Bombing and gunnery practice – the former at the continued expense of the 96BG, and the latter sometimes at the expense of the local cattle – was steadily expanded. The persistent dust storms were a major hazard, but nevertheless no B-17s were to be lost or even seriously damaged at Pyote. The sustained training pressure was to culminate in the dispatch of 36 aircraft formations. The groundcrew proved equally vigilant in their efforts, and a full schedule of operational B-17s was maintained.

February saw the completion of the Command structure, with Capt Leroy Wilcox arriving as Group Adjutant on the 9th. The structure was as follows:

532BS

CO	Capt Post
Operations Officer	1 Lt Robert E Nelson
Flight Commanders	Capt Joe Alexander
	2 Lt Marvin D Lord
	2 Lt Jack H Owen

533BS

CO	Capt Landon C Hendricks
Operations Officer	Capt John H Hamilton
Flight Commanders	1 Lt Robert L Withers
	1 Lt Martin Schrader
	1 Lt John L Martin

Group line-up at Pueblo shows civilian contractors still working in foreground. Three B-17Fs revealing their serial numbers and closest to camera were to experience vastly different fates. Nearside aircraft crashed on landing at Ridgewell on 9 June '43 and was salvaged. Next to it is 42-29976 "Sad Sack" (532BS), which was MIA on 25 July '43. The third bomber is 42-30018 "Old Coffins," which transferred to the 305BG on 22 August and returned States-side on 20 March '44.

534BS

CO	Capt David E Kunkel
Operations Officer	Capt George G Shackley
Flight Commanders	1 Lt Alan F Tucker
	1 Lt Weldon L Simpson
	1 Lt Reinhard M. King

535BS

CO	Maj. William H Ingenhutt
Operations Officer	Capt Arthur F Briggs
Flight Commanders	1 Lt Orlando H Koenig
	1 Lt Charles W Dowell
	1 Lt Melvin R Hecker
Group Bombardier	Capt William G Fullick
Group Navigator	Capt Norman C Mackay
Group Communications	1 Lt Warren Dewlin
Group Armaments	1 Lt Gerald Platz
Ground Executive	Maj William J Reid

Maj Reid had arrived on 5 March, and his background and general demeanour provided the perfect liaison between Col. Nazzaro and the Ground organisation.

On 25 Feb. a practice mission to Wilcox Dry Lake, AZ, officially completed first Phase training, and 2nd Air Force duly authorised Phase Two, which was to involve even more Sqdn and Group formations flown over much greater distances. Although this in turn placed an equally increased pressure upon the labouring groundcrews, they still maintained a minimum aircraft availability of 80%. Combat crew arriving during this Phase made a necessarily more rapid transition from First to Second Phase readiness, but this factor was readily accepted and taken in hand. The S2 Sections were filled up, and it was in this period that several Medal Award ceremonies involving the 19BG took place. Such occasions were scarcely appreciated by the hapless 381BG personnel forced to parade in the heat and dust!

On 31 March Col. Nazzaro flew to Pueblo, CO, where the final training Phase would take place, and the Group transferred on 4 April. The bulk of the Air echelon traveled alongside the groundcrew in two special trains, which completed the 180 mile journey over two days. Met by a brass band, all ranks were obliged to march to their new base, which pleased nobody. Pueblo was a very welcome change from Pyote, since it was an established Base with full facilities and located close to the equally well-established town whose name it bore.

"Colonel Joe" Nazzaro peers backwards from the cockpit of his B-17F, below which is the nick-name accorded the 381st's Group Commander by Capt Post (532BS CO). He had one of his men apply the name during the night preceding departure from Pueblo. The Colonel's co-pilot on 42-30034 was the slightly built Col. Hall, and the equivalent title applied below his cockpit window was "Peewee!"

It was here that the Group allocation of bombers it would take into action occurred. A final figure of 41 B-17Fs was taken on charge, of which one (42-3219) would be re-allocated to the 94BG and one (42-30025) would be left behind. Twenty-seven came from the Boeing production blocks BO-70, 75, 80, and 85, ten from Douglas DL-35, one from DL-25, and three from Vega VE-25:

25-DL	42-3092				
35-DL	42-3211	42-3215	42-3217	42-3219	42-3220
	42-3221	42-3223	42-3225	42-3226	42-3227
25-VE	42-5845	42-5846	42-5847		
70-BO	42-29789				
75-BO	42-29888				
80-BO	42-29950	42-29953	42-29954	42-29958	42-29976
	42-29978	42-29988	42-29992	42-30009	42-30011
	42-30012	42-30013	42-30014	42-30015	42-30016
	42-30018	42-30020	42-30021	42-30024	42-30025
	42-30026				
	42-30027	42-30028	42-30029		
85-BO	42-30034				

What was at first sight a collection of anonymous and character-less aircraft was soon to take on the mantle of personalities for both the combat and groundcrew. Given the natural penchant for vesting their aerial charges with a variety of titles – ranging from polite to unprintable! – it was not long before 42-29888 became THE JOKER, or 42-5846 converted into TINKERTOY. In common with all other Bomb Groups entering combat during mid-1943, there would be just a handful of these "original" B-17s on hand after six months; the vast majority were fated to end up as MIA statistics, although a few would be "written off" due to accidents. A similar and even sadder rate of attrition would be realised among the ranks of the "original" combat crews; death or captivity awaited the greater majority, although a surprising proportion would slot into the fortunate category of "evader" and return safely to England. In turn the Nazi war machine would feel the weight of well-directed ordnance as the 381BG was welded into an effective fighting unit.

Final stage training was even more strenuously indulged in, and the B-17s were further modified. Adaptations included new-pattern brakes, 58 inch wheel tires, and – more significant for future combat operations – forward-firing flexible gunmounts with a single '5 machine gun in the center of the nose Plexiglas. The latter modification was a tacit acknowledgement of the effectiveness of the head-on attacks being made against the bombers by the Luftwaffe fighters and the increasingly desperate attempts to combat them. In any event, it would only be the introduction of B-17Gs equipped with Bendix chin-turrets which would provide any realistic counter-measure.

Now the emphasis within briefing sessions was on missions over Europe, a clear hint of future Group deployment. Another pointer in this direction was the dropping of Japanese aircraft from recognition classes and ground school training tending to concentrate upon European conditions. It was while the Group was at Pueblo that the sole serious accident occurred. A mechanic who was servicing a ball turret got in the path of an accidentally discharged gun with fatal consequences.

Missions of note included a leaflet drop on behalf of a War bond Campaign at Denver. The culminating mission took place on 21 April with a five-day sea search sortie out of Harmer, CA. No "abortions" were recorded, and the sole mishap occurred when a 500 lb bomb, borne by each B-17 in case enemy vessels were sighted, was inadvertently dropped on a sled target along with the allotted practice bombs; once again, there were no takers for the prize among the crews! Naval reports of B-17s firing on a freighter bound for San Francisco were also politely refuted. A night flight over San Francisco and Los Angeles permitted U.S. Army searchlight units to operate, but the experience of being "coned" in the blinding beams was not to the liking of the fliers.

Final leaves were being granted, but the apparently generous six day periods allotted took no account of the chaotic state of the railroad system in Wartime, and many men suffered the consequences of arriving back late and therefore being treated as AWOL. The Group strength at Pueblo had been increased by three "non-established" members, all of them canine. "Meatball" and "Spaghetti" were taken on hand by two Sgts., and "Nick" gravitated to Capt Fullick. "Spaghetti" was fated to go missing prior to departure for England, but the other pair went to War. Capt Post sanctioned clearance for "Meatball," but "Nick" traveled on board the QUEEN ELIZABETH on the QT!

This is a 532BS group of "original" officers prior to overseas movement, a number of whom would be MIA statistics within a few weeks. Lt. Phil Dreisun (Standing on left) would become a POW on 25 July, and his bombardier, Jim Houck (kneeling second from left), would be killed. Other POWs would be Lts. Lloyd Duke, Bill Lockhart, and Leo Jarvis (standing fifth to seventh from right). More fortunate would be Lts. Marvin Lord (three along from Dreisun) and Will Baltrusaitus (kneeling on left), although Lord would be KIA flying with the 91BG on 3 Feb. '45.

The final period at Pueblo witnessed strenuous efforts to bring the physical condition of the groundcrew up to scratch, but the results were indeterminate. The Medical Section was concerned that not all personnel had received the full ration of inoculations and used several methods to trap those avoiding treatment. Capts Bland and Robson stood by the head of the chow line and refused access to any miscreant until he had accepted the needle at the dispensary. Capt Wymer's remedy was equally drastic, and consisted of hauling the individual out of his bed around midnight and refusing him leave to return until he had been "stabbed!"

As April ended all equipment was being checked and packed for when the Overseas Movement order was issued. This duly arrived on 2 May, with the first Advanced Party led by the Ground Executive (Now promoted to Lt Col) and heading for Atlantic City, NJ, where it would fly on the 12th to Prestwick, Scotland, in a C-54. Moving to New York in order to proceed with the Advanced Ground Echelon were Capt Goodrum and Lt Denby.

Lt. Painter was assigned this B-17F prior to departure overseas. During the Group's arrival at Ridgewell she was "bellied-in," losing the No. 3 propeller, which can be seen tucked under the wing. Bomber was declared "Category E" and was relegated to "Hangar Queen" status.

The first B-17 departed for Salinas, KS, on the 5th bearing Col. Nazzaro, Maj. Hall, Capts Mackay and Fullick, and several other key personnel. Over the ensuing 48 hours the remainder of the Group followed their aircraft. Lt Lord lost a main gear wheel on take-off but managed to stay aloft. He headed for Oklahoma City as ordered, where there was a Repair Depot, and skillfully put down his B-17 for a smooth crash-landing. He and his crew were later picked up by Capt Post. The Pueblo Base staff had watched the errant wheel bouncing down the runway, but all their efforts to retrieve it proved fruitless – which was hardly surprising, since enterprising 534BS groundcrew had promptly secured the wheel for addition to their inventory! The average stopover at Salinas was to last 14 days, during which the crews received quotas of the very latest in personal flying equipment.

Salinas was vacated from the 15th onward. "Col. Joe" (his unofficial title among the men) again led the protracted internal route to Gander, Newfoundland, which staged through Selfridge Field at Detroit and Bangor, Maine. From this easternmost point the crews would face a daunting Trans-Atlantic flight lasting up to 14 hours and proceeding via Greenland and Iceland. The CO was first off on the 12th and touched down at Prestwick next morning at 0900. Here he was eventually joined by the others, although three crews were "sweated out" during their time over the route before turning up safely. The final stage of the wearisome transit haul occurred on the 20th and

This is 42-30020 a short time later presenting a sorry sight. Already she has lost her outer-wing sections, center-fin, and rudder and stabilisers for use on other damaged Group B-17s.

was a relatively short hop South to Bovingdon airfield West of London. Here a two to three week period of orientation instruction was given on subjects ranging from British flying procedures to Luftwaffe fighter techniques.

By contrast the progress of the groundcrew to their English base was to span almost one month. Special Order 138/8 May '43 was immediately followed by the provision of four trains, which departed Salinas between the 9th and 10th. All four snaked their torturous way East towards the Embarkation facility of Camp Kilmer, NJ; two of these were routed through Ohio and Pennsylvania, the third went via Nebraska, and the fourth headed up into and then back down out of Canada. The Camp was reached on the 12th, and the Group personnel were swallowed up within its immense spaces. The food provided was the worst yet experienced, and it was only the purchase of hamburgers and sandwiches from the various PX locations which sustained the appetite. The series of hikes and commando courses the men were put through helped to take the edge off their boring surroundings, while the issue of passes permitted visits to nearby New York.

The final suspension of telephone calls and telegrams coupled with instructions to pack two barrack-bags, or one footlocker and one bag in the case of officers, provided ample evidence of impending States-side departure. May 26th arrived, and all staggered along under a wealth of equipment and baggage to the railroad station for the short journey to the Bayonne Ferry. Waiting in the pouring rain at Pier 44 was the majestic bulk of the Cunard liner QUEEN ELIZABETH, into which upward of 17000 Service personnel were being directed. "Nick" nearly didn't make it, as his several attempts to bound up the gangway were promptly repulsed by the Transportation officials; he was finally smuggled aboard tucked under the folds of a GI's overcoat. (During the voyage he was detected and faced with being thrown overboard as demanded by Army regulations. Fortunately, the Officer of the Watch was a much more kindly disposed individual and told "Nick's" owners to ensure he was kept out of sight.)

Blackout regulations were more than ever observed, given that the vessel was sailing independently. Sleeping space was at a premium, with the enlisted men discovering they were even worse off than the officers, due to there being only enough berths for half their number. Hence, alternate nights were spent out on the open deck where the chilled atmosphere was at the other extreme to the internal areas, which were as hot as Hell! Boat drills were run through daily, but the scene of mass confusion as the personnel milled around raised the gloomy specter of a disaster should the unthinkable occur and the liner be torpedoed.

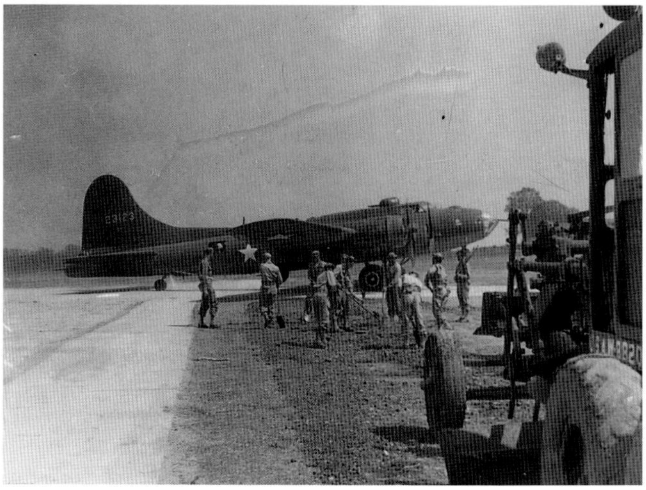

Although this B-17F did operate with the 381BG, the picture (shot in May 1943) depicts the bomber while with its original unit, the 96BG. Transfer to Ridgewell occurred on 16 July when it was assigned to the 535BS and named "Ron-Chee." It was ultimately MIA with Lt. Kemp's crew over Bremen on 8 Oct 1943.

With but two days left of what was so far a smooth crossing, the situation rapidly degenerated into chaos as a full-blown gale developed. The tally of seasick "Sad Sacks" abandoned the Mess halls to the hardy few, and even some of the latter gave up in a hurry when confronted, for example, with kippers for breakfast. It was with undoubtedly thankfulness that the hills surrounding the Firth of Clyde were sighted on the morning of 1 June and final anchorage off the port of Gourock was achieved in the afternoon. A small detachment of nurses were on board, and as they disembarked ahead of the men they were regaled by the sight of countless balloons floating down from the upper decks.

While awaiting their turn to land a number of Group personnel took the opportunity to exchange money with a party of Australian aircrew, and thereby gained an advance insight into the complexities of the British currency system compared to that of the U.S.A. It was later in the day before the Group commenced dis-embarking, and early evening before they were aboard the train which would take them Southward to what would be for most their "home" for nearly two years. The rail route went through Glasgow and East to Edinburgh before heading across the Scottish/English border and down the East Coast. It was early next morning when the train finally rolled into Great Yeldham station, where trucks were on hand for the short journey to Ridgewell.

The airfield with which the Group's fortunes were to be inextricably linked was located in the NW of Essex, close to the boundary with Suffolk, and was the single USAAF heavy bomber base in the County. It was bounded by the triangle of Great Yeldham, Tilbury Juxta Clare, and Ashen villages, and had formerly housed the Short Stirling bombers of No. 90 Sqdn, RAF. The nearest towns of any size were Haverhill seven miles West and Braintree, which was a similar distance Eastward. Built in 1942 to typical Wartime construction standards, its facilities were rather basic. Two T-type hangars graced the main flight-line, which at this time possessed 36 dispersal points, a number later increased to 50 during 1943/44 in acknowledgement of the much greater aircraft establishment for a USAAF heavy bomber unit compared to its RAF contemporary. The main runway of 6000 ft lay on an East/West axis, and two subsidiary runways of shorter length completed a layout resembling a cross between a triangle and a figure 4.

Although the main support buildings were grouped around the southern hangar, all other work and domestic sites were set in or on either side of a shallow valley a little further to the South and out of sight of the flight-line. Other than Cambridge about 20 miles distant, the closest link to "civilisation," as probably understood by the base's new residents, was London. To reach this social Mecca from Great Yeldham's LNER rail station entailed a journey of about two hours jammed into the cramped compartments of what was dubbed the "Toonerville Trolley." (Facilities on American trains were considerably more expansive and therefore more comfortable than those in Britain).

Having settled in over the ensuing four days the men were greeted by Col. Nazzaro, who now arrived on the 6th. Three days later the novel sound of Wright Cyclone engines brought the local people out into the village streets as the B-17s slanted into the circuit from the SW and eased their way onto the runway. One of their number (42-30020) was fated to end its career even before it had begun by crash-landing on touchdown. Having been deemed too severely damaged to repair, it was "written off" to become a "Hangar Queen," providing spare parts for fellow 532BS bombers.

2

BAPTISM OF FIRE

Early on the morning of 22 June the fateful call came for the combat crews who, after breakfasting, then filed into the briefing room. The mission outlined to the expectant men was in accordance with the procedure for "freshman" Groups – a short-range, diversionary effort, in this case on the Ford and General Motors factories in Antwerp, Belgium. Sharing the mission but flying as lead Group was the equally un-tested 384BG from Grafton Underwood. The diversion was linked to the main 8USAAF thrust that day upon a synthetic-rubber plant at Hüls/Recklinghausen in the Ruhr, and the anticipated effect was that the Luftwaffe fighter strength would be dissipated in trying to counteract the twin strikes. The two new Groups were to be provided with a strong fighter escort for their short Channel crossing and incursion into enemy territory.

To the men – many of whom were barely out of adolescence – who were nervously assembled in the room it must have seemed only yesterday since they had sat through "mock" briefing sessions at Pyote and Pueblo, with some perhaps feeling a sense of boredom and even a little sleepy. But here they listened and listened attentively to every last word spoken by the various officers mounting the rostrum. School was truly over, and the impending opposition was all too real, as well as playing for keeps. During the briefing it was announced that Brig. Gen. Hunter, commanding the 8th Fighter Command, would fly the mission as co-pilot to Lt. Withers in 42-30024.

This first day of combat was to bring varying degrees of fortune, with the crews of Lts. Shenk and Inman Jobe being tested to the very limits of their endurance. The teams of Lts. Horr (532BS) and Martin (533BS) would taste the bitter seeds of failure, as would S/Sgt Brinton, one of Lt. Shenk's waist-gunners, and S/Sgt Arnold Lorick, tail gunner to Lt. Hedin (533BS).

Briefing over, the crews gathered their flying equipment together and assembled outside for the big 6 x 6 trucks to bear them to the scattered dispersals, where the groundcrew had laboured long through the short Summer night to ready the big Fortresses. All 20 aircraft involved in the impending mission were on top line, and there would be no "aborts." The "start engines" flare was shot from the control tower, and what was initially a ragged series of coughing, spluttering motors soon blended into a constant, dinning roar which pounded through the quiet English countryside. A second flare signalled "start

Gen. Frank O'Donnell Hunter (CG 8th Fighter Command) has just returned from Antwerp on 22 June '43 having flown in a 533BS bomber with Lt. Withers. He is handing over some of his flight equipment to his RAF driver prior to attending the mission de-briefing session.

Capt. Landon C. Hendricks shakes hands with Gen. Hunter. The 533BS CO would soon be promoted to Major, but was fated to be the third of the "original" Sqdn. COs to go missing on 9 Oct during the Anklam mission. Unlike the other two, he would not survive and is listed on the Wall of the Missing at Madingley Military Cemetery, Cambridge.

taxiing" to the pilots, and each B-17 heaved itself out of its dispersal and onto the perimeter track in a pre-determined order. The line of bombers waddled along in elephantine fashion with brakes squealing in protest until all were stationary behind one another. The Lead bomber now turned onto the runway-end, revved up to full power against the brakes, and at 0709 eased its way sonorously and majestically away from the column. Within ten minutes the entire Group was airborne on what would be the first of 297 missions during the next 22 months.

The local civilians were to grow accustomed to the sight of the American bombers circling and forming into their distinctive defensive formations. They would also become all too accustomed to seeing depleted and scattered Group formations returning after a rough mission, with flares popping from those B-17s bearing wounded or dead crewmen. There would be other occasions when the detonation of a crashing bomber would assail their ears, telling of a tragic outcome for some or all of the ten young American airmen on board the stricken machine.

Link up with the 384BG was made without any problem. The plan of attack had called for the 381BG to fly in trail to Col. Bud Peaslee's Group. The full formation climbed steadily to operational altitude and steered a SE course for the North Foreland in Kent, from where a direct course for Antwerp would be set. The mission's short duration, coupled with the bomber crews' obvious lack of combat experience, had been acknowledged by the provision of P-47 and RAF Typhoon fighters which should have rendezvoused with the B-17s at the English coast. A message sent to Peaslee stating the fighters were 40 minutes late in taking-off and advising him to take the appropriate delaying action was unfortunately not received. Consequently, the crews searched in vain for the "Little Friends" as they bore on towards hostile air space.

Col. Peaslee was having to balance the possibility of his relatively small force suffering heavy losses should they be attacked while on their own against the fact that "aborting" the mission would deny the Huls force any indirect succour. He quickly decided to press on in the hope of the Allied fighters making interception before the Belgian coast was crossed. Progress to this point was un-opposed, which must have seemed like a miracle to the tension-laden crews. As the target was being approached, hopes must have been steadily rising that a "milk-run" would be the end result for this inaugural strike.

The main villain in the piece was on the point of shattering such expectations. The first and stunning evidence of this emerged in the form of brilliant, winking flashes from directly ahead. The reaction of Lloyd Duke (N) to this first brush with the Luftwaffe may well have been typical – he wondered why Morse code signals were being flashed by the encroaching aircraft! All the training in the world could not condition new crews to this aspect of combat any more than to the skidding, swerving motions of the Fw 190s and Me 109s, nor the manner in which tracer trails appeared to move slowly until the last moment when they whisked by. The initial encounters with flak proved equally unreal, since the silent smoke-puffs from the expended shells were only translated into a lethal message whenever the shell fragments impacted with the aircraft's skin or with human flesh.

Aerial view of the aftermath of the bomb-loading explosion on 23 June '43 which blew 42-30024 to pieces on her 533BS dispersal, along with 22 combat and ground crew. Left-hand dispersal normally housed the Sqdn's 42-29992, in which a 23rd airman (Lt. Tull, bombardier) was killed.

Closer ground view of the explosion site reveals an uncowled engine as the sole identifiable segment of 42-30024. The crater created by the blast is quite shallow and confirms eye-witness reports that its pattern was primarily upwards.

The acolyte Groups were receiving a harsh baptism in the effective head-on attack angle practised by their redoubtable adversaries, and it is unlikely very much return fire other than a few scattered bursts were brought to bear on the enemy fighters as they shot through in tight groups of five or six. But battle had been joined, and the bombers' salvation at this parlous stage was entirely in their own hands. And so, as the fighters combed through the formation and turned to engage from behind the Fortress gunners began to recover from their shock and to deliver counter-attacking fire. The initial Luftwaffe assault had been made by one of the two sub-formations from the battle-tested JG 26, led by its Kommodore Oberst Josef "Pips" Priller.

No aircraft had been taken down during this first assault, but Lt. Shenk's B-17 flying No. 3 in the High Sqdn's second element had suffered a "runaway" propeller on the No. 2 engine, and all attempts to "feather" the blades were in vain. The B-17F (42-29984) staggered along while gamely hanging onto its position. The formation was by now running into the flak-defended approaches to the target and was momentarily freed from the enemy fighters' attention. During the run-up from the I.P. one B-17, believed to be Lt. Horr's 42-30016, sustained strikes, causing it to fall out of formation. De-briefing reports indicated that as many as five or six parachutes were seen to emerge from the dying Fortress, which crashed near Terneuzen with the loss of two out of the ten crewmen on board (this bomber's loss was later credited to Oberst Priller). Both Groups achieved a fair bombing result, with their Lead Bombardiers having tended towards under-aiming in order to avoid an overshoot, which would have affected a civilian housing estate. The bombs walked their way across open fields and finally onto the plant.

Turning off the target, the crews awaited the resurgent fighter attacks. Priller's formation had by now been joined by the Geschwader's second sub-formation under the command of Hauptmann "Wutz" Galland. However, the enemy pilots were now fully engaged in combating the belated but welcome appearance of the P-47s and Typhoons. Despite this, any straggling bomber was still fair game, and one such aircraft was 42-29984. She had been straggling from the moment her element leader had gone down. (This was Lt. Martin in 42-30021, who was reported to have been pursued in its dive by an Fw 190, which was struck by return fire from its prey's gunners and which accompanied it to a watery grave. Lt. Harry Long (N) was recorded as the sole survivor.) S/Sgt Charles Brinton (WG) was knocked out of action, and S/Sgt Jim Sloan (TG) was also wounded, although he did initially manage to keep operating his guns. Calls for assistance brought T/Sgt John D Sinclair

This is 42-29992 prior to the explosion of 42-30024. The severe degree of damage inflicted on the 533BS bomber by the explosion was sufficient to merit her being salvaged on 1 July.

from his radio-room to the waist, where he gave what attention he could to Brinton before taking over his gun. The B-17 was under constant attack from all quarters, and the effect was beginning to tell.

Damage to the oxygen system forced such a rapid descent that observers from the fast disappearing formation reported Shenk's B-17 as a definite loss. During this stage Sinclair received a leg wound and had the waist gun that he was operating rendered out of action.

Despite bleeding profusely he crawled back to the tail where Sloan was by now unconscious. The physical effort of dragging his buddy forward to the radio-room must have been extremely exhausting. However, having realised that his bomber was completely vulnerable to attacks from the rear he quickly returned to the tail and spiritedly snapped out calculated bursts of fire.

Only Shenk and two other crewmen were still unscathed, and the twisting, gyrating B-17 was being torn apart under the relentless battering. Happily, salvation in the form of P-47s arrived halfway towards the English coast. Although freed from the Luftwaffe's attention, Shenk and his co-pilot still had much to do to keep the bomber airborne. The loss of No.1 meant they were down to two functioning engines, which left them wallowing along at minimum speed and altitude. Sighting an airstrip at Framlingham they made hurried preparations to land. When selecting GEAR DOWN Shenk discovered this was impossible due to a total failure of the gear electrical operating system. The subsequent force-landing went off without incident, which says much for the pilots' skill, and the wounded men were hastily extracted and whisked away to the nearest hospital.

Shenk's experience was mirrored in almost every respect by another 533BS crew led by Lt. Jobe. No less than three observers stated they had seen 42-3226 crash, although the time and location varied; after several misleading bulletins the B-17 was declared MIA. But she was far from dead.

Trouble had first struck during the bomb-run. The No.2 engine was knocked out by shell fragments and a hole torn in one wing through which the ground was visible. Veering out of formation she was promptly set upon, and a 20mm shell bursting around the top-turret put it out of action, as well as stunning S/Sgt Lindsay. Trailing the Group over the target, Lt. Larry Potenza (B) found he could not release the bombs even with the manual trip mechanism due to hydraulic failure. Evasive action – difficult enough in normal circumstances – was being maintained in the face of attacks which immobilised No. 4 and shot out big chunks of aileron, forcing Jobe to fly on his elevators and automatic alone! Suddenly, the B-17 dipped sharply, and it was only by a miraculous effort that it was brought back on an even keel. A few minutes later another sudden stall forced a similar Herculean effort out of the pilots.

All the time the gunners were desperately warding off the fighters up to the Belgian coast, but ammunition was running low and the crew's solo run seemed doomed. Directly over the coast the Fws were seen to falter and then flee in the face of determined P-47 counter-thrusts. However, although the enemy's worst attention had been survived, the crew was still far from out of the woods. Attention was focused on attempts to release the bombs, but it was some time before they cleared the bomb-bay and splashed into the English Channel, which was hurtling past none too far beneath the crippled B-17. All excess equipment, including the guns, were ditched as the bomber was hard-pressed to maintain level flight, especially after No.3 engine caught fire and "died" as the Kent coast loomed up.

A mere 700 ft altitude remained as the shore slid by, but Jobe found he could not hold her aloft anymore, and a hurried

This is Lt. Julius Eichenbaum, the 533BS Ordnance Officer. He was one of five personnel later awarded the Soldiers Medal for their positive conduct following the explosion of 42-30024.

search for a suitable crash-landing site revealed only a potato patch directly ahead. At around 120 mph the burning B-17 roared in for a landing whose initial impact was surprisingly gentle. Suddenly, to the horror of those up front with a forward view, a hitherto un-seen concrete post made contact with the left wing. Extreme good fortune was riding on the crew's shoulders; instead of blowing up or rolling herself into a disintegrating mass, the bomber had the wing neatly sheered off at the fuselage joint, and the dismembered remnants careered to a dust-shrouded but safe halt! Not a single crewman had even been slightly injured during the incident, which was a fitting climax to "Little Chuck's" brief but valiant operational spell.

And so the 381BG was finally home from its "breaking-in" mission. Back at the base talk flowed like a river as the men tried to re-live their experience for the de-briefing staff, albeit with a varying degree of success. Of the 20 B-17s heading out for Antwerp just a few hours previous, two were broken hulks in Belgium or under the North Sea. Lt. Hedin brought his crew home, but S/Sgt Lorick would never know this as he had been killed at his post early on in the air battle.

And what of the two crews who had come halfway home? With but one exception the wounded men on Lt. Shenk's bomber made a full recovery. S/Sgt Brinton had been rushed to the 12th Evacuation Hospital at Diss and given blood transfusions, among the donors for which were his bombardier Lt. Williams – all to no avail, as the Sgt died on 29 June. As for Lt. Jobe's crew, they returned to Ridgewell and resumed operations on the day of Brinton's death. Resulting from the severe battle damage suffered, their B-17 became the first Group bomber to be declared Category E (fit only for scrap).

As a final postscript to the 22 June mission, a few weeks later an award of the Silver Star – America's third-highest military decoration – was granted to T/Sgt Sinclair for his supreme courage that day. It is pleasant to relate that the Sgt went on to complete his 25th mission during the following winter, and shortly after returned States-side.

Around mid-morning on the 23rd and down on the flight line a mix of combat and ground personnel were hard at work preparing the bombers for the day's effort against St Martin Bernay airfield. At 42-30024 Lt. Eichenbaum (Ordnance Officer) was supervising the loading of bombs and ammunition; then, at 1057 he jumped into his Jeep and motored 'round to the adjacent ammunition area. In the adjoining dispersal squatted 42-29992, with Lt. Jim Alexander standing by its nose talking to W/O Joe Nutt; up in the nose Lt. Tull (B) was checking out his bombsight. Among this B-17's mechanics were T/Sgt Balasa supervising bomb loading and S/Sgt Pinter standing by his Jeep. They were about to be joined by Sgt Miller who, acting on W/O Nutt's order, had followed him 'round from 42-30024. S/Sgt Francis E Owen, a gunner on Lt Ballinger's B-17, parked on the other side of A/C 024, was engaged in gun maintenance. W/O Platz (also from the Ordnance Section) had returned to his office after dropping off Nutt, and a third Ordnance Officer, Lt. Bannon, was several hundred yards distant in the bomb-dump. All those men, with one tragic exception, were about to be principal witnesses to the shocking event now unfolding.

At 1100 there was a rush of air, and 42-30024 erupted into smoke and flame. Scarcely had the base personnel recovered from the literally stunning effect of this initial blast when there was a second, which a distant witness later said "blew the ship from the face of the earth." A mere 45 seconds had elapsed between the twin explosions, but in that period one officer and 22 enlisted men had perished in an instantaneously horrible manner. It later transpired that loading-up had been carried out with the nose-fuses in position. Whether a dropped bomb was the cause of the accident would never be fully determined, as there were no survivors among either the loading detail or the other airmen around or inside the B-17.

Maj. William Ingenhutt was the original commander of the 535BS. His jacket bears the Sqdn. badge consisting of a bomb-carrying imp. This diminutive but forceful officer was shot down on 8 Oct. '43 to become a POW.

Those working on the surrounding B-17s were either frozen into momentary immobility, galvanised into erratic action, or in one instance left lying injured on the ground. Hearing the first explosion S/Sgt Owens jumped out of his B-17 and started to run towards its tail – then sighting what he described as a "hail of corruption" hurtling towards him he promptly turned 'round. Hearing a weak call for assistance belonging to PFC Glenn W Burkland, and fearing further and possible fatal injury to the hapless man in the event of further blasts if left in his precarious position, Owens gallantly went back and dragged the airman behind a piece of loose concrete curbing. No sooner was this act completed than the second blast occurred.

Lt. Alexander and W/O Nutt were blown from one side of their B-17 to the other, and the latter sustained an injury as well as ending up under one of the engines. On regaining his feet Nutt "took off" from the vicinity, but ran into Lt. Eichenbaum. He had seen the smoke pall, and after ordering an MP to keep all other personnel out of the affected area he arrived to render assistance. He remarked on Nutt's injuries, which the W/O shrugged off as superficial and asked for his help. Sgt Miller, who had been walking from 024 to 992, was picked up on the way over to the latter B-17. The trio now came across Owens and Burkland; fearing further injury to Burkland should further explosions occur, and despite the obvious pain the PFC was suffering due to a compound fracture of a leg, Lt. Eichenbaum had him moved on a piece of wood over to a vehicle.

The task of rendering 42-29992 safe was then begun with additional help from T/Sgt Balasa and S/Sgt Pinter (Balasa had scattered, and Pinter had hidden behind his Jeep in the interval between the blasts.). As Eichenbaum clambered into the rear fuselage Lt. Alexander went up front, where he had the painful experience of coming across the body of Lt Tull, who had been struck in the head by a big chunk of flying metal. His corpse

Up to 15 bombers can be seen taxiing along the runway and perimeter track towards the 535BS and 534BS areas of the airfield. They are probably completing a practice flight, since normal operational procedure required the runways to be kept clear. Picture taken during the first few weeks at Ridgewell, as confirmed by the trio of RAF Stirling bombers occupying the 534BS dispersals at top left of picture.

The Western end of the 534BS dispersals displays the unfamiliar sight of RAF Stirlings belonging to No. 90 Sqdn., who occupied Ridgewell before the 381BG. This trio was still on the base after the Group moved in. Note how the private house is not fenced off from the airfield.

was gently eased out of the nose hatch and down to the waiting W/O Nutt and Lt. Bannon (who had just arrived from the bomb-dump), and laid down on the ground to await carriage to the mortuary. The young officer's combat career had been closed within a mere 24 hours. This unhappy detail completed, some of the men set to fighting fires around the B-17's tail surfaces and surrounding ammunition boxes, while bomb de-fusing was made by Lts. Eichenbaum and Bannon, who gingerly handed the detached fuses down to Nutt, Balasa, and Pinter.

By now Cols. Nazzaro and Fiegel were among those being admitted to the disaster zone, but there was little more to do than hose down the remnants of 42-20024 and commence the grisly task of picking up whatever was left of the mens' bodies. With the impending mission in mind, Col. Nazzaro called for the taxiway to be cleared of debris. A Cleatrac was brought in, to which 42-29992 was hooked-up for towing away. The crisis over, all that remained was the relatively mundane duty of clearing up so that the base could begin to function again. All non-essential personnel dispersed to their duties with the exception of W/O Nutt, who despite protesting was directed by Lt. Kohler (Flight Surgeon) to accompany him to the hospital.

Priority telegrams were soon on their way to the deceased mens' families. Sixteen of those were "ground-pounders" whose seemingly safe and repetitive (but equally vital) duties were largely shunned by Wartime publicity sources, but the grief borne by their relatives was just as real and deep as if they had gone to their deaths in a broken and doom-spinning B-17. No headlines were likely to be created by this incident. The remaining seven men were 42-20024's gunner complement and Lt Tull.

Most of the principal witnesses to the disaster would soldier on at Ridgewell over the next two years. One who would not was S/Sgt Owens, who would be listed MIA with Lt Olaf Ballinger 11 days later. The recommendation that he be granted an award for his gallant action would never reach fruition. As for B-17F 42-29992, she was so badly damaged that she was "written off" on 1 July. "Black Wednesday" soon became a distant fragment of the Group history, as its personnel experienced further days of tragedy – but surely none with such a joint involvement of ground and combat crew.

Full entry into the "Big League of Sky Fighting," both in respect of the duration and intensity of the mission, occurred on the 25th when the Group went to Hamburg – not that some of the crewmen would have noted a material difference after their bloody initiation over Antwerp. (It was ironic that groundcrew casualties were so far almost on a par with the combat crews; 16 men as opposed to 20 MIA, two KIA and seven killed on the 23rd at Ridgewell). Cols. Nazzaro and Fiegel led 24 B-17s in an 0545 take-off to bomb the Glockner aeroplant. In the event, cloud cover prevented accurate bombing and only 14 aircraft released their loads within the assigned area. Flak and fighter opposition varied between meager and moderate, but one B-17 was MIA, its loss continuing the run

This still anonymous B-17F is making a test flight from the Douglas plant in Los Angeles during April 1943. It was assigned to the 381BG while the Group was at Pueblo and became "Damfino" of the 532BS. Lt. Harry Smith took her to England, where she and this crew were to become one of the eleven bombers failing to return from Schweinfurt on 17 Aug '43.

A mixed formation of 532BS and 533BS Fortresses reveals how the former Sqdn started off with its VE code letter allocation, whereas the OQ code for the other Sqdn would soon change to VP. Several researchers have suggested the nearside B-17F is bearing the Group-identifying letter L. This is a coincidence of letter-usage, and actually relates to 381BG practice (prior to introduction of the "Triangle L" insignia) of placing the aircraft letter above the serial.

of bad luck for the 533BS. This was 42-30027, flown by Lt. Schrader and carrying the Sqdn. Operations Officer, Capt. John H Hamilton. There were no survivors among this crew following their aircraft's crash at Bengerseil. T/Sgt Goucher on Lt Frick's 534BS crew was slightly injured, with this being the first of several similar experiences.

Another 534BS crew, that of Lt. Lishon, lost their No. 2 engine on the way in. Shortly after this occurred, fighter strikes by three Fw190s killed S/Sgt Ivan Tieman, one of the waist gunners, and wounded his companion, Sgt Pedrosky. The bomber then absorbed further punishment that knocked out a second engine and damaged the controls. By now on its own, the straggler was being pursued by up to 16 Fws as a friendly cloud layer was slipped into and the crew threw out all weapons and other detachable equipment. The cover dissipated over the Friesian Islands, and almost at once a Fw 190 swooped in from behind. Sgt Bill Marques (TG) now had no guns with which to challenge his deadly opponent, and in desperation started to throw out anything on hand, including ammunition boxes – and even his boots! Whether or not this unorthodox form of defensive fire affected the enemy pilot would never be confirmed, as he went into a steep dive and disappeared. All expendable gear continued to be jettisoned, and the prospect of "ditching" was real, but "Whaletail" was held up long enough to regain friendly shores and divert into the RAF airfield at Foulsham in North Norfolk.

This same day burial services for the personnel killed on the 23rd were conducted down at Brookwood Military Cemetery to the South of London. This facility dated back to World War I, but would be displaced towards the end of 1943 by a new Cemetery at Madingley to the West of Cambridge, whose grounds were granted to the American authorities by the British. Chaplain Brown led the Service, as well as a Memorial Service next day back at Ridgewell.

A similar degree of frustration to the Hamburg sortie was experienced on the 27th when Villacoubley air depot was found to be "socked in." This time no bombs were dropped by the 19 aircraft dispatched since there was a distinct risk of causing

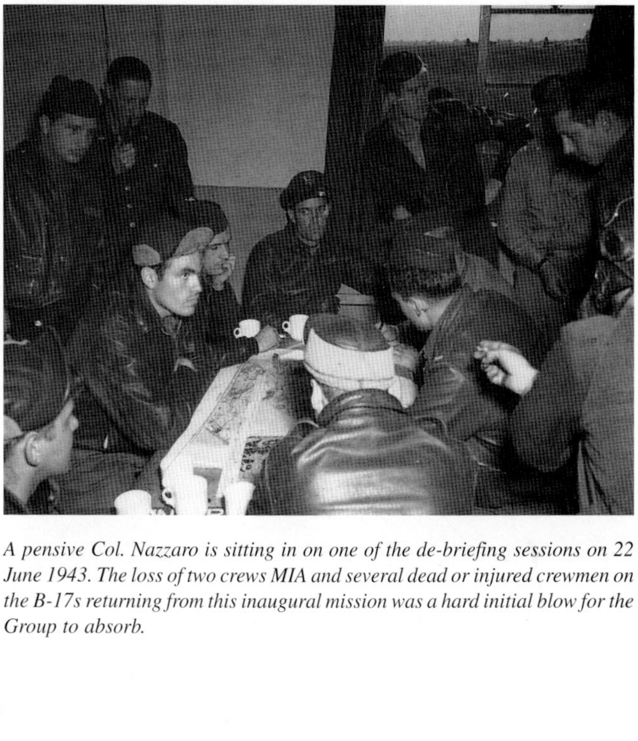

A pensive Col. Nazzaro is sitting in on one of the de-briefing sessions on 22 June 1943. The loss of two crews MIA and several dead or injured crewmen on the B-17s returning from this inaugural mission was a hard initial blow for the Group to absorb.

This picture was taken during the first mission de-briefing. Three days later (25 June '43) Sgt Ivan Tieman (in center facing left), a member of Lt. Lishon's 534BS crew, was killed by a cannon shell. The baby-faced airman facing camera on left is Lt. Don Rutan, Lishon's co-pilot; he finished up with his own crew in December when barely 20 years old!

casualties among the French population. (This was of little consolation to the 384BG, who lost five B-17s in the process of adhering to this strict principle.) The penultimate June run on the 28th involved 22 crews and was directed at a target upon which the 8USAAF had cut its teeth over the past eight months. St Nazaire's submarine-pens were about to receive their final aerial assault before the 8USAAF turned its full attention on the German aircraft industry, as agreed within the terms of the "Pointblank" Directive. This time Col. Nazzaro was leading the full CBW, and the 381BG planted its load of 2000-lb ordnance squarely upon the Aiming Point. June operations were rounded off next day with another abortive mission when solid cloud cover was found on approach to and over Triqueville airfield in France. Only two Sqdns led by Capt. Briggs (Assistant Group Operations Officer) participated as part of what was a diversionary tactic for a 1st Wing run to Villacoubley. Back at Ridgewell one more fatal statistic was added to groundcrew ranks when Sgt Bob Anderson was accidentally shot while he was discussing the readiness-state of Sgt Miller's sub-machine gun!

The six missions so far briefed had resulted in three B-17s and their crews MIA, along with two crewmen KIA. The bombing results on the three completed runs had varied between "uncertain" and "concentrated." Enemy fighter claims were 9-2-13 (destroyed – damaged – probable). The Group had acquitted itself well, despite a relatively adverse start, and was now ready for the imminent and sterner task of striking at the heart of Hitler's Empire – a process that would see rapidly fluctuating fortunes for both it and the 8USAAF.

Up to the end of June the heavy bomber units had borne little markings other than individual aircraft and Sqdn codes. This situation was bearable during the early days of the Offensive when the few Groups on hand meant that unit and Wing assembly problems arising from mis-identification were at a minimum. The recent sizeable expansion in the overall strength of the 8USAAF dictated that a more distinctive identification system be introduced. This was mandatory in order to ensure not only that Groups and CBWs assembled properly, but also to ensure that elements of 1st and 4th Wing did not inter-mingle. (The latter situation was one that could arise given the enormous aerial space required for forming up the overall Task Force.)

The vertical fins above the serial number and the right upper-wing surfaces were painted with geometric designs, triangular for 1st Wing and square or rectangular for 4th Wing, within which was applied an alphabetic letter. In Ridgewell's case this was "L." Application of the markings caused a degree more effort for the 381BG groundcrew compared to the other 1st Wing Groups.

Prior to the new arrangements it had been policy to apply the aircraft letter below the serial number on the fin; for some unknown reason Ridgewell aircraft bore these letters above the serial. Cynics might have equated the issued letter "L" with the Group's "freshman" status, but in retrospect the expression "L for Leather" was to prove a more apt connotation!

Yet another crew are reportedly being de-briefed at Ridgewell after the first Group mission. Presence of Lt. Inman Jobe (on right and pointing to map) tends to contradict this date. At time of de-briefing on 22 June '43 Jobe had just crash-landed 42-3226 "Little Chuck" in a Kentish field.

Capt. John Hamilton was the 533BS Operations Officer and is photographed while the Group was at Pueblo. On 25 June '43 he was co-pilot to Lt. Schrader in 42-30027 when all ten crewmen were KIA over Hamburg.

Lt John Carah was co-pilot to Lt. Ballinger (533BS). Both airmen managed to evade capture after their B-17 was shot down on the Le Mans mission of 4 July '43. John is snapped, still wearing his flying coveralls, in the company of the French family who sheltered him during the first stage of his evasion and eventual return to England.

July 1–23 1943

On 1 July the 8USAAF's ranks had swelled to twelve B-17 Groups, capable between them of dispatching up to 300 bombers. This was in stark contrast to just three months previous when the six operational B-17 and B-24 units could barely muster much more than a third of this figure. The "Point-blank" Directive was primarily aimed at German aircraft production and the dispersal of such aircraft to depots and operational airfields, with the initial attacks focused on locations in France. It was appropriate that the first of these missions occurred on 4 July when 24 aircraft under Lt. Col. Fiegel hit the Ghome-Rhone factory at le Mans; other targets were concurrently struck in a well co-ordinated plan to split the German defences. Only one B-17 was lost, but again this meant more heartache for the 533BS when Lt. Olaf Ballinger, flying in 42-29928, went down.

Lt. John Carah (CP) recalled how Fw 190s raked the B-17 during run-up to the target. Both waist-gunners and the ball-turret gunner were killed, and the oxygen system was knocked out. Out of formation the bomber received further attention from three Fws whose strikes resulted in the elevators and rudder jamming and forcing it into an uncontrollable climb. Realising the inevitable stall-out would be fatal, the bale-out

Lt. Ed Manchester's original B-17F is photographed on its 535BS dispersal in June or early July '43. This bomber, which was named TS, was "written off" after force landing at Manston on 14 July, having survived a mid-air collision with a Fw 190. Its replacement 42-29941 became "TS TOO"!

bell was rung. Up in the nose Lt. Williams (B) had spilled his chute, and although gathering it together declined John's suggestion he jump. John delayed opening his chute until near the ground, but when nearly down was horrified to spot an Me 109 bearing down on him; the pilot did not fire, but his "prop-wash" rocked the American back and forth. The B-17 was seen to crash close by, and just before it impacted a body (assumed to be Lt. Williams) squeezed out of the nose hatch, but sadly failed to get clear in time. The bombs were still on board, and their blast again severely oscillated John's chute.

He landed in an orchard, buried his chute and all insignia, and, using his compass, took up a Southerly route. Coming across a farmhouse, John took the advice previously offered at the Security briefings to observe the premises for several hours before considering an approach to the inhabitants. Although there was no guarantee the occupants were supporters of the Allied cause, he still knocked on the door and endeavoured to convince the woman who answered what his status was using sign language. His act was convincing enough for him to be invited into the house, and fortune was with him because his plight was brought to the attention of the local Resistance. So began a process spread over many months and involving regular moves, but which culminated in John's return to England. He was initially escorted through to neutral Switzerland, but in Jan. '44 volunteered to try a new escape route going to Spain. On one occasion near the village of Frangy, close to Mont Blanc, his party was captured by German and Vichy police, only for the Resistance to counter-attack and secure the fliers' re-release! Lt. Ballinger had similar good fortune to John in regaining friendly shores.

Six days elapsed before yet another attack on Villacoubley was made. The formation leader, Maj. Ingenhutt, was forced to "abort" with engine failure, and his place was taken by Col. Hall. Once again a complete cloud cover forced the bombers to return home with their ordnance.

By the middle of July eight full missions had been briefed. Field Order No.74 on the 14th (Bastille Day) called for an attack on Amiens-Glissey airfield in Northern France. Opposition from the two French-based Geschwadern JG 2 and JG 26 – the principal Luftwaffe forces defending this sector of Festung

Ed Manchester stands second from left, along with his crew and their B-17F "TS" on 15 July '43. Damage caused the previous day by the colliding Fw 190 is clearly evident. Ed is holding the remnant from one of the fighter's cannon barrels that was found lodged in the bomber's bomb bay! The bomber was considered too badly damaged to be repaired and was declared surplus to operational requirement.

Another 535BS "original" B-17F was "Lucifer Jnr." An unusual location for what is a devil or snorting bull has been applied behind the Sqdn code letters. This aircraft was one of several transferred to the 305BG on 22 Aug and was MIA on 14 Oct '43 during the infamous "Black Thursday" mission to Schweinfurt.

Europa – could be counted upon as ever. For three of the crews attending the briefing the day's events were to bring huge and tragic variations in personal and corporate fortunes. Lt. Holdom's crew would end up as MIA, while an arguably crueler fate would await most of Lt. Hedin's crew. The third crew, led by Lt. Manchester, would live through an experience never to be forgotten by those members who would in time complete their 25 missions.

Maj. Post was in charge of the 24 aircraft taking off, of which only 17 would make effective sorties. One of the seven "aborts" was "Red Hot Riding Hood" (42-3223), but instead of returning to her dispersal the B-17 was to become a pile of twisted wreckage strewn across Rattlesden airfield. During the prolonged group assembly the No.3 engine was observed to be smoking and then catching fire by Sgt Potts (ROG). He suggested that it be "feathered," but almost straight away as Lt. Hedin said he was taking this course of action the Sgt gave out with "Whoops, it's gone!" Potts must have blacked out at this point, because when he came to it was to discover he had exchanged the enclosed space of his radio-room for the open space of mid-air. Pulling his ripcord, he floated down while all the time watching the death throes of his aircraft. The bomber had

What is reputed to be the last Short Stirling to depart from Ridgewell is just lifting off. Its massive two-stage landing gear left the cockpit area no less than 22 ft. up from the ground! In spite of its bulky appearance the aircraft proved to be very manoeuvrable, but its inability to gain operational altitudes much above 12000 to 14000 ft left it particularly vulnerable to flak and night fighters.

"Sad Sack" was assigned to, and flown over to England by Lt. Jack Owen (532BS). It was his crew who went down over Hamburg on 25 July '43; all ten crewmen baled out into captivity.

This Group formation picture has been taken just after the introduction of the Divisional triangle system in July '43, since the Group letter L appears to be missing from the triangles. Presence of aircraft letters on fuselage indicates bombers are from the 533BS – the only Sqdn. at Ridgewell to regularly repeat the letter in this manner.

split in two behind the radio-room, and after descending a few thousand feet the outer wing sections were seen to detach themselves and the nose folded back against the truncated fuselage. Only three other crewmen survived the incident, about which a Group Medical Officer made the very pertinent note in his diary "Sometimes you do not need combat to suffer losses." Lt. Frank Cappel's (B) memory over the next few days was totally expunged, and such was the traumatic effect upon him that he never resumed combat duties and was finally medically discharged almost a year later. The cause of the aircraft's disintegration was traced to the No.3 master cylinder rod fracturing and creating a progressive destruction of the engine, which in turn fatally affected the wing structure.

Some 53 B-17s of the 101PCBW (Provisional Combat Bomb Wing) got through to the target, of which only one – that flown by Lt. Holdom in WIDGET (42-30011) – went down; reports subsequently received confirmed the deaths of all ten 535BS men on board. By all rights there should have been one more 381BG bomber added to this MIA tally, flown by Lt. Manchester. This was 42-3211, which bore the simple inscrip-

Lt. Charles Hedin (533BS) brought this B-17F across from the States. Given the original Sqdn. code letters OQ, she was more identifiable as "Red Hot Riding Hood." Both crew and bomber survived until Group mission No. 9 (14 July '43) when they were involved in a particularly tragic incident.

The crumpled fin and rear fuselage section belongs to "Red Hot Riding Hood." On 14 July '43 the 533BS B-17F broke up during assembly and fell to earth right on the edge of Rattlesden airfield in Suffolk. Only four of the ten crew survived the grim incident.

This is 42-29954 "Devils Angel" of the 534BS, which became the regular mount of Lt. Bill Wroblicka. Picture was taken in late June or early July when Division geometric designs were being applied to the fins and right-upper wing surfaces. The de-icing boots have been removed from wing and fin leading-edges, but only from one stabiliser.

tion "TS" on its nose. Lt. Bob Weniger (CP) hailed from Texas, and the official explanation for the initials was "Texas State," whereas the true interpretation was "Tough S...!" This latter expression reflected the sense of defiant apprehension with which the American bomber crews approached their daunting task.

One of the potential penalties for the Luftwaffe fighter pilots in making head-on attacks was the tremendous closing speed of anything up to 450 mph, and the prospect of a collision with one or more of the bomber formation if prompt evasive action in the form of a downward half-roll was not taken. As "TS" was making her turn off the target, Lt. Weniger called in a pair of Fw190s who were climbing at full rate on a parallel course, and when far enough ahead reversing their course to make what he later described as a "balls to the wall" forward pass. The ensuing events are best related in his own words:

"Prior to coming into range you could see their wings belching fire. All our gunners were firing at max rate, but they kept on coming. At this point I knew we were in for a real problem. The Lead fighter rolled to the left and Split S down some four or five lengths ahead of us. Sgt Tucker (BT) shouted out 'He almost took my guns with him!' The wingman to the right was either dead or dammed mad at us for bombing his airfield when he also rolled left for a Split S. His aircraft was perpendicular when he crashed into us between the No. 3 engine and the fuselage. His nose section and propeller became unglued and departed over the top of No. 4, cutting a deep gash in the nacelle top, which immediately poured forth a big black stream of oil resembling a Texas 'oil gusher' into the air.

The crashing Fw. continued on down the fuselage, embedding one of his 20mm guns in our bomb-bay and part of his fuselage lodged in our aircraft; I still have one such piece with the dates and names of my crew, as well as the gun. (The author actually handled the latter item, which was a section of a 20mm gun-barrel, during a visit in 1977). With this evidence there is no doubt of the head-on collision, and to my knowledge the only such collision where one of the aircraft got back.

Sgt Budzik (RWG) was holding his gun when the Fw hit the barrel. He reported the shock was so great that it threw him to the floor. The Fw's progress knocked the dorsal fin out of alignment and heavily damaged the right horizontal stabiliser and elevator. The tail-gunner stated

A formation shot taken during the first weeks in England picks out two B-17Fs of the 535BS. Nearest to the camera is 42-29953 "Man O' War," which departed Ridgewell for the 305BG on 22 Aug. The other bomber is 42-29950 "Forget Me Not," which was MIA on 12 Aug '43 with F/O Evans and crew. PL codes were changed to MS during July '43.

that the Fw left the scene in an un-controlled cartwheel – that's the hard way to knock down one of Jerry's fighters, and is not recommended for longevity for bomber crews!

Due to the impact 'TS' was in a dead stall. Acting on reflex, Eddie and I rammed the yokes full forward to their full extent and pushed the throttles forward for maximum power. This was then the time for a little prayer while we sat to see if TS would either fly or fall off one wing and into an irretrievable spiral or spin. I believe I shall never forget that moment, and if Eddie were still with us I am sure he would have the same feeling. Like the good old airplane that the B-17 is, after shuddering, groaning, and her instruments going all crazy, 'TS' began to fly again.

The controls gave a heavy vibration due to the severe damage suffered, but we were flying – we hoped. As I looked down Sgt O'Donnell (Eng.) was lying between the seats with his head against the pedestal. The concussion had knocked him from his top turret platform, and our first thought was that the pass had killed him, but within a few he came up fighting and said 'What the Hell is going on?' What a relief! The No. 4 engine was still gushing oil and was 'feathered,' leaving us with Nos.1 and 2, which were now advanced to full power and pulling 70 degrees of mercury. The intercom system was out, and the entire electrical system had ceased to function, which included the top and tail turret guns. O'Donnell went back to check, but returned to report no injuries, and that the ball turret was being cranked manually back into the exit position.

As the Group began to fade into the distance and we were letting down at 500 ft a minute to maintain flying speed, 'Smitty' (Lt. Marvin Smith, navigator) came up from the nose to report all was OK and that the nearest base was Manston. We could see the Channel when to our surprise and bad luck we flew over a flak battery, and big black smoke-puffs appeared all 'round. We received a number of hits, happily none direct; evasive action was very limited due to TS' condition. After running out of range (we later counted over 1000 holes in TS) we were sure nothing else could happen, although we were flying on a wing and a prayer. In this we were soon proved wrong!

O'Donnell, on his second return from the rear, called in German fighters. When asked if he thought they would attack the question was answered a moment later when a 20mm exploded under Eddie's seat. There was no doubt they were in for the kill of our crippled B-17. Sgt McCook (TG) later stated the fighters were making pursuit passes from the high right angle. He also said that one of his guns had jammed during the fight, and in the heat of battle while attempting to clear this weapon he pulled the cocking-lever clear off! (He showed it to us after our crash-landing). O'Donnell used his wisdom and training to fire off continuous red flares, seeking help from any friendly fighters around. At this stage the outlook was very grim, and although nobody wanted to admit it, the odds were the Luftwaffe was going to eat us up in quick time.

Then, with a stroke of luck provided by that Man Way upstairs, word came from aft that P-47s were attacking the Fws, and we began to witness a dogfight. After the Fws were driven off one P-47 flown by Capt Jack London (the first 'Ace' in the ETO) appeared off our right wing – the most beautiful sight I believe any of our crew had ever seen. After a few waves of friendly greeting and indicat-

Another early picture shows 42-5845 "Whaletail II" sitting at her 534BS dispersal. Group practice of placing aircraft letters above the serial was a relative exception to 8USAAF rules stipulating that aircraft letters be placed below. JZ codes were altered to GD at the same time as the 533BS and 535BS code-alteration.

"Georgia Rebel," an "original" B-17F of the 535BS, went to Heroya, Norway, on 24 July '43 but did not return. Maj. Osce V. Jones and Lt. George Mackintosh had the dubious distinction of flying the first USAAF aircraft forced to divert into Sweden after their aircraft received flak damage.

ing we had no radio we asked for continuous escort by using sign language. All was well, except that we were running out of altitude. Could we possibly clear the Channel, or would we be forced to ditch? The order was given to throw everything possible out; we were going to England, come Hell or (hopefully no) high water! One seldom realises how long it takes to cross that strip of water, but our trusty old 'TS' did it. The day had turned hazy, and we looked desperately for a landing strip. There then appeared a number of barrage balloons in front, and the thought ran through our minds that we just could not have come so far and been on the razor's edge for so long to wind up flying into one of these!

Things were looking grim when a shout from Smitty and Black (Lt. Bob Black, bombardier) came that a landing strip was in sight, and Capt London dipped his wing to indicate its direction. We had to turn in order to line-up; this was made cautiously, hoping 'TS' would not stall out and quit on us. Our indicated air-speed had been 120mph since the collision, and we were not going to change it now since we were starting down final with one good engine (No. 1), a sick No. 2, and Nos. 3 and 4 'out.' In all my

An enterprising photographer took this shot of "Georgia Rebel" passing overhead as her pilots were seeking out a suitable location for putting down their damaged B-17.

years of flying I have never seen two men so well co-ordinated as Eddie and I at this time. No flaps or landing gear, RPM at the peg from the point of collision onward, and power being very cautiously reduced. (If you have power do not turn it off too soon; you may need it later, and it may not come back).

Over the runway end and then full power reduction; we floated, and then 'TS' the Queen at last settled in easily and rolled down the dirt strip in a 'gear up' attitude upon the protruding main wheels. So smooth was the landing that the IFF equipment detonators did not explode. At the end of the roll and without directions the crew evacuated in seconds, expecting TS to explode and burn. After grouping together and watching her smoke a little we returned to admire that great old aircraft that had brought us home safely. The English Aerodrome Officer arrived shortly to advise us we should not have landed on that runway because it had been mined in the event the Germans tried to land. Eddie dryly remarked to him 'We just did.'"

So the 14 July 1943 mission passed into history. Three B-17s had been summarily struck off the Group records, TS being so badly shot up she was declared Category E. Also gone were 16 of the 30 crewmen on board these bombers, while a maligned fate awaited several of the survivors in the months ahead.

July 14 was the final act for a sergeant gunner whose diary notes were anonymously quoted in "Target Germany," a fine, under-stated official account of the 8USAAF's first year in combat and produced in 1944. His brief record stands as a simple tribute to all who failed to run the gauntlet of flak and fighters, or died over England in what were euphemistically described as "operational" crashes:

"June 22. Our first engagement. Antwerp was our target. Our part was a minor one intended to keep the Germans' attention divided while the main force hit Huls. We were hard hit by Fw190s and had our share of flak. The two other ships in our Flight never returned, taking three of the men in my barracks down with them. Our tail gunner was killed by the only shot to enter our ship. He was a fine fellow.

June 25. Today, Hamburg. Rather a wasted trip. A large formation dropping bombs through thick cloud obscuring the target. Flak and fighters with us. One B-17 went down, taking more of my friends and our Operations Officer.

June 26. Target a French airport. We turned back over the Channel when No.1 quit. Others went in, but weather bad and only a few bombed.

June 28. Big game, big formation. We made the Germans at St Nazaire aware of our presence. Our bombs raised submarine pens to heaven. Encountered clouds of flak and fighters. On way back picked up two fighters

Curious onlookers cluster 'round "Georgia Rebel," following her safe crash-landing in a bog near Vannacka. Bomber's momentum stopped just short of the large pole located in front of the right wing.

which made repeated attacks on our tail. Had the unpleasant experience of seeing 20mm shells exploding close to our tail. Stopped at an RAF field overnight. They treated us wonderfully.

June 29. Flying today with Lt. L. All enlisted men in hospital with the exception of one who is dead. We go well into France looking for our target, which is cloud-covered.

July 4. Another Independence Day quite unlike any other I can remember. A German aircraft factory in France got a look at some American fireworks. Our crew went as spares and had to return just short of France. Today we are heavy-hearted because Lt. B's crew did not return.

July 8. No mission today. I received the Air Medal for the successful completion of five missions."

The diary postscript in "Target Germany" baldly states: "Six days later the author did not return from a mission and is listed as MIA." In fact, a comparison of the 533BS records over the diary period indicates the author to be either Sgt Marhefke or Sgt McDonald from Lt Hedin's crew. The June 22 fatality appears to be Hedin's TG, Sgt Lorick; Capt. Hamilton (the Sqdn's Operations Officer) was MIA on June 25; finally, Lt. Ballinger's crew were MIA on July 4. The author's loss coincides with 'Red Hot Riding Hood's' loss. The fact that those on board who were killed had died over English airspace rather than going MIA over Europe was no less tragic for themselves or their families. Such a brief combat career was to be paralleled by many Ridgewell personnel, as the German defences bit ever deeper into the 8USAAF ranks. In the course of this trial the "self-defending bomber" theory was to be dealt blow after blow, causing it to degenerate into its bloody demise over Schweinfurt on 14 October.

A return to German targets occurred on the 17th when 30 B-17s took off at 0705 under the command of Col. Nazzaro and Capt Kunkel (534BS CO), and with part of the Group flying a composite formation led by Maj. Ingenhutt. The Maj. was forced to "abort," along with four others. Solid cloud over the Hanover synthetic factories briefed for attack forced a diversion to a Target of Opportunity (TOT), later established as Geringhausen, which was accurately struck. Estimates of between 65 and 75 attacking fighters led to gunners' claims of 7-3-2.

There now followed a seven day lull in operations broken only by a notable social event when Lt Manchester's crew were taken by the 535BS PR Officer, Lt Saul Schwartz, down to London, where they made a broadcast account of the 14 July mission. The first ten Purple Hearts were handed out by Col. Gross, the 101PCBW CO, along with 120 Air Medals and two Oak Leaf Clusters. Few of those present, apart from Gross and the Senior Group staff, could have been aware that the morrow would initiate a seven day test of physical and mental strength for all personnel. Long-range weather forecasts were indicating a sustained spell of clear conditions over Central Europe, and the six full-scale missions that would be launched between 24 and 30 July would go down in history as BLITZ WEEK.

3

BLITZ WEEK TO BLACK TUESDAY

The crews called to briefing in the early hours of 24 July must have been surprised at both the target choice and duration of the planned mission. The map ribbon, instead of stretching into the Low Countries or Germany, was aligned NE towards Norway. The 1st Bomb Wing was to raid the recently commissioned Nordisk Lettmetal aluminum plant at Heroya, and a simultaneous attack on Trondheim further up the Norwegian coast was laid on for 4th Wing.

There were two novel features to the mission. Today was the first intended use of Splasher Beacons (British medium frequency radio stations spread throughout East Anglia), which would facilitate Group and PCBW assembly in overcast conditions. Then, instead of climbing to altitude over England as was the normal procedure prior to departing the coast, the bombers would head out at around 2500 ft and only rise to bombing altitude when on approach to the target. The latter tactic appeared to have fooled the enemy radar chain, which in turn could provide no early warning of the B-17s' direction to the waiting fighters.

Aerial opposition to 1st Wing was nil, and only meager flak greeted the Groups as they unleashed a lethal bomb pattern which rendered the plant largely out of operation for the duration of the War. The lack of opposition was of little consolation to Lts Osce V Jones and Mackintosh piloting "Georgia Rebel" (42-3217). Flak strikes forced them to a hurried sanctuary in nearby neutral Sweden, the first such 8USAAF aircraft to do so. The B-17 was crash-landed in a bog near Vannacka and barely missed colliding with a big wooden pole as it slithered to a halt. Mackintosh was the 535BS Operations Officer and had displaced Jones' co-pilot for this mission. Over the next six months the crew was repatriated to England, forsaking an undoubted lotus-eating life-style for the prospect of

On 2 August '43 Ridgewell was officially handed over by the RAF. Double rows of RAF and Group personnel flank the two officers who are completing the ceremony outside Station Headquarters. The RAF Ensign has just been lowered from the flagpole, and "Old Glory" will take its place.

Lt. Jack Painter's "King Malfunction II" sits on her 532BS dispersal. Her de-icing boots have been removed from fin, stabiliser, and wing leading edges. Bomber shared the fate of nine other Ridgewell B-17Fs over Europe on 17 Aug '43. Lt Painter was KIA, but Capt. Bob Nelson (Sqdn. Operations Officer) and S/Sgt Genz (TG) managed to regain English shores. The remaining seven crew became POWs.

a return to combat duties. In the event, both Mackintosh and Jones were fated to be shot down a second time on separate missions and wind up in the same POW camp!

John C Donovan was a replacement navigator arriving in England as a member of the Saunders Provisional Group and assigned to the 532BS on 14 July. Flying his first mission with Lt. Bill McDaniels, he awaited his first contact with the Luftwaffe in a natural mood of trepidation. Approaching the target the bombardier called in "enemy fighters at 11 o'clock" as a mass of aircraft bore in. John's fears were not yet to be fulfilled, since the "fighters" were gradually transformed into the comforting shape of B-17s from preceding Groups which had already bombed. The flak which had accounted for "Georgia Rebel" and left a couple of other B-17s with "feathered" propellers also nearly left its mark on John. The puff of dust he noticed coming up off the cabin floor during the bomb-run was later determined to have been caused by a flak fragment which struck alongside his position.

Any lingering sense of euphoria felt by the crews at the ease of the Heroya run and the possibility that it could herald a series of similar missions was swiftly and brutally wiped out next day when Hamburg was the briefed city, with its Glockner aero-plant as the assigned target. A mis-understanding in procedure during PCBW assembly found the 381BG vainly endeavouring to catch up with the 91BG and 351BG. In addition, six B-17s, including the designated Lead aircraft, "aborted"

A second "original" B-17F transferred to the 305BG on 22 Aug '43 was 42-30015. She lasted a few weeks longer than "Lucifer Jnr." before going MIA on 26 Nov. Photo taken before Sqdn. code change from OQ to VP, and introduction of Divisional triangle on fin.

The 305BG received a third Group B-17F on 22 Aug. '43. This was "Old Coffins" of the 532BS. She proved luckier than the other transferred-out bombers, since she survived combat over many months and returned States-side around June 44. The artwork on this B-17F is a simple skull-and-crossbones design.

the mission to leave Capt George Shackley (Deputy Lead) in charge. These problems were compounded at Hamburg when the target was discovered to be shrouded in a pall of dense smoke pouring up from the previous night's RAF raid. (What had been the first in a series of Bomber Command attacks intended to raze Hamburg to the ground bore the grimly appropriate code-name "Gomorrah." It would owe much of its success to the first use of "Window," metallic strips designed to drift down in clouds and blind the German radar system.)

Shackley continued to attempt catching up with the PCBW elements by cutting across the briefed target approach, but this stratagem bore no positive result and the Group skirted around Hamburg and headed for home while seeking out a suitable "target of opportunity." A few miles from the coast lies the small town of Heide, and its railroad marshalling yards and junction felt the weight of 15 bomb-loads. Two remaining B-17s should also have bombed had they not already dropped out as Hamburg was being cleared; these were the 532BS's 42-30013 "Lethal Lady" (Lt W Moore) and 42-29976 (Lt Jack Owen).

Lt Phil Dreisun, Moore's navigator, recalled how his bomber had swung wide at a turning point and was taken out by head-on fighter attacks. Lt Houck (B) was fatally wounded by a 20mm shell, and Lt Dale Wendte (CP) was also killed, along with two gunners. Dreisun's parachute pack had absorbed the worst effects of a shell. Consequently, he suffered an extremely rapid descent under the partially destroyed canopy, and the impact on landing completely knocked him out. He came to a few minutes later with a soldier sitting on his torso and rifling through his pockets, whereupon he gathered enough strength to contort his body and throw the German off. His B-17 impacted with the ground some 40 miles West of Hamburg and South of the River Weser.

Lt Owens' B-17 was seen by his wingman, Lt Baltrusaitus, to develop a fire around No. 2 engine and to sustain damage to the fuselage with pieces ripping off. Two parachutes emerged before the B-17 started down into the thick haze. Post-war reports by both Owens and Bill Bohan (CP) confirmed that all ten men got out, although T/Sgt Roy Slater (ROG) suffered a dislocated hip when he struck the tail section. Bohan suffered a more serious injury when a German civilian shot him through one lung shortly after the Lt. landed, but he thankfully made a full recovery.

The reduced Group headed out from the coast, but about 30 miles towards home Capt. Joe Alexander, flying 42-30153, banked off to the left and headed back into Germany. Ever since being struck by flak over the target one engine had suffered progressive vibration. This was now so severe that Alexander doubted the B-17 could make it back to England, hence the reason for his reluctant course reversal. The ailing bomber was soon picked up by five Me 109s, which were content to circle and take up station around their charge with the clear intention of directing its pilots towards an airfield. The Germans were ever keen to capture Allied aircraft intact for evaluation purposes, but the Capt. was not about to oblige if he could help it. He accordingly faked his approach, and finally belly-landed the B-17 in an open field. Sadly, the very open nature of the terrain and the presence of a Polish forced-labour camp in a nearby forest meant all escape attempts were totally thwarted, and the crew joined Lt Owens' team and the survivors from Lt Moore's B-17 in captivity. As Germany's second city and a major seaport and industrial complex, Hamburg was ever a hotly contested target, and on this occasion claimed 15 of the 127 American attackers.

A pair of P-47s is parked in the 532BS area. VE: K "Nobodys Baby" was very lucky compared to VE: E (42-30013) to the left, which was MIA over Hamburg on 25 July '43. After serving the Group, the 305BG and No. 100 (Radio Counter-measures) Group, RAF, 42-30034 was retired to training duties in March '44.

Barely had the Wright Cyclone engines had time to cool and the hard-pressed groundcrew time to patch up and repair the B-17s when the call for a return to Hamburg was outlined in the small hours of 26 July. Lt Col. Fiegel (soon to depart to take command of the B-24 equipped 93BG) led 22 bombers

Normally fighters protected bombers, but the reverse happened here. The Spitfire pilot reputedly called in to say he had problems and sought cover from the Group B-17s. Whether true or not, no self-respecting fighter pilot would come this close to the bomber formations, since he would accordingly be unable to combat any assault by the Luftwaffe.

One of the P-47s was "El Jeepo," whose pilot was Capt. Charles London. In this picture he is one short of the five "kills" which will make him the first 8th Fighter Command "Ace" in World War II

Photo taken from the original "Whaletail" (42-3221) picks out the trail which the crash-landed B-17F made through a Norfolk wheatfield. Rapid power-loss in three engines forced Lt. Bill Wroblicka into this drastic action on 29 July '43. Nobody was injured, and the bomber was salvaged a few days later.

"Nobodys Baby" leads a section of the Group through smoke created by several spent shell-bursts. Aircraft letter repeated on fuselage was not normal practice for the 532BS.

back over the same penetration route, but with withdrawal made to the South of the city this time. The Primary target of the Blohm und Voss U-boat yards was covered by a combination of bomb-damage smoke and that created artificially by chemical-screens, and recourse was had to striking the Howaldswerke U-boat yard, which was in the clear. Fiegel's bombardier, Lt. Thomas Hester, made an accurate sighting despite suffering a frozen hand. An incident arising during this mission would give rise to a "jinx-ship" reputation surrounding the 535BS's 42-5846 "Tinkertoy." A flak fragment killed Lt Sidney Novell, who was a replacement navigator on his first mission. Otherwise, all aircraft got back to Ridgewell.

No mission was called for on the 27th. The COs for the 532BS, 533BS, and 534BS must have been pleased, not only on account of the respite from combat, but also by confirmation of their promotion to Major. (The sole holder of this rank as a Sqdn CO prior to overseas deployment had been Bill Ingenhutt). The pace of operations was picked up next day when 20 bombers went out to the Fiesler aero-plant at Kassel, fully 100 miles East of the Rhine, but bombed the Hentschel tank factory at Altenbuna instead. Kiel was the focus of attention 24 hours later. No MIA losses were incurred among the 38 aircraft involved in these two missions, but there was to be one "Category E" loss.

Returning from Kiel Lt Bill Wroblicka suffered progressive engine failure over Norfolk. With just a single functioning engine he was rapidly forced to take 42-3221 "Whaletail" in for a crash-landing in a wheat-field near Thetford. On board were Capt Briggs (Operations Officer) and Capt Mackay (Group Navigator). The 534BS B-17 was "written off," but it

Second full picture of "Whaletail" shows her with bent propeller blades; it is probable these were spinning in the slipstream despite the B-17 being down to one functioning engine at the point of contact with the soil. Aircraft name and five mission symbols can just be made out on the lower nose area.

Maj. Bob Post (left) was the original commander of the 532BS. On 30 July '43 he became the first of the Sqdn. "original" COs to go missing. Post was one of nine survivors from Lt. Humason's crew, although he suffered the loss of an eye and a broken leg after the B-17F, which had been crash-landed, was strafed by an Fw 190.

was not long before Capt Lishon, having claimed regular ownership of "Whaletail" and given it this name, conferred the title "Whaletail II" upon its replacement 42-5845. The farmer's ire at the damage inflicted upon his crop by the skidding aircraft was more than matched by Bill. He quietly but rather caustically reminded the Englishman of the very pertinent reason for the bomber's presence there, and the fact that he and his crew were fighting for their mutual survival!

Although all the participating bombers returned to England off the Kassel and Kiel missions, there ought to have been one MIA statistic. Lt McDaniels, flying 42-29761 "Martha the II," was for no apparent reason lagging 800 yds back as the run for home was commenced. The lone B-17 all too soon became the focus for a number of Me 110s and Me 410s, which worked her over. A 20mm shell penetrated behind No.2 engine, which was "feathered," and over the next 30 to 40 minutes the gunners frenziedly beat off all assaults, as well as causing at least one pilot to abandon his fighter. Further damage was inflicted on an elevator, and a strike on one of the life-raft hatches destroyed its priceless contents. Despite the power loss McDaniels succeeded in finally catching up with the Group. Ammunition was running low, as what transpired as the final attack was initiated by three line-astern fighters slicing in from 9 o'clock. Lt John Donovan (N) sighted and fired on the leader, who promptly dissolved in a flash of flame, at which point his companions peeled off and headed home. John's reaction after the mission was to feel that if the Germans were to get him at this stage of his "tour," he would at least have extracted a price from them in the form of four missions – plus one fighter!

What was to be the final mission in a wearying week's effort was directed at Kassel and its Fiesler aero-plant on the 30th. One B-17 was MIA from the 18 despatched, with the 532BS suffering the loss not only of Lt Humason in 42-3100, but also its CO, Maj. Post. Crewmen on the Lead ship stated that the B-17 took hits, which disabled No.3 engine and also blew out the No.2 gas-tank on the already disabled engine. The bomber veered off to the right under heavy attack from five Fw190s, and at least two parachutes were sighted before it descended into cloud near Ascheberg. On board the B-17 the pilots were contending with three failing engines and loss of ra-

Capt. Martin Shenk (Standing on left) is pictured with the bulk of his crew in front of their B-17F "Linda Mary." Bomber was named after Shenk's daughter and was fated to be the last "original" B-17 to fall in combat when it was lost on the Berlin mission of 6 March '44.

Col. Nazzaro stands in the center of Lt. Manchester's crew. Manchester has his back to the camera, and Lt. Bob Black (B) kneels next to Nazzaro. Lt. Bob Weniger (CP) is third from the left.

The 532BS "original" crew of Lt. Leo Jarvis (kneeling second from left) poses for the photographer. Lt. Bill Lockhart (B) kneels on the right. B-17F is probably "Margie Mae," one of three Vega-production Fortresses with bulged cheek-gun frames on the left side, which were assigned to the 381BG. The other two examples were "Whaletail II" and "Tinkertoy."

dio and oxygen facilities. Four men did in fact abandon the bomber, but Sgt Anderson (WG) was almost certainly fatally injured when he hit the tail. All but one of the remaining six crewmen were wounded, and the aircraft was finally brought in for a crash-landing near Appeldoorn, Holland, where it was strafed by at least one of the Fws. Maj. Post's injuries involved a broken leg, and worse still, the loss of one eye – a scale of injury which later merited his repatriation to the States during 1944.

The relative success of "Blitz Week" and the concept of striking at aero-production centers by way of blunting the Luftwaffe's impact upon the bomber forces can now be viewed in a more objective context. Although the bomb concentrations were generally good, the policy – particularly on the 25th – of dispersing the 8USAAF's strength among no less than three separate targets, as well as dividing that strength between two targets on the other five days, tended to minimise the extent of the damage that full concentration on just the one location might have better achieved. The mix of high explosive and incendiary content in overall tonnage was reasonably sound. The former ordnance type had better ballistic properties, despite a Post-war survey indicating that one in every ten bombs failed to explode. However, heavy plant machinery often withstood the worst blast effect, but was much more susceptible to the heat-distortion of its refined parts, which could only be brought about by the use of incendiary weapons.

Gunnery claims reflected the intensity of operations, with an inevitable inflation well above subsequently confirmed Luftwaffe losses. Swinging a heavy .5 machine-gun on a flexible nose or waist mount and firing from what was a constantly swaying aerial platform was not guaranteed to produce a high degree of accuracy. Even the power-operated turrets had their

This B-17E had a short life at Ridgewell. Assigned to the 533BS in late July '43, it was gone within one month. Its new home was the Combat Crew Replacement Center (CCRC) at Bovingdon. Name of the bomber was "Annie Freeze."

Examples of artwork on the original batch of 381BG Fortresses were not too numerous. "Ole Swayback" actually arrived from the 96BG on 16 July '43 and was photographed on 8 August. Nine days later she was a shattered pile of metal at Ebrach, SE of Schweinfurt. Lt Leo Jarvis baled out his 532BS crew safely, although Lt. Bill Lockhart (B) lost an eye after being struck by a cannon shell.

This 533BS Fortress was one out of the original cadre brought over from the States. The title "Strato Sam" straddles a spanner-wielding airman. Its combat career was ended on the same mission as "Ole Swayback" (17 Aug. '43) when all but one of F/O Hudson's crew abandoned her near Munstereifel. The unlucky exception was Lt. Ken Robinson (B), who was killed at his post.

limitations. The concentration of fire produced by any one bomber was never great due to the widespread nature of the gun positions, and it was virtually impossible to achieve an agreed fire-concentration between bombers flying in the same formation. (During 1939/40 the Luftwaffe used "fire controllers" within specific bombers to co-ordinate the formations' fire-pattern, but the rather unimaginative RAF Fighter Command attack methods initially used did allow much more scope for these German specialists, at least up to the early stages of the Battle of Britain.). At best the bombers' firepower could blunt the otherwise overwhelming weight of fighter assault, and any destruction inflicted among the attackers was a distinct, albeit accidental, bonus.

The true savior of the B-17s and B-24s seeking to carry out the Daylight Precision Bombing policy would be the long-range escort fighter. Unfortunately, the P-47 Groups currently available were restricted by lack of range. Although the 28 July mission had seen some of the Thunderbolts penetrating as far as the Dutch/German border, it was still an unpalatable fact that when a deep-range mission was suspected the Luftwaffe could afford to stand off and only commit its full strength when the bombers were bereft of their precious cover. The first jettisonable fuel tanks had allowed the P-47s to gain their enhanced range, but problems with tank pressurisation and leakage were rampant and would not be cured for some time. Consequently, the bomber crews would have to endure their lonely crucifixion over Central Europe for the remaining bulk of 1943.

In this period two particular missions would test the 381BG to its limits. The first of these was only 17 days distant, and the choice of target would be attributed to an over-optimistic attempt to close a perceived "bottle-neck" in the Nazi industrial structure. On a more basic level the name of the target was to be forever burnt into the hearts and minds of the combat crews – SCHWEINFURT. The name of this town had been much on the minds of the 8th Bomber Command HQ staff. The initial plan was for a strike involving some 16 Groups to strike the ball-bearing plants located there. The anticipated effect of drastically reducing these specialist supplies to the German indus-

"Yankee Eagle" is seen among other 381BG aircraft on 8 Aug '43. She was never assigned to Ridgewell, but fluctuated between the 91BG and 379BG, with one short spell at Snetterton Heath (96BG). Indirect confirmation of non-assignment to the 381BG lies in the photo-date; aircraft's nose carries 19 mission symbols, but the 381BG had only flown 16 missions up to this point!

Three officers of a 535BS crew are being de-briefed after a mission in June or July '43. Man sitting on the table wears his distinctive Sqdn. badge consisting of a bomb-carrying devil. His hand action probably describes the attack manoeuvers of Luftwaffe fighters.

trial machine was destined to become something of an obsession during 1943, with the off-set effect of alternate supplies from other German plants supplemented by Swedish and Swiss sources seemingly ignored.

In contrast to the original planned involvement of both British and North African-based units, the final plan of attack concerned only the 8USAAF and was drawn up just four days prior to its execution. The date planned would coincide with the first anniversary of the 8USAAF's inaugural mission. At Ridgewell the men's minds were more concerned with the simpler issue of survival. In 39 days eleven B-17s and 106 crew had been culled from the Group strength – stark statistics which represented 27% of the aircraft and personnel brought over to England. With a combat tour currently set at 25 missions, the prospects of survival were not good, and were to worsen between now and October.

Almost two weeks of August passed by before enemy air space was again penetrated. (Schweinfurt was the subject of a scrubbed briefing on the 9th). Sixteen of the 20 bombers heading for Gelsenkirchen in the Ruhr made effective sorties, but only upon "targets of opportunity." Three of the four Sqdns lost one aircraft each. The 534BS suffered its first combat loss with Lt Wroblicka's 42-29958 "Devils Angel." Assailed by fighters, Bill finally baled out his crew, but delayed his own departure for several minutes. He managed to evade capture for several days and headed West with the hope of getting into friendly hands in Belgium, but was taken near Aachen, close to the Belgian/German border. The 532Bs's Lt Moon in 42-5847 "Margie Mae," and 42-29950 "Forget Me not," flown by F/O Evans (535BS), completed the trio of losses.

The 15th and 16th both involved "milk-run" strikes in Holland and France. An airfield near Flushing (Vlissingen) was hit by 23 aircraft, and the next day Le Bourget airfield received 20 bomb-loads. Only four of the 246 crews involved were MIA, with none from the 381BG, a fact which reflected the solid cover provided by around 140 P-47s. It was all the more unfortunate that next day the bombers would again be largely on their own; the Luftwaffe, with its superbly honed strength, would hand out a particularly brutal lesson as the B-17s strove to complete their deepest thrust to date into the German hinterland.

Schweinfurt

The basic failure of the overall plan for the mission flown on 17 August 1943 has been thoroughly documented, particularly by Martin Middlebrook in his excellent book "Schweinfurt/ Regensburg Mission." The original ten minute separation between the 4th Bomb Wing bound for Regensburg and thence to North Africa and the 1st Bomb Wing detailed for a return flight to and from Schweinfurt was thwarted by the delayed departure of the latter force by several hours. Fog conditions were retrospectively claimed as the primary reason for the delay, but the same conditions over 4th Bomb Wing bases did not prevent their departure barely one hour behind schedule. Not only would the Schweinfurt Force have to fight its way in both directions, but the revised I.P. forced upon the bombardiers would be located over what was featureless terrain, while the run-up to the target would be down-wind. In addition, tactical

The burnt-out remnants of VE: A1 lie close to trees at Appeldoorn, Holland, on 30 July '43. On board with Lt. Humason was Maj. Bob Post (532BS CO), who lost an eye and suffered a broken leg when the bomber was strafed after crash-landing. Bomber had only arrived from the 95BG ten days before.

Lt. Frank Chapman (on right next to the American Red Cross man) poses with his 535BS crew after return from a mission. The coffee and doughnuts are an undoubted welcome bonus. Fourth from left is Sgt. Ed Myers, Chapman's ROG and the Group's first successful evader. On far left is Lt. Melvin Hecker (CP).

manoeuvers by the Force Leader, Col. Gross, would arguably add to the Wing's difficulties.

These malign factors were way ahead of the Ridgewell crews, as they were alerted once more in the early hours, breakfasted, and assembled for briefing. Take-off time, originally scheduled for 0630, was repeatedly postponed until almost Noon, when 26 bombers with Maj. Hall in command lifted off and ultimately departed the English coast. The basic Group formation comprised 20 aircraft flying Low Group within the 101 PCBW. The remaining six aircraft from the 533BS took a Lead Sqdn slot within the PCBW's Composite High Group

Capt. Baltrusaitus' crew were among the most experienced at Ridgewell with 16 missions behind them, but the choice of target stunned those crewmembers present at the briefing into shocked silence. Sgt Tom Murphy (TG) was to record a graphic account of the mission, and especially the three hours spent over enemy territory without escort. Fighter attacks were in evidence even before the P-47s and Spitfires were forced to turn for home. The Luftwaffe assaults were to reach a peak of intensity extending from Eupen in Eastern Belgium as far as approach to Schweinfurt. However, two 534BS B-17s had already been taken down before Eupen; these were Lt. Weldon Simpson's 42-30245 "Lucky Lady" and Lt. Forkner piloting 42-3227, whose aircraft crashed near Turnhout and Meerlaan. Simpson was his crew's sole fatality, while Forkner not only got himself and all others out safely, but was listed as evading along with three other crewmen.

Sgt Murphy's ship 42-29888 "The Joker" had been thrown upwards by a flak burst into the preceding element's slipstream, and the pilots had a hard time fighting the resultant turbulence, which threatened to throw the Fortress out of control. Murphy then recalled yelling to the pilots to pull up in order to avoid an incoming rocket, which streaked through the formation to impact with a leading bomber. (Analysis of the mission does not support the use of such a form of weaponry, although these were used later in 1943.) In reality, it was to be the conventional attacks from ahead which proved the chief form of execution on this day. Very little firepower could be brought to bear by the American crews upon their tormentors as the Fw190s and Me 109s came in from this angle.

Five more Group bombers were lost prior to the formation's skirting to the South of Frankfurt. First down was Lt N Wright's 42-30028 "Sweet Le' Lani," with the 534BS crew succumbing to fighter attacks over Düren, but not before all ten men jumped.

"Margie Mae" of the 532BS has her right stabiliser detached, which suggests it had been seriously damaged either in combat or in a ground accident. Bomber came from the same Lockheed-Vega batch as "Whaletail II" and "Tinkertoy." It was finally MIA on 12 Aug '43 when flown by Lt. Moon.

"Strato Sam" (42-3092) was a 533BS bomber flown by F/O Hudson, which fell to a combination of flak and fighters at Pesch. Almost immediately 42-30140, in the charge of Lt Painter (532BS), fell out and down to impact SE of Munsterfeld at Esch; Painter was the only fatality, and two of his crew not only evaded capture, but started out on an epic return to England. The bombardier, Lt Duke, was to later record that his reaction to the bale-out order was annoyance, since he was fully occupied with operating the nose gun and indeed was almost enjoying the experience! The fourth loss was 42-29983, which came to earth at Keeseling and bore Lt Challon Atkinson (P) and Sgt Jim McGoldrick to their deaths. The quintet of losses was completed when yet another 534BS crew, that of Lt Reinhard King in 42-29978 "Hells Angels," was taken down by fighters. Sgt Cecil Floura (Eng.) recalled Lt King calling for the bombs to be salvoed before issuing the bale-out order, whereupon all ten cleared their doomed bomber, which crashed at Bad Schwalbach, NW of Wiesbaden.

Nineteen bombers were left when the I.P. was reached, but official records state that only 18 made effective bomb-runs. However, although the B-17s of Lts. Harry Smith (535BS) and Leo Jarvis (532BS) crashed East and SE of Schweinfurt, respectively, de-briefing reports stated the former aircraft fell out of formation at a point where the Group was turning for the home leg. Smith's own Post-war observations confirmed that he bombed and the B-17 was abandoned directly thereafter. One of this crew, Sgt Elsberry, stated that he came down near Bamberg and was free for the next 13 days. All ten crew survived, but Lt Gwinn (B) suffered a 20mm wound. Their B-17 42-3220 "Damfino" came down near Marksteinach, five miles East of Schweinfurt.

The crash location of Lt Jarvis's B-17 42-29731 "Ole' Swayback" was believed to be at Ebrach, 19 miles SE of Schweinfurt. As the Group turned off left from the target a flak strike knocked out all power on one side of this B-17, causing her to complete an involuntary roll. Apart from the loss of one eye suffered by Lt Bill Lockhart (who recollected that he suffered this injury after the bomb-run), he and the others all got out safely. Lt. Jarvis was fortunate to get out, however. Having called for the navigator to attach a chute pack to Lockhart, he then reached under his seat for his own pack – only to find to his horror that Lockhart's pack had been grabbed from this position! Managing to stabilise the bomber, Jarvis hastily scrambled into the nose for the bombardier's pack, clipped it on, and followed the others out.

Following the bomb-run and re-assembly there was a merciful lull in fighter attacks for upwards of an hour until the Rhine was being reached, after which the by now badly depleted force was assailed by fresh waves of Fw 190s and Me 109s. The 381BG's severely depleted ranks were to remain intact until the Belgian/German border was being traversed. It was then that Lt Loren Disbrow's 42-3225 "Chugalug Lulu" was forced out of formation. The B-17 gradually descended as a result of steadily failing power, but there was still a chance of at least clearing the Belgian coast, if not getting across the English Channel. That hope was brutally shattered when Fw190s spotted the straggler near Liege and inflicted fatal damage. Lt Chapin (CP) was to recall that his emotions went from joyful anticipation to complete numbness in just a split second as the "abandon" signal was given. All ten crewmen jumped, leaving their B-17 to pile into the ground close to Tongeron. From this crew no less than four – T/Sgt Bruzewski (Eng.), T/Sgt Tom Moore (ROG), S/Sgt Joseph J Walters (BT), and S/Sgt Kiniklis (TG) – were to return to home via the Underground system. Although all four were at one time in the same place of concealment at Liege, the ultimate fate of a fifth evading crewmember, Sgt King (returned to England before or after Belgium's Liberation or capture at some stage), is unclear from Group records. The other five men, among them a badly wounded Lt Jones (N), were less fortunate in ending up as POWs.

And so the Group left ten B-17s and their crews, totalling 101 men, behind as the sorely battered formation crossed the Belgian coast in the early evening sunshine. Although a total of five crewmen KIA was low, for 85 there was beginning the strange and shadowy existence of a "Kriegsgefangener," or

This 535BS B-17F was regularly flown by Lt. Loren Disbrow. It sports a neat piece of artwork and ten mission symbols, but only one more symbol would be added before Disbrow's crew failed to bring it back from Schweinfurt on 17 Aug. Picture-angle picks out the twin pitot-masts borne by all B-17 variants up to the F-Model.

POW. The remaining eleven men were to experience the great good fortune of regaining friendly shores. In the case of Capt. Bob Nelson (532BS Operations Officer) and S/Sgt Raymond Genz (TG), who had survived the demise of Lt Painter's aircraft, their return was effected by the end of October – this after coming down well inside German territory!

Fifteen Group aircraft were now well out of danger from attack, but the sixteenth had been straggling home on its own for some time. Lt George Darrow's 42-29735 had suffered engine problems on approach to the target and had drifted inexorably back and down through its own and succeeding formations. The B-17 eventually struggled to within a few miles of the Kent coast before gently settling into the mercifully calm Channel waters. All the crew survived the potentially lethal act of "ditching" to be soon fished out by RAF Air-Sea Rescue launches and delivered to the nearby RAF field at Manston – one of three Emergency Landing Fields spread along the Eastern coast of England.

The bright promises for a successful mission in terms of bombing results coupled to low casualty rates had been shattered. The bunching up of the four Provisional Combat Bombardment Wings (PCBWs) on approach to the target had made for hurried and largely inaccurate bombing runs. This failure was probably caused by Col. Gross' previous decision to lower the height of the two PCBWs under his charge. This was made in order to avoid flying through what was seen as a solid cloud barrier at the briefed altitude. He then regained the briefed altitude. This was a measure that the other half of the Task Force did not follow, as it flew all the way at the briefed altitude. The scale and intensity of the fighter opposition had taken a terrible toll of the 183 B-17s penetrating enemy air space, with no less than 36 of this figure MIA. (A similar proportion of loss was suffered by 4th Bomb Wing when 24 were MIA out of 124).

This attrition rate was insupportable if continuing to reoccur, and highlighted the pressing need for long-range escorts. Unfortunately, these were still months away, and in the interim period the 8th Bomber Command would be forced to proceed with its policy and leave the bombers fully naked to the aerial threat posed by the Luftwaffe. Schweinfurt was still treated as a top priority target, and a second strike could surely be counted upon before the onset of winter with its short days and uncertain weather might force a halt to this venture.

In one savage day's combat the 381BG losses had been virtually doubled, and barely half the "original" crews were still on hand. The Group had earned the dubious distinction of suffering the highest loss-rate for any participating 1st Bomb Wing unit, although its 91BG partner had lost just one B-17 less. Morale must have been just a word, and the chances of coming through a tour of 25 missions seemingly worse than the chances of a victim of deep-seated cancer making a recovery. The sense of depression spread to the groundcrews. Mission pressures were none the less real for being in the hearts and minds of these "back-up" teams. Throughout World War II it was a regular feature for small groups to collect all around the airfield hours before the bombers were due to return, the casual air generally adopted concealing their apprehension at the thought of their specific B-17 failing to be part of the returning formation. All too often (131 times in fact) some of them would gaze Eastwards in growing and numbing disbelief as their dispersal remained starkly empty after all the bombers were down. Without their patient and physically demanding efforts the combat crews could not have guaranteed their own safety, particularly in the hostile environment over "Festung Europa." The outwardly casual relationship between fliers and groundcrew often concealed what was a bond born out of mutual respect.

Col. Nazzaro was no exception to the depressive mood enveloping his base. Indeed, and in the immediate aftermath of the mission, the need to declare a "non-operational" status for the Group was discussed. This was successfully argued against on the grounds that continuing involvement in the next mission would prevent the Germans from realising how hard the 381BG had been hit. Although not a totally convincing line of thought, given that Luftwaffe Intelligence was efficient enough to promptly establish both the Group and Task Force

"Sweet Le'Lani" (42-30028) displays the forward-firing .50, a standard mounting on Group "original" bombers. There was little chance for the four mission symbols to be added to, as this 534BS B-17 was downed with Lt. N. Wright's crew on 17 August '43. All ten crew became POWs.

loss-scale, the positive line of reasoning won the day. What amounted to a token force was assembled two days later.

Three airfields in Belgium and Holland were selected for attack on the 19th, with Gilze-Rijen and Flushing allotted to 1st Bomb Wing. The total force despatched was only 125, of which 93 made bomb-runs; Ridgewell's contribution was seven and five, respectively. Lt Orlando Koenig had headed the 535BS "model" crew during the early days at Pyote. Today he and Lt Len Spivey (N) were part of a composite crew comprised of 535BS and 533BS crewmen. Their B-17 was 42-3101, which had been transferred-in from the 95BG in late July. Heading in to strike at Gilze-Rijen, the run was cancelled in its final stage, and the crews prepared to circle around for a second run. In this period fighters caught up with and knocked down Koenig's aircraft. Lt Spivey was one of the fortunate survivors, along with Koenig, but a proportion of the crew was not so fortunate, the ball, waist, and tail-gunners all being killed.

For the rest of August the 8USAAF stuck to close-range targets, with 1st Bomb Wing striking Villacoubley (24th), Watten (27th), and Amiens/Glissey (31st). It was a clear measure of the battering borne by the 381BG over Schweinfurt that just 17 aircraft in total were sent to the first two targets; only over Amiens/Glissey did the Group return to near-normal strength when 19 participated. And so the general tone of morale was steadily if cautiously resurrected from the nadir reached on the 17th. However, these missions were but an interim measure and were not likely to last, at which point the immeasurably harder option of facing unimpeded enemy opposition would recur.

Lt. Will Baltrusaitus brought over "The Joker" from the States, and his crew flew the bulk of their 25 missions in this B-17F. Their good fortune at surviving their combat tour (excepting Lt. Sample, who took on his own crew but was KIA on 8 Oct '43) was mirrored by the bomber's career; it completed around 50 missions and returned to the states via AFSC in August '44.

4

RECUPERATION

By 3 Sept T/Sgt Ed Myers and S/Sgt Bang were combat-tested members of Lt Frank Chapman's 535BS crew, having completed 10 and 11 missions, respectively. Myers was rated as one of the best Sqdn. ROGs, while Bang's enthusiasm to remain with his crew overcame a broken leg suffered during training; the doctors recommended his retention in the States, but he evaded their control to come over by boat with the groundcrew! By contrast, Lt Benjamin Zum's crew were facing just their second mission. Therefore, the reason for Myers' and Bang's attachment to Zum was, to say the least, questionable. Taking off in 42-29789 "Big Time Operator," a 532BS ship normally flown by Lt Lord, they headed out along with 21 other bombers for Romilly's air depot. Only 19 bombed, and this figure was further reduced shortly after when "Big Time Operator" was observed to lose position before falling victim to fighters. Ten chutes were reported coming out of the doomed aircraft.

On board Lts. Willis (N) and Clark (B) prepared to jump, with the latter indicating the nose hatch be opened as he was fastening on his remaining loose parachute harness attachment. Lt Willis lost consciousness as he was pulling the emergency release and only fully revived when on the ground and with metal fragments embedded in his hands and legs. Clarks' fate was initially undetermined, but conflicting statements among the other eight survivors regarding the B-17 blowing up – when allied to a Resistance member's mention of the burial of an

The hoisting-beam on this specialist vehicle is about to lift a 500-lb bomb from among the stack of ordnance on the trailer. It will then be trolleyed under the belly of "Whaletail II" and placed in position within the bomb bay.

This is the main entrance to Ridgewell. The main collection of Nissen huts linked by covered passageways comprises the Base Hospital, and the single hut at top is the mortuary. A magnificent Memorial now occupies the base of the Guard hut at left of entrance.

The bomb-dump at Ridgewell was located up off the NW corner of the airfield. It consisted of parallel rows of ramps covered over with camouflage netting. Light colored track surfaces tend to negate the attempt to camouflage this potentially volatile section of the base.

S/Sgt Joseph J Walters was one of four crewmen from Lt. Disbrow's B-17F who evaded capture following their bale-out over Belgium on 17 August 1943. He is photographed in the company of two out of a group of Resistance workers. Walters was later got into Spain, from where he returned to England towards the year's end.

airman whose chute had failed to open and whose description fitted Clark – seemed to confirm that he was dead or unconscious before being thrown clear of the aircraft. (Lt. Clark and his crew had arrived at Ridgewell on 22 August and his combat career had lasted a mere four days.).

The two veterans among the crew were to have very different experiences. Whereas Sgt Bang quickly ended up in a POW camp along with five others, Myers was in friendly hands within two days and fated to return to England via Paris and a Breton fishing-boat by late October. (One of Zum's regular crew, S/Sgt Floyd Terry, was also able to avoid capture and was fed down the Resistance lines and back to England, while Lt Hoover (CP) made a similar "home run" before the year was out).

Ed Myers was later to state that Lt Zum seemed to be experiencing great difficulty in holding proper formation. After abandoning the B-17 he drifted down into a field within which a group of farmers were working. While he was disengaging his harness he noticed the men gesticulating in a manner which indicated he should hide in the trees forming a small copse. Here he was destined to remain for the next 48 hours, during which time several civilians came by but generally without making contact. The exception to this rule was two young children who ventured up to the young flier. In an attempt to com-

A typically murky English atmosphere forms the background to a line of returning Group B-17Fs. After completing the landing run, it was standard practice for the bombers to taxi on the outboard engines only.

The beautiful artwork on 42-30721 "Sweet and Lovely" is as yet unsupported by any mission symbols, although the Sqdn. badge is added below the cockpit. Originally assigned on 20 Sept. '43 from the 482BG, this 533BS bomber ran up a string of missions. On 25 April '44 it was assigned to Radio-Relay duties for the 65th Fighter Wing.

The use of British-designed inflatable air bags proved invaluable to the Groundcrew. In this case an outer wing section is being raised into position for attachment to a B-17. Picture taken on 1 Aug '43.

municate with the boys Ed made what could have been a fatal mistake; he knew neither French nor German, but acting on some illogical impulse uttered the word "Ja," whereupon the children fled! He was extremely lucky that details of the incident did not filter back to the Resistance. Had this proved the case he might well have been summarily disposed of as a suspected Nazi or Milice infiltrator, not withstanding that he had been seen to descend by parachute.

He had baled out on Friday, and by Sunday decided to seek assistance since none had so far come his way. Despite all the strictures contained in Security lectures given in the States and at Ridgewell about what not to do in these parlous circumstances, Ed would break several cardinal rules during this stage of his evasion. For a start, he walked down the middle of a small town's main street just as the populace were emptying out of the churches; no Germans were among the congregations who totally ignored this odd "stranger." Later the same day he committed an even graver error which could have cost him his life. For a civilian to go anywhere near a railroad track, let alone walk its length, was an act inviting a bullet from any intercepting member of the Wehrmacht or SS. Rail systems were regarded as a prime target for sabotage, and the soldiers were issued with "shoot to kill" orders. Great good fortune was riding on his shoulders in that nobody was sighted during this spell of trackside wandering.

On 21 Aug '43 Col. Nazzaro presented America's third-highest military decoration, the Silver Star, to T/Sgt John Sinclair. This was granted in recognition of the Sgt's gallantry, despite his own wounds, in attending to other wounded buddies during the first mission on 22 June '43. Sinclair completed his missions early in 1944.

The Station dance band was known as the "Rockettes" and comprised ten musicians. The clear influence of Glenn Miller shows up in the mix of trombones and saxophones. The band is playing in the Red Cross Club on this occasion.

Clambering back onto the road, he trudged on for some time before being over-taken by a civilian riding a bicycle. The man stopped and indicated he would render assistance – Ed was still wearing his coveralls and so must have stood out like a sore thumb, but the Frenchman still took a chance on Ed being an Allied airman as opposed to a German infiltrator.

There now ensued a protracted journey extending over two to three weeks. In this period Ed was destined to be transferred from several locations which culminated in his arrival in Paris. His stay at one house was rudely interrupted by the imminent threat of a German "swoop" upon the property, and he was hustled away into a depression in the ground where he spent several uncomfortable hours. His spell in Paris was relatively uneventful, and he saw few Germans, which was a situation causing him no loss of sleep. He also witnessed the bombing of a factory within the city. (This was on 15 Sept, as it was the sole attack on Paris during Sept/Oct. The raiders striking the Renault and Hispano-Suiza plants were from the 3rd Bomb Division, the revised title for the 4th Bomb Wing introduced on 13 Sept).

By now Ed's clothing had changed from official issue to a more Gallic garb. His profession as an umbrella maker – a deaf and dumb one at that – was eccentric, but his perceived aural and verbal deficiencies served to conceal his total lack of French expression. A further series of moves towards the NW coast of France was to conclude in an upstairs room above a bakery in the Naval port of Brest, one of the most heavily fortified bases in France. Within the premises were gathered no less than 40 Allied evaders, the majority airmen. What seemed a potentially suicidal act of assembling so many personnel within the heart of a Nazi troop concentration could be justified on the "Scarlet Pimpernel" technique – that is, placing yourself where your adversary would least expect you to be! In any event, the technique appeared to be paying off.

Lt George Darrow (532BS) points to the map during his crew's de-briefing session after the Schweinfurt mission of 17 Aug '43. Men on either side of Darrow wear RAF battledress jackets. Crew was outfitted at RAF Manston following their rescue from the North Sea, into which Darrow had been forced to "ditch" his battle-damaged B-17F.

Being as the final escape to England would be by boat it was natural to gather the evaders close to where the vessels were moored. Such a refinement was scarcely on the mens' minds on a Sunday morning when the critical move from bakery to dock-side was carried out. Grouped in pairs they were led to the quay and down into the stuffy hold of a typical French fishing-boat. Only seventeen of the party had been transferred when all further movement was brought to a halt and none were subsequently added to those already embarked.

Any chance of a quick release from the rather unhygienic conditions existing within the vessel's bowels was totally dashed. In fact, with the weather conditions becoming too bad for fishing to take place, a further six days and nights elapsed before the boat was ready to stand out to sea. Moderate weather the following Saturday involved a mass of vessels casting-off for the fishing grounds. Prior to the evaders' boat doing so, German guards ordered the two-man crew to open the hatches for inspection. The check was thankfully cursory; it is likely the guards were repelled from entering the hold for a thorough scrutiny thanks to the undoubted pungent smell emanating from that area – caused by a combined odor of fish and unwashed human beings! Setting course for the fishing grounds along with their companions, the crew waited until out of sight of land before taking up a Northward heading. (Fishing fleets were generally "escorted" by German vessels, so their apparent absence on this occasion in order for anybody to get away in this manner was surprising.)

It was almost certain that severe restrictions on the fishing fleet would have followed the disappearance of Ed's boat. Whatever the outcome, it seems the plan of escape was far from being a precipitate act, but rather was well thought out beforehand. The safe return of 17 valuable Allied airmen must have been calculated as a price well worth paying by the Breton sailors, whose loyalty to the Allied cause was unquestioned. Two days elapsed before a very welcome landfall was made off the SW English coast. Following attention by the local authorities, Ed was transferred to a London location where he remained for the next two weeks while going through numerous de-briefing sessions. In this time he was identified by his regular pilot, Lt Frank Chapman. His Continental odyssey had

"Battlin' Bombsprayer" lands off the 9 Sept '43 mission to Lille/Nord airfield in France. Aircraft's code letters are dulled-down, and the individual letter is (unusually for the 534BS) repeated on the fuselage. One calendar month after this photograph was taken the B-17F was one of three MIA when flown by Lt. Loftin.

been undertaken over an amazingly brief period, added to which he was the 381BG's first evader, a tale with which he could regale his children in years to come. (It is sad to relate that Ed's only child was fated to die as a paratrooper in Vietnam, a shocking contrast with his father's good fortune in World War II).

Back at Ridgewell a second consecutive mission to Romilly was "scrubbed." Two days later came the first deep-penetration run since Schweinfurt, which entailed a strike on ball-bearing plants at Stuttgart in South/Central Germany. The force CO, Col. Travis, had reputedly advanced the operational theory now put into practice on the 6th. Instead of climbing to altitude over England the bombers were to make a steady ascent into Europe, flying at just medium altitude until target approach when bombing altitude would be sought. The theory did not take into account the possible malfunction of turbo-superchargers. Any B-17 suffering from this deficiency would by then be so deep into "Indian Territory" that its safe return home was very problematical, given the inevitable detachment from its Group and consequent isolation.

Cloud conditions over the target added to sighting problems, and nearly 60 minutes passed by before bombing was completed. This left those crews whose B-17s were not fitted with "Tokyo Tanks" to worry over the possibility of running out of fuel before even reaching the English Channel. One such crew was that of Lt Paul Gleichauf (533BS). Sgt Comer (Eng.) was to recall that all four gas-tank warning lights were on as they cleared the French coast, and it was a miracle that 42-5846 "Tinkertoy" managed to stagger into an RAF airfield on the South coast. A second crew fortunate to make it back was that of Capt. Lishon in their regular aircraft, 42-5845 "Whaletail II." (Companion to "Tinkertoy" off the Lockheed-Vega production line). His crew was jettisoning equipment for part of the return flight and finally managed to get into an airfield close to Ashford in Kent. Twelve other crews were not so lucky and

The pewter-like surface of an unusually placid North Sea passes beneath a neat but well spaced out practice formation. GD codes on bottom-right B-17 suggest this is the 534BS. All are F Models, and within a few weeks of picture date (25 Sept '43) some will probably be MIA statistics arising out of "Black Week."

were forced to "ditch"; the calm sea was a key factor in ensuring all twelve were put down intact and the 118 personnel on board rescued by RAF launches. However, a further 33 crews remained behind on the Continent.

The next 20 days saw a resumption of the short-range mission. From Ridgewell a total of 35 bombers struck at Brussels/ Evere (7th) and Lille Nord (9th) airfields. Romilly's facilities were struck on the 15th by 17 Group bombers, and the next day Nantes Chateau/Bougon airfield felt the weight of 18 bombloads from the 20 aircraft despatched. Fully half the 22 crews heading for Nantes on the 23rd turned back, while there was a total Group recall when heading for Meulan on the 26th.

The month ended on a higher note when Emden's port installations were selected for attack. The mission was notable for two reasons. Use of the RAF's H2S blind-bombing device was indulged for the first time. The virtually solid cloud greeting the crews prevented any visual observation of the bomb strikes. On the other hand, such a weather pattern provided a reverse benefit in that the Luftwaffe was largely absent. The small scale of fighter opposition was ironic because the bombers were being escorted over a greater distance than ever before by 262 P-47s, whose post-mission claims for 21-2-6 might have been even greater had clearer conditions existed. The fighters' range had been enhanced by what was the initial use of 108 gal. drop-tanks made in America and signalled the 8th Fighter Command's growing ability to range ever further Eastward. Flak over Emden and the Friesien Islands damaged four Group bombers, as well as wounding four crewmen.

Lt Dan Hagarty's 534BS crew were on their 15th mission, and their B-17 received more than its fair share of attention from the Luftwaffe. One burst in the waist tore a leg off Sgt Jim Dunn and badly wounded Sgt John Crawbuck on the hip with a blow described as seeming like one made by a baseball bat. A tourniquet was swiftly applied to Dunn's leg and morphine administered before John went forward to get assistance from the ROG who was too busy; it was only then that the dull ache in his lower torso made him realise he had been hit. Everything possible was being done to lighten the bomber as Hagarty and Lt Rick Rylands skillfully held their aircraft aloft and finally brought it back over England. Prompt medical attention saved Sgt Dunn and soon restored Sgt Crawbuck to combat duty. He was awarded the Silver Star for his conduct on the Emden mission, but it was inevitable that his spell in hospital placed him behind his crew when they finished up in November. His luck would run out when flying with another crew on 11 Jan. '44, but at least he would survive as a POW.

September, in stark contrast to July and August, had culminated in minimal aircraft and crew casualties. Now that the 8USAAF had brought its available strength back to the point where upwards of 400 bombers could be launched its Commanders were ready to initiate another sustained campaign into the enemy heartland, with the ultimate intention of again striking at Schweinfurt. Hard times were again looming up, and October would prove to be a watershed in terms of strategic bombing – but not in the positive manner anticipated by Washington and "Pinetree."

Lt. Marvin Lord's "Big Time Operator" (42-29789) only lasted until 3 Sept '43 when it went down over Romilly-sur-Seine on 3 Sept. Its replacement was "Big Time Operator II," which was assigned from the 303BG on 7 Sept and operated until April '44 when it returned States-side. Although painted over, the PU codes from its previous unit are still legible.

"Lucky Strike" of the 532BS displays the Sqdn. tendency to apply its code letters on over-scale size. Bomber was originally with the 305BG and transferred to Ridgewell on 11 Sept '43.

5

BLACK WEEK

Many of the men filing into the briefing room on Friday 8 Oct. had flown the month's initial missions to Emden (2nd) and Frankfurt (4th). They had experienced no losses, relatively little damage to their B-17s, and best of all, no crew fatalities or injuries. Two of the pilots taking part today were close friends from their spell in the Coastal Artillery who had transferred to the AAF at the same time – Capts. Ed Manchester and Dexter Lishon. Ed's battle-hardened team were currently within six missions of finishing their tour; their co-pilot, Lt Bob Weniger, would not be with them, as he was riding tailgunner/observer in the Lead ship flown by Lt Bill Cormany and bearing Maj. Ingenhutt as Group Commander.

Dexter's crew were equally experienced, but his original co-pilot, Lt. Don Rutan, had recently assumed command of his own crew, and his bombardier, Lt. Darrell DeBolt, had taken up the option of a 24 hour pass up to London. Capt. Baltrusaitus' original co-pilot, Lt. Arthur Sample, was another recent Airplane Commander appointee. At the opposite end of the experience scale was Lt. Bob Miller setting out with Lt Ed Klein (B) and his other crewmen on their first mission. The impending "Black Friday" run to Bremen would leave its mark on all these participants, whether measured in hours or a lifetime. Two crewmen in particular would be involved in a horrific incident, and the controversial reputation of their B-7 would be further enhanced.

The assigned B-17s were a similar mix of veteran and novice aircraft. "Tinkertoy" (42-5846) had crossed the Atlantic in May, and Lt Jack Pry's "Feather Merchant" (42-30009) was another "original." Having had TS "written off" on 14 July, Capt. Manchester's replacement was 42-29941, which was christened "TS Too." A relative newcomer to the 535BS during July was 42-3177 "The Hellion." Capt. Lishon's "Whaletail II" (42-5845), which had accompanied "Tinkertoy" all the way from the Lockheed /Vega production line, would remain behind while her crew operated in 42-30722 "Bobbie."

Group and Wing assembly were carried out without incident as the 381BG dropped into the Low Group slot of what was now designated the 1st CBW. (This title replaced the former PCBW designation; in addition, the "Bomb Wing" titles for 1st and 4th BWs had been changed to 1st and 3rd Bomb Divisions with effect from 13 Sept.) Although de-briefing reports were to talk of fighter attacks which spanned over two hours, these appear not to have caused much bother in the period be-

The proper packing of parachutes was a vitally important duty. Canopies are being hung up to eradicate any trace of moisture, after which they will be laid out onto the packing table. One airman is patently ignoring the notice prohibiting staff from sitting on the table surfaces!

The official photo caption states "Pilot briefing his crew." In fact, the "pilot" is Lt. Marvin Smith, navigator to Lt. Manchester, who stands second from left. Beside him with hands on knees is L Weniger (CP). Lt. Bob Black (B) crouches in front of Weniger.

tween crossing the enemy coast and reaching the I.P. It was only then that Lt Weniger recalled "All Hell breaking loose" as flak batteries found the range and peppered the formation. By contrast, Ed Klein was of the opinion that trouble in this form only struck as the Group was turning right off the revised target of opportunity located at Vegesack, a course of action forced upon it by cloud cover over the Primary. He thought that in attempting to skirt Bremen laying to the SE the Group may have swung too far over and thereby permitted an element of the 600 guns allotted to that city to engage. Regardless of these varied observations, a foreshortened version of what befell the Group at Schweinfurt was about to run its course.

Ed Klein's B-17 took a burst which caused Plexiglas fragments to strike his face. Hastily clearing his vision, he was dumbstruck upon peering forwards. Where there had just been a number of aircraft ahead of "Our Mom" (42-29832) the sky was now vacant. On querying the situation with Miller and Lt. Joe Doerfler (CP) he was told to look downward, where his still shocked gaze took in the sight of B-17s either falling away or struggling in various stages of distress. "Our Mom" appeared to have also found itself detached, because Ed remembers the pilots attempting a successful link-up with two other stragglers. However, as the gap was being closed his B-17 came under fighter attack with cannon shells blowing the rudder off its supports and killing Sgt Steve Klinger (TG) instantly. The immediate upward surge probably caused by this drastic strike was countered with much difficulty by the pilots. On recovering control they realised their companion stragglers' condition with smoking and "feathered" engines would hinder the trio from catching up with a larger formation up front, and so "Our Mom" pulled ahead. Once inside this "formation" Miller's crew noted a number of different Group insignias, including some from the 3rd Bomb Division! This tangled situation confirmed just how rough the Bremen mission was proving to be, but at least "Our Mom" got back home.

One of the B-17s seen by Ed to be in difficulty was undoubtedly the Lead ship. Bob Weniger remembered how shrapnel kept rattling against the fuselage amidst the constant presence of innumerable flak bursts. Ingenhutt and Cormany still strove to head the Group on the bomb-run, and as far as the Rally Point when they finally relinquished the position. The No. 2 engine was well ablaze, and now free of the formation an attempt was made to extinguish the flames by diving. This action only succeeded in blowing off the cowling panels, and with the flames threatening to penetrate the firewall protection for the gas-tank the order to bale out was signalled as the pilots levelled out at 17000 ft.

A P-47 of the 4FG based at Debden is ready to start-up from a Ridgewell dispersal. The 108 gal. capacity drop-tank proved a vital factor in extending the "Jug's" limited range when solely dependent upon its internal fuel capacity. Even so, the bombers were forced to "go it alone" when striking into Central Germany, a course of action which finally caused an insupportable loss ratio in 1943.

Part of a 535BS formation is caught flying over a virtually solid undercast. B-17F taking the lead is 42-3180 "Forget Me Not II," in which Lt. Herbert Carqueville's crew went to their deaths on 9 Oct '43; all ten from this 533BS crew are commemorated on the Wall of the Missing at Madingley Military Cemetery, Cambridge.

Bob was sure all crew got out intact, but the Post-war "Missing in Action" report cast doubt on whether Lt. Bob Black, Bob's bombardier buddy on Manchester's crew, did in fact survive, since no trace of him had been found at the time the report was made. (Sadly, he did die and is now interred at Margraten Cemetery, Holland.) Falling free, Bob delayed pulling his ripcord until under 1000-ft. He remembered the descent as "one of the most peaceful experiences in my life," with the increasingly muted sounds of combat intermingling with voices and animal noises as he neared the ground. He landed awkwardly and was dazed by the contact. While gathering in his chute prior to running away he heard a woman's voice call out "American airmen must get drunk to fly over Germany," to which he responded in his pigeon German "You are a fool; that's not true." Almost at once he found himself surrounded by rifle-brandishing soldiers, one of whom uttered the classic Wartime expression "For you the War is over!" Bob would spend 52 days in "solitary" before being transported to a POW camp.

As Cormany was starting down Lt Eichhorn, navigator to Lt Hopp, noted how Ed Manchester banked right to avoid the Lead ship, and it was his opinion that TS TOO must have been struck and disabled at this point, since it never did regain position within the Lead Sqdn's first element. One of Hopp's gunners, Sgt Hanson, reported the same B-17 with No. 2 engine on fire and No. 4 "feathered" as it disappeared out of his vision. The final minutes of its existence are uncertain, but according to Lt Moore (B) fire was taking hold of the fuselage. Manchester had called for a bale-out, but the inter-phone was then knocked out. No gunfire had been heard from Sgt O'Donnell's top turret since crossing over the target, and S/Sgt Tucker had requested permission to vacate the ball turret on account of the danger posed by leaking gas. Meanwhile, Sgt McCook had moved the injured Sgt Berk, who had been replaced on Zum's crew by Sgt Bang for their fatal 3 Sept mission, to the tail.

An explosion blew in the nose and threw Moore and Lt Smith (N) back as far as the escape hatch, whereupon one of them hurriedly kicked the cover open and jumped. Although Moore recollected Capt Elton Jukes (535BS Ops. Officer) pressing close behind him, he did not survive; it was believed that he was either suffocated by the scorching heat or that his chute caught fire. What is certain is that TS Too broke in half, with the forward section wrapped in flames while the tail section spiralled to earth bearing Sgts Berk and McCook to a miraculously safe, if heavy, landing!

The end for two 532BS crews occurred almost simultaneously and within ten minutes of completing the bomb-run. Lt Arthur Sample's "Old Flak Sack" (42-29854) was already carrying two wounded crewmen when it suddenly went out of control and almost immediately exploded to blow out Lt Cytarzynski (CP) and S/Sgt Forbes as the sole survivors. The B-17's shattered remains fell to earth near Diepholz. Lt Jack Pry's "Feather Merchant" (42-30009) was deep in trouble, hav-

"Chugalug" (42-30765) leads another 535BS B-17F and a pair from the 533BS over a fleecy undercast. Picture taken between 20 Sept '43 when "Chug-A-Lug" arrived and 14 Oct when VP; P (flying on right of picture) was MIA with Lt. Yorba and crew.

"Old Flak Sack" of the 532BS is down on her belly on one of the runways. Cables are being attached to the wings with which she will be pulled clear by a Cletrac. Assigned on 16 June '43 she would be lost with all but two of Lt. Arthur Sample's crew over Bremen on 8 Oct.

ing been crippled just after bombing, and was reckoned to be some 15 miles SE of Bremen when detaching from the formation. The reverse experience to Lt Sample occurred in this case, with only two out of the ten crewmen failing to survive as POWs. One was S/Sgt Johnson (LWG), whose chute spilled out inside the fuselage. S/Sgt Lapointe helped him to gather up the canopy, but Johnson resisted all inducements to jump. He was viewed as an excitable individual and was thought to have "frozen" at the prospect of baling out, thereby going down with his B-17. The other death, that of S/Sgt Smith (BT), was attributed to his being killed at his post either by 20mm shells or flak.

Three more aircraft were lost during this mission. Capt Lishon and crew were all successful parachutists from "Bobbie." Their fate contrasted starkly with Lt Kemp's crew; no official information is on hand as to when and how this 535BS team met their deaths in "Ron-Chee" (42-3123). The seventh and final bomber failing to return to Ridgewell was "Nip N' Tuck" (42-29765) flown by Lt Jim Hartje (533BS), who was one of those on board ending up as a "Kriegsgefangener."

The tattered Group ranks were shorn of seven B-17s, but the most shocking incident was to occur on a surviving bomber. Lt Hal Minerich's "Tinkertoy" received a burst of cannon shells which tore off the nose Plexiglas; two of the shells penetrated the cockpit through the left-hand windshield frame to take the head completely off the hapless pilot before impacting inside. Lt Minerich could not have suffered, but the effect on his co-pilot, Lt Thomas Sellars, must have been traumatic. The blood-spray from the headless body of his fellow pilot shot all over the cockpit floor, rendering the top turret plinth so slippery T/Sgt Miller could no longer man his guns, and so he now bent his energies to assisting Sellars fly the bomber by handling the throttles. The windshield was smeared with blood, and S/Sgt

The date of this picture is 7 Oct. 43. A mere 24 hours later Capt.. Dexter Lishon's 534BS crew would be one of seven crews MIA over Bremen. Lishon is second from left and his navigator Lt. Bob Gluck is on the right. Kneeling between them is the unfortunate 'stand-in' co-pilot Lt. Carlton Long whose first mission this was! At least all baled out safely to become POWs.

John Wood (BT) recalled urinating on a piece of rag in order to wipe away the worst effect on forward visibility. Back at Ridgewell the errant B-17 completed its landing run with a sharp ground loop. Sellars had suffered wounds to his left arm, while up in the shattered nose both Lt Palas (B) and Stickel (N) suffered varying degrees of injury. A more pleasant sequel to this gruesome incident was the award of the Distinguished Service Cross, America's second highest military decoration, to Sellars – one of only two granted to 381BG personnel during World War II. Such was the effect on Sellars arising from the experience that he only returned to combat operations after several weeks.

Taking account of all post-mortem suppositions as to whether or not the formation had swung too close to Bremen or had impinged upon hitherto unrecorded flak concentrations, the sober fact was that the 381BG had again been dealt a harsh blow to rank alongside the disaster of 17 August. Flying in the Low Group position was also proving an unlucky experience. The 8USAAF had lost a total of 30 B-17s, to which the Group had contributed nearly one quarter. Group gunners' claims for 21-1-5 reflected the intensity of the battle.

Despite the beating handed out on the 8th the groundcrew were able to muster 16 bombers at the runway end next morning for what would be one of the longest penetrations to date. The crews were facing a 1500 mile round flight up to the Baltic coast to strike the Arado aero-plant at Anklam. T/Sgt John Comer on Lt Gleichauf's crew had accordingly arranged with his crewchief for extra ammunition to be carried, giving an

T/Sgt Dean Carrier and Capt Clayton Greenwood (535BS Engineering Officer) point to the holes made by two 20 mm cannon shells in "Tinkertoy"'s cockpit frame. Heavy damage to the nose Plexiglas left Lts. Stickel (B) and Palas (N) with moderate wounds. Bulged, frame-less cheek-gun position was a feature on the Lockheed-Vega production batch from which this B-17F originated.

T/Sgt Dean Carrier holds a measuring rule to the left cockpit frame on "Tinkertoy" the day after the 8 Oct '43 mission to Bremen. Holes indicate where the two cannon shells entered to decapitate Lt. Hal Minerich before exploding inside the 535BS B-17F.

enhanced total of over 13000 rounds, but adding more weight to the already critically laden B-17. Comer had ensured the added capacity of 6000 rounds was all stacked in the radio-room, then went about his business as the engineer.

Take-off in 42-27719 "Hellcat" – one of the first B-17G models equipped with the Bendix chin turret recently assigned to Ridgewell – progressed normally up to the point where the un-stick speed was reached, and then exceeded with the B-17 still firmly glued to the surface! Almost too late the bomber skimmed over the perimeter-end and rose a bare few feet before starting to sag towards the ground. Lt. Gleichauf decided upon drastic action to forestall the inevitable fatal crash by calling on Lt Kels (CP) to lower the landing gear. The Essex soil was mercifully firm and level as the wheels impacted to throw the B-17 back into the air and then grant enough time for the airspeed to pick up to a normal level. Moving aft Sgt Comer was horrified to discover that the boxes holding the excess ammunition had been dispersed among the waist and tail-gun positions. Worse still, Sgt Legg had gone into the tail before take-off. These twin factors had thrown the bomber's already critical center of gravity into a potentially lethal state; it was only thanks to a combination of pilot skill and favourable geography that the situation had been salvaged, otherwise one aircraft and ten men would almost certainly have been struck off Group records.

In contrast to the 3rd BD's brilliant performance over the Focke-Wulf production plant at Marienburg, results for the 1st BD at Anklam and Gydnia were only judged moderate to poor.

Lt. Sellars, the co-pilot on "Tinkertoy," stands on left, along with most of the Minerich crew, including S/Sgt John Woods (BT) who is next to Sellars. Despite the severe frontal damage Lts Stickel (N) and Palas (B) were only moderately injured. The controversial B-17F displays upwards of 20 mission symbols below the cockpit.

John Comer's apprehension about the possibility of regular attention from the Luftwaffe was to be justified, although the punishment handed out was spread among the six participating Groups, with 18 out of the 106 B-17s which bombed being culled from the formations. Three of these came from the 381BG, one of which was the Lead ship 42-30012 being flown by Lt Withers and carrying his 533BS CO Maj Hendricks. The Danish coast was just looming up on the way back when Hendricks dropped the landing gear as a signal for the Deputy Lead to take over and then immediately dropped away. Back at Ridgewell it was reported that the bomber might have been "ditched" after apparently taking ferocious punishment from several Fw190s. However, the formation's altitude coupled with the time taken for the Withers/Hendricks ship to get down to sea level indicated a distance separation of between 15 and 20 miles – too far for a visual sighting. All ten men are commemorated on the Wall of the Missing at Madingley.

Also MIA were Lt Carqueville (533BS and Comer's original pilot) in 42-3180 "Forget Me not" and Lt Loftin (534BS) flying 42-29958 "Battlin' Bombsprayer." (The former crew was fated to join the Hendricks crew on Madingley's Wall of the Missing). Added to this figure of 30 men MIA were four crewmen from Lt Winter's bomber in what seemed a bizarre incident. The Danish coast was being crossed when an explosion in the region of his cockpit temporarily knocked out Lt Doug Winters. As he was hazily recovering he noted some of the crew saluting in his direction before filing into the nose. On regaining his senses Winters discovered his fellow-officers and the Engineer had baled out. Putting the B-17 on auto-pilot he went back to extinguish a small fire and then returned to his now solitary post to bring the aircraft safely home. Evidently the departing quartet had thought their pilot to be fatally wounded, but this assumption was premature, to say the least! Winters' action would be recognised with the award of the Silver Star.

The ranks of the 40 "original" crews had been further pruned by six during the first two missions of what would become known in some circles as "Black Week." The casualty rate among the "original" B-17s was equally severe, having almost reached the 50% figure. Some of the replacement aircraft had arrived not from the Air Depots, but were displacements from the 3BD. Such examples were bombers not fitted with Tokyo Tanks in the outer-wings, and since the 3BD had been given first priority for such configured aircraft it came about that numbers of non-Tokyo Tank B-17s already on hand were transferred into the 1BD. From Mid-August the B-17G started to come into service. Although the first Douglas batch consisted of B-17F airframes without large cheek-gun windows in the nose, the presence of the Bendix power turret permitted a steadier stream of defensive fire to be directed at the Luftwaffe fighters. The new turret also meant the "jury-rigged" flexible gun -mountings in the nose cones could be dispensed with.

Revised appointments on the 9th involved Maj. Shackley (Asst. Group Operations Officer) and Lt Sherwood assuming the places of the missing Maj. Ingenhutt and Capt. Jukes as the 535BS CO and Operations Officer, respectively. Four days later Frank Chapman replaced Shackley, who then moved over to assume command of the 533BS in place of the Late Maj. Hendricks, while Lt Armstead replaced Sherwood on the 20th.

Aircraft availability on the 10th was such that only seven B-17s were sent out to hit Munster. The reduced formation was led by Col. Dunlop and Capt Fricks (534BS), and took up position at the head of the 1BD as the Lead Sqdn within a Combat Box shared with the 91BG. Two crews "aborted" to leave the other five making effective sorties. Apart from making an "S" turn on target approach with which to place the Group into the correct bombing interval the overall mission proved uneventful, and the mixed loads of 2000 lb bombs and 100 lb incendiaries were deposited slightly right of the MPI (Mean Point of Impact), which was smoke-shrouded. Only 20 to 25 fighters – mainly Me 110 and 410 "twins" – were sighted, but these did not attack. Flak was moderate until over Munster when it rose to an "intense" level. The mission's easy nature for the 1BD was not paralleled by the 3BD, whose in-aptly numbered 13CBW lost 25 of the 30 bombers crossed off the 8USAAF inventory. This was also the occasion when the 100BG strengthened its "Bloody Hundredth" reputation by losing 12 of its 13 aircraft. Although Munster was an important railroad center, the designated Aiming Points had been the city center, a decided departure from the stated aim of Precision Bombing.

A four-day break from operations provided an extremely welcome break for combat and groundcrew alike. In fact, two missions (both to Emden) on the 11th and 13th were briefed in this period, and the crews were in the process of taking off on the second occasion when the "scrubbing" signal was issued.

Group records for 14 Oct state that the mention of Schweinfurt as the assigned target "shocked the crews into complete silence." There was an expressed sense of resignation at the slim chances of survival, given the Group's experience during the previous venture to this location. Unlike 17 August when only the 1BD had been allocated Schweinfurt, this time around the full strength of the 8USAAF would be sent to seek a knockout blow. Maj. Shackley would head a force of 17 aircraft which would once again assume the Low Group slot in the 1CBW – a chilling prospect in view of recent events. However, Fortune was to display much greater favour to the 381BG on this mission compared to 17 August and 8 Oct.

Assembly difficulties for both the 40CBW and 1CBW left one Group from each formation (305BG and 381BG respectively) milling around the skies in search of their fellow Groups. Not being able to get in visual contact with his own CBW, Maj. Normand elected to take up the still-vacant slot within a CBW up ahead, which was the 1CBW's Low Group position. The subsequent rendezvous with the now complete 1CBW decided Maj. Shackley into pulling up level with the 351BG flying High Group. Due to what he later reported as the disruption to his 40CBW caused by the absence of the 305BG, Col. Bud Peaslee, Air Commander for the entire force, decided to hand over to Col. Milton leading the 1CBW while still completing the mission with his sharply reduced sub-force.

All three Groups from Peaslee's CBW were to be decimated, whereas the 1CBW in the lead would suffer just three losses. Although located within the ranks of the 1CBW, the 305BG were set upon by the Luftwaffe to such an extent that only two of the 15 bombers despatched came back home! Ridgewell's loss factor was reduced to one bomber. Lt Yorba had been assigned to the 534BS during September, but now he and his crew had gone down in 42-29803 with the Lt. becoming a POW. It was supremely ironic that his B-17F had recently been re-assigned from the 305BG!

An element of B-17Fs from one of the Group Sqdns is formed up into a tight defensive triangle. The angle of the photographer's Fortress suggests its pilots have cut across the path of the oncoming bombers and are hastily clearing out of the way!

Dropping a much higher proportion of incendiaries to high explosives compared to that employed on 17 August, the bombers had struck a much more effective blow at the ball-bearing plants, but a shockingly high price of 60 bombers and their crews had been exacted in return. It was clear that the Luftwaffe ruled the skies over Germany, and that further expansion of the Daylight Bombing Policy was stalled if not fatally compromised unless and until that grip could be broken, and broken permanently. The remainder of 1943 would be devoted to retrenchment and a build-up for a renewed and (hopefully) decisive Offensive against the Nazi industrial and military machine.

In the period between "Black Thursday" (as Second Schweinfurt was to become immortalised in aviation annuls) and the month-end there was a series of briefed missions, several of which were launched before being re-called. On 18 Oct seven crews were briefed at another airfield for Düren, but the Composite Group formation was recalled before crossing the English coast. Two days later with the same target and formation in mind the bombers reached as far as Cambrai, Belgium, but adverse weather both at home and over the target forced a recall; mission credit was nevertheless granted in this instance.

"The Hellion" (535BS) displays the heavy engine exhaust staining that soon disfigured B-17 wing surfaces. Lighter color on the control surfaces is due to paint fading quicker on the fabric covering compared to the aluminum airframe. National marking on wing is greatly over-scale. This B-17F transferred to the RAF on 25 Jan '44 to become part of No. 100 (Radio Counter-Measures) Group, which was tasked with confusing the Luftwaffe night fighter and ground defences.

An interesting lecture on the 24th involved the recently returned evader Sgt Ed Myers. His account of how he was sheltered and assisted back to Britain by the Resistance was well received.

Two days prior to Myers' lecture notification came through of two more Group evaders, Capt. Bob Nelson and S/Sgt Raymond Genz. The story of their success was in one respect even more incredible; whereas Myers had landed in friendly territory, this 532BS duo had come down at least 60 miles inside Germany when they baled out of Lt Painter's B-17. Both landed in a wood where they ran across Sgt Kellogg (BT), who was badly wounded in one foot and who decided to await capture where he could be given proper medical attention. All three hid up until the following morning when Kellogg was left by a roadside. Using a compass a SW course was taken up, and for the next week or so all habitation was strictly avoided as both airmen tried to exist on a diet of beetroot, blackberries, apples, and grain. They experienced good fortune when coming to a bridge with a sentry box, which turned out to be unoccupied and across which they promptly slipped.

One day Bob observed a motorcycle bearing LUX on its numberplate. By this stage Genz was suffering badly from pyorrhea and expressed himself ready to give up. However, he did agree with Bob's suggestion that they walk through the nearby town – if they were not apprehended at this time then Genz would keep on going and never again mention the subject of surrender. Despite a prolonged route which took them twice through the main thoroughfare they were unmolested and kept on Westward. Having traversed a small stream a day or so later they blundered straight into a fisherman, whom they greeted with their usual expression "Guten Tag" before asking for a cigarette. Bob now decided to gamble and said "Americano pilato kaput," the reaction to which was for the man to lead them down into a creek. Spreading out his escape map, Bob enquired where they were and received the response "Luxembourg," The first, and certainly most hazardous, stage of their evasion attempt was over!

Having been shown the direction that would take them into Belgium they set off, but soon were so hungry that they wandered into a farmyard hoping to come across some source of food. Here they were spotted and accosted by four men. Bob explained who he and Genz were, which seemed to satisfy the party. They were instructed to secret themselves in a wood where a package of soap and razors was later dropped off. From now on the pair were in the hands of the Resistance Movement, after they had satisfied their interrogators that they were genuine Americans and not Nazi "stool pigeons." Mov-

"If it looks good, it flies good" was a statement which fully applied to the B-17. This is the fourth Douglas-built B-17G to arrive at Ridgewell on 27 Sept. '43 and assignment to the 533 BS. All were B-17F-75 airframes re-configured to G Model status by the inclusion of Bendix chin-turrets, but lacking cheek-gun windows. Named "Gremlins Delight," she came safely through combat duty to be transferred out to AFSC on 19 May '44.

ing from Kolmar in Luxembourg, after some ten days they were guided across into France and then on to Paris. On one occasion complicated instructions were given for both to proceed on their own across town to a concealment point; a bad fall down a hidden embankment resulted in Bob's clothing being badly torn, but they did attain their goal.

Several more transfers via Clermont and Toulouse (including one unforgettable ride in among the inhabitants of a sheep-laden lorry) got them within range of the Pyrenees Mountains, and what was to prove the hardest physical aspect of their protracted evasion-run. Fully eleven days passed by before the guide's monotonous answer "Mañana. Mañana!" to the question "When will we reach Spain?" was finally fulfilled. In that period they had scaled heights of more than 10000 ft, often through deep snowfields. Arriving by train in Barcelona the entire party of fifteen were headed towards the British Embassy through whose doors they gratefully scrambled.

The final stage of the journey to Gibraltar was via Madrid and the British Consulate located there. A final de-briefing interrogation and an issue of G.I. clothing in Gibraltar was soon followed by the flight back to England. Yet one more interrogation in London was followed by two Group colleagues arriving to make a positive identification. It was not until 4 Nov. that both airmen turned up at Ridgewell when Bob gave a lecture on evasion techniques to a packed hall. (George Shackley remembered that one of the points stressed was the matter of oral hygiene. Bob said he had used a twig or similar item to pick at his teeth each morning, and the sense of freshness engendered by this simple act provided a distinct boost to his mental, as well as physical, well-being. It is probable that the poor physical state of Sgt Genz was exacerbated by the pyorrhea, which he might have brought under control had he taken the same precaution.)

6

TIME FOR REFLECTION

November 1943 was the month from which point onward regular use of H2X was indulged in by the 8USAAF, since some degree of pressure had to be kept up against the enemy in the face of ever deteriorating weather conditions. This blind-bombing device at least allowed a large area, such as a city, to be pin-pointed, but bombing accuracy suffered, and many debriefing statements of "bombing results believed good" were really euphemisms for what could only be termed "area precision bombardment." Targets on the coastal fringe of Germany gave better pointers than locations within the Continental landmass, and Bremen in particular received constant attention during the final two months of the year.

Action commenced on the 3rd when Wilhelmshaven's naval facilities came under assault. The bomber formations stretching out of sight in either direction of the 381BG's position in the column dropped their ordnance through 10/10 cloud in the face of a light flak barrage, and the crews were further heartened by the presence of P-38 escorts. T/Sgt Goucher, who was injured on 25 June, suffered a further blow when he fell out of his top turret and fractured his humorus as his B-17 was in the act of "aborting." The pleasure of the 26 crews who bombed and who traversed a heavily defended target with impunity was evident to the interrogation staff.

A 0920 take-off for 21 aircraft occurred on the 5th with Gelsenkirchen in the Ruhr as the target. Weather conditions again forced the use of H2X, but had the apparent reverse benefit of keeping the Luftwaffe grounded. This limitation in no way affected the flak guns, and they delivered a heavy and accurate barrage. (The deflection of flak away from the bombers could be achieved by the use of the metallic strips known as "Window," or "Chaff," but this counter-measure was not yet in regular use by the 8USAAF).

Twenty crews made it back, unlike Lt Don Hopp's 42-30852 "Blowin' Bessie," from which ten parachutes were reported to have emerged. It was all the more sad that the bomber's fate close to Moerdijk in Western Holland was shared by all but three of the crew, who probably fell into the estuarial waters of this region to die by drowning or from exposure. (The aircraft wreck was recovered during Post-war dredging operations).

Koos Overwater, a Dutch civilian, witnessed the final moments of the B-17 as it was spiralling down to its fiery demise. He spotted a parachute, below which hung T/Sgt Alex

Lt. Alan Tucker (standing third from left) is photographed with the bulk of his crew in front of B-17F "Battlin' Bombsprayer"; both belong to the 534BS. Holding his chute pack is Lt. Rick Rylands (N), while T/Sgt Bill Savage (Eng.) stands on the extreme left. Alan suffered a bad reaction following the Schweinfurt mission on 17 Aug '43, but later returned to combat and finished up during the Winter of 1943/44.

"Bacta Th' Sac" was the very first B-17G to be assigned to the 381BG. She arrived on 16 Sept '43, but only flew five recorded missions with the 535BS. She was MIA with Lt. Hess and crew on 1 Dec '43, one of four Group losses on the mission to Leverkusen.

Girvan (ROG), and which floated down into a field. He and two friends approached the airman, who seemed reluctant to appear from behind the large tree acting as his cover. Only when sure he was among his Allies did the Sgt emerge and enquire about directions intended to take him to – Sweden! He was swiftly dis-abused of the idea of escape to that far-off country, and after destroying all necessary items he went along with his "rescuers." Some German soldiers who had been despatched to pick up survivors but who had previously failed to spot Girvan's descent finally appeared on the scene. Before Girvan was taken away the local Burgomeister somehow persuaded the soldiers to note the American flier's personal details, including his home address, so that the Red Cross could be notified! Girvan expressed his doubts about receiving fair treatment at the hands of his captors, but these were allayed by the Feldwebel in charge, who assured him he would not be shot but sent to a POW camp.

In the Lead ship both pilots Lts Charles Ohl and Martin Downey had suffered serious wounds, with the former hit around the groin. Lt "Pappy" Heintz, flying his last mission, removed Ohl from his seat to administer First Aid while Lt Stralser (N) took the vacant seat.

With Downey's assistance – whenever the co-pilot had not lapsed back into unconsciousness – he completed the bomb-run and turned for home. Finally finding himself unable to hold formation, Stralser dropped the landing gear to signal that he was pulling out, whereupon the other pilots in his Sqdn followed him down! Such action was totally contrary to all 8USAAF defensive principles, as stragglers were regarded as expendable, and the sub-formation was fortunate that it met no fighter opposition while getting safely out over the North Sea. Lt Ohl was rushed to hospital, and his condition was such that the possibility of emasculation was raised. Happily, this grisly prospect was averted by skillful surgery, and indeed the Lt's subsequent marriage produced several offsprings!

The second incident on 5 November involved Lt Butler's 532BS crew, six of whom baled out reputedly on orders issued by the co-pilot. A seventh airman, Lt Brown, had a miraculous escape from death. Having removed his oxygen-mask prior to jumping out of the nose hatch he lost consciousness, and in slumping forward managed to accidentally pull his rip-cord. The deploying parachute streamed outside to wrap itself round the ball-turret, and the pressure of the canopy cords exerted on one leg pulled it out into the slipstream and tore off Brown's boot. A state of oxygen starvation usually resulted in death within a few minutes, so the Lt. should have expired long before the Group descended to normal breathing altitude. Amazingly, he not only survived, but suffered only minimal frostbite despite a –40 degree temperature at the 28000 ft operational altitude flown!

Poor weather persisted for the raid on Wesel (7th) when its marshalling yards were struck using H2X. The P-47 escort kept the Luftwaffe at bay, and the sole casualties were six cases of frost-bite to neck and face induced by the murderous -40 degree temperature existing at the bombing altitude of 26000 ft. Four days later a second sortie to Wesel was cancelled. How-

M/Sgt Fitzgerald, who is seen in the middle of his team, supervised "Forget Me Not II." This airman was destined to hold a Division record for consecutive non-abortive missions (169) by VE-Day. On the right is Sgt Dave Martin, who later rose to crewchief status within the 535BS.

ever, with the Lead CBW inside Holland and the 381BG headed by Maj. Lord (532BS CO) approaching the Dutch coast, the Division Air Commander decided to "abort" the mission when faced by mounting cloud conditions expected to force the B-17s up beyond 30000 ft.

The mission sent out on 13 Nov. involved an early take-off with Group assembly at 9000 ft over the base. Wishing to witness this in the target-towing B-17 were Col. Hall, Capt. Delano (534BS Navigator), Maj. Gaillard, a 535BS doctor, Capt. Wymer, and an Equipment Section Sgt. Cloud-masses extended up to 20000 ft, and with only three oxygen-masks on board it was ill-advised for the five men to proceed higher, but this they did. A "comic opera" scenario then ensued, with the most obvious anoxia case being handed a mask until he had recovered. Worsening the situation was the fact that the B-17 was fitted with "constant flow" oxygen facilities, but two of the masks were "demand" pattern. In addition, all five were dressed for a much lower altitude and were paying the inevitable penalty of extreme discomfort in the sub-zero temperature. Subsequent notes by one of the participants stated "The whole exercise was a tribute to individual and corporate stupidity." It was doubly ironic that the mission was cancelled. However, Lts Deering (533BS) and Reece had lost contact with the Group and missed the "recall" signal. Advancing into Europe on a solo "Drang Nach Osten" (Drive to the East), it was only the deteriorating weather and close attention from flak that persuaded them to turn back. An official diary note recorded that the said crew had been returned to training status!

Lt. Frank Chapman (left) lines up with six of his crew; the other three are perched on the No. 2 propeller and nacelle of their B-17F "Chaps Flying Circus." Chapman became 535BS CO after Maj. Ingenhutt was MIA on 8 Oct. '43 and held the post until the end of the year. S/Sgt Wardell, sitting on the propeller, was later commissioned, as were at least two other crewmen, S/Sgt. Gugenheim and T/Sgt Crowley.

This is the original nose window configuration on interim and late B-17Fs. Large flat panels with "nipple" gun mountings were installed. The left side window was placed in the center as demonstrated by "Nobody's Baby." Also added was a single forward-firing gun through the nose Plexiglas with which to counter head-on attacks, against which the side guns were largely ineffective.

Attention on the 16th was switched towards Norway when Knaben's molybdenum mines were bombed with un-determined result. Fresh falls of snow and the concealed nature of the mine-shafts created doubt as to whether the Primary had even been hit; worse still was the fact that nearby townships suffered a sizeable number of dead and injured among their populations. Bomb-loads varied between 3000 lbs and 6000 lbs, with the former quantity carried in B-17s not equipped with Tokyo-tanks and having to mount a bomb-bay tank on one side. Capt Will Baltrusaitus and crew celebrated the end of their combat tour, but for Sgt Wallace McGaughy (BT) it was nearly a fatal finish. His turret back-plate became detached, and the next few minutes were hectic to say the least as he strove to hold his precarious position before cranking the turret vertically and exiting.

Two "scrubbed" briefings preceded the last monthly mission flown on the 26th when 23 out of 29 aircraft bombed Bremen. Over 500 bombers dropped with minimal flak interference through cloud, and the estimated figure of 50 enemy fighters were all going after B-24 Groups. The grim jest "Who needs fighter escorts when the Liberator boys are around?" was a reference to the Luftwaffe's alleged preference for striking at the B-24 units, and appeared to have been played out once again on this occasion. In truth, both heavy bomber types were almost equally vulnerable to fighter attack, and no German pilot was going to waste time on seeking out B-24s from B-17s when the destruction of them all was imperative. The

The equivalent large nose window on the right was directly behind the nose Plexiglas as depicted by "Full Boost!" This bomber carries twin .50 machine-guns up front, as well as what appears to be a sheet of armor in front of the weapons. It proved impossible to insert the Norden bombsight in these circumstances.

In an attempt to bolster forward firepower the B-17F's flat panels were replaced by "wedge" shaped frames as carried on "Shoo Shoo Baby." Despite this, it was really only the nose-mounted gun or guns, which had the ability to engage the Luftwaffe fighters as they made their highly effective "twelve o'clock" approach.

381BG lost no aircraft, but seven frostbite cases resulted from another minus 40-degree temperature-level, and three other crewmen sustained burns due to faulty electrical-suit wiring. The severely frost-bitten state of Sgt Homer's face merited his B-17 landing away from base so he could receive urgent treatment at Waterbury's RAF Hospital.

The 535BS records for 29 November note the return of "The Deacon," S/Sgt Joseph J Walters. He was Lt Disbrow's ball-turret gunner who, after baling out near Liege on 17 August, was almost immediately picked up by the Belgian Resistance. (A picture exists which shows Walters standing between a father and son not long after landing and ready to be spirited away into hiding). Moving by foot, bicycle, and train, he ended up walking across the Pyrenees Mountains into neutral Spain. His closest shave came when two German officers entered his train compartment and asked for the occupants' Identity Cards. His fellow-evader was a Canadian who produced not an Identity Card, but a revolver with which he despatched both Germans; Walters helped to dispose of the bodies out of the speeding train. He was flown back to England in a British civilian transport, having actually gained weight. He turned up at Ridgewell sporting a fez and that rare Wartime commodity – bananas! Walter's promotion to M/Sgt soon followed his return.

Returning around the same time was Lt Hoover, co-pilot to Lt Zum. Baling out over France on 3 Sept., he made a delayed drop, but landed smack into a tree where he was forced to abandon his parachute and pass an uncomfortable night in bushes. Contact was first made with a farmer who quickly passed him over to the local Resistance. Like Sgt. Myers he was channelled down the escape routes as far as Paris. His subsequent movements from the French capital paralleled those of Sgt Walters, using a combination of train and bicycle and finally scaling the Pyrenees. Several of the men in his party had footwear made out of paper-based material, which fell apart in the snow-covered slopes. A direct result of this basic defi-

On Lockheed/Vega's VE-25 production batch of B-17Fs the flat gun panels were reversed, and an unframed and "bulged" Plexiglas section was inserted on the left side only. "Margie Mae" (42-5847) was assigned to the 381BG from this batch, along with "Whaletail II" and "Tinkertoy."

ciency was for three of them to ultimately collapse, forcing their abandonment and almost certain death from exposure.

Two missions to Bremen (29th) and Solingen (30th) were "scrubbed" with massed cloud being the primary reason in both instances. The latter location would be indirectly resurrected as a target just 24 hours later and would leave its mark upon the group. The average combat crew gradually accustomed itself to the loss of contemporaries, which was a necessary factor for its own survival. What was even more upsetting than watching other B-17s taking their buddies to their deaths or into captivity was the inability to recall how or when bombers and their crews had been lost. There was a heightened sense of shock and depression on 1 Dec., particularly among the 535BS. Three of the four B-17s MIA were out of this Sqdn; not only that, but all four crews were regarded as having been allocated relatively "safe" positions in the High Sqdn. This apart, the mission had been regarded as something of a "milk-run," which only increased the frustration at bearing such losses.

To one of the pilots, Lt Warren O Hess (535BS), there was no sense of having flown a "milk-run." The mission plan was for the bombers to skirt around the target to the South and swing 'round to come in from the East. Warren remembered a mention at the briefing of the abnormally high incidence of aircraft "aborts" during November with the crews now being exhorted to cut down such frequency as much as was consistent with ultimate crew safety. For example, engine failure was to be

Brig/Gen. Williams (center) is seen on 18 Dec. '43 flanked by four winners of U.S. top military awards. Second right is Lt. Thomas D Sellars, who along with Williams earned the Distinguished Service Cross – in the Lt's. case, for the 8 Oct '43 mission. Also granted the DSC was Lt. Hudson (91BG), next to Sellars. Second left and wearing RAF wings to confirm his status as a former Eagle Sqdn. pilot is Lt. John Morgan (92BG), who was awarded the Congressional Medal of Honor.

This is Lt. Sellars after the award of the Distinguished Service Cross, whose medal is being admired by a member of the W.A.C.

treated a minimum basis for "abort" action. Hess's bomber 42-3540 "Bacta T' Sac" was the first B-17G arriving at Ridgewell, and he found he was having to draw an inordinate degree of power just to keep up with the other 25 aircraft. A 90 knot tailwind whisked the force into Germany, but just as the turn to the left was made towards Solingen the No. 3 engine was disabled; the wallowing B-17 fell down and behind the Group, and sight of the formation was lost even before the I.P.

A twin-engine fighter now positioned itself at six o'clock and delivered a burst of fire, which probably took out No. 2 engine. Hess had little recourse other than to jettison the bombs, while he and Lt Charles Smith (CP) fought their bomber's tendency to nose up by using a mix of variable power and the ailerons. With the windshield iced-up, oxygen bottles exploding, and several guns out of action Lt Randle (N) gave a course for home and fighter support was called for. One P-47 did appear, but the bomber crew were scarcely buoyed up by this – the Thunderbolt was going down vertically in flames as it narrowly missed colliding with "Bacta T' Sac!" A temporary reprieve loomed up in the form of a cloud layer, but once traversed it was not too long before two Me 109s came into sight. One circled while its partner positioned itself out ahead to the right. Lt Randle opened fire on the latter, but his gun jammed after he had fired a short burst. Unimpressed by this the Me swung back around, and his firing pass knocked out all remaining power. With the inter-phone "out" the bale-out order was passed verbally to those in the rear and all ten men jumped.

Sgt Bill Macklin (BT) had earlier been injured in one foot, and its condition was such that it was later amputated in a Ger-

A 535BS crew head away from "Tinkertoy," the Group's reputed "Jinx Ship" during mid-1943. A problem with No. 2 engine has caused the propeller to be "feathered." The pilot is Lt Harold Henslin (wearing dark glasses), who would be KIA along with six of his crew on 28 April '44 when only a few missions short of completing his combat tour.

man hospital. Sgt Edgar Delp (TG) was also wounded, but landed all right to be later incarcerated with his pilot in a jail. He was later removed to hospital, but unlike Macklin he succumbed to his injuries. At the other end of the fortune-scale Lts Smith and Wernersbach (N) were not captured and would succeed in adding their names to the growing list of 381BG evaders.

The other three losses involved F/O Noxon in 42-31111 "Four Aces," F/O Sunde in 42-31097, and the 532BS crew of Lt Duncan in 42-29506 "Full Boost!" Almost all of Noxon's crew were 16 mission veterans just returned from a Rest Home. A fifth bomber crash-landed in Kent, and Lts Hytinen, Cronin, and Maustead sustained varied fracture injuries that after temporary treatment at Rochester saw them transferred to the 38th Station Hospital near to Southampton. Their B-17G 42-39808 was salvaged. Once again the German defences had handed out a smart rebuff to the 8USAAF by taking out 24 of the 281 crews granted mission credit. Solingen had been the planned Secondary to the briefed target at Leverkusen, but the PFF-assisted bombing had achieved very uncertain results.

A Paris mission sent out on 4 Dec. involved 30 aircraft, but the weather conditions were too marginal for safe bombing to be made. Of much more import for the weary bomber crews was their first sight of the newly arrived P-51B Mustang. The slim lines of the North American fighter when compared to the bulk of the P-47 gave little indication of its "Seven League Boots" range capacity; this would be a material factor in taking its "Big Friends" into Central Europe with relative impunity, as well as being the principal tool which would sweep the Luftwaffe from the skies. The marriage of the Rolls Royce Merlin 61 to the Mustang's technologically advanced aerofoil surfaces was the perfect technical combination with which to pursue the goal of fighter-to-fighter supremacy. Happier times were ahead for the bombers, although some hard knocks would still have to be borne.

One problem affecting the new escort fighter was its distinct resemblance to the Me109. It is fairly certain that the pilots were instructed to stay clear of the B-17s and B-24s even more so than their P-47 contemporaries – bomber gunners shot first and asked questions later! The P-51's presence over Paris was small in numbers, since only the one Group (354FG) was on hand. It was an apparent contradiction that this unit was assigned to the Tactical 9USAAF. Fortunately, it was swiftly realised that the much harder-pressed "heavies" were in urgent need of its protection, otherwise, the wresting of air superiority from the Luftwaffe might have been more in question. The 354FG was to remain within the 9USAAF, but would come under the operational control of the 8th Fighter Command for its first few months in Europe.

The middle of December involved a succession of strikes at North German ports with Bremen the principal source of destruction. Emden was briefed on the 11th, and take-off was carried out in a snowstorm whose thinning flakes were soon dispersed by a watery sun; wing surfaces had previously been

Maj. Dave Kunkel was the first CO of the 534BS and held the post well into 1944, as well as being promoted to Lt. Col. He is wearing the heavy pattern combat jacket and trousers. This clothing item tended to be too cumbersome for many personnel when combined with a "Mae West" life preserver and a parachute harness.

Lt John Donovan was a 532BS navigator who commenced his combat tour on 24 July 1943 and completed his 25th mission at the end of December. He was at the Rest home on 8 Oct when his crew, led by Lt. Sample, were MIA over Bremen. A second piece of personal good fortune saw him finish one mission ahead of his re-assigned crew under Lt. Cecil Clore's charge. On 4 Jan. '44 all ten crewmen were KIA following a crash on take-off.

Lt. Dan Hagarty was a Group "original" member. He arrived in England as co-pilot to Lt. Ohl, but was subsequently assigned his own crew. Having completed his tour in November, he was re-trained on fighters and joined the 78FG based at Duxford. His luck, unlike that of Lt. Donovan, ran out on 12 May '44 when he was forced to bale out of his stricken P-47 and ended up a POW.

swept clean to obviate the risk of black ice. The 535BS were scheduled to form part of a Composite third Group within the 1CBW. This revised arrangement was becoming a regular feature brought about by the transfer of the 351BG to the 92CBW and the current absence of a third Group to take its place. In fact, this reduced situation was to remain in place until April 1944 when the 398BG would be integrated into the 1CBW on its arrival in England.

Rendezvous problems with the Composite Group caused by the failure of the 91BG element to appear were partially redressed by several of that Group's stragglers linking up with the 535BS to form a 12-plane formation. In the months ahead the Composite Group arrangement would have its detractors due to several unfortunate incidents – all blamed on the 91BG by the 381BG chroniclers! Perfect visibility over the target permitted the dropping of 500 lb bombs and 100 lb incendiaries within the NE quarter of the city, but there was a permanent 10 /10 undercast to and from Emden which left one officer to aver that the mission was a weather-made success!

Two days later occurred the first of three runs to Bremen when 29 out of 30 crews made PFF-directed drops through a solid undercast. Moderate flak bursting well below the formations still left 12 bombers damaged and injured one crewman. Pressure was maintained on the 16th with PFF direction once more necessary in the face of solid cloud layers. Seven aircraft were struck by flak, and some unidentified fighters were called in which did not engage. With three relatively easy missions under their belts there was a risk the crews might again slip

"ChugaLug" has a distinctive scoreboard on her nose – she has twice as many enemy fighters to her credit as she has flown missions! Arriving on 20 Sept. '43, her time with the 535BS ended on 29 Dec. The second picture shows her perched on a hillside. The B-17 struck trees near Salisbury while on a "slow-time" flight in the charge of Lt. Bill Ridley. She was salvaged next day. (Note how the gaps in the bomb symbols shown in the first picture have been filled in with similar symbols as recorded in the crash picture!).

into a complacent mood. Completion of the third Bremen mission would dispel any such thoughts.

B-17Fs 42-5845 "Whaletail II" and 42-5846 "Tinkertoy" had enjoyed lengthy operational careers stretching as far back as Pueblo when they were respectively assigned to the 534BS and 535BS. "Whaletail II" had featured in a production scene used in the Deanna Durbin film "Hers to hold," while "Tinkertoy" had enjoyed a mixed reputation within its Sqdn in particular and the Group in general. Today (20 Dec.) the duo would accompany 26 other aircraft to Bremen. Among the number would be a relatively new B-17G, 42-31075 "The Rebel," also belonging to the 535BS and carrying Lt. Waldo Crossan's crew on their seventh mission.

Take-off was at 0815, and around three to four hours later the Group was reaching for the target. At 1147 enemy fighters made a sudden slashing lunge from 11 o'clock. The brunt of this assault was borne by the Low Sqdn's second element, of which only the No. 2 aircraft, 42-30765 flown by Lt Urban, escaped unscathed. "Tinkertoy," flying in the No.3 position, was rammed in its tail section by one of the Me 109s. The veteran bomber was variously seen to fall out of formation but regain contact for the bomb-release before disappearing two minutes later, or staying momentarily under control and then flipping over to spin down in flames. Lt John Anderson (N) was to confirm that "Tinkertoy" went into a spin and blew up not many hundred feet below the formation. In those brief seconds Anderson and Lt Johnson (CP) had scrambled to the escape hatch that was kicked open, and Johnson was shoved out by his fellow officer. Immediately pulling his ripcord, Johnson could see no other chutes, which was hardly surprising as the B-17 had blown up directly after his exit. He landed in a vacant lot located in Delmenhorst's main street and was picked up and escorted to a large Army barracks. That evening he was shown a list that quoted Lt. Mitchell's (B) name and serial num-

Col. Reed is presenting Capt Bob Nelson with the Silver Star. The award relates to his action in regaining English soil after the B-17F in which he was flying was shot down North of Koblenz on 17 August '43. Ceremony was held at Station HQ on 20 Dec '43.

The extremely inhospitable and snow-covered Norwegian mountains are skirted over by a Group formation on 16 Nov '43. Target was a molybdenum plant at Knaben. Bomber at top left is "Winsome Winn/Hilda" of the 534BS. (The "Hilda" part of the title was apparently added after this mission.)

ber. The German holding the list then drew his finger across his neck and said the bombardier was dead. Unknown to Johnson, Lt. Dorman Lane (P) and S/Sgt Peanoski (ROG) had also made good their exit. (All three officers would be re-united in Stalag Luft I, Barth.)

The second element leader was Lt Crossan. Disabled by cannon fire, "The Rebel" also fell out but managed to complete the bomb-run to momentarily tuck itself under Lt Urban's wing before drifting back and out of sight in the thick vapour-trails exuded by the Group aircraft. In the meantime, three more Me 109s inflicted further punishment upon the lone B-17. Lt Curran (B) recorded that Lt Jim Opitz (CP) was killed by a 20mm shell in the neck at the point of baling out. S/Sgt Steve Bulsok vacated his ball-turret after the oxygen bottles were shot off and was just donning his chute pack when a cannon shell struck S/Sgt Klima (WG) and probably also wounded Bulsok. Klima was thrown against the side of the ball-turret

P-38s of the 20FG or 55FG pass over the 381BG during a mission flown in late 1943. B-17G in the foreground is either 42-37721 "Sugar" or 42-37754 "Whodat," both from the 534BS. At bottom right is that Sqdn's "Whaletail II," which would soon be lost in the North Sea on 20 Dec.

Maj. Arthur F Briggs was the first regular Operations Officer for the 535BS. He was later destined to become the last wartime CO of the 398BG at Nuthampstead.

This is a closer view of "Whaletail II," whose engine cowlings are already well-stained after completing around ten missions. Code letters are over-scale in width. National insignia also appears over-sized and still bears the red outline which was officially superseded by blue in Sept '43.

and shared Opitz's fate, along with S/Sgt Eloe (TG). (The fact of Eloe's death was subsequently communicated to Bulsok by an orderly in the hospital to which he was admitted). "The Rebel" crashed close to Wesermunde, NE of Bremen, and her three dead crewmen were buried four days later in the nearby cemetery of Albstedt.

Two more bombers were to be culled from the formation – the 532BS' 42-3563 flown by Lt Hollenkamp, and "Whaletail II" in the hands of Lt Leo Canelake. The latter was in the exposed No. 3 position within the High Sqdn's lead element and was badly hit by flak which almost removed the left elevator. Even with all four engines still functioning the B-17 began to swing in an erratic manner vertically and horizontally as was being noted by the second element leader, Lt Richard Niederitter. However, the aircraft cleared the German coast still in formation, and the prospect of her safe return to Ridgewell rose with every minute the North Sea was passing below.

It was not to be. Niederitter glanced back at a point some 70 miles out from the English coast and sighted what turned out to be "Whaletail II" low down on the water and making a 180 degree turn; he had been distracted from recording the fact that the B-17 had dropped out. Although he now requested his tail-gunner to check the cripple's movements, the rear canopy was badly frosted over and the gunner was unable to witness the final impact with the waves. The remorseless North Sea had swallowed up another ten souls in its dark maw; even with a successful "ditching," the chances of lasting very long in the freezing December waters were minimal, as were the chances of being located by the Rescue Service. (All ten crewmen are featured on the Wall of the Missing at Madingley). "Tinkertoy" and "Whaletail II" had come into being at the same time and had shared many a hard combat experience, just as now they were inextricably bound in their passing from the records of the 381BG.

Twenty-two aircraft headed out to Osnabruck and its communications centers on the 22nd, of which 19 utilised the PFF markers in the face of the almost inevitable heavy cloud. Just a single bomber was hit by flak, and it was probably its navigator, Lt Len Meier, who suffered the sole recorded wound. That same day a B-17G was delivered (42-39895) with whom Meier's 535BS crew, led by Lt Lee W Smith, would become identified.

Osnabruck marked the 381BG's first six months in combat. In the course of 52 completed missions the vast bulk of the "original" aircraft and crews had succumbed to enemy action. On the other hand, many of the Group's senior figures had managed to come through, and their example was an undoubted key factor in sustaining both morale and efficiency at Ridgewell. But the time was fast approaching when the top command would witness a change. "Col. Joe" had been marked for higher authority and would officially depart the base on 1 Jan. after handing over to Lt. Col. Harry P Leber.

There was no let-up in operations even with Xmas impending. Preparations of a less festive kind were evident over 23/24 Dec., and the crews were duly called to a morning briefing for a short run to bomb what were code-named "Noballs" and what later evolved as V-1 launch-sites located in the Pas de Calais region of NE France. Among those participating was a Medical Officer who recorded his reactions during what was his first mission. No fear or even apprehension was felt until his B-17 received flak hits, at which point the observer wondered "What the Hell am I doing here!" His attempt to locate the source from where the shells were coming was rightly thwarted by one of the waist-gunners, who unceremoniously hauled him back into a sitting position. In addition, his enthusiasm to take pictures almost proved fatal; the aircraft turned sharply towards his side of the fuselage, and he just held on at the waist-window. During the de-briefing he said he was now experiencing a sense of lassitude, and his overall impression of the day's events was that he would enjoy combat – but on reflection, only for a time!

In the run-up to Xmas it was mooted by the Chaplain, Capt. Brown, to Col. Reed (Ground Executive) that the children attending the local schools be given a treat by laying on a party at the base. The anticipated figure of 250 had swollen to nearly 400 on the day the G.I.s collected them by truck. A film in the Base Cinema was followed by a veritable feast of food in the Red cross Club as they watched Maj. John Goodrum perform a series of magical tricks. Then Santa Claus in the form of Bob Nagle, Maj. Brown's assistant, handed out crayon packs, coloring books, soft toys, dolls, and games. To these children, long conditioned to the very basic amenities of ration-bound Britain, the sight of oranges, bananas, and in particular ice-cream was a pure and delightful dream.

On Xmas Eve a Carol Service was held in the Chapel when a mixture of traditional songs were sung by all present; these were supplemented by violin solos from the Chaplain, tenor solos by Lt Leon Wagner, and finally, several hymn renditions by the Chapel Quartet. Next day a solemn religious service was attended by an equally large number of personnel. Thus, for at least 24 hours the travails and horrors of aerial combat – though ever present – could at least be placed in the recesses of each man's mind.

"Full Boost!" bears an impressive list of mission and fighter "kill" symbols which was built up during service with two Groups. Originally assigned to the 305BG in Feb. '43 and named "Ye White Swan," the B-17F came into 532BS hands on 22 Aug. The majority of Lt. Chason Duncan's crew were KIA in this bomber on 1 Dec '43.

Neat artwork on "Four Aces" is a reference to the B-17G's last four digits in its serial number (42-31111). This Fortress lasted barely six weeks with the 535BS, going down with the Noxon crew on 1 Dec '43. It was the joint-first G Model to be MIA from Ridgewell, along with 42-31097 flown by Lt. Sunde and 42-3540 flown by Lt. Hess (both 535BS), who were also MIA on 1 Dec.

The fifth Xmas of World War II arrived with the Allied camp in a mood of sober confidence that the end of the conflict was beckoning tantalisingly over the far horizon. The overall feeling was not so much if the War could be won, but how soon could the enemy be vanquished. The Xmas period was one of relaxation for the 8USAAF, broken only by a small-scale fighter sweep over the Dutch coast (28th) and at Ridgewell a "scrubbed" briefing for the airfield at St. Jean/D'Angely that same day. The sole flying incident at the base affected the 535BS's 42-30765 "Chugalug." Lt Bill Ridley was conducting a "slow time" flight on the 29th. In the poor visibility a turn made near Salisbury resulted in one wing striking the tree-tops. The B-17 was vibrating so badly that a forced-landing was quickly made close to Warminster. There were no injuries among the crew, but the bomber was salvaged the next day.

The next briefing on the 30th was more productive when the 8USAAF resumed full-scale operations. A wearying flight was in prospect to bomb the port areas and oil installations at Ludgwigshaven on the Upper Rhine. This medium-range penetration made by 28 bombers signalled the last occasion on which "Col. Joe" would be in charge of the Group. Fighter opposition tended to concentrate on the following formations, and 10/10 cloud dictated the use of PFF techniques with bombing results unobserved. After landing off the mission Col. Nazzaro was given no time to say his farewells to his men. Orders from above demanded his immediate presence next day at 8USAAF HQ, and it would be the following July before he could make a belated return to Ridgewell to express his thoughts!

For one airman, S/Sgt Clarence Hickman, the "milk-run" nature of the Ludwigshafen mission was academic; the 533BS gunner was found slumped over his seat by the ball-turret gunner 45 minutes before reaching Ridgewell. When examined he was cyanotic, his pupils dilating, and was frothing at the mouth. Emergency oxygen and application of artificial respiration failed to revive him. A check of his mask outlets revealed pieces of ice whose presence may well have caused exhalation problems with the unmodified A14 "demand" type used in this case. The "male" part of the connection plug was catching in the "female" part before full insertion and required a pull of 25/30 pounds to effect separation. The ball-turret gunner stated that the mask hose was disconnected when he first checked Hickman. That there were more insidious dangers in combat flying other than those posed by the enemy had once again been borne out as poor Sgt Hickman had posthumously demonstrated. His body was removed to the 121st Field Hospital, Braintree, for an autopsy.

There was no pause for New Year celebrations, and indeed the final mission for 1943 was one of the longest to date, with the "heavies" reaching down to within a short distance of the French/Spanish border. The Primary was Bordeaux/ Merignac airfield, with the Secondary at Chateaubriand airfield. Approach to the target would be over the Bay of Biscay prior to cutting in over the French coast South of Bordeaux and then turning North. Progress as far as the coast was relatively easy for the 26 bombers, with the exception of Lt Earl Duarte (535BS) flying in 42-39910 and in No. 2 position within the High Sqdn's second element. According to reports from several sources his B-17 was hit by fire from one of several Fw190s, after which he fell back and jettisoned his bombs. He then regained an approximate contact with the formation, but with the bomb-doors still extended. As the Secondary was looming up he made a turn to the right back in the general direction of Spain.

On board the stricken Fortress the nose Plexiglas was destroyed and a hole torn in the lower right of the nose. Gunfire had seriously wounded Lt Grimball (B) in both legs, and with the No. 2 propeller "windmilling" and No. 3 smoking the chances of winning through to neutral Spain were steadily receding. The entire crew finally baled out near Toulouse, and their aircraft hit close to the city's Western boundary. Lts Duarte and McCabe (CP) were fortunate to be picked up by the Resistance, who later spirited both through Spain to England. Both officers saw Sgt Balesh on the ground, but he was not so fortunate; although also picked by the French, his arrival at Dulag Luft interrogation center on 24 Feb. was later noted.

S/Sgt Jevons remained at large for upwards of two months before he too was captured. The remaining six crewmen were captured on landing. Lt Grimball was sent to a Paris hospital for treatment, and Lt Heintz (N) received similar attention for his wounds.

The returning crews ran into marginal weather conditions, which forced a number to seek bases in SW England. The 535BS did get back to Ridgewell, and on board Capt Chapman's 42-30029 "Chaps Flying Circus" was that Sqdn's first enlisted man to complete 25 missions – quite a manner for Sgt Gugenheim to celebrate bringing in the New Year! The previous day three tour-expired officers were ordered home. They were: Lt Paul Gleichauf (533BS), who was the Group's very first replacement pilot; Lt Richard Niederitter, (534BS) who had arrived with his crew on 20 August; and Lt Harold Stralser, the 534BS navigator who had been instrumental in bringing his B-17 home on 5 Nov. when Lts Ohl and Downey were both incapacitated by serious wounds. Good fortune had held for this quartet, unlike so many of their colleagues.

A member of the groundcrew cycles unconcernedly past a line-up of bombers as the late autumn sun highlights a beautiful mackerel cloud-layer. "Four Aces" of the 535BS is last in line and confirms picture was taken between her assignment on 19 Oct and loss on 1 Dec '43.

7

SECOND WIND

Lt Cecil Clore's crew had arrived at Ridgewell on 20 Aug. and was assigned to the 532BS. The crew had weathered many rough missions, but now on 4 Jan. '44 as they filed into the briefing-room their thoughts were not so much on where they would be sent for what was the Group's first New Year's mission, but rather on the priceless bonus awaiting them on return to base – the completion of their tour and then rotation back to the States.

Up at the Combat Crew Replacement Center (C.C.R.C.) at Stone, Staffordshire, was Lt John Donovan (N), who had completed the final few missions of his tour with Lt Clore, and who was now awaiting the arrival there of his pilot, who had been one mission behind in terms of numbers. John had already experienced two slices of fortune on 19 Aug, and especially on 8 Oct. On the latter occasion, and despite his protests, he had been sent to a rest home while his regular crew, headed by Lt Sample, went to Bremen, where the bulk of the crew, including the navigator, were killed. Fortune would prove to still be riding on John's shoulders this January day.

The assigned target was Kiel, and Clore's B-17G 42-31278 took its place in line, rolled down the runway, and eased up into the gloom. The bomber was still low over the Essex countryside when the Lt. called up to say he was having a problem maintaining airspeed and was turning back. He was fated never to achieve this primary objective. Having jettisoned his bombs he must have stood at least a marginal chance of getting the bomber down in a field adjoining Bloom's farm at Sible Hedingham. It was later conjectured that the left wing-tip caught the edge of a copse of trees and swung the aircraft into full contact with the tree-trunks; the resultant impact and explosion of the full gas-tanks left only ten shrivelled and dismembered corpses for the Medical team to attend to.

In the minds of the combat crews this fate was one of the cruellest imaginable to strike home. Instead of a relaxed passage home there remained for Clore, Lts Newell (CP), Dille (B), and Waldman (N), the tall, quiet S/Sgt Bozette, and S/Sgts Howard and Ingmire (the latter awaiting the birth of his first child) the short funereal journey to Madingley Military Cemetery; there they were interred under the caring administration of Chaplains Brown and Colette. It was a shocked and chastened John Donovan who, in response to his telephone enquiry a few days after as to the non-appearance of Lt Clore at Stone,

"Our Mom" (42-29832) was transferred in from the 305BG on 22 Aug '43 and was then assigned to Lt. Bob Miller's crew, for whom it proved a good luck token. Apart from Sgt. Klinger (TG) killed on the crew's first mission, all nine men returned States-side, while their B-17 also survived to be transferred to Air Force Service Command on 5 April '44.

The strain of combat is etched into the faces of these 535BS crewmen as they queue up for coffee and chocolate bars prior to de-briefing. In the center is Lt. Melvin Hecker (CP), whose face still bears the pressure lines from his oxygen mask. Hecker completed his tour in early 1944.

was confronted with the grim details of his crew's gruesome fate.

Clore's B-17 was a recent Sqdn. replacement; in contrast, 42-29923 "The Lucky Strike," also of the 532BS, had come in from the 305BG on 9 Sept. and was now a veteran. However, the Kiel mission was to signal her demise when she was crash-landed at Cawston Norfolk by Lt Evans, which resulted in the deaths of Lt Kraut (B) and Sgt. Rivera (BT) and serious injury to Sgts Deasy and Burckhalter. Much more fortunate were two 535BS members, Capt Frank Chapman and S/Sgt Harriman (Once attached to Capt Manchester's crew), who were finishing up. The mission itself proved a success, with a square strike on the target as P-38s kept the Luftwaffe at bay.

Next day the Group went to Paraday/Mesley airfield at Tours, France, when Lt Wood and his 532BS CO Maj. Marvin Lord flew the Lead bomber. Given an uninterrupted run from the I.P. a solid concentration of ordnance was accurately dumped on hangars and machine-shops. The B-17 flown by Lt Zeman (Also 532BS) was struck by a rocket while the bomb-bay doors were still open. The doomed bomber described a slow turn to the right, which was then reversed before it finally nosed over into a spin. Reports of as many as eight chutes were made. Zeman's aircraft was a relatively long-term survivor assigned on 19 Sept., and for it to have come through the "Autumn Crisis" of 1943 was no mean feat, but now 42-30676 had gone down the same terminal path as many of its Boeing partners.

Sgt Morrison in 42-29888 not only witnessed Zeman's departure, but also stated that the B-17 lost a wing during the final stage of descent and burst into flames upon impact. All but one of the crew would escape, but there were conflicting reports among their number as to how many were confirmed in doing so, such was the often stunning confusion created by the trauma of being shot down. For instance, Zeman said he saw two others clear the bomber, Sgt Leroux (BT) sighted one chute below and two above him, while Sgt Chevraux (LWG) was initially certain he was the sole survivor because the B-17 disintegrated when he was halfway out!

In fact, the sole fatality was Lt Bill Walker (B). According to Lt Frank Biscagna (N), a fighter had raked the B-17 from stem to stern, setting the oxygen system on fire and shooting away the controls. Attempts to extinguish the flames and to inform the pilot failed, and so after donning his chute Biscagna crawled up into the cockpit to inform Lt Zeman. On returning he found Walker's chute-pack missing, but remembered a spare located behind Zeman, which he secured and passed over to the bombardier. He then pulled the escape hatch release and

The forward compartment on the B-17 was very cramped, especially for the bombardier. Forward-firing gun is mounted into a lozenge-shaped bracket which is supported by curved bracing-bars.

The first B-17Gs were actually F Models from the final Douglas production batches DL-70 to DL-85. These were modified to accommodate the Bendix "chin" gun turret. "Gremlins Delite" was the seventh B-17G assigned to Ridgewell in Sept '43 and flew with the 533BS until transfer to AFSC on 19 May '44. She bears the long equi-shaped nose Plexiglas.

A proportion of the initial B-17G batches was introduced into service without side-gun panels, such was the urgency to make this Model operational. "Shack Rabbit" is from the Boeing BO-5 production-run, and arrived at Ridgewell on 13 Jan '44. The twin pitot-masts on the B-17F were replaced by a single fitting higher up the leftside fuselage, as depicted here. This bomber was transferred to AFSC the same day as "Gremlins Delite."

must have immediately passed out, since he could not recall either baling out or pulling his rip-cord. However, on landing he noted some of the canopy cords were severed (possibly by a 20mm shell), which allowed the chute to filter out through its ripped cover.

Sgt Cator (WG) was among the last to jump from the tumbling bomber, getting out below 1000 ft and being sure Walker was still inside. When sitting in a truck waiting transport to hospital a soldier placed a blood-spattered chute in beside him and said a body had been found beside the wrecked B-17. Sgt Sinquefield (Eng.) was informed during interrogation that his pilot was dead due to chute failure and was asked for his (Zeman's) name. The Sgt later met up with Zeman, and knowing the co-pilot had survived, as well as Lt Biscagna, with whom he had travelled to Dulag Luft, he deduced the dead airman was Lt Walker.

Lt Wilson (534BS) brought back his B-17 with an engine "out" and his ROG suffering a bad spinal wound. Holding formation, he arrived over England in the face of rain-filled darkness and a hovering 2000-ft ceiling. Over-shooting Ridgewell, he called four times for "Darky" to provide a QDM for his base. The response from the female operator at what was an RAF Mosquito airfield was "Come on in and land, 2000 ft runway." The subsequent hospitality provided for the crew was well received.

The Tours mission was destined to be the last under which the 8USAAF would operate as an independent entity. From this date on the United States Strategic and Tactical Air Forces (USSTAF), headed by Gen. Spaatz, would co-ordinate the policies and functions of both the 8USAAF and the Italian-based 15USAAF (Along with the respective 9th and 12th Tactical Air Forces) from Bushey Park. However, a separate Eighth Air Force HQ formed from the disbanded VIII Bomber Command was established at High Wycombe. Gen. Eaker was now displaced by Gen. Doolittle and transferred to the Mediterranean Theater of Operations.

The reintroduction of the side-gun panels on the B-17G resulted in their positions being reversed compared to the B-17F. "Honey" (42-40007) is a Vega-produced bomber, and is fitted with the fore-shortened version of the nose Plexiglas that increased the angle of incidence for the bombardier's optically-flat sighting panel.

"Patches N' Prayers" of the 535BS reveals an interesting field modification to her armament. The "wedge" frame for a cheek-gun mounting has replaced the original small panel fitted to this early Douglas-produced B-17G. A similar fitting can just be seen on the forward rightside of the nose.

The 6th involved only a "scrubbed" mission to Cocove, France, which doubtless would have involved further bombing of "Noball" sites. On a personal level the day witnessed the final act of burial for the Clore crew. This was attended by 12 officers and 32 enlisted men from the 532BS. Each coffin was suitably draped with "Old Glory," and the grave-side service lasted 30 minutes.

Next day another lengthy probe into Germany was initiated with a return to Ludwigshafen. One of the 534BS pilots, Lt John Silvernale, noted how another of his Sqdn pilots was carrying out a very thorough scrutiny of his escape and evasion equipment – Lt Arden Wilson. The bulk of the 35 B-17s were led by Maj. Shackley with Lt Bill McDaniels in 42-30721 "Sweet N' Lovely," with the rest slotting into the Composite Group headed by Capt. Lord and Lt. Ridley in "Big Time Operator II." Conditions dictated bombing by PFF, and the "Little Friends" ensured the Luftwaffe was generally conspicuous by its absence.

Lt Wilson was at the controls of another veteran B-17F 42-3078 "Winsome Winn/Hilda," whose title alluded to his wife. The bomber had been assigned seven days prior to operations commencing on 22 June and wore an impressive tally of mission symbols; now she was limping home on half power. One engine (newly installed and being tested in combat for the first time) had suffered a "runaway" propeller, and a second had been affected by flak; to compound the problem both were on the same wing. Despite this the crew were confident they could win through, as the formation was coming up towards the French/German border.

The Luftwaffe intervened at this point to shatter such hopes, and "Winn" was cut out of the Group ranks to be last seen disappearing into the undercast with fighters snapping at her heels. These assaults killed S/Sgt Kucher (ROG), an unlucky replacement for S/Sgt Nisbet, who was seriously wounded on the Tours mission, and S/Sgt Greco (TG). The survivors were to express their satisfaction that they had knocked down three of their adversaries. The B-17 was finally abandoned when

The solid undercast being overflown by the 381BG proved all too typical of weather conditions over Europe during World War II. Use of H2X in such conditions did provide a means of sustaining pressure on Nazi industrial resources, but the accuracy factor was greatly reduced compared to visual sighting of targets.

Ground personnel gather around the East side of the control tower to "count" the bombers in as they return from a mission. One B-17 can be seen settling down on the runway. It was not unusual for the men to collect in such groups around the field, and often hours before the Estimated Time of Arrival (ETA) of the formation.

This otherwise perfect formation is short one bomber from the High Sqdn, which probably denotes one MIA crew to be deleted from the Group strength. This was a scenario repeated 131 times at Ridgewell during 22 months of unremitting combat.

smoke and fire from the left wing's ruptured gas tanks penetrated through to the fuselage. "Winsome Winn" ended her 35th mission as a shattered pile in a field after her crew floated down to begin 17 months of captivity, with the officers incarcerated in Stalag Luft I and the enlisted men in Stalag XVIIB in Austria.

Approximately three months had passed since "Black Thursday" and the restriction on regular deep-penetration missions into Germany. In this time-span not only had 8USAAF strength been built up to a point where between 600 and 700 bombers could be despatched, but the advent of the Merlin-powered P-51B promised to deliver effective all-round protection for the "Big Friends." P-51 numbers were admittedly still modest, but when allied to the ever-increasing ranges being achieved by its P-38 and P-47 brethren through the medium of fully pressurised drop-tanks, such a promise looked ever more capable of fulfillment.

Oschersleben

It was now acknowledged at USSTAF HQ that the breaking of the Luftwaffe had to be achieved in the near future, otherwise not only the Combined Bombing Policy, but also the projected "Overlord" Invasion of France would be placed in jeopardy. Gen. Eaker's successor, Gen. Doolittle, faced little option other than to force the pace of air operations with this critical objective in mind, and it can be conjectured that the 11 Jan. mission formed part of this thought-pattern.

For the Ridgewell crews today's mission was just one more occasion on which to bitch at the Top Brass and the seemingly fickle manner in which they operated. All three Bomb Divisions were to participate in hitting the aircraft-assembly plants situated in Oschersleben and Halberstadt, both of which lay some 100 miles SW of Berlin (Itself a potentially "hot" though yet virginal target for the USAAF and the subject of fearful conjecture among its crews). Opposition was expected to be severe, but with several hundred escorts on hand it was hoped the Luftwaffe's sting could be drawn. The 1CBW would lead

A Group formation leaves non-persistent contrails as it heads out on a mission. B-17G in the foreground bears over-sized 532BS code letters and red borders to the national insignia. This Fortress arrived as one of the first G-Models, and survived from assignment on 20 Sept '43 until 19 May '44 when it also transferred out to AFSC.

Broken cloud formations outline a pair of B-17Fs of the 534BS. Picture was taken not later than 11 Jan '44 when 42-3118 "Green Hornet" at top was MIA. The other bomber is "Mickey Finn," which was salvaged following a crash-landing at Ridgewell on 4 Feb '44.

the Division, with the 91BG up front and the 381BG contributing 33 aircraft within its own and the Composite Groups. The name of Oschersleben was destined to be woven into 381BG annuls in a similar negative manner to Schweinfurt, with the 533BS's nine participating bombers bearing the brunt of the punishment.

Steadily deteriorating weather, which arose during assembly and as the formations were crossing into Europe, caused "recall" signals to be relayed in general to the 2BD and 3BD. The 1BD was well on its way towards the target by this stage of official action, and its segment of the overall Task Force was left alone. The weather was also mainly responsible for failure of the escorts to make full rendezvous with the bombers, who were therefore left to experience ever-increasing Luftwaffe attacks from the Dutch/German borders onwards. These were intensified as the forces sent to intercept the other two Divisions were freed from this duty to join in the battle.

Penetration of the enemy coast was made over the vast inland stretch of water in Northern Holland known then as the Zuiderzee and re-titled the Ijsselmeer after World War II. Flying over water provided a doubtful sanctuary from the German defences, but it at least left the bombers free from flak. This was a point of academic interest to Lt Nason and crew in 42-37719 "Hellcat" as they were struggling to hold in formation. They were flying on their fourth or fifth mission, which was fated to be their last. Turning back over the Dutch border the B-17 retraced its steps. It appears that No. 3 engine then caught fire, and the co-pilot's call for a bale-out was acted upon fairly promptly by several men. This was despite the warning from Lt Anagnos (N) that they were over water – no place to jump out and into in the summer, let alone in January.

Sgt John Lantz (WG) remembers his fellow waist-gunner, Sgt Beus, adjusting his harness prior to jumping, after which John followed him out of the burning B-17. John also observed Sgt Stonich (BT) as he drifted down below with a further number of chutes above. Their good fortune at escaping a fiery death in the plunging B-17 was to be cruelly eclipsed for all bar John, who was fortunate to be picked up after some 15 or 20 minutes by Dutch fishermen. Death by drowning or exposure was the common fate of the other four parachutists, with

Part of Lt. Dan Hagarty's 534BS crew pose in front of 42-3118 "Green Hornet." The pilot is standing second from right, while Sgt. John Crawbuck (winner of the Silver Star and wearing a Bunny Suit) is next to Hagarty. Lt. Rick Rylands (B) squats on right; he was the designer of the Sqdn's badge.

"Sugar" was the first Ridgewell B-17G from the Douglas DL-10 batch. She is modified with a single gun through the center side-window and a similar fitting through the front-left window. The original heavy-framed top turret was still standard on the Fortress in late 1943. This 534BS bomber was returned to combat duty following her collapsed gear incident and survived to be transferred to AFSC on 19 May '44.

Anagnos and Sgt Fiery the only bodies recovered three months later. A marginally kinder fate awaited those crewmen still on board "Hellcat," since they were probably killed instantly when the aircraft exploded, a fact also reported by Sgt Lantz.

Lt Saur's crew was of similar operational experience to Lt Nason's, and they were also struggling to maintain contact with the Group as it bore into German air space. Fighter attacks were constantly being called in, whose strikes finally shot away part of the tail on 42-37962 and caused the B-17 to fall into a spin before breaking in two. Only Sgts Bernard Keane and L.T. Paterson (both WGs) managed to bale out, and it was Keane's opinion that centrifugal force held the other eight within the craft until final impact. He was also told by a 532BS gunner shot down on a later mission and in his POW camp that Sgt Prestwood was said by "Lord Haw Haw" to have been found in his ball turret deep in the ground. Keane also saw the jacket of Sgt Brogden (Eng.) laying in a truck next day and was shown the flying jacket and escape picture of Lt Warren (N). The garment had a large hole in the pocket, probably caused by a shell, which led the Sgt to suppose (correctly) that the Lt. was dead.

Gunnery was deceptively easy when indulged in from a static ground position. In truth, operating the 65-lb weapon from a flexible mount inside a bouncing, bucking B-17 was a very different matter, and was not much easier from the turrets. It was accordingly not surprising that the main executioners of the Luftwaffe were the USAAF fighters, supported on some occasions by RAF Fighter Command.

The regular crew of "Winsome Winn/Hilda" is seen during States-side training. The pilot, Lt. Arden Wilson, is second from left at the front, and Lt. Harry Ullom (B) is on the right. Sgt Bob Geraghty (BT) stands third from right, and Sgt Greco (right) was one of two fatalities when the B-17F and its crew were shot down on 7 Jan '44.

"Wolverine" of the 535BS was one of three B-17Gs assigned to Ridgewell on 20 Oct '43. Absence of cheek-gun windows up front and open waist windows were features of early G Models. Lt. Bob Deering's crew were MIA in this bomber on 30 Jan '44.

Keane had landed barely 75 ft away from Paterson, whose canopy had snagged in a tree, but by the time he got to the tree Paterson had gone. Their capture was noted at 1120, ten minutes after their B-17 crashed at Gallenbeck/forest section Mittelberg. The eight dead crewmen were buried at Achmer airbase cemetery at 0830 on 13 Jan.

Around 1130 the 381BG was approaching Osnabruck when Lt McEvoy's B-17F 42-29999 "Fertile Myrtle" was seen with a smoking No. 4 engine, and shortly after it went into a slow spin with no chutes coming free before it disappeared. Fortunately, all ten men did bale out, and the 533BS bomber fell to earth near Eickhelt South of Mille with several German witnesses at Achmer attesting to its destruction by an Fw 190 or Me109. Seven of the crew were promptly arrested around Neukirchen, two recorded as seized at Halle, and the tenth listed as "dead," but the latter observation was happily incorrect.

Lt Ernest Klein's battle-hardened team had survived a bad time on an earlier mission to Bremen. Iced-up Plexiglas and instrument failure due to faults in the vacuum pump's control valve forced their B-17 out of formation and kept them badly lagging behind on the way in. Lt Klein still "pressed on regardless" to bomb after the bomb-bay doors were cranked open and then headed home within the ranks of another Group. The crew were now facing imminent death or capture as 42-31417 had Nos. 2 and 3 engines set on fire and once again lost contact near Hildesheim. Up in the nose Sgt Jim Counce (nose gunner) had been mortally wounded by several bullet strikes as the other nine got ready to jump. In any event, only eight got

Another transferred in B-17F from the 96BG was "Fertile Myrtle," which arrived on 16 July '43. The 533BS bomber survived almost six months of combat. Then, on 11 Jan '44 she was one of six Sqdn and eight Group aircraft MIA over Oschersleben; happily, all ten of Lt. Matthew McEvoy's crew baled out.

clear, with Lt Klein finally opening his chute at what Lt Chelf (CP) claimed was a perilously low height. S/Sgt Wright's body was sighted close to the crash-site near Harsum by Klein. There was to be an ironic twist to the later meeting between T/Sgt Pope and his pilot, because the latter had thought that the body in the nose was that of Pope. (The unfortunate Sgt Counce had but one or two missions left of his combat tour, having been a member of the Gleichauf crew that with several of its members already tour-expired was now dissolved.)

There is a degree of confusion as to when Lt Gordon Crozier's B-17G 42-37730 became detached from the Group, with Lt Monaco stating this happened a few minutes away from the I.P. and Lt Hannon (N) saying this occurred ten miles South of the target. Three witnesses noted No. 3 engine wreathed in flames and two chutes emerging as the bomber turned off to the right. On making his way to the rear exit Lt Hannon noted T/Sgt George Balmore (ROG) slumped in his seat. Closer inspection revealed a gaping hole in his skull and wounds to his back, his face blue, and no pulse to be felt. Hannon's opinion was backed by his pilot, after which both airmen baled out to end up with the other seven as "Kriegies." Their bomber flew on to come down 10 miles North of Gallenbeck, close to where Lt Saur's aircraft had earlier crashed. (Balmore was the second unlucky member of Lt Gleichauf's crew, who was also within one or two missions of completing his tour). One of the survivors was S/Sgt Bob Osborne, who on a previous mission had assisted his wounded bombardier, as well as helping to fly the B-17 back – actions which saw him bestowed with the Silver Star.

Up in the nose of the 1CBW Lead ship all was not well. The bomb-sight had been knocked out by 20mm shells, so it was little wonder the 91BG's bombing effort was ineffective. This inauspicious start to the attack was brilliantly countered by Capt Darrell DeBolt (534BS). Acting in his capacity of Lead Bombardier he precisely directed the 381BG's bomb pattern, which smothered the factory and was an example generally followed by succeeding Groups.

Group personnel sift through the jumbled wreckage of a 532BS B-17G on 4 Jan '44. The mission should have witnessed a successful end to the combat tours of Lt. Cecil Clore and the majority of his crew. Instead, all were killed in an attempted crash-landing when their bomber developed problems shortly after take-off.

"Lucky Strike" "struck out" returning from Kiel on 4 Jan '44 when Lt. Evans managed a heavy crash-landing at Cawston, Norfolk; sadly, two crewmen were killed in the attempt. Aircraft had transferred-in from the 305BG on 11 Sept '43. She had completed 26 missions prior to this date.

The punishment being handed out up to now had resulted in unavoidable losses. However, on the way back the crews were to complain of some very indifferent guidance from the 1CBW Lead Navigator, which it was reckoned took the formations through some of the worst flak concentrations in North/Central Germany (some crews said the Ruhr). This being the case, it would appear that the briefed return route had been badly strayed from.

Three more Ridgewell crews were MIA by the mission's end, and two of these losses would exemplify the extremes of fortune in combat as these affected Lts Larson (534BS) and Perot (533BS). Sgt Defenbaugh was flying as a "spare" gunner, and also on board was S/Sgt John Crawbuck who was back in action after hospitalisation after the 27 Sept mission when he had earned a Silver Star. "Green Hornet" (42-3118) had just bombed when she was reportedly hit head-on by an Me109 and broke into four sections which fell East of Hannover. The fact that both pilots and the bombardier baled out several minutes after the others cast doubt on such a report. In fact, only one death occurred, which was the "substitute," Sgt Defenbaugh, who was seen by the ROG lying with severe head wounds.

"Winsome Winn/Hilda" ("Hilda" was added later by Lt. Arden Wilson in honor of his wife) tucks in close to the photographer's B-17. The 534BS Fortress was assigned on 14 June '43 and had eight completed missions at this time. Group letter on the fin has been applied in relation to aircraft's ground attitude – either that, or the airman responsible was intoxicated at the time!

The reported collision involving "Green Hornet" almost certainly applied to Lt Perot piloting 42-5878. Sgt Besley (WG), who was on his tenth mission, had gone through Phase training with this crew but was currently not a regular member. He noted an Me109 coming in and was clipping on his chute-pack when the German fighter impacted between Nos. 1 and 2 engines. The B-17 then exploded, but Besley's next conscious recollection was of coming-to on German soil. Why he donned his chute-pack is unclear, but in his own words stated in his Post-war de-briefing report; "Had I not done so I would not be around to relate the story!"

The eighth and final Group loss involved Lt Chason (533BS) in 42-3514, and to add to the deep sense of gloom the dispirited survivors were not even able to get back to their own base. Fog conditions over the Home Counties forced a diversion into the 44BG airfield at Shipdam, near to Norwich, from where the crews were transported to Ridgewell by bus. Total losses for the 1BD amounted to 42 out of 291 bombers despatched, of which 13 came out of the 1CBW. Oschersleben had yielded bloody evidence of the continuing power of the Luftwaffe – a power that only a more than adequate U.S. fighter force could hope to neutralise.

Lt. Bill Farrell (B) to Lt Flaherty in 42-31443 "Friday the 13th" was initially wounded in one leg by fragments from a 20mm shell exploding in the nose. Then, on the bomb-run he incurred a second more serious set of wounds to head and one arm; this time the 20mm blew him off his stool and tore off his oxygen mask. He nonetheless crawled back to his bombsight and completed the run, then continued to operate the nose guns in the face of continuous fighter assaults. F/O Ben Saporta (N) had also been wounded during the action. Lt Farrell noticed his companion was getting steadily weaker from his thigh wound, so he attended to Saporta by administering sulpha drugs and a morphine shot before bracing the leg with a splint. Although he had earlier communicated the fact of his injuries to his pilot, it was only when the bombers were again clear of fighter attack that Farrell submitted himself to medical attention. His great gallantry was recognised by a Silver Star award. A second such decoration went to Saporta.

Over the next ten days just a single mission was launched by the 8USAAF (14th), and although the 381BG was briefed

"Chaps Flying Circus" (535BS) displays an impressive number of mission symbols totalling over 30, as well as eleven "kill" stars for enemy fighters. The veteran B-17F met a sad end on 30 Jan '44. Shortage of gas forced Lt. Carl Baer into a "ditching" from which none of the ten crewmen emerged alive; Baer's body was the only one recovered.

"Winsome Winn/Hilda" is seen trailing smoke from her No. 1 engine. Shortly after the photograph was taken she peeled away and down to be intercepted and shot down by Fw 190s. Two of Lt. Arden Wilson's crew were KIA and the others became POWs. Date was 7 Jan '44.

for several targets, such as Gotha and Frankfurt, in this period, it was 21 Jan. before Col. Leber led a force striking at installations connected with enemy secret weapons at St Adrienne and Belleville-en-Caux just across the Channel. The Col. later stated; "The mission was a bombardier's dream; we spent 90 minutes over the two allotted targets with an average of six bomb-runs for most ships and ten for one Sqdn." This latter sub-unit may well have been the 535BS, which achieved no result due to 10/10 cloud and brought its bombs back. Apart from one Group, which was caught by the few fighters around, "meager" was the description for both this form of opposition and flak. One of the returning B-17s flown by Lt Hansen (42-39997 "Big Mike") was bearing an odd mix of experience. S/Sgt Basil Johnson was finishing-up, Lt J Brunning (N) was flying his 13th mission (diplomatically referred to as No. 12A), and Lt Hal Roling (P) was just starting out; he would soon take over his own crew, but would go down on 22 Feb. Lt Hansen remarked wryly; "As the undertaker who married the mid-wife said – we catch them coming and going!"

Lt. Nitikin (CP) hands his chute-pack to a Red Cross representative as Lt. Henry Lipsky (N) looks on. Both were members of Lt. Matthew McEvoy's 533BS crew, which baled out of 42-29999 "Fertile Myrtle" over Germany on 11 Jan '44.

By now the originally wary attitudes of the local people around the base towards the military "invaders" from overseas had mellowed to the point where many of them now talked about the rough experiences "our boys" were facing in combat. The numerous hostelries around Ridgewell were well frequented by the American airmen, and none more so than the "White Hart" in Great Yeldham. There the middle-aged landlady had struck up a friendship with one young gunner who had somehow developed a perfect Cockney accent. His favourite line with guests travelling through was to engage them in conversation. When they would point to the apparent contradiction of the gunner wearing an American instead of a British uniform he would convince them that he had served in the RAF but had transferred to the USAAF thanks to the lousy pay and feeding conditions! One evening John Howland and his 535BS co-pilot, Bill Doherty, who had witnessed the gunner's act many times, made their way to the "White Hart." They soon noted that the atmosphere was unusually tense and that the landlady seemed almost in tears. It transpired the gunner was MIA, and she remarked she was terribly tired of War, and it might be best for all concerned if (as John put it) "We Yanks stayed on base." Her attitude was far from being anti-American; rather, it highlighted how involvement with their Allies was liable to create such an emotional reaction to recurring tragedies of this nature within the community

By this stage in the Group's combat career there were very few of the B-17Fs brought over in June still on hand. One of these was Capt Frank Chapman's 42-30029 "Chaps Flying Circus'es." Six of his crew, including M/Sgt Myers, the Group's first evader, had already finished their tours. Today they were joined by Lt Wilson Cupp and T/Sgt Otha Frost to leave only T/Sgt Crowley and S/Sgt Wardell to join their fortunate ranks. Unlike those who had entrusted their lives to the Boeing machine, "Circus'" existence was fast running to a tragic conclusion.

A controversial note was struck on the 24th. A mission to Frankfurt was in progress, and the Group had just crossed the enemy coast when a "recall" was broadcast, but to the crews' chagrin they were not granted mission credit. To reach this point for no result was particularly depressing for the already highly stressed personnel. Re-assigned on this day was T/Sgt Otto Bruszewski (Eng.) who had jumped from "Chug A Lug Lulu" on 17 August. Lt. Carl Dittus was again in trouble with the authorities when arrested after a brush with an M.P. Lt Ridley's errant bombardier had already been cleared of an affray in London. He had been wounded in action and held the Purple Heart, but the 535BS diarist dryly noted this was one combat for which he would receive no decoration!

After two false briefings the Group set out for Frankfurt on the 29th, and heavy flak was encountered as the formations unloaded with PFF guidance. Although the Luftwaffe was up in strength no contact was made with the 381BG, who nevertheless was to mourn the loss of two more crews, both from the 534BS. Lts Mohnacky flying 42-38045 and Mickow in 42-37884 were the unlucky duo. Brunswick was the selected target next day, and the last mission for January. Among the 535BS contingent was the venerable "Chaps Flying Circus," containing Lt Carl Baer and crew. PFF bombing methods were again mandatory due to the solid undercast. For the second successive day losses were suffered, three this time around. Two of this number were Lt Deering – a 533BS pilot, but flying 42-31047 "Wolverine" from the 535BS – and Lt Steele (533BS) in 42-29761 "Martha the II." (Lt Deering was the "lone warrior," who on 13 Nov. had missed both the Group assembly and subsequent "recall" signal and proceeded as far as Holland before realising his precarious position and turning back). The Lt., along with his navigator, Lt Barer, and four of the enlisted men are all buried at Margraten Military Cemetery, in Holland. Lt Steele's B-17 was attacked by Fw190s, lagged behind for 15 minutes, and finally peeled off into the clouds. A fire in the left wing gained in intensity, and the "jump" signal was finally given. Sgt Eason (ROG) was dragged out of his seat by Lt Settle (CP), and although he got clear of the bomber, his body was found on the ground with his chute unopened. Sgt Hylnsky (WG) suffered a cruel end when he drifted backwards into a fence and broke his neck in the collision; a priest summoned to the scene administered the Last Rites. Two bodies were claimed found by some Dutchmen in the wreckage, and Lt Steele later surmised that Sgts Lee (BT) and Holtz (WG) may have "frozen" at the thought of jumping. The remainder of the crew survived.

An even sadder loss was about to occur as the Group was clearing the Dutch coast. Lt Baer called up to say he was faced with "ditching" thanks to rapidly drying gas-tanks. He sounded quite composed and even cheerful over the intercom. Contact with the Air-Sea Rescue Service indicated the situation was in hand, and a successful pick-up of Baer and his crew was con-

This 381BG line-up was not taken at Ridgewell, but at Shipdam (44BG) the day after the disastrous Oschersleben mission of 11 Jan '44. Last in the left-hand line is 42-29832 "Our Mom" (534BS), and bringing up the right-hand line is a PFF B-17G from the 305BG.

fidently anticipated. The hours passed with no news of any such outcome, and the next day those ten souls on "Chaps Flying Circus" were posted MIA. The pilot's body was subsequently picked up, but his fellow-crewmen were never found and are like so many others commemorated on Madingley's Wall of the Missing.

February 1944

By February 1944 the Senior Command structure at Ridgewell had involved several changes. Col. Harry P Leber (His Lt. Col. status on arrival was not altered for the first few weeks of his command) had assumed charge of the Group with effect from 9 Jan., although he was already on the base towards the end of December. Of a rather more flamboyant nature than Col. Nazzaro, the new Group CO was able to maintain the high level of overall efficiency, although the presence of seasoned veterans such as Col. Hall and Maj. Shackley assisted him in this respect. Maj. Charles L Halsey had arrived after duties with an anti-submarine Group to take over the 535BS, and Maj. John Fitzgerald arrived to hold the same post in the 532BS. (Fitzgerald had been involved in the training of pilots practising "short take-off" procedures for their impending Tokyo raid launched from the carrier "Hornet" in April 1942). Replaced by Fitzgerald was Maj. Lord, but his career would blossom further. He later transferred to Bassingbourn, and as a Lt. Col. assumed the Group Operations Officer post, but was tragically fated to die over Berlin on 3 Feb. 1945.

A handful of "original" combat crew were still on hand, but given the scale of personnel loss in the intervening seven months it was inevitable the vast bulk of the fliers were replacements, largely of one or two months' standing. They could be regarded as the "second generation" for the 381BG, who would see it and the 8USAAF through the climax of the aerial contest with the Luftwaffe, a climax which would witness the inexorable slide into oblivion for that hitherto formidable Air Force. A deceptively easy start to February was made on the 3rd when a ten-mile long bomber stream poured over Wilhelmshaven on what was the Group's 63rd accomplished run out of 121 Field Orders handed down. Capts. Briggs and Tucker (534BS) were in charge of 35 bombers, which reached the target in double-quick time thanks to a 110-mph tail wind! Bombs were released through an undercast, and a strong escort ensured the mission was easy-paced as far as fighter opposition was concerned. The flak over the primary naval port was not so easily dispelled. For Lt. John Silvernale and his ROG, Sgt. Ernie Neves, the run was a repetition of their combat debut exactly three months previous. All aircraft came home with little damage and no casualties. Sgt. Reilly (ROG) on "Homing Pigeon" spent a very breezy few minutes in the bomb-bay as he was trying to release four incendiaries which had "hung up," a task made more difficult by having to hold onto his "walk-around" oxygen bottle and work away with just one hand!

Maj. Shackley stands on the left alongside Maj. McDaniels and other 533BS crewmen. Behind is 42-29761 "Martha the II" with an impressive 38 mission tally. Only a few more symbols would be added prior to the B-17F going MIA on 30 Jan '44 with Lt. Steele and crew.

Frankfurt was visited 24 hours later by 27 crews who made a concentrated drop through the 10/10 cloud while facing a flak barrage of some 15 minutes duration. Flying his final mission was Capt. Bill McDaniel, leading the Group with Lt. George Sandman in 42-30721 "Sweet N' Lovely." Although no losses were incurred, much bitter recrimination was directed at the CBW Lead Navigator, who was adjudged to have led the force off-course and over regions providing sustained flak opposition – naturally, it was the 91BG up front again! A family reunion awaited Sgt Dick Hamilton (BT) when his brother Merrill (a S/Sgt based in Northern Ireland) was on hand to greet him.

Tailing the formation home was Lt John Kuhl in 42-30834 "Mickey Finn," with Nos. 3 and 4 engines knocked out by flak. Arriving over Ridgewell, Kuhl found himself faced with a similar situation to that on 20 Dec. when he "bellied-in" 42-37754 "Whodat?". The B-17F's right landing gear was jammed in the retracted position, and the left only partially extended. The Lt. made a steady approach and eased the bomber into a soft landing alongside the runway. He could have landed at an RAF Mosquito base in Norfolk to which he had been directed, but he chose instead to make a "home run." Shortly after posing

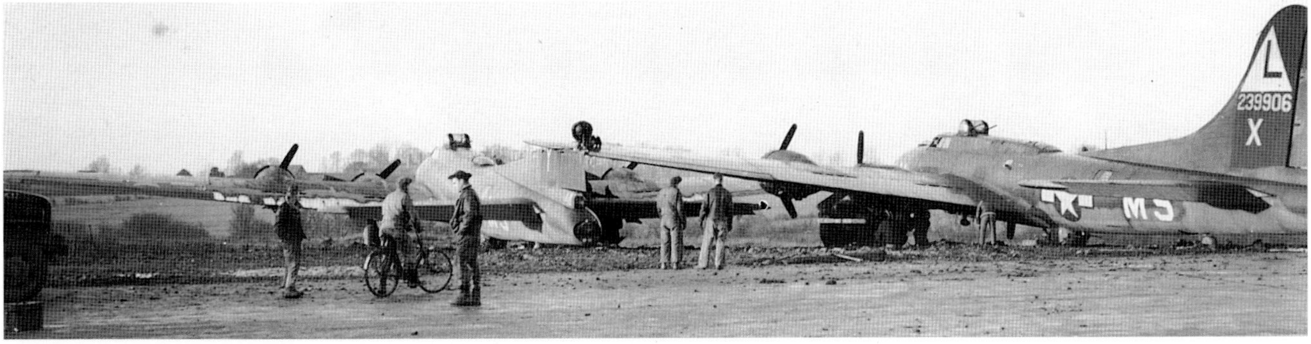

On 21 Jan '44 and while landing off a practice mission, "Squat N' Droppit" got too close to "Return Ticket" (42-39890) and slashed its left wing-tip across the latter B-17G's fin and rudder to cause the damage recorded here. Despite its severity, "Return Ticket" lived up to her name by being repaired and resuming combat duty. However, she was finally lost on the expensive 24 May '44 mission to Berlin.

for a picture with his crew by the aircraft's nose Kuhl suffered a mental relapse that left him with no memory of events over the course of the next few days. In any event, he recovered from this condition to finally complete his run of missions.

"Mickey Finn" was adjudged too badly damaged to be repaired and was declared "Category E" on the 7th. A similar fate awaited 42-30732 from the same Sqdn. Lt Hytinen had flown the aircraft on a passenger-carrying hop to Little Staughton. A touchdown short of the runway left the B-17 minus its left landing gear, which was sheared off by the impact. Hytinen was re-directed to Alconbury, where a crash-landing was effected in the dark, the short February day having faded by this time. "Category E" status was declared the very same day.

A relatively short-haul mission was laid on for the 5th when Col. Hall took 28 aircraft to St Avord airfield, located South of Paris, with Maj. Fitzgerald heading the Composite Group element. Crystal-clear conditions gave full scope for Capt Bill Fullick (Group Bombardier) to set up a perfect drop. The resultant concentration of ordnance pulverised the main hangars and maintenance buildings with not one bomb dropped off-target. Several aircraft attempting to taxi out and take-off were caught in the blast of the pattern. The heavy escort of P-47s and P-38s kept the Luftwaffe at bay.

The fourth daily mission in a row was also directed at a French airfield Nancy/Essey, but a solid undercast meant no bombing was carried out. Lt Henry Putek (535BS) was holding formation in his regular B-17 42-40025 "Touch the Button Nell" when at 1115 an explosion occurred between the top-turret and bomb bay. The blast ripped out the cockpit side-windows and cracked the windshield on the right side, as well as springing the left side bottom frame, and disabled the top-turret. Smoke and flames filled the cockpit, and Putek quickly pulled out to one side as he rang the "bale-out" bell; he was unaware that his own chute-pack had been burnt beyond recognition. Meanwhile, T/Sgt Lifford French (Eng.) dropped out of the turret to grab a fire extinguisher with which to extinguish the fire, but incurred severe facial burns in the process. By now only Putek was left of the officer complement. The Sgt contacted the remaining crew to tell them the "bale-out" order was rescinded and then returned to assist his pilot.

The B-17 was now on its own, and its gunners fully alert for possible fighter attacks, which began all too soon as three Me 109s materialised from six o'clock. Sgt Vinovich (TG) blew up one and Sgt Shortell (RWG) took out the second, whose fire landed four strikes on the ball-turret, which seriously wounded Sgt Burgasser in one eye. The enemy trio's claimed destruction was completed by S/Sgt Viner (ROG). It was very fortunate that the German pilots never had the opportunity to discover their adversary's total vulnerability to frontal attack, the consequences of which would surely have been fatal for "Nell."

Wallowing along at 4000 ft with no navigator, bomb-doors jammed open, a large hole in one wing, and hundreds of perforations all over the fuselage, bomber and crew faced a desperate struggle to get home. The persistent undercast inconveniently thinned as they flew close to Paris, and flak pasted them for what seemed an interminable length of time. Putek and French were having recourse to use of oxygen masks thanks to the boreal gale punching through the windshield. For well over two hours the B-17 was shepherded home until a landfall was made near to a town on the Southwest coast of England.

With the radio shot out Viner could not respond to the AA gunners' challenge, who naturally acted in a hostile manner, especially on sighting an aircraft with bomb-doors open; Putek had no option other than to turn away out to sea. (The reception momentarily instilled doubts in the pilot's mind as to whether or not he was over England!) A quick scan of the geography soon settled such doubts, and this time around the AA batteries permitted his B-17 unfettered access to an airfield close to the town, which was the U.S. Navy base at Dunkeswell.

Sgt French had refused medical attention up to now, so he and Sgt. Burgasser were whisked off to hospital, where the latter airman's injured eye was removed. When his buddies later visited him he joked about his bandaged head and referred to his limited vision in this manner: "It's not too bad – just like being in a London black-out!" The actions of T/Sgt French were to earn him the sole other Distinguished Service Cross awarded to 381BG crewmen, and an equally well-merited Silver Star went to Lt. Putek. "Nell" was considered too badly shot-up for repair and return to operational duty and was "scrapped."

The 535BS records noted that on 8 Feb. M/Sgt Charles Stormer was assigned as the first Enlisted navigator in its strength. He had previously flown with an RCAF Sqdn. operating on Bristol Beaufort torpedo-bombers but had recently transferred over to the 8USAAF. His promotion to Flight Officer or 2 Lt. was anticipated soon.

A "scrubbed" Leipzig mission (9th) was followed on the 11th by yet another foray to Frankfurt and its marshalling yards. The 1BD put up 223 B-17s, of which 157 attacked the Primary. The 381BG records, however, indicate that its aircraft trailed a PFF B-17 to what proved to be Ludwigshafen, over 100 miles South of Frankfurt, where bombs were released through broken clouds and with results rated as "fair." Only four bombers were missing from the total force, but one of these was 42-31099 "Tenabuv" flown by Lt. Laux (532BS). The B-17 was one of three 'stragglers' taken down by JG 26 over Belgium or France, in this instance by Unteroffizier Guttman of 8 Staffel. One of this crew was Sgt Glennan, a former radio mechanic who had volunteered for combat duties and had spent seven days at a Gunnery School in order to qualify. The Sgt was one of a sizeable number of groundcrew who were to forsake the more sedentary life of the support personnel in order to experience the sharp edge of aerial combat, and today was his third mission. Amazingly, no less than seven of the crew would avoid their potential captors and eventually return to England. Lt. Laux, after bringing his bomber down near Haussez, SE of Forges-les-Eaux, France, concealed himself in available buildings, as well as the local woods. He was then discovered by a Frenchwoman who contacted a local

Close-up view of the damage caused to "Return Ticket" by her sister-ship on 21 Jan '44.

Resistance Group into whose charge he was taken. On 26 March he arrived back in England, having been evacuated by a Royal Navy motor-torpedo-boat. (Bob Laux was Vice President of the Air Force Escape and Evasion Society)

Another 532BS bomber in trouble was flying its 41st mission; "The Joker" was carrying Lt. Ridley's veteran crew. On the way in its oxygen system failed, which forced the tail and waist-gunners to exist on emergency bottles. The ball-turret gunner was hauled out of his position after he lost consciousness and was placed in the radio-room. Then a failure of the bomb-release gear added to Ridley's problems. Attacks by three Me 109s and a single Me 110 left numerous strikes, including one that hit the ball-turret gunner as he lay in the radio-room. The violent evasive action at one point threw T/Sgt Kaufman (ROG) up against the Plexiglas, which temporarily knocked him out. Other crewmembers were similarly shaken about, but their B-17 was brought back into formation and made it home. ("The Joker" was one of a handful of B-17Fs still on hand, as well as being a Group "original" aircraft. Its mission tally would increase to around 50 before it was honourably "retired" back to the States in April).

Although the other two Bomb Divisions were twice active over the ensuing nine days, the 1BD was not called upon at all. In this time yet another Group "evader" in the form of S/Sgt Floyd Terry came through the Ridgewell gates. He had followed Sgt Ed Myers out of France after both were downed in Lt. Zum's aircraft. Arriving on the 12th, he was promptly promoted to M/Sgt.

Up to now the names applied on bomber fuselages had generally been at the inspiration of the combat or groundcrew. In the winter of 1943/44 the British Public had raised large sums of money under the auspices of "Wings for Victory Week" schemes. A decision was now taken to name four B-17s after four of the most badly blitzed London Districts, mainly those in the city's East End. Two of these B-17Gs, "Rotherhithes Revenge" and "Bermondsay Battler," were 381BG aircraft. They were gathered together, along with "Bermondsay Special" and "London Avenger" at Kimbolton (379BG) on 15 Feb. when "Revenge" was the specific subject of a christening ceremony; this bomber was the sole operational "virgin" among the quartet.

Bermondsey Borough had previously raised £800,000, of which a quarter was used to "buy" the B-17s. Councillor E.J. Gibson, Chairman of the War Loans Committee, smashed a bottle of Bermondsey-produced ale over the chin-turret guns, and Councillor Starr presented a scroll as a token of the Borough's friendship and admiration for its American Allies. Col. Leber then responded by saying that he felt the Group would now be carrying the ball for the Londoners. "Bermondsay Battler" was already a 535BS nine-mission veteran whose regular pilot was tall, sandy-haired, and slow-speaking Lt. Lee W Smith, a mid-Westerner hailing from Battleground, Ind. A complete combat record was being kept on both bomber and crew. (The 91BG's "London Avenger" had five missions in, and "Bermondsay Special" had just broken its duck with the 379BG). The ultimate fate of these four B-17s would reflect the high and low points of the Daylight Bombing Policy, although only one would be MIA.

The 8USAAF was fast approaching another, if not the critical, stage in its Campaign. Although the bulk of escorts were still P-47s and P-38s (only two P-51 Groups were currently operational), the provision of efficient drop-tanks was granting solid support well into Central Germany for the "Big Friends." The destruction of aero-plants was high on the agenda, and so Gens. Spaatz and Doolittle decided upon a sustained campaign of attrition against this source, whose anticipated success would literally "ground" the Luftwaffe for want of both aircraft and spares. They acknowledged that a high level of bomber losses was likely to be borne by the 8USAAF and its Italian-based twin, the 15USAAF – a figure as high as 200 was regarded as the possible wastage factor arising from the first mission alone! It says much for the rapid build-up of the ETO Air Forces that serious consideration could be given to this very negative aspect of the Bomber Offensive. However, America's industrial capacity was at its peak, while the training schools were turning out more than sufficient human resources to make up for crew casualty rates.

Lt. John Kuhl (kneeling on left) and his 534BS crew give a "thumbs up" sign as they cluster 'round the nose of their B-17F "Mickey Finn" (42-30834). The bomber had lost all power in its right-side engines thanks to flak damage that also knocked out the hydraulics for the right landing gear. However, the pilots managed to bring off a smooth crash-landing. Incident occurred on 4 Feb '44, and the Fortress was salvaged three days later.

8

BIG WEEK

Sunday 20 Feb. dawned with low-cloud conditions extending over many 8USAAF bases. Field Order No. 226, which signalled the start of the planned series of operations against German aircraft production plants and storage depots, despatched the 1BD to four primary locations in the Leipzig/Oschersleben/Bernberg region. Operation "Argument" – forever to be referred to under its more pungent title of "Big Week" – was on. The first two targets were the focus of Group attention by 17 and 24 crews, respectively. Despite the very poor weather over England, assembly of the near 700 bombers went off well. Varying weather conditions were encountered over Germany, with Lt. Ridley's contingent striking Leipzig/Mockau airfield which was in the clear, and broken cloud opening up at the last moment for Lt. Col. Kunkel's force to unload visually.

The 835 escorts on hand gave more than a one to one cover for the entire 1BD Task Force, and in the 381BG's Leipzig element resulted in fighter attacks being kept to a very minimum. However, one Me 110 out of a small group which did evade the P-47s landed strikes on Lt Cogswell's 42-3562 just before the target. The bomber fell out around 1342 but managed to link up with another Group on the bomb-run; that was the last sight Group witnesses had, as it was MIA at the end of the day. Col. Kunkel said his formation had no escort, but the weather tended to render their presence unnecessary. Flak was absent over Oschersleben and moderate at Leipzig. The first punch of "Big Week" had been landed, and the overall loss of 21 aircraft from among the hundreds launched must have created an overwhelming sense of relief among the Brass at "Pinetree."

With but the one break on the 23rd the crews were to add four more missions to their tally by the 25th. It was as well they were unaware of the latest physical and mental task looming up as they circled to land that Sunday. The loss factor was to steadily rise over these five days, and the 381BG would have its share with seven more crews following on Lt Cogswell's exit from combat.

Lt Bill Borrego was Cogswell's co-pilot, and was to recall that today's mission was his crew's third full run, although he had flown as a substitute on 11 Feb. when his B-17 "aborted." Difficulty in assembling had caused their bomber to stall-out and nearly collide with another stalled B-17 closing in on their blind side. The complete element failed to turn with the formation at the I.P. at Halle, and it was then that the Me 110s struck

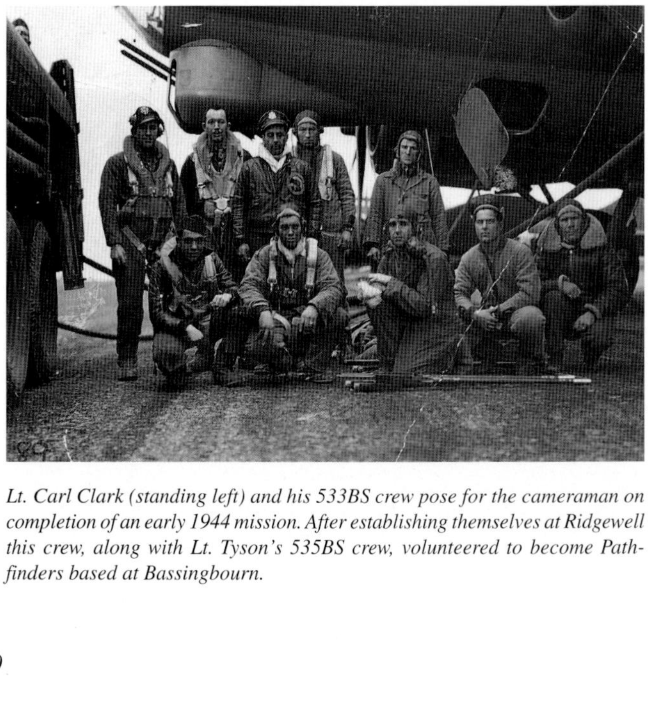

Lt. Carl Clark (standing left) and his 533BS crew pose for the cameraman on completion of an early 1944 mission. After establishing themselves at Ridgewell this crew, along with Lt. Tyson's 535BS crew, volunteered to become Pathfinders based at Bassingbourn.

Aerial view of Ridgewell in Feb '44. The original 36 dispersal pans were expanded to 50 to accommodate the much larger aircraft establishment of USAAF units compared to the RAF. Main flight-line is left-center, with the 535BS dispersals extending anti-clockwise from here around to the right of the NW/SE runway. Sited on picture's rightside are the 534BS and 533BS dispersals (the latter directly below the bomb-dump). Finally, the 532BS dispersals are at the top and clustered 'round the Northern hangar. Administrative and domestic sites are mainly located within the picture's left side.

with a force calculated at nine fighters. Cogswell's B-17 was raked from end to end, and the explosion of the shells was akin to a thousand sticks beating on a tin roof. The navigator's compartment was thoroughly sieved and the top turret similarly shredded, yet neither occupant was injured. The engineer was knocked out as he was cranking down the bomb-doors and was revived by Bill, who used oxygen from his own mask. A flak burst caught the left side of the nose. The blast killed power to Nos. 1 and 2 engines, holed the wing, left the aileron dangling, and in damaging the control cables below the cockpit set the B-17 on fire.

Bill's attempts to extinguish the flames were to no avail, and he returned to assist his pilot. Sgt. Lecces (Eng.) looked through to the bomb-bay, and his gaze settled on a fire licking 'round the auxiliary gas-tank formed from black rubber and occupying one side of the bay. The bombs were still in position, and the order to abandon the fast expiring aircraft was issued. Bill is not sure how the crew in the rear fuselage were informed, but they all exited with the exception of Sgt. Duncan (RWG), who had been killed outright by a 20mm shell. Sgt. Miller (TG) had his right knee-cap blown off and also suffered bullet wounds; despite this critical condition he dragged himself to the rear hatch after attending to Duncan in the mistaken belief the gunner was still alive. The bomb-load was salvoed, and the pilots prepared to get out as their B-17 was now far behind the formation and in a left descending spiral. (The air-

Lt. Bill Johnson is seen with Lt. Renalds (Chemical Warfare Officer). Unable to squeeze through into the bomb-bay to eject an incendiary bomb jammed across the walk-way, he did a risky balancing act by sitting on the beam and stretching out a foot to kick the lethal object free. The B-17 involved was "Martha the II" from Johnson's 533BS. This officer won a DFC for tackling a blaze in his bomber's nose compartment during a subsequent mission.

Cameraman in this aircraft has caught the control tower during a low pass. The two-floored design with small framed structure on top was to be seen at many Wartime airfields. Letters RD identify Ridgewell. The "T" frame inside the signal-square indicates the runway direction for landings, and barbell shape informs pilots that landings should only be made on the runways since the grass is not prepared for this function.

This Ju 88 bomber belongs to the RAF's No. 1426 Flight, known as the "RAFWAFFE." It was one of several captured Luftwaffe aircraft flown around Allied airfields in Britain to give the crews an impression of their adversaries' general performance. Several groundcrew at Ridgewell are gathered 'round another Flight machine in the right background, in this case an Fw 190.

craft was so ablaze that some de-briefing reports stated it had exploded with no chutes seen to deploy).

Bill experienced the common feeling among survivors of being scared and trembling at the thought of hurling himself out into a rushing void. He did not hook up his chute pack properly first time 'round, and it fell on the legs of Sgt Leccese as the engineer was about to jump. Fortunately, he hesitated and handed the pack back, whereupon Bill ensured it was secure, put one foot on the top turret base, and went out through the bomb-bay. As he was falling through space his reaction was not one of fear, but rather one of hysterical elation coupled with nervous and uncontrollable laughter. As soon as he deemed himself well clear of the B-17 he pulled his ripcord. This left him with the bulk of 25000 ft from which to drift down, and which passed astonishingly slowly in the very cold winter atmosphere. Landing in four feet of snow close to a Russian POW camp he noticed a civilian and a German guard rushing from either side. The civilian unhappily won the race and administered a pistol-whipping 'round the aviator's face, which split a lip before the guard prevailed on his countryman to desist. After being ordered to carry his chute Bill was escorted to the POW camp.

He was later reunited with Sgts. Kangas and Miller and Lt Meehan (N). Miller complained of the cold and pain to one arm and leg, and Bill had a scuffle with the guard before he could persuade the German to return the morphine in the First Aid kit strapped to his confiscated parachute harness in order to attend to Miller's needs. All four airmen were transferred to a basement in what Bill understood to be a "Lebensborn" center, where selected women and men of Aryan physique were paired off to produce pure offsprings. The potato soup brought in to the Americans was incapable of being appreciated by Bill at least, as he was by now suffering from a dreadful headache probably induced by the concussive effect of the 20mm shells. Miller's condition had further worsened, and the Germans were gradually persuaded to bring in a doctor who arranged for the Sgt. to be removed and for Bill to be given aspirin tablets.

A second transfer was preceded by the removal of all personal effects, and a preliminary interrogation occurred at this time. Next morning after sleeping on wooden table-shaped beds

Councillor Gibson, Chairman of Bermondsey's War Savings Committee, is christening "Rotherhithes Revenge" (533BS) with a bottle of Coca-Cola. The B-17G was one of four subscribed to by Rotherhithe, a badly blitzed London Borough, and would go on to repay the citizens' trust by surviving through to VE-Day.

It appears that "Rotherhithes Revenge" earned the honor of a double christening. In this picture Councillor Gibson wields what looks like a spirits bottle. Group records state the christening was made with a bottle containing Bermondsey-produced ale, so it is debatable if this shot depicts the correct event! Maj. Shackley (533BS CO) stands on left of Col. Leber.

they were put on a train for Dulag Luft at Oberursel NW of Frankfurt-am-Main. Standing dressed only in their blue electric suits and heated boots, the airmen were reviled and spat upon by civilians prior to entraining. Arriving late evening in Frankfurt they were housed in the station basement and only moved out in the morning. At Dulag Luft they were each photographed and allotted a room with high windows, which were barely big enough to house a cot. Food was limited to a morning cup of ersatz coffee without sugar or milk and lunch and evening servings of watery turnip soup. Toilet requests were indicated by pulling on a chain whose action raised a red flag outside. However, in Bill's case the sight of an armed guard standing over one with his machine pistol cocked and pointed direct at his squatting figure was enough to discourage him from calling very often upon this basic facility!

Bill was to face three interrogation sessions, each time escorted by two guards and an Alsation dog. The usual range of unanswerable questions were posed and responded to by "name, rank, and serial number only" utterances. Finally, the interrogator would try to unsettle Bill by claiming his fate would remain closed to the Allied authorities and by extension to his family until and unless the questions were answered. The cigarette proffered at the start was usually snatched back, and the German would then stamp out of the room. A variation in the techniques employed was the appearance of an elderly man claiming to be representing the Red Cross. He would pose the same general range of questions, to which the same dusty answers were given by Bill.

After three or four days Bill was allowed to join his crew in a barracks which lacked glass in the windows, through which the snow blew. The men all huddled together between the windows with an extra (stolen) blanket covering those on the outside. Next morning each was handed a hard cardboard suitcase, along with socks, shorts, field jacket, shirt, RAF greatcoat, and hob-nail boots; the latter item appeared to transmit rather than repel the cold! An air raid alert around noon saw the crew herded into a trench covered over by railroad sleepers and earth, but the anticipated attack thankfully never materialised. That evening they marched to the station to be loaded onto trucks designed for carrying 40 men or eight horses. Some 20 to 30 men were distributed on one side with six guards

Two 535BS B-17Gs flank a compact bomber formation during Feb '44. Right-hand aircraft lasted from 5 Jan. until 22 Feb. when Lt Downey's crew were lost. The other B-17 was assigned on 2 Feb. and was named "Georgia Rebel II"; the original "Georgia Rebel" was interned in Sweden on 24 July 1943. Seven of Lt. Henslin's crew were KIA in this aircraft on 28 April '44.

This group formation is pulling thick, persistent con-trails. In these conditions it was all too easy for the already pressurised pilots to become disoriented by the blinding effect of flying through the trails, and cut across another B-17's path, with disastrous consequences.

"Martha the II" is pictured flying in the company of a fellow 533BS Fortress 42-37719 "Hellcat." This duo were MIA during Jan '44, with "Hellcat" first down on the 11th when all but one of Lt. Nason's crew perished. Both bear red borders to their national insignia.

on the other and a potbelly stove in between. The over-crowding forced the POWs to sleep in turn, but this discomfort might have proved an academic issue had the RAF raid made that very night affected the railroad station area of the city. However, the marshalling yard containing their train remained untouched.

During the protracted journey to a permanent POW camp stops were normally made in the morning for bodily relief, but the time allotted was barely sufficient. So it was that the guards permitted an alternative for those desperate to seek relief in easing their discomfort – his buddies held the man concerned out of the open truck door. Anyone falling out, however inadvertently, was likely to be fired upon on the assumption he was trying to escape! The final stop for Bill and his fellow-officers was Stalag Luft I, Barth, up on the Baltic coast, where he and they spent the next 15 months. Bill's active war had proved short, but still filled with incident.

The 381BG was assigned to lead the 1CBW on 21 Feb, and the Group Lead ship was piloted by Lt. Jones (535BS), whose co-pilot was the Wing CO, Col. Gross. Gutersloh airfield was to be hit by 32 bombers, but cloud-cover on this and the Secondary forced the choice of Achmer airfield upon Capt. Fullick. His sighting resulted in tight bomb-patterns among the main complex of buildings, which he was to assert "wrecked the joint." T/Sgt John Sinclair, whose bravery during the very first Group mission won him the Silver Star and Purple Heart, added to the latter decoration today when he was nicked in both heels by a 20mm shell bursting over his radio-room hatch. Just the one B-17 downed from the 70 credited with sorties so far in "Big Week" must have left the crews hoping that this streak of fortune would continue – a dangerous assumption, as events on the morrow would again prove.

The indifferent weather conditions persisted on the 22nd as the 1CBW was briefed for a target well remembered from 11 Jan. – Oschersleben. Although 31 bombers led by Maj. Fitzgerald and Capt. Hecker took off, persistent thick cloud at higher altitudes forced all but 12 crews to "abort," and these formed up with 15 Bassingbourn aircraft. One of the Ridgewell contingent was "Bermondsay Battler," with her regular "tenant" crew headed by Lt. Lee W Smith. Penetration of the enemy coast was made without opposition, but also without es-

Another shot of "Martha the II" catches her with bomb-doors open and in company of a 532BS B-17G. Latter bomber is from the 10-DL batch produced by Douglas, which did not have cheek-guns fitted. Both are flying against a thick mass of contrails from preceding formations.

Although no name is carried by VE:M of the 532BS, it was christened "Friday the 13TH." This was probably an unwise choice, as the bomber only lasted from assignment on 6 Jan '44 to 22 Feb. Then it was MIA during the Oscherslebem mission while flown by Lt Francis Flaherty. B-17G positioned above is "Squat N' Droppit" of the 535BS.

An absolutely solid undercast forms the backcloth for a 381BG formation during the Winter of 1943/44. B-17G in right foreground is from the 532BS and was to be the final Group loss during BIG WEEK. It was crash-landed near Willmandingen by Lt. Henderson with the fatal loss of six from the ten crew.

cort. This deficiency was not to prove initially critical, since although the formation was visible in the clearing skies the Luftwaffe was also out of sight. It was all the more ironic that the first fighter thrusts came in as the cloud cover was reforming. A number of P-51s were now on hand, but were badly outnumbered, and so the bombers were faced with seeking their own salvation in the face of what was later estimated were between 200 and 300 individual fighter assaults. Fully two hours was to elapse before these efforts ceased, during which time the 381BG would lose half its number.

The Luftwaffe fighters' pattern of attack seemed for one B-17 at a time to be singled out and dispatched. Fitzgerald reported losing two sets of wingmen in the battle, and it was highly likely that the first to be downed was Lt Smith flying No.2 to the Major. S/Sgt Perdue (RWG) noted that the first attacks hit "Battler" and set No.3 engine on fire, while S/Sgt Rosata said Nos. 2 and 3 were ignited. Both men agreed that Smith slipped down under their Lead B-17, probably doing so in an attempt to blow out the flames before levelling out some 3000 ft lower. Shortly after sight of the straggler was lost. Tragically, there would be no survivors among the entire crew when the bomber was downed some 10 miles NW of Hiddesen, near Dettmold, but the exact circumstances of their deaths remains unclear. All ten were buried in Hiddesen cemetery.

Lt Hal Roling's B-17 42-39946 was taking steady punishment as the formation passed Bielefeld, and with his No. 2 engine disabled he called his crew to say he was pulling out. On the ground at 1214 the gunners of a Heavy flak battery operating 105mm guns observed what was the 1CBW overflying their position on a SW-NE course. Using their MALSI fire-director set they engaged the force for around two minutes and fired 48 shells in volleys. Halfway through this engagement the battery telescope-sight observer noted one bomber falling behind and going into cloud; two minutes later what was surely Roling's B-17 emerged in a dive and crashed SE of the gun-sites at Leopoldshohe, 12 kilometers East of Bielefeld.

The five gunners in the rear managed to bale out, but this possibility was denied the other five because returning crews stated the aircraft's nose was totally excised by the flak. The

This photograph of Lt. Lee W. Smith's crew (Smith is kneeling on the left) is taken in front of the 535BS B-17G "Bermmondsay Battler," with which they were linked as part of a "Wings for Victory Week" fund-raising drive. Only eight days after photo was taken on 14 Feb '44 aircraft and crew were MIA. All ten men on board were killed, and only Lt. Sherwood (CP), seen next to Smith, was spared, being absent for this mission.

Operation ARGUMENT ("Big Week") commenced on 20 Feb '44. The mission flown that day by the Group to Leipzig was a happy one for at least one 533BS crew headed by Lt. Bill Butler, as it was their last. Butler is pictured with the Group Chaplain Capt. James Brown.

Another very happy man returning from Leipzig on 20 Feb '44 was Capt. Alan Tucker, an "original" pilot of the 534BS. He is seen signing-in while watched by S/Sgt Charles Raglin.

hapless engineer, S/Sgt Asbury Thompson, was in the nose working on the Bendix chin-turret at the time, otherwise he might have survived had he been in his usual top-turret post. S/Sgt Jemiolo was informed his dead buddies were buried in the bomber. This assertion was refuted given that the bombs were still in their racks and would have blown the machine to pieces on final impact. (A correct assumption, because German records confirmed the B-17 hit at an angle of 45 degrees and was 98% destroyed.) The exact nature of his aircraft's loss would not be related to Jemiolo and his buddies until they were in Stalag Luft VI – presumably by one of the returning crewmen who had himself become a "Kriegie" in the interim period!

Two more Group aircraft were shot out of the sky before approach to the target. The weather again intervened, with cloud obscuring the Primary and forcing retention of bombloads for use on a Target of Opportunity as the turn for home was made. P-47s picked up the beleaguered force some 20 minutes later, and an unspecified location at Bunde SW of Minden suffered the attention of the bombardiers. There was still some opposition facing the crews, but only in the form of a snowstorm, which Fitzgerald would suggest was "adding insult to injury." T/Sgt Fred Berg (Eng.) on the Lead ship suffered severe frostbite to one hand when cranking open the bomb-doors – perhaps not too high a price to pay compared to 60 other crewmen. Only four of the 381BG bombers returned to base, with the other two diverting, one due to mechanical reasons and the other for reasons of dire emergency.

MIA along with Lts. Smith and Roling were the 535BS crews of Lts. Hustedt in 42-31696 and Downey in 42-31533, Lt. Fridgen (533BS) in 42-97474 "Homing Pigeon," and Lt Flaherty (532BS), whose 42-31443 was unwisely named "Friday the 13th". With several of his crew already dead, Fridgen managed to put his B-17 down for a heavy crash-landing, out of which only he and two other crewmen emerged alive. S/Sgt Lowell Slayton (TG) would return to the region in 1986, where he was reunited with several of the local populace who had run to the crash-site at the time. One of the Germans was a young woman in 1944. She told Lowell that she had cradled one of his buddies in her arms as he was slowly dying – so exposing one of the contradictions of any war, namely how hostility could turn to compassion even in the midst of what was a bitterly contested conflict.

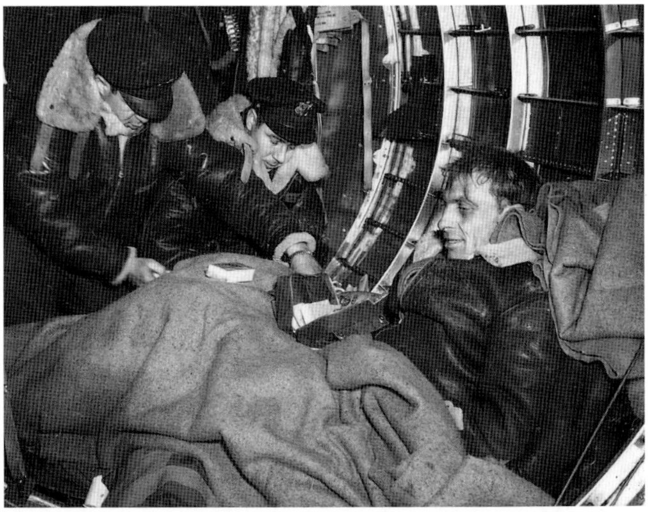

Two Medical Section officers are attending to a crewmen injured off the first mission of "Big Week." His injuries must be fairly serious for him to have to be treated in his B-17's fuselage before removal to an ambulance.

The B-17 making the emergency diversion was 42-38079 flown by Lt Armor Bowen (532BS). On the way in the No. 2 engine supercharger had failed, and the aircraft continued on three engines. Just after "bombs away" No. 4 engine was completely destroyed by 20mm strikes, and the engineer collapsed with a critical neck wound. A drop into the undercast did throw the pursuing fighters off their immediate trail, but progress back to the Dutch coast proved fraught with further attacks being delivered whenever clear air-space was once more encountered. Lt Julian O'Neal (CP) was able to un-feather No. 3 (loss of the supercharger was superfluous, as it was not required at the lower altitude now being flown), so the crippled bomber was again functioning on three-quarters power. Lts. Pilger (N) and Matty (B) were alternating between attending to the engineer and manning the nose guns. Back in the tail position S/Sgt Tom LaMore was frantically manoeuvring his .50s, which despite his best efforts finally "burnt out." He then clambered forward to continue operating from the waist.

The struggling bomber was nursed back across the forbidding North Sea. Every single parachute had been rendered useless by cannon fire, and it was uncertain if the life rafts were similarly affected, assuming a safe "ditching" could be achieved if called for. Thankfully, this option was never exercised and the B-17 was brought in for a skillful crash-landing at an 8th Fighter Command base on the Suffolk coast (Leiston). Over 200 holes were counted in its airframe, and the Fortress was still languishing there come the end of March. It had been assigned to Ridgewell on 20 Feb., so its operational career was brief in the extreme!

When set against this day's loss-factor the prospect of further deep-penetration missions looming in the near future surely cast a pall of gloom over the combat crews. The available fighter cover just could not guarantee blanket cover for the bombers, and it was a fact that this situation would persist in a diminishing degree right up to VE-Day. There would always be some scope for the Luftwaffe to strike somewhere within the bomber stream. Unbeknown to the bomber crews was the fact that retribution was hovering around the corner for their aerial adversaries. The P-51 element of the 8FC was up into three figures and would constitute at least a third of all the Command's sorties by the end of March. In that period the pilots in their North American, Republic, and Lockheed "pursuits" would begin to take the Fw190s and Me 109s apart, not only in the air, but also on the ground. An important element in that defeat would be the recently introduced practice of sending relieved Fighter Groups with un-expended ammunition down to strafe any suitable ground target. From now on no Luftwaffe pilot could guarantee his freedom from assault, even when taking off or landing – two of the most vulnerable stages of any flight.

A valuable 24-hour respite was granted the crews, and then it was back to action on the 24th with a target well known to the Ridgewell veterans – Schweinfurt. The officer leading today was no stranger to the ball-bearing plants, having participated in both previous missions and as Leader on the latter. The 30 Group B-17s were the fourth unit to bomb, and perfect weather conditions contributed to generally good results. Maj. Shackley was to report that evening that he believed the knockout blow had been delivered to Schweinfurt by the smothering effect of the bomb-patterns. This was an optimistic assessment, because the developed strike-photos over the entire 1BD revealed several important areas untouched, although in the 381BG's case its assigned zone was well hit. Flak and fighters were both "meager," which was a decided relief to the fliers.

The Field Order issued next day was the 133rd received at Ridgewell and would result in the Group's 73rd completed mission. It is worth reflecting on the proportions of the second figure compared to the first; for every mission completed virtually one was "scrubbed" at some stage, mainly before entering enemy air-space, but with several proceeding that far. One of the major reasons for so many false alarms lay in the unpredictable weather patterns over NW Europe as well as Britain. These false starts inevitably increased the great stress-factors

De-briefing forms along with "Lucky Strike" cigarette packs litter the table as Maj. Linn Kidd interrogates Lt. Tyson (standing) and his 535BS crew. Lt. Doherty (CP) sits with cigarette in hand next to Maj. Kidd. Officer with pencil poised above his navigator's computing disc is Lt. John Howland – known as "John the Giant" due to his being all of 5 ft. 3 ins. tall! Picture taken the same day as Lt. Butler's last mission (20 Feb '44).

The 533BS B-17G of Lt. Francis Fridgen has broken in half and discarded its No. 3 engine during a desperate crash-landing near Hamm on 22 Feb '44. The bomber was one of six MIA from the second and equally disastrous mission to Oschersleben. Only Lt. Fridgen, along with Sgts Abernathy (RW) and Slayton (TG), survived.

borne by the combat crews, who were already geared up in their minds for the approaching air-battle.

One of the thirty-two crews going out to the Messerschmitt plant at Augsburg was that of Lt Don Henderson (532BS), who were embarking on their final mission. They were flying in 42-37786 as No. 2 to Lt Woods (Composite Group CO) and ten other B-17s, while Lt Silvernale led a further 20 bombers as the 1CBW's Low Group. Over 400 tons of ordnance was dropped by the 196 attackers, but the flak gunners were to deny this act to the Low Group. Thundering in from the I.P. with bomb-doors opened, a chance shell fragment sliced into the Lead Ship's bay to set off a smoke-marker bomb. Faced with a fire and possible explosion, Lt. Silvernale had little recourse other than release his complete load. The main limitation of the "bomb on Leader" technique was now highlighted, because many other bombardiers in the Group took this as a signal to also let go. The result was that almost the entire mass of bombs fell harmlessly short.

The main Group formation came home intact, but the watchers clustered around the control tower might well have noticed one gap in Woods' smaller force. Lt Henderson had fallen victim to an Me109, whose fatal strikes had finally brought his B-17 down at Wilmandingen near Stuttgart; only he and three others survived the incident. As with Lt Clore on

The separated rear fuselage further demonstrates the severe force with which Lt. Fridgen's bomber "Homing Pigeon" struck the ground. Second view of this aircraft section (opposite page) shows a German policeman wearing his distinctive helmet and badge and scrutinising the body of an unidentified crewman. The bag in his hands is probably intended to hold any personal items removed from the unfortunate airman's clothing.

4 Jan., the very last combat hurdle had proven cruelly impossible to surmount. In contrast, another 532BS "original" did finish up over Augsburg. This was Lt George Darrow, who had successfully "ditched" during the first Schweinfurt mission. Despite the misfortune to his Low Group, Lt Silvernale said, "We really rang the bell today," a view endorsed by his bombardier, Lt Happy Hendryx, who stated that the M.P.I. was covered in hits.

"Big Week" was over, and evaluation of the effect on German aircraft production brought an optimistic response from the U.S. authorities. The heavy destruction wrought upon many of the plants gave an ultimately false impression of the scale of production-loss. The available types of American ordnance could not guarantee the total destruction of heavy plant machinery. Incredibly, Germany was still not fully geared up to possible War production levels, and Post-war studies confirmed that the aircraft production rates had materially increased between "Big Week" and VE-Day.

What was to signal the death-knell of the Luftwaffe was the release of the U.S. fighters from their original "close escort" limitations, and adoption of the much more flexible and effective tactic of seeking out their opponents well before they could bring their large and all-too-often unwieldy concentrations into contact with the bombers. (This tactic was initially adopted by the Luftwaffe in the early stages of the Battle of Britain. Known as "Freiejagd," or "Free-hunt," it resulted in severe losses to RAF Fighter Command. Fortunately, it was later abandoned in favor of the greatly stultifying tight escort of their own bombers, which cost the Luftwaffe dearly.) The Americans were simply reversing the experience of the Luftwaffe in 1940. This act was to have an increasingly devastating effect on the enemy pilots' ability to survive, let alone inflict casualties upon the B-17s and B-24s. The Luftwaffe would simply bleed to death for a lack of combat-tried pilots rather than equipment.

No more February missions were flown by the 381BG, whose records continued to highlight the stark contrast between life and death. T/Sgt Floyd Terry (535BS) was sent to 8USAAF Intelligence in London; his active service as a combat crewmen and evader was effectively over. On the other hand, the 532BS record noted the burial on the 28th of Sgt. Bill Seifermann who had succumbed to wounds suffered four days earlier over Schweinfurt. His burial service at Madingley was attended by his brother and his crew.

9

"BIG B"

March 1944 can arguably be regarded as the most critical month for both Bomber Commands in prosecuting the European Air War. RAF Bomber Command's ability to hammer the main German industrial cities (and by extension, their citizens) into a state of abject surrender was by now badly blunted thanks primarily to the German night fighters. The Command's own "Black Thursday" occurred on March 30/31, exactly one day before the date predicted by Air Chief Marshal "Butch" Harris as the point at which the German collective will to fight on was expected to collapse under his crew's Offensive. Fully 94 Halifaxes and Lancasters were pulled out of the skies to and from Nuremberg on this infamous night. The Command would survive this final blow to its 1943/44 Campaign, known as "The Battle of Berlin," and continue to inflict serious damage on the enemy's economy. However, this would be made under the vastly more favourable circumstances of a steadily compressed defensive network and with the support of No.100 Group's aircraft fitted with a sophisticated range of radio counter-measures.

A reverse trend from hardship to relative ease would be the experience of the U.S. heavy bombers, as their aerial tormentors were drawn into a series of air battles from which they would never recover. The focus of a number of these combats was Berlin, or "Big B," as the Nazi Capital City became known among the 8USAAF personnel. It was thought that the Germans would put up a most ferocious effort in defence of the city. Apart from this supposition, the length of time taken to penetrate as far as Berlin would almost certainly guarantee a strong response since the Luftwaffe would have more than ample time to marshall its strength.

Although Berlin briefings had been conducted as far back as November, March actually opened with a run to Frankfurt on the 2nd. Eight B-17s were contributed by the 532BS, along with 81 crewmen, but the extra person was a very special inclusion. Chaplain Brown was the sole officially appointed padre at Ridgewell. A gifted scholar and writer, he had long wished to fly in combat, since he felt he could not administer spiritual comfort to the combat crews without literally sharing their experience of war. An initial approach to Col. Nazzaro on the subject was met with a firm "No!" – an eminently reasonable decision given Brown's "non-combatant" status under the Geneva Convention. A later approach to Nazzaro's successor was more openly responded to with the words "Oh, you might

Lt. Harold Henslin (kneeling on left) with his crew during States-side training. He was KIA on 28 April '44 along with three of those standing – Sgt Bill McLaughlin (left), Sgt Sell next to him, and Sgt Karr (right). Sgt Bill Blackmon (standing third from right) was one of only three survivors of the 535BS crew. The other five in the picture were either grounded or baled out on other missions while flying with another crew.

Dramatic view of a 534BS B-17G on the bomb-run. The walkway frame dividing the bay along its short eleven foot length were joint limiting factors in the B-17's maximum ordnance capacity; the largest bomb capable of internal stowage was 2000 lbs, while the average bomb-load was rarely more than 6000 lbs. This bomber was lost over Eschwege with Lt. Rayburn and crew on 19 April '44.

get yourself killed." Being more than capable of making a positive interpretation of Col. Leber's words, Capt. Brown was now dressed and ready to join Capt. Woods, whose crew welcomed him aboard the 533BS's 42-31761 "Rotherhithes Revenge."

Combat was very much a young man's game, which says much for the padre, who was in his early 40s. He was very careful to accede to any request to act as instructed; he was also conscious of the fact that he was taking up valuable space and oxygen facilities.

The generally cloudy weather proved a mixed blessing for a sizeable proportion of the 375 bombers involved who were forced to seek out Targets of Opportunity. Fighter reaction was patchy, with none affecting the 381BG and only nine B-17s were MIA. Unfortunately, one of this number was 42-39891, flown by Lt Schultze (533BS). Capt Woods managed to bring his "supernumerary" back intact; however, this was only the first occasion Brown would venture into combat. (Unconfirmed reports indicated he was offered the chance of earning an Air Medal by Col. Leber, for which award a minimum of five missions had to be completed!).

The last sight of Lt Schultze's B-17 had been over Belgium, when up to eight chutes were counted coming out, but in fact all ten men survived. The pilot managed to evade capture until 29 April when he was taken at a railroad station, but Sgt. Farr (RWG) was never apprehended. In sad contrast to Farr's luck was that experienced by his fellow crewman, Sgt. Trapnell (BT). He failed to live through a subsequent forced-march from Stalag Luft IV in 1945, his death being due either to exposure or to being shot by a guard.

The long-dreaded call to go to Berlin came next morning when the Primary targets were listed as the Erkner ball-bearings plant and an aviation factory at Oranienburg. Participating in the mission was a total of 748 bombers. Routing to Berlin was over Schleswig-Holstein and North of Hamburg before turning SE. Lt Fred Beardsworth (N), on Lt Dan Henry's 534BS crew, later stated the cloud-tops were still looming up above the bomber-stream even when it was at 29000 ft, and the mission was finally "aborted" at a point NE of Hamburg. An element of the 381BG did unload on a Target of Opportu-

The original title "Mis Abortion" for this B-17F caused great offence to Col. Leber, who ordered its deletion. However, Sgt John Randall, the bomber's crewchief, had a keener understanding of British humor, and applied this substitute name directly behind the female figure, which was never queried! The 534BS bomber carries an impressive total of 30 mission symbols.

The reason for "Assend" was not due to the pronunciation of its pilot's name – Lt. Enos (kneeling on left) – but to the fact the crew were fed up with always being in "Purple Heart Corner" within the Group formation! Next to Lt. Enos is Lt. John Hallecy (CP), who later commanded his own crew. Left rear is T/Sgt Buren Cook (Eng.), with Sgts Bud Church and Robert Smith (WGs) second and third from right.

This groundcrew member is about to change a tire on a main wheel. Purpose of the wheel's surrounding frame is to prevent injury or even a fatal effect should the air pressure blow out in the case of a faulty fitting.

nity identified as Oldenburg, and the Group crossed out over Heligoland Island. Some units ended up on collision courses, which resulted in a number of head-on crashes. One of these involved a 94BG B-17 (4CBW) and two 91BG bombers. Some of the debris fell on another 1CBW aircraft and probably caused its loss; the B-17 so unluckily affected was 42-37986, flown by Lt. Rogers (534BS). All ten crewmen survived the loss of their bomber, which crashed in Holland.

Berlin was again "on" for the 4th with the Erkner ball-bearings plant as the specific target. Col. Hall and Lt. Henslin (535BS) were up front, but penetration well in towards Berlin was finally reversed by a "recall" signal. This was thanks to similar poor weather conditions as met the previous day. Once again the Group sought a Target of Opportunity and finally dropped on Dusseldorf under PFF guidance with unobserved results.

Lt Keyes (532BS) had earlier turned back, but failed to come home. His B-17F was 42-30151 and bore the name "Spare Parts," which proved a very apt choice. It had originally been assigned on 16 June 1943 and had quickly earned the reputation as a "lemon." The Keyes crew had recently flown over in a new B-17G and were heart-broken at having to surrender it in favor of this Sqdn. "black sheep." The previous day Sgt. Van Voorhis had reported a bad oil leak in one engine, and this was attended to with the bomber back on the flight line and ready for the crew to take to Berlin on what was only their second mission. On the way in an engine had gone "out," and then a second started to falter through lack of – oil!

The decision to turn back was promptly followed by the bomb-load being salvoed, but the bad luck continued with the refusal of the bomb-doors to close. A continuous strong vibration coupled with a self-destructing No. 3 engine and consequent loss of altitude induced the pilots to seek a forced-land-

"Linda Mary" is the sole B-17F in this picture shot in early 1944. She would earn the dubious "honor" of being the very last Group "original" bomber to go MIA during the first full Berlin strike of 6 March '44. "Big Mike" (42-39997) is a fellow 533BS bomber later re-titled "Frenchys Folly," and a third 533BS B-17G (42-97454) leads the quartet completed by "Our Desire" (42-31357) of the 535BS.

Probably the worst stage of any mission for bomber crews was experienced on the bomb-run. This had to be flown straight and level, often in the face of flak barrages. Spent shell-bursts are bracketing "Whodat" of the 534BS as her bomb-doors gap open, ready for the release of her ordnance.

ing near St. Omer in NE France. (On reflection, Sgt Van Voorhis was to suggest it was just as well they had come down over land instead of being faced with possible "ditching," especially as it was still Wintertime!) Any hope of dispersing and seeking assistance from the local population was firmly quashed when a horde of soldiers based at a nearby garrison surrounded the crew and herded them towards the first stage of "Kriegydom!"

Arriving on the 4th was S/Sgt Eugene Copp assigned from 1BD HQ. He was a States-side gunnery instructor sent over to complete three missions in which enemy fighters would be encountered before his return home. Given the current rate of Luftwaffe involvement with the Group, Sgt. Copp could expect to be around for some time. He had arrived at Ridgewell with another un-named Sgt. on the same assignment and recalled that this man's operational career was to be even shorter than his own, being as he went down on his first! In fact, Eugene's tenure at Ridgewell would be over in 16 days, but not in the manner he might have hoped for.

It was to prove a case of "third time lucky" in mounting an assault on Berlin, not that the crews would have thought in terms of this expression. In fact, Lt. Sherwood, a 535BS pilot, recollected that the queues to the briefing-room toilet were three times as long as usual! The Aiming-point was again the Erkner plant, and the 30 bombers would be led by Capt. Woods, who was flying his 25th mission, and Capt. Doug Winters (both 532BS). The greatly improved weather worked to both sides' advantage, with the bombers getting through but meeting the heaviest aerial resistance for some time; despite an escort figure totalling just over 500, the Luftwaffe still culled 69 bombers out of the 672 making bomb-runs. The carefully assembled Geschwadern struck hard to inflict punishment on all three Bomb Divisions, particularly the Third, where the "Bloody Hundredth" alone lost 15 B-17s.

Three of the 18 aircraft lost by the 1BD came from the 381BG. Lt. "Slick" Coyle (532BS) was riding in 42-3215 "Linda Mary," which was the Group's last "original" bomber. When in the vicinity of Madgeburg, just 30 minutes short of Berlin, a fusillade of cannon shells smashed into the aircraft, flying in its element's No. 3 position. Two crewmen in the element leader's B-17 reported how the underside of the B-17F caught fire, with the flames enveloping No. 3 engine. The bomber momentarily held station and then peeled off under apparent control as the nose and waist hatches flew off. John Wierman (CP) was on his third mission and was to relate what seemed a confusing sequence of events that saw his swift transfer from the relative safety of his cockpit into a chilling void over enemy soil. Sgts. Mendoza and Peter W Smith were wounded, but they and seven others ended up as POWs.

One fatality was S/Sgt Raymond Legg (TG), who was either killed at his post or trapped within his position. Legg had flown most of his 25 missions, during which he had several bad experiences. One of the worst was on 9 Oct. when his ill-chosen decision to ride in the tail during take-off, along with extra ammunition stacked around him, was one major factor in the ground-hugging departure by Lts. Gleichauf and Kels. He was the third member of this crew to fall at the very end of his combat tour

Lt. Haushalter was one of five KIA when his B-17G 42-31553 was downed by fighters during the bomb-run. A head-on thrust by Fw190s or Me 109s was swiftly followed by an

On 2 March '44 the Group Chaplain, Capt. Brown (kneeling second from left), flew with Capt. Woods (seen on Brown's left) to Frankfurt for what was the crew's penultimate mission. Not only did Woods's crew complete their tour, but "Rotherhithes Revenge," in which they operated this day, got through World War II with well over 100 missions to its credit.

attack from the left by Me 110s, which set the interior on fire. The B-17 dropped away, and Lt. Haushalter gave the bale-out order, after which the bomber impacted between Niederlerne and Wernsdorf. A third loss occurred during the return to England: Lt Fastrup's 42-31448 became detached from the Group and was brought down near Julich by a leading "Ace" of JG 26, Oberleutnant Matoni. All ten crewmen were later reported as POWs.

The fighter attacks persisted right through to and even during the bomb-run, and few gunners had time to study the scene below as they were too taken up with resisting the assaults. Typical quotes were:

"There were moving clouds of fighters circling over the target waiting for us, which we could spot from 25 miles away." (Capt. Woods)

"All I saw of Berlin were the Jerry fighters over it. Everything from Me 109s painted like our P-51s to Kondor bombers and Ju 88 nightfighters." (S/Sgt Stewart Hanson)

"These Jerry pilots were the best. They went at us on the bomb-run through their own flak as if none of us had a gun!" (S/Sgt Joe Cuttadauro)

"We didn't look at Berlin – too dammed many Jerries! The ball-turret and I got an Me109 right over the city, hitting him at 600 yards as he crossed in front from left to right. He started smoking like hell, and pieces flew off in all directions before he went down leaving a wide smoke-trail." (S/Sgt Jesse Norman)

The reported Kondor bomber was almost certainly a case of mistaken identity, while the fact that the Me109 was smoking could well have been the normal trail exuded by most German aero-engines when a fighter was flown in this attitude, as opposed to resulting from any terminal damage. This in no way discredits the bomber gunners, but highlights the inordinate pressures placed upon them, especially during a running battle.

It was on this mission that Sgt. Arnold Farmer, the Tennessee tail-gunner on Lt. Tyson's crew, provided one of those flashes of unintentional humor that often arose in the heat of battle. His natural instinct to talk in his State accent made his excited first call that he had nailed an Me 110 sound unintelligible. His pilot reminded him of the need to call in his observations in a clear manner. A few minutes later he again pressed his microphone-switch to state in a very deliberate manner; "Tail-gunner to pilot. Tail-gunner to pilot. Lt. Tyson, there are four Dee OH two seventeen EEEs back of us hyah and they're a shootin' rock...OH LORDY...Nevah' mind, they missed us." As John Howland (N) was to remember; "The entire crew yelped with joy and roared with laughter; truly a release of pent-up emotions."

The flak by contrast was surprisingly light for such a heavily defended region and appeared like little winking neon lights to S/Sgt Moe Kluger, who had assisted Sgt. Norman in taking down the Me109. The 1CBW was fronting the entire 1BD, which was the first Division scheduled to bomb. The Lead bombardier was lining up on the Erkner plant when it was obscured by cloud. It was by then too late to adjust for a radar-assisted bombing of the Friederichstrasse railroad station in the city center, and so the succeeding Groups were advised to seek Targets of Opportunity. It happened that the 381BG was destined to be the first 8USAAF unit to bomb this day, with its loads striking around the village of Zernsdorf, SW of the Primary. Return to base proved a long-winded affair, but

A weary looking Capt. Brown (Group Chaplain) is snapped standing by "Rotherhithes Revenge" on his and the bomber's return from Frankfurt on 2 March '44.

26 aircraft with their weary crews finally settled down on the runway as the short winter daylight faded. The 27th B-17 (42-37983) had struggled most of the way across the North Sea before Lt Cahill was forced into a "ditching," but the Douglas-built machine did not fail her 532BS crew, who were soon picked up by the Air-Sea Rescue Service.

The Nazis had been well and truly "bearded in their den," but the mission was only the first in a planned series of strikes against the Big City. The adverse weather conditions over Berlin had resulted in somewhat dispersed bomb-patterns, and in several instances (as with the 381 BG) the Targets of Opportunity were of very marginal benefit to the Allied War effort. Two days later continued clear weather was forecast, and Erkner was again the focus of attention. Lt. Col. Kunkel, an "original" from Pyote days and now Group Operations Officer, flew in "Rotherhithes Revenge" with Capt. Melvin Hecker (who was on his 25th mission) to take charge of the 1CBW. The continuing strong fighter reaction anticipated by the bomber crews was almost totally absent, and the bombing results of the preceding 3BD were sighted 50 miles away. Capt. Hester, the Lead ship bombardier, reported the loads of four Groups striking as he synchronised his bomb-sight, and his aim was equally true. A smoke column up to 15000 ft hung over the city and was visible from 75 miles. Only Lt Thomas Pirtle (532BS) in 42-38029 failed to return. His B-17 was reported shot down near the Dutch town of Meppen by a leading "Experte" of III/JG 26, Major Klaus Mietusch.

Capt Hecker's return was the culmination of a combat tour extending back nine months. The 23-year-old pilot was a former mechanical engineering student at St. Paul University and had the distinction of being one of the few pilots with a "kill." Riding as tail-gunner/observer during an early September mission he fired upon and was credited with an Me109. The de-briefing over, he engaged in a telephone conversation with his brother Bob, a Bomb Division Flight Surgeon. T/Sgt Ed Knauth (ROG to Hecker) was also blessed with the precious gift of his 25th completed mission.

It was a grim fact of life on Wartime airfields that nobody, be he combatcrew or groundcrew, was safe from injury or death from the moment he approached an aircraft until he was well clear again. During the night of 7/8 March a 534BS mechanic, Sgt. Michael Babines, was acting as co-pilot while the B-17 he was in was undergoing its normal pre-flight inspection. One of the engines caught fire when it started up, and the Sgt was instructed to go out through the nose hatch with a fire-extinguisher. When he jumped out he appeared to stumble and fell backwards or sideways into the revolving propeller blades. It was a miracle he was not killed outright in the process. However, his lease on life proved tragically short, because although he was transported to the 121st Hospital, Braintree, and given the best of treatment, he expired in the early hours of the 8th.

Heading in over a solid undercast for the third Berlin strike on the 9th were 21 bombers under the command of Lt. George Sandman (532BS) in "Rotherhithes Revenge," which dropped their ordnance with H2X guidance. A thick black plume emerged through the clouds as the B-17s and B-24s were on their way home, and the sole incident of note among the 381BG contingent was a flak injury to one gunner's leg. Only eight bombers were MIA from the total of 490 getting through to bomb, and although over 800 escorts were on hand, their final haul of "kills" was – nil! This was also the mission when an anonymous pilot was heard to utter the immortal expression "Ho Hum!" over the inter-phone as a pertinent observation on the routine nature of events this day.

The absence of the Luftwaffe was not to continue, but there was little doubt that the trio of completed Berlin assaults had at least temporarily wrested control of the Continental air-space from its hands. Although the loss of 82 of its fighters to the Allied escorts (plus a number claimed by the bomber gunners) was not a critically high percentage of its overall strength, what was becoming critical was the steady attrition among its "Experten" (German for "Ace"). Worse still for the Nazi cause was the inexplicable policy of not resting such leading pilots and utilising their skills in briefing new pilots while they stood

Lt. David Keyes and his 532BS crew were fated to go down on only their second mission (4 March '44), although all survived the crash-landing of 42-30151 "Spare Parts" near St. Omer, France. The officer on the right and enlisted man standing second from left were not part of the crew that day.

down from combat. The "Clobber Colleges" established by 8th Fighter Command, whereby fighter pilots "on rest" gave orientation lectures for new arrivals, were an unknown luxury to its Luftwaffe adversary. This and similar basic errors of omission were to prove terminal from the Spring of 1944 onward.

A full week passed by before the Group re-entered the fray. A social event of note in this time was the 535BS's first party, at which no less than 14 casks of beer were consumed. The very late cancellation of three truck-loads of women guests was brilliantly countered by Lt Keating, whose efforts brought together a selection of WAAFs, Land Army girls, some social ladies, and four WACs. Capt. Tansey (Sqdn. Adjutant) was in charge, and the party was judged a fine success. On the 14th, yet another evader returned in the form of Lt Glenn McCabe, the co-pilot to Lt Duarte, whose crew was MIA on 31 Dec. Departing for the States was a fellow-evader, T/Sgt. Floyd Terry.

Long-range missions were now the order of the day, and 33 bombers visited Augsburg on the 16th. Col. Leber flew as Group/CBW Lead, and the Composite Group was led by Maj. Halsey and Lt. Sandman in "Rotherhithes Revenge" – surely a current favourite B-17 for this duty! Cloud cover again forced a resort to PFF bombing technique. The flak was described as moderate until after the bomb-run when it intensified, and little fighter activity was noted. One B-17 ran into internally imposed difficulties when fire erupted in the cockpit due to a probable short-circuit. Lt. Rudolf Duncan pulled out of formation, while T/Sgt John Eylens (Eng.) tore out smoking insulation and beat out the flames with his bare hands after he had exhausted the fire-extinguisher contents. Though not severely burnt, he still paid a price in frost-bitten hands through holding the extinguisher without his gloves on. Lt. Franek (CP) had called in the blaze over the inter-phone, and it was this action which probably induced S/Sgt Yancek (LWG), flying his first mission, to "hit the silk." Anxiously awaiting the outcome of this drama was T/Sgt Carl Wilson (ROG). He said Eylens did a swell job in fighting the fire for 15 minutes, and added this was one mission on which he didn't want anything to happen – a not surprising reaction since it was his last! Another crewman finishing up was Lt. Thomas D Sellars (535BS), the saviour of "Tinkertoy" on 8 Oct. '43 after Lt. Minerich (P) had been decapitated.

Next day separate sets of Fields Orders for Augsburg and Frankfurt were issued but later cancelled. Returning from hospital via 12 R.C.D. was S/Sgt Burgasser, who had been badly wounded in Lt. Putek's B-17 on 6 Feb. with the subsequent loss of his left eye. In direct contrast to the weather prevailing on the 16th, the 30 bombers crossing over Oberpfaffenhofen on the 18th unloaded in CAVU conditions. Lt. Bob Miller, in his regular ship 42-29832 "Our Mom" and on his final mission, was partnered as Group Lead by Lt. Wayne Schomberg. The aero-assembly plant under attack was thoroughly ploughed up by the accurate bombing, and a massive smoke-column rapidly built up. Apart from the Target of Opportunity hit on the 6th, March had not provided an opportunity for visual target-

S/Sgt Emory Y Naha (A Tewa Indian known as "Little Beaver") stands up into a shell hole torn in the left elevator after the 4 March '44 mission. The same shell shot out his oxygen lines, but he still managed to man his guns. On the right is S/Sgt Clinton, who was one of two survivors off Lt. Bob Bobrof's crew on the 4 July '44 mission. Both gunners were regular members of Lt. Liddle's 535BS crew when this picture was taken.

sighting, and the Group bombardiers were well pleased to observe the results of their efforts. On the way in four Fw190s did start in towards the formation, but they were scattered by 12 P-38s according to S/Sgt Jerry Petska (Eng.) on the 532BS bomber "Mizpah." For Lt. Bill Loftin (B), his joy at getting a sight of where his bombs struck was overtaken by the greater joy of release from the pressures of combat, as this run was his last. Promoted to Maj. was Osce V Jones (535BS Operations Officer), who was also sent to London to identify the remaining eight members of "Georgia Rebel's" crew. They were newly returned from internment in Sweden following their diversion into that country off the Heroya mission on 24 July '43, when Jones had been the pilot.

Capt Doug Winters (532BS) had his share of incidents during his time at Ridgewell. He was piloting 42-97471 "Male Call" to Mannheim on the 20th. The overall mission was uneventful, with all crews returning to base. However, as Winters settled his B-17 down on the runway, the landing gear abruptly folded up, leaving the bomber to skate along on its belly. It was a shaken crew, which hastily evacuated their aircraft, fortunately without suffering any injury. "Male Call" had only been transferred-in from the 457BG on 12 March, and the damage she had suffered was sufficient for salvage action to be initiated. This was only the first of two crash-landing incidents for Winters during the first half of 1944.

The final March mission to Berlin was sent out on the 22nd. Maj. Jones and Lt. Charles Enos (535BS) led 29 B-17s aloft, and the force coasted in over a solid undercast that extended virtually all the way to the target. The 535BS diarist summed up the day's effort as "29 up, 29 over, and 29 back." The early stage of the bomb-run was temporarily free of cloud, but the cover moved in again, forcing a recourse to what was described as "navigational aids" for the drop, which Group records stated was actually on the Secondary. T/Sgt Steve Gaspar (535BS) added a culinary contribution to the bomb-load. The previous evening he had eaten a dish of sauerkraut that had reacted on him during the bomb-run. He scribbled a note saying that since the Krauts had invented the stuff he hoped every string of the product would spoil. He also added a footnote stating that the Führer's town did not look so good from the air, attached the note to the sick-bag, and tossed it out into the slipstream!

10

OUT OF WINTER'S SHADOW

Lt. George Mackintosh was one of the relatively few "original" combat personnel still at Ridgewell by mid-March 1944. He had come into the Group as a member of Lt. Koenig's "Model Crew" at Pyote. While at Pueblo he was reassigned as Sqdn. Operations Officer and actually followed his colleagues across the Atlantic in the "Queen Elizabeth." Flying only when required, he had ended his second mission as co-pilot to Lt. Jones in "Georgia Rebel" in the shadowy security of Sweden on 24 July '43.

Both men were repatriated to Britain between Xmas and New Year and recommenced operations with the 535BS. Mackintosh still had no regular crew, and so "filled in" by taking on crews whose pilot was temporarily unavailable. On 21 Feb. he was piloting 42-31357 "Our Desire" when a sudden slashing fighter attack set the B-17's nose on fire. Lts. Pietarski (B) and Burgreen (N) were wounded, and with their compartment full of smoke they promptly baled out. F/O Scarborough (CP) and T/Sgt Padgett (Eng.) put the fire out, and the aircraft narrowly missed colliding with others in the Group as it dropped out. The long flight home was further hampered by the bomb-doors stubbornly refusing to close, making the possibility of a safe landing doubtful in the pilot's mind. Happily, no such problem arose, and George's action in bringing the stricken B-17 back was rewarded with a DFC.

The Mannheim mission on 20 March was George's 14th. Flying in 42-31381 "Jaynee B," along with Lt. Bill Bartlett's crew, he slotted into formation as a Flight Leader. Extremely bad cloud conditions found the force flying in a horizonless space between the layers. Less than half the 1BD Force of 231 made effective sorties, and the homeward flight was to result in formations straying up to 100 miles South of their intended track. The already apprehensive crews must have been startled when they reached the French coast, not over the Pas de Calais, but over Normandy. "Jaynee B" had been trailing the Group ever since she had suffered an engine failure in the target zone, whose propeller refused to "feather." The resultant bad vibration forced the engineer to abandon his turret, and some of the cockpit instruments were being shaken out of their mounts.

George was uncertain of his exact position at the coast, but thought he had flown over Belle Isle; by now his low altitude had attracted a mass of ground fire. Two more engines

Lt. John Rickerson's 532BS crew are seen during States-side training; Rickerson is kneeling on the right. His crew survived a mid-air collision on 24 March '44 and crash-landed at Carvin in NE France. Third from left at rear is Sgt. Durward Williams, who evaded capture but was later betrayed to the Germans along with a fellow crewman, S/Sgt Tom LaMore (TG).

"Magnificent trails of treachery" was the apt description accorded to contrails in a prominent Wartime documentary on the 8USAAF; they could be seen for miles in clear conditions and compromised any chance of visual concealment for the formations. B-17F in foreground is 42-3411 of the 532BS, which was assigned on 21 Sept '43 and flew missions until 19 May '44 when it was transferred out to AFSC.

began to falter and fail under the onslaught, and the decision was very reluctantly taken to turn back to the coastline and "ditch"; the prospect of a "ditching" in mid-Channel had to be discarded as suicidal. Choosing a location about one mile offshore, he and Lt. Fowler (CP) slid the B-17 smoothly into the frigid waters, where it remained floating for between 15 and 20 minutes. Only one life-raft was operable, into which eight men scrambled as George and the ill-starred S/Sgt. Eugene Copp hung onto the raft-lines. (The States-side instructor was flying what was the last of his three missions before return home!) The fairly prompt arrival of a French long-boat manned by civilians, but carrying German guards, was thankfully welcomed by the half-frozen Americans, even if it meant an enemy Stalag for the rest of the War.

Their immediate adventures were not yet over, as their arrival in Frankfurt coincided with an RAF raid. The 60 minutes that ensued must have been terrifying, as bombs hailed down and they lay under the rail carriages. But even more daunting was the understandably angry reaction of the local civilians in the shelter they were escorted to after the raid. George was certain they would have been killed but for the protection of the Luftwaffe guards.

Assigned to Stalag Luft III's South Compound, George was strolling 'round the circuit one day when he looked across to the West Compound, where his astonished gaze took in the sight of Osce V Jones, his fellow Swedish internee who had been downed over St. Avord on 28 April. After the end of hostilities and while located in Camp Lucky Strike he ran into Lts. Pietarski and Burgreen, who until then had been convinced they were the sole survivors from the 21 Feb. '44 mission when they had baled out!

Contrasting with McIntosh's grim experience was Lt. Beckman flying on his last mission. Along with Capt. Winters in 42-97471 "Male Call" he had been Composite Group Lead. On touchdown he was well into his landing run when the landing gear suddenly folded and the B-17 skidded to an ignominious halt. The crew's reactions were not recorded, but were sure to be a mixture of profanity and perturbation. This was hardly the best way for the Lt. and seven of his crew to finish, but the expression "Any landing you walk away from is a good one" must have occurred to them!

By 23 March 1944 S/Sgt Tom LaMore was a seasoned combat flier with 18 missions under his belt who was now flying with Lt. Rickerson. Frostbite suffered on the 22 Feb. mission had landed him in hospital, and his place on Lt. Bowen's crew was taken over by the time he was released. That evening, with a mission alert in the offing he was approached by a 532BS gunner yet to fly a combat mission, but who was expecting the call for his crew in the morning. He explained that he was not only apprehensive about how he might conduct himself under fire, but was scared that he might display such feelings before his pilot Lt Kenneth Haynes and thereby let himself down. Over the next hour or so Tom outlined his thoughts on how Sgt. Plows should conduct himself. As he shook hands and turned to leave the room he said to Tom "The cold ones are on me tomorrow evening."

The weather was very poor on the 24th as the B-17s taxied out for Schweinfurt. Lt. Rickerson lifted off and eased his

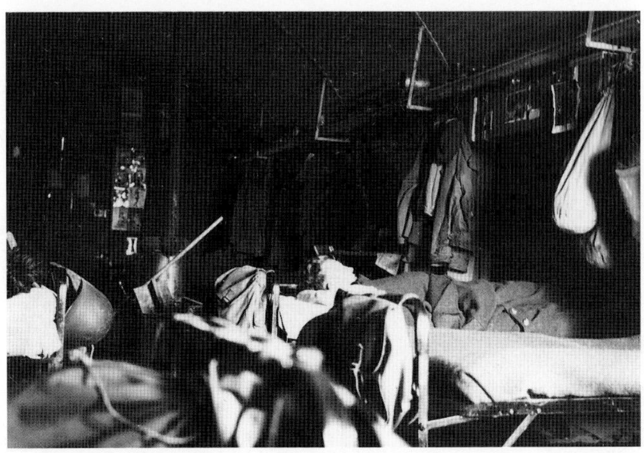

The Nissen huts in which both combat and groundcrew tried to live were primitive structures. Space was at a premium, as can be seen in this example. Airman on right is sleeping under his greatcoat. This is not surprising, since the pot-bellied stove was fuelled by coke, which gave off a very poor level of heat.

This party of 381BG groundcrew is belting up ammunition. The man nearest to the camera is ensuring the belt is tracked into its box in perfect alignment; otherwise, there could be a risk of the belt jamming at a vital moment during a combat action.

path steadily away from the mist-shrouded airfield. As Tom stared casually back from his lonely outpost in the tail he was jolted to attention by the flash and glare of an explosion back along the take-off route. He was not destined to know for many years that what was certainly a Group bomber impacting with the ground had borne Lt. Haynes and the hapless Sgt. Plows to their deaths – the young gunner's combat career was over before it had even started. Taking-off for the first time with a heavily laden bomber in very marginal winter weather must have been too much for the inexperienced pilots. Whatever the cause of the crash, ten more airmen were to be added to the lengthening human tally at Madingley Cemetery. (The duties of a Medical Orderly were difficult when handling this type of incident; the task of collecting up severed limbs, separating clothing remnants forced into flesh, or picking dog-tags out of charred remains must have affected the soul of the most hard-bitten staff member.)

Conditions during Wing Assembly were little improved, and the nightmare of collision in the ever-deteriorating skies over Europe loomed large in the crews' minds. In fact, the bulk of the attacking force sought out the Secondary at Frankfurt. It was at this stage of the mission that two more B-17s were "written off" the Group inventory to make a total of three lost to other than enemy action. Lt. Rickerson had Lt. Tompson on his right, but as his aircraft swung off in that direction, the latter flying 42-40008 did not respond at all. Thomson's No.1 engine propeller completely removed 42-31490's nose

Caption for this picture states "crew of a B-17 Fortress." In fact, the "crew" are British soldiers (probably from the Home Guard) who are being shown 'round Ridgewell by their two American escorts. They are standing beside "Big Time Operator II" of the 532BS.

Of the six "original" 534BS Line and Flight Chiefs standing at the back, T/Sgt Percy Casey (second from left) was later transferred to the 20USAAF during 1944, while the other five remained at Ridgewell for the duration. Lt. Paul Stull (front, right) was the Engineering Officer for the Sqdn. and was one of six killed in "Mis Abortion/Stuff," which crashed while landing off a local flight on 31 March '44.

A trio of 535BS crewmen are talking animatedly during a mission de-briefing. Lt. Vernon Nicholson (N) on left has one mission left from which he will return, and Lt. Bill Ridley (P) is well through his ultimately successful combat tour. Happiest of all is T/Sgt Lester, for whom today's mission is his last

Plexiglas, and his cockpit in turn was ripped asunder by Rickerson's No. 4 propeller. The duo of giant bombers locked together in a death-tumble extending down through several thousand feet.

Tom LaMore had suffered serious injuries to his head and upper body caused by impact with his guns, and his blood had smeared the turret Plexiglas. As he rubbed a clear patch and strove to orient himself he witnessed Tompson's B-17G falling away on its own, only to explode in a huge mushroom of flame and smoke as its load of 300 lb bombs detonated. It was but a few seconds previous that he had caught the attention of the other tail-gunner who had waved back – now he and his crew had been cruelly consumed in their bomber's demise.

Returning crew said Rickerson's B-17 had split in two, but they were mistaken, although the badly damaged bomber was fated never to return. One of its engines had been rendered powerless and set on fire as a result of the collision, but Lt. Wilson (CP) managed to get the fire extinguisher to operate. No. 4 engine bore a "windmilling" propeller, and the right wing was damaged. All disposable equipment was thrown out as the pilots fought their errant charge back across Germany and into Northern France. Despite their efforts, the chances of clearing enemy territory gradually receded. And so it was that several townsfolk of Carmin in the Pas de Calais were startled by the appearance of the B-17 looming up at minimum altitude out of the gloom to the Southeast and banking gently prior to heading in for a belly-landing in a field close by.

The news that they were crash-landing came as a relief to Tom, because his chute-pack had "popped" during the collision, thus making a bale-out very hazardous. He now moved to a position behind the radio-room and waited for the impact. Touchdown in what he thought was a potato field was smooth, and the deceleration was equally smooth and rapid. Despite his injuries he gathered together four incendiary devices carried for the express purpose of destroying the intact aircraft in order to deny access to new or secret equipment that might be installed. In his semi-conscious state he had little recollection of getting away from the burning aircraft. His hazy vision took in a small copse of trees in the distance towards which he alternately ran, walked, or even crawled. Coming across a cyclist he was advised to alter direction, but his injuries soon forced him to flop into a ditch-row bordering a field, and there he collapsed. From this vantage point he noted a farmer ploughing the field and steadily working his way in Tom's direction over the next 30 minutes.

Monsieur Gilbert Marmuse was fully immersed in his work as he came to the edge of the field, and the 20 year old Frenchman must have been virtually frightened out of his wits when an apparition in flying coveralls made his presence felt with a loud "Pssst!" His apprehension was apparent, and for good reason – was Tom a friend or a foe? Was he indeed an Allied flier, or either a member of the detested Milice (French collaborators), or a "stool-pigeon" sent out to trap anyone showing favor to the Allied cause? Staring around motionless for a minute or so, Gilbert finally gestured to Tom to remain where he was and indicated he would return later to pick up the wounded American.

It seemed no time at all before Gilbert returned with an ox-driven cart. Climbing down he assisted Tom into the cart

On 24 March '44 Lt. Kenneth Haynes (flying his second mission and taking his crew on their first) lifted off the darkened runway in 42-38102. Within a few minutes the 532BS bomber was a crumpled mass at Baileys Farm to the West of the airfield, having taken its crew to their deaths.

containing straw and a large tarpaulin beneath which he was concealed. Now began the perilous journey of several kilometres back to the Marmuse farm. The cart lumbered along at a painful pace as a look-out was kept for German patrols scouring the countryside for any sign of the recently arrived "Luftgangsters" (Several of whom managed to avoid capture until the Allied advance in August/September liberated the region.)

Arrival at the farm in Provin saw Tom helped into a barn, where a bed in a straw pile was hastily prepared. Still in intense pain and with a body aching all over, cold, and on the edge of exhaustion, he gradually dozed off as the warm surroundings relaxed him. He awoke as another Frenchman entered. This man attended to his dislocated shoulder by popping it back into position. He then placed a splint on the right upper arm before tending to a deep puncture wound in Tom's forehead. Handing over some painkillers, he departed as silently as he had arrived, never to be seen again by his patient. (In 1995 Tom discovered he was not a doctor but a chemist) Ahead of the American airman as he lay recovering from his present condition were actions that would test his physical and mental endurance to the limit.

The remaining Group bombers completed a ten-minute bomb-run through "tracking" flak, but the tight bomb-pattern fell through the undercast with its effect naturally unknown. No further losses occurred, but this factor still made it all the harder for the 532BS, to whom all three B-17 casualties belonged, along with the 30 crewmen killed or MIA.

Every March mission to date had involved a deep penetration, so it must have been with some incredulity that the crews

The burnt-out remains of this 532BS aircraft were snapped by a French Resistance worker despite the dangerous presence of German soldiers. Lt. John Rickerson "bellied-in" the B-17 near Carvin in the Pas de Calais region of France on 24 March '44 after surviving a collision with Lt. Tompson on the way to Schweinfurt. All ten crewmen got out, and several evaded capture, including Rickerson.

"Whodat" (42-37754) of the 534BS is recorded on another B-17's strike camera. The blast from a flak shell has punched out the fuselage around the waist-windows and almost cut her in two, as well as killing all three waist and tail gunners. Target was Rheims/Champagne on 28 March '44.

studied the target choice on the 26th – a "Noball" site at Marquise/Mimoyeques in the Pas de Calais, constituting one of the shortest missions to date. The 24 crews were over enemy territory for no more than ten minutes, and Capt Winters in the lead noted a 90-second bomb-run through moderate flak, while Capt. Hester (B) recorded a precise bomb-strike. However, the flak intensified as the Group headed back out over the Channel, and Lt. Ewing Watson saw two B-17s blow up. This was the third consecutive mission with no "aborts," and the month's overall record was almost as perfect in this respect.

A second French target followed next day when St. Jean D'Angely airfield was visited by 30 aircraft, with Col. Hall and Capt. Winters assuming CBW Lead. The perfect weather coupled with a total absence of flak or fighters allowed Capt. Hester to indulge in directing a precise strike, with hangars and other buildings seen to collapse under the weight of ordnance. There was even time for a 360 degree turn to observe results.

The penultimate March mission continued the trend towards French targets, this time to Rheims/Champagne airfield in Central France. A force of 21 bombers under the charge of Capt. Franek and Lt. Sandman took up the Low Group position in the CBW (533BS), while Lt. Pluemer (535BS) took another nine into the Composite Group's High Sqdn. slot. Flying in the former formation's Low Sqdn. as second element leader was Lt. Dan Henry and crew on their 22nd mission, and Lt. Liddle taking up No. 3 in the same Sqdn's rear element.

Neither B-17 was destined to see Ridgewell again, and their crews would have greatly varying experiences.

Take-off was at 0815, with cross-out over the English coast at Beachy Head at 1036. Approximately 90 minutes later the bombers were engaged on the bomb-run, and their loads released without incident. Another "milk-run" appeared to be on the cards, even though flak was speckling the sky.

When the blast came it must have seemed like the end of everything to the crew on 42-37754 "Whodat" – that is, for those surviving the flak shell which had impacted against the rear fuselage to leave the tail hanging on by a few strips of metal, as well as abruptly snuffing out the lives of S/Sgts Norcom and Toler (WGs) and Kurtz (TG). What had hitherto been a fairly routine mission for Henry's combat-tested crew was sharply transformed into an uphill battle for survival as the B-17 dipped towards the earth.

The crew and aircraft were both well known around Ridgewell. The former had with one exception been together since crewing-up, and six months training had culminated in assignment to the 534BS. Then, while at the Rest Home S/Sgt Moe Kluger (BT) had broken a leg and was replaced by S/Sgt Kyle Wheatley. As for "Whodat," she was two missions ahead of her crew and had had her share of near things. During her 11th mission to Bremen on 20 Dec. she had suffered the loss of an engine and shrapnel hits on the right landing gear that prevented its being lowered when Lt. Kuhl entered the landing circuit. In spite of this serious handicap, he brought off a successful belly-landing which enabled the groundcrew to jack her up, roll her into a hangar, and soon bring her back into service. Now she was facing her second and final ordeal.

As the bomber fell out of the sky Lt. Henry rang the bale-out bell, but quickly countermanded the instruction before anybody could react. Apart from an arm wound to S/Sgt Carl Mongrue (ROG), the seven men left were unscathed. The pilots, having pulled the B-17 out of its dive, were fighting to keep the B-17 level, but this was difficult with the elevators jammed in the "up" position and the rudder cables severed. Little could be done about freeing the elevators, but T/Sgt Sebastian Quaresma (Eng.) grabbed some wires from the bomb-bay and lashed the rudder cables together to provide a form of directional control. Altitude could only be lost in a perverse way by pulling back on the control columns, but at this time every effort was being directed towards holding altitude.

The luckiest man on board was S/Sgt Wheatley. The Fortress was hit as it was clearing the target, and the ball-turret gunner still had the turret in the vertical position. He was able to vacate his position, but when he later attempted to rotate it into its normal fore-and-aft angle he found the operating mechanism jammed. Being unable to wear a chute-pack inside the constricted space, it is clear what his fate would have been had he been operating the turret in other than a vertical configuration at the time the B-17 was struck.

The full extent of the almost mortal wound to "Whodat" was now realised by Wheatley and Quaresma. The latter tried to work his way back to the tailwheel to check it out, but was confronted by a tangle of wires, tubes, and aluminum. He noted the hole to the right was big enough to drive a Jeep through, and that on the left was only marginally smaller. The waist-gunners were huddled together, and their state was such that he said he never wanted to see anything like it again. No contact could be made with the tail-gunner, and it was assumed (correctly) that he was also dead.

At least the B-17 was no longer alone. Having spotted her plight Lt Chet Hallberg led his group of eight P-38s from the 20FG towards the bomber, which he noticed was heading away from, rather than towards, England. Frantic directional signals by hand from Hallberg ensured Lts. Henry and Crisler took the necessary course-correction action. Safe within this protective circle, concentration could now center on the task of getting back home. The virtually truncated fuselage was still weathering the tremendous air pressure, but the pilots must have pondered on the possibility that they and the crew would be unable to bale out should the remaining strands of metal give way and throw the bomber into an uncontrollable spin. It was obvious that the men had full faith in Lts. Henry and Crisler,

Lt. Dan Henry (left) and his co-pilot, Bob Crisler, were responsible for bringing back "Whodat" on 28 March '44. They baled out the other five survivors while orbiting over Ridgewell before abandoning the Fortress over the Suffolk coast.

since nobody raised the issue of jumping even when the English coast had been crossed.

And so it was that observers at the base first saw the B-17 as it wallowed in overhead. An earlier order to divert to another base for a crash-landing had initially been acceded to, but bad weather en route had decided Henry into coming back to Ridgewell. The knot of men by the control tower watched for the first chute to emerge, for it was all too obvious that an attempted crash-landing would likely end in disaster. To Lt. Bob Van Buskirk, standing with the others in Lt. Zapinski's newly assigned crew, it must have been a chastening foretaste of what combat could entail just to gaze up at "Whodat." (In any event, this crew was to have several rough experiences of its own in the weeks ahead).

The first chute puffed out South of the tower bearing Lt. Jasiask (B), who touched down near a parked B-17 and had already gathered in his canopy before being picked up by the Station Flight Surgeon. Then, followed by an ambulance, the same surgeon headed off the base and across some fields to collect T/Sgt Quaresma. Sgts. Mongrue and Wheatley came out simultaneously, with the ROG's arm wound not impeding him from pulling his ripcord and drifting down into a field where a passing civilian picked him up. Finally, Lt. Beardsworth (N) made a heart-stopping free-fall almost to ground level before deploying his chute. The pilots were now only left with the sad duty of heading the doomed veteran B-17 out towards the Suffolk coast where they baled out. The abandoned bomber performed perfectly to the end of the line by coming down harmlessly into the North Sea. A few weeks later the body of S/Sgt Kurtz was washed ashore, but Sgts. Norcom and Toler remain missing to this day.

Lt Liddle's B-17 did not get as far as the target. Instead, a malfunction on No. 3 engine of 42-37933 resulted in the propeller "windmilling," and so slowing the aircraft that the mission was "aborted." Luckily, no fighters were encountered, but the ailing engine caught fire with the flames intensifying as the B-17 descended into the ever-denser atmosphere. At 12000 ft over Kent the bale-out bell rang. S/Sgt Ken Schmitt noticed Sgt. Emory Y Naha (TG), a full-blooded Tewa Indian, accidentally pulling his rip-cord and ending up with a pile of silk and cords. Ken kicked open the rear door, then helped Naha into a sitting position on the doorsill before pushing him out. He quickly followed, but still had time to notice two other crewmembers imitating Naha's error.

Ken experienced no sensation of falling, and after getting far enough down he opened his chute. The descent was normal, but ended 12 ft above the ground when he swung into some trees. Shortly after he heard a voice calling out, "Are you there, are you there?" and duly responded by directing the questioner to his location. Looking up, the Englishman shouted "Smashing show!" He wore a pair of binoculars around his neck, and Ken asked him if he had sighted any other chutes, and if so, how many. He had been following the bomber's course the whole time, and confirmed all ten men had got out, ending his short account with another loud "Smashing show!" Two GIs now turned up, and one of them responded to Ken's plea

Four B-17Gs of the 535BS are straining for altitude as they head outward during the winter of 1943/44. Bomber on photo right side is 42-31357 "Our Desire," which was MIA with Lt. Jim Mullane's crew on 13 April '44. Formation in background seems to be badly strung out, and will be in trouble if not tightened up before crossing the enemy coast.

This is Site No. 3, which contains the gymnasium (top left), the church just below the gymnasium, and the enlisted men's Mess-hall. The B-17 design is applied to the bath-house tower and is part of the artwork for a War-bond Drive or similar money-raising exercise conducted on an inter-Squadron basis.

for a knife with which he could cut the canopy cords on one side and swing down to the ground.

This achieved, the soldiers took him to an RAF airfield in the vicinity, where he met the other members of the crew. (The civilian's enthusiastic remarks struck Ken as humorous, making the entire incident appear as if it had been for his benefit!)

Lt. Joe Scott (N) also jumped via the rear door. He recollected that Naha had initially balked at the thought of jumping, but had been firmly persuaded to do so by Joe's superior rank! This was the third incident in the tail-gunner's combat tour in that he had survived a crash-landing, and during a later mission was knocked out by a 20mm explosion which made a "window" in the turret Plexiglas bigger and wider than his head. Joe sustained a sprained ankle on landing near to a corn-threshing machine operated by Land Army girls. By the time he had shared some tea and a conversation with them and got ready to depart with British soldiers to the local police station he had given away his helmet and his chute had disappeared. Both he and Sgt. Hanson were "billeted out" at the "Saracens Head" Hotel in Ashford, where Joe displayed his initiative to overcome a lack of ready British cash – he sold the French Franc element in his escape kit! The hotel manager's enquiry about how the apparently money-less airmen were settling their costs was met with this explanation, whereupon the manager loaned Joe a further ten pounds. This bonus allowed Joe and Sgt. Hanson to live well until Maj. Halsey (535BS CO) arrived to pick them up by aircraft. (The manager's generosity was promptly settled by return cheque).

Brunswick closed off operations for March when Maj. Shackley and Lt. Tyson in a PFF B-17 led both the "A" Group and 1CBW, and Lts. Putek and Watson headed the Lead and Low Sqdns in a separate "B" Group. The Primary was obscured, and a run was made instead on factories in nearby Waggum. Fighter opposition was the most intense since the first Berlin mission, although mainly directed at succeeding CBWs. However, the P-51s and P-47s did their usual efficient job of tangling with the Fw190s and Me 109s to come out on top, scoring 44 "kills" against 12 losses. T/Sgt Lifford French noted a B-17 from another Group drop out under harassment from an Me109, but not only did it evade the fighter's fire, but its crew brought their opponent down.

One Group bomber was fortunate to get back. This was the Group/CBW Deputy Lead 42-40007 "Honey," flown by Maj. Halsey and Lt. Milton Tarr (533BS). Cannon fire disabled No. 3 engine and tore up the radio-room, destroying the equipment and blasting a large hole in the room's left side. It was amazing that Sgt. Philip Smith (ROG) was only knocked to the floor to suffer no more than a bruised elbow – no Purple Heart for him! A total of thirteen out of the 31 B-17s were forced to land away from base in the face of solid ice-forming cloud.

This detached upturned wing with exposed landing gear comes from one of the 131 B-17s MIA from Ridgewell. Lying in the background is the crushed rear fuselage, identifiable as part of a B-17 by the Y-shaped aperture for the tail wheel. Severity of the impact suggests aircraft was completely out of control, with anybody still on board at this point unlikely to escape from his aerial tomb.

March loss statistics were ten B-17s MIA and three "Category E" as regards combat operations. Now, the last day was to throw up a crash incident with particularly cruel overtones for one of the victims. T/Sgt Don Carr had flown around 20 missions as Lt. Silvernale's engineer, and had sworn never to fly with anybody else. On the 31st he was persuaded to make up a skeleton crew of six for a "slow-time" flight in the 534BS veteran B-17F 42-29751 "Mis Abortion/Stuff." Lt. Wayne Schomberg and Capt. Paul Stull (534BS Engineering Officer) occupied the pilots' seats. Left behind was the crewchief, Sgt. John Randle. He should automatically have been included for a test-hop of this nature, but a chute pack was not on hand – a piece of great good fortune for him.

Whatever happened as the bomber prepared to land off the short flight was never fully determined, although there were persistent rumours afterwards that Capt. Stull might have had the controls under Lt. Schomberg's guidance, being as he had regularly expressed the desire to fly an aircraft. Some distance short of the runway threshold the veteran bomber was seen to dip sharply, roll over, and plough at an angle into the ground where it exploded on contact. There were no survivors, and Sgt. Carr's doubts had been proven to be grimly accurate. His body was interred at Madingley Cemetery, where it currently still rests.

11

BUILD-UP TO D-DAY

In April 1944 there occurred a significant, if short-term, change from strategic bombing to the tactical bombing of pre-Invasion targets within France and the Low Countries, which involved both RAF Bomber Command and USSTAF forces based in England. This (enforced) move at Gen. Eisenhower's request was not welcomed either by Gen. "Tooey" Spaatz or his RAF counterpart, "Butch" Harris. The latter commander had argued against the use of his crews in striking at specific sources such as marshalling yards on the grounds that their destruction could not be guaranteed without incurring many casualties among the civilian population. (Harris was to subsequently admit his aircrew had proven his dire prediction to be wrong with a number of pin-point assaults on this category of target during the next two or three months.)

As far as the 8USAAF was concerned May and June would accelerate the trend away from strategic targets, but even in April this was discernible. A study of 381BG missions reveals the following pattern:

	German Targets	Other Targets
April	Nine	Six
May	Twelve	Seven
June	Three	Twenty

Gen. Spaatz had a probable sound reason for advising maximum concentration upon strategic targets. The real "Achilles Heel" for German industrial output was its strong dependence on synthetic oil, especially now that natural oil-well complexes such as Ploesti in Romania were coming under threat of Russian seizure. If major synthetic plants like Merseberg/Leuna, Lutzkendorf, and Politz could be rendered useless, then overall production would inevitably "dry up." This process was especially relevant to the bomber crews, since the Luftwaffe would be one of the principal victims of fuel deficiency on such a scale.

As Spring faded into Summer the pace of daylight operations was hugely stepped up. As an example, where the 381BG had taken over nine months to complete its first 88 missions, virtually the same number (85) would be added by the end of August. This pace had a knock-on effect for the crews in shortening the period for completion of their tours. (These had recently been raised from 25 to 30 missions on 19 March. This was a measure which created understandably hostile reaction,

"Squat N' Droppit" seemed to have a penchant for accidents, seen here after her final effort occurred on 15 April '44. She was taxiing in from a local flight when she caught fire. All efforts of the personnel to douse the flames failed. These.two men are braving the ignition of the B-17G's ammunition as they continue with their vain endeavours.

Official caption ascribes this damage to enemy action, but in fact it was self-inflicted. On 9 April '44 Lt. Souder ran out of runway while making a third attempt at take-off. Nobody was injured among the crew, but B-17F/42-30613 was promptly salvaged – apart from her center fin, which for some reason was fitted to "Tomahawk Warrior," but without a change to that B-17G's serial number of 42-97267!

This picture depicts the hoped-for result of precision bombing – a tight pattern of bomb strikes smothering the target (In this case Rheims/Champagne airfield). Weather conditions were not often as clear as this, with an inevitable deterioration in bombing accuracy as these became worse.

even though those men close to completing their 25 missions on that date had proportionately less than five missions added in).

No missions were flown from Ridgewell during the first week of April. In that period one evader arrived back and two former evaders departed for home; all three were 535BS personnel. Lt. Alfred Coffman had been Lt. Putek's co-pilot on 6 Feb. when he baled out along with the two officers up-front in the nose. Lt. Glenn McCabe (CP) and T/Sgt. Russell Jevons (Eng.) were the fortunate duo out of Lt. Duarte's B-17 MIA over Bordeaux on 31 Dec. (Duarte would also evade capture).

After two "scrubbed" missions on the 6th (Oberpfaffenhofen) and 7th (Oldenburg), the latter was again selected on the 8th. Briefed take-off at 0800 for the 29 aircraft was delayed due to fog until 1000. Lt. Pluemer (535BS) was in the lead and took the force over the haze-shrouded airfield. The 91BG had already covered the MPI with their bombs, and it was into the smoke created by this strike that the Ridgewell bombardiers let go. Moderate to heavy flak was encountered at this stage only. All crews returned, but Lt. Leslie Bond's "Carolina Queen" was faced with a belly-landing due to an inoperable landing-gear. To worsen the situation, the special tools normally carried to release the ball-turret in such an emergency were missing. Col. Hall hit upon the idea of placing a spare set in a soil-ballast bag and dropping the bag in through the open radio-hatch. The initial attempt to do so using the Group's L-4 Piper Cub was thwarted by slipstream-effect. Hall landed and substituted a B-17 for the Cub in order to equalise his speed more precisely with Bond; he also tied a longer piece of rope to the bag. After a short spell of "fishing," the bag was delivered and the ball-turret then jettisoned. "Carolina Queen" was belly-landed with minimum damage and no crew injuries. (It is sad to record that the majority of this crew's tenure on either life or freedom had but eleven more days to run.)

The 9th was the inaugural mission for Lt. Zapinski's 532BS crew, which included Lt. Bob Van Buskirk (B). He was never to forget the occasion, although the reason was a macabre one. As his B-17 joined up with 28 others and headed NE for Gydnia,

"Minnie the Mermaid" came to the 381BG in Jan '44 and served on combat status for almost eleven months. On 29 Nov. she force-landed on the Continent, but was declared surplus to requirements only on 27 Jan '45. Black divisional triangle on what is a camouflaged B-17 is unusual, as white was normally used. Aircraft letter is positioned higher up fuselage than the Sqdn. letters, a feature on 533BS aircraft.

Living facilities on "tin shack" airfields like Ridgewell were rather basic. These are the Nissen huts, which housed the 532BS crewmen. In each would be either the officer or enlisted complements from two crews. They proved extremely difficult to heat, especially in the damp East Anglian atmosphere.

Lt. Leonard "Zip" Zapinski's crew seen during States-side training in Jan '44 prior to assignment to the 532BS. Standing {L-R) are Zapinski, Widosh (CP), Dave Fuller (N), and Bob Van Buskirk (B). After completing 20 missions from early April they were shot down on their 21st on 30 May.

Poland, his "epitaph" kept flashing up in his mind; "Bob Van Buskirk, born 9 April 1922, died 9 April 1944" – not the most pleasant of birthday memories! Happily, this fate was to be denied to him because the Group abandoned the mission, and in fact he would go on to complete a further 20 missions before becoming a POW.

A hair-raising occurrence involved Lt. Souder (535BS). The Sqdn records state he made three attempts to take-off, with the third recording 160 mph and a mercury reading of 39 inches as he over-shot the runway and tipped the B-17F onto its nose. The nose section was crushed, but the bomb-load did not explode. However, what was surely a miraculous escape from "the Grim Reaper" once again proved but a temporary reprieve for the crew, who slipped over into the MIA lists soon after. There is some mystery over mission credit for the 9th. Although the mission does not appear on official lists, the 535BS diary states that credit was granted simply because a single 534BS crew followed another Group to the target. (The crew in question are equally convinced to this very day that the credit granted against the next day's completed run was relevant to the 9th!)

Brussels (10th) involved a split effort when the majority of the 32 crews formed up under Maj. Briggs and Lt. Kesley in "Sweet Patootie" to lead the 1CBW, and the rest went into the Composite Group led by Capt. Winters. Two bomb-runs towards the industrial sites in the city were nullified by heavy cloud gradually building up from the coast onward. Briggs turned North towards Woensdrecht airfield, where a cloud-break allowed a sight of the Aiming Point and a 40 second run delivered what was described as "a good, though unobserved, result." It was to be hoped this optimism was justified in view of the rule that only visual attacks should be made over Nazi-occupied countries. The Composite Group also carried out two runs on its particular Brussels site with better luck the second time around. Lt. Tidwell (Lead Bombardier) said bombing was "good," and other crewmen said they saw bursts landing on factories and a possible oil refinery.

Crewchief for "The Joker" (532BS) was Sgt. Charlie Ayers (right), who is dwarfed by one of his assistants, Steve Drosdek. On the left is Sgt Andrew "Whitey" Strednak, who later became crew chief for "Flak Magnet." "Joker"'s lower nose displays 48 mission symbols. Bomber transferred to AFSC during May '44.

A quartet of runs into Central Germany commenced the next day when the 8USAAF made for Fw. Aero-plants at Cottbus and Sorau. Flak commenced right from the coast and harried the twin elements of the 32 aircraft, in particular over Hanover and in the target zone. Maj. Osce V Jones reported that fighter attacks commenced 20 minutes into Germany and persisted most of the way in. Numbers were estimated at 150, with groups of between 12 and 15 striking after breaching the screen set up by the sometimes out-numbered escorts. The attacks were fortunately focused on other units, and especially one flying B-24s. The 381BG was the sole 1CBW Group to hit the Primary, which was found to be severely damaged according to the strike-photos. The other two Groups bombed the Secondary, and Lt. Reese's segment of the Composite Group landed an equally positive strike.

One flak burst knocked out the rudder controls on 42-38194 "Baboon Mcgoon," and the B-17 dropped 2000 ft before Lt. Schindler managed to level off. Six P-51s picked up the bomber, and apart from a quick foray to dispatch an unwary fighter, the escorts took their "Big friend" all the way back to Ridgewell. While the crew piled into the radio-room to assume crash-position, the pilots made very skillful use of throttles, ailerons, and elevators to bring off a perfect landing.

Two interesting observations from this mission were the downing of a tri-motor transport by the P-51s and a successful distraction from attack on a preceding Group by an Me 410. The latter action was staged not by a fighter, but by a B-17. The bomber in question had been straggling, and was diving to gain speed when it picked upon the Me 410. The pilots took the opportunity to turn into the German, and their gunfire harassed him so much that he just dived down and away! It was pleasant to record that this bomber turned fighter did come home, but its good fortune was not matched by the 534BS's Lt. Hesse, who was MIA in 42-31497; at least all nine men survived to become POWs.

The fourth Group mission to Schweinfurt took place on the 13th. A total of 154 B-17s out of 172 dispatched by the 1BD unloaded over 340 tons of explosives and incendiaries on the infamous ball-bearings complex. Situated around 100 miles East of Frankfurt, this location had always promised stiff opposition, and today was to prove no exception. High altitude haze and a 3/10 undercast cleared on approach, but flak hit hard from thereon in. Fighters were active, with 50 to 60 making a sweeping lunge at a Group to the right and taking down six of its B-17s. Direct assaults on the 381BG were limited to one pass at each section of the 32 bombers sent out, Capt. Franek having split off 12 from the Lead Group to head for a separate target. Maj. Halsey was riding with Lt. Chuck Enos in 42-38061 "Georgia Rebel II," and his assessment of the day as "plenty rough" found echoes from everybody. Bombing results were not seen since smoke from preceding strikes totally cut out a visual sighting.

Lt. James Mullane's crew had commenced operations with the 534BS, but were then transferred to the 535BS. Being well on their way to finishing up, they had headed out in their regular B-17 42-31357 "Our Desire." Lt. Sherwood (CP) recalled the sight of the single fighter pass when Fw190s had shot across the formation from one side to another hotly pursued by P-51s.

"Mis Abortion" survived over a year of combat operations. Assigned from the 96BG on 16 July '43, its name caused offence to Col. Leber, who ordered its deletion. In its place, the crew chief, who possessed a good sense of rough English humor, applied the single word "Stuff" behind the bending female figure – an act which was never subsequently challenged!

Non-combat flights did not guarantee safety from danger. "Mis Abortion/Stuff" of the 534BS was landing off an engine "slow-time" test on 31 March '44 when she faltered and crashed. Lt. Wayne Schomberg, a "tour-expired" pilot, Lt. Paul Stull (Sqdn. Engineering Officer), and four others were killed. Crash-angle was steep as indicated by the three engines buried into the soil.

He felt that the scene was something akin to a Western movie, like "Stagecoach," with the German "Indians" being driven off by the aerial Seventh Cavalry, and experienced a great urge to stand up from his seat and cheer them on!

Flak hits on "Our Desire" while over the target disabled Nos. 3 and 4 engines, as well as destroyed the co-pilot's controls. It was inevitable that the crippled B-17 was unable to hold its formation position and was forced to soldier on for home alone, as well as slowly losing altitude, which was but a few thousand feet as it came up to the Rhine. Further ground fire left Lt. Mullane with no option but to push the bale-out bell, and the crew all departed to land intact, with the exception of S/Sgt Tarczinski, who broke a leg.

During Lt. Sherwood's subsequent interrogation at Dulag Luft he was informed that an unidentified airman had been found trapped under the wreck of the B-17. It was suggested to him that if he would not reveal the man's name it would surely lead to continuing heartache for the dead man's relatives, since the German authorities would lack this vital detail in order to transmit it to the Red Cross. What the interrogator did not know was that Mullane's crew was one of the first within the 381BG to fly with only nine men, one waist-gunner having been deleted from the original ten in accordance with 8USAAF policy. Furthermore, the Lt. was well aware that his buddies had all got out safely, so the German's blandishments cut no ice with him!

The bombers remained on the ground for four days before lifting off on the 18th for a multi-pronged thrust at targets in the Oranienburg and Brandenburg regions. The 381BG went to the former area to bomb a Heinkel plant 12 miles North of Berlin. Capt. Winters in "Whirlaway" was forced to lower his formation when confronted by a cloud-layer at the briefed run-in altitude, but the bombardiers made the most of visual conditions to put down a tight bomb-pattern. Once again an unusual type of enemy aircraft was spotted being shot down by P-51s as it took off. Lt. Yank, a 533BS bombardier, described it as a "six-engine job" (probably an Me 323 transport known as a "Gigant") which crashed in a ball of fire about 300 yds from the runway-end.

Targets like Cottbus, Schweinfurt, and Oranienburg entailed many hours flying; for example, the first-named location involved an 11-hour flight. The briefing for Eschwege on the 19th must have brought groans of resignation from those crews who had flown all the previously mentioned missions, and the heart-felt expression "Oh, my achin' back!" echoed around the room. It took no small effort even for relatively fit crewmen to sit in a pilot's seat or be bundled up in a ball or tail-turret for long spells. Post-war spinal, hearing, and associated medical conditions were surely prevalent among 8USAAF

On 8 April '44 Lt. Leslie Bond (534BS) had to crash-land his B-17G "Carolina Queen" (42-97214). This picture was snapped as the bomber was set down safely on the runway after the ball-turret had been jettisoned.

bomber crews, if the experiences of their RAF contemporaries were anything to go by. Other factors, such as the noise generated by the engines and the extreme temperatures, could easily induce a tremendous sense of lassitude.

Col. Hall took the 1CBW Lead with the 38 B-17s split between the Lead and High Groups. A 7/10 cloud pattern threatened to foul up the prospect for a visual bomb-run, but a convenient gap allowed Capt. Fullick (befitting his status as Group Bombardier) to again earn his money with a perfect sighting and drop. Aerial attacks were short but severe, with an estimated 200 single and twin-engine fighters of which 50 made one mass assault in the target area. It was the High Group which received their exclusive attention at the cost of two 534BS crews. Lt. Bond in 42-3525 had made a successful crash-landing on the 8th, but his luck was out on this mission. His Fortress exploded shortly after being struck by 20mm shells, and only Lt. Mason (CP) and Sgt Clyman got clear. (This crew's fate had been paralleled the day before by Lt. Souder (535BS), who had survived a take-off crash on the 9th but who had gone down in 42-37733 "Patches N' Prayers") The other 534BS loss over Eschwege was 42-38004, piloted by Lt. Rayburn. His B-17 was seen to catch fire following the first fighter thrust, and in falling away barely missed Lt. Kuhl in Deputy Lead position. One chute came out, but the bomber later broke in two, killing Rayburn and Lt. Craft (CP), as well as throwing out S/Sgt Peterson (Eng.) without his chute pack. On return to base it must have been galling to make a formation fly-past for the benefit of Gens. Spaatz, Doolittle, and Williams; it would have cut little ice with the weary fliers, and especially with the one crew bringing home a dead buddy!

A welcome break from long-haul operations was a strike 24 hours later at several "Noball" sites near Croisette in the Pas de Calais (These were still known as "rocket sites," because the existence of the V-1 Flying Bomb was as yet unknown and would only be revealed with the launch of the first of the weapons in mid-June). A late take-off at 1600 was to prove fruitless because a solid overcast across France prevented any chance of bombing. The German gunners were not similarly inhibited and inflicted heavy damage on at least five B-17s.

S/Sgt Gugenheim was sworn in as a 2 Lt. the next day to join former Sgts. Wardell and Crowley in elevation to officer rank; all were former members of Capt. Chapman's 535BS crew. On this day there occurred the first aircraft "christening" ceremony since "Rotherhithes Revenge" back on 15 Feb. Laurence Olivier and Vivien Leigh, Mary Churchill, and Alfred Lunt were the center of attraction for the many personnel thronging 'round a 535BS dispersal on which squatted a camouflaged B-17G. The Prime Minister's daughter did the honors with a bottle of Coca-Cola smashed over the chin-turret guns. The bomber's previous anonymity had given way to the title "Stage Door Canteen," in recognition of the sizeable facility for U.S. forces located down in London. In fact, she would carry her name through more than 100 missions right up to the War's end.

Another and surprising late take-off for Hamm was scheduled on the 22nd, which it had been calculated would bring the bombers back around 2200. Marshalling yards in the city were a long-time target for RAF Bomber Command, whose crews had composed a very ribald song about the advisability of avoiding this part of Germany! A total of 1528 tons was carried and dropped on the yards by the 8USAAF. The 381BG duly returned in the gathering dusk, and the final landings were completed in the blaze of the runway lights. Further to the NE were other "blazes," which in a number of cases belonged to B-24s of the 2BD. These had been brought down either by one of the Me 410 Intruders which had followed the formations back to England, or by their own nervous AA gunners who had opened up in the confusion. In fact, one B-24 did divert into Ridgewell after being warned off from its own airfield. Why the Luftwaffe no longer indulged in this attack-method on Allied airfields was all down to Hitler. In 1940/41 the Fernnachtjager (Long-range intruder) units had been tasked with this duty, and the resulting harassing tactics over its airfields had terrible consequences for RAF Bomber Command. However, the Führer then decreed the Ju 88s and Do 17s had to restrict their operations

Darkness had already fallen when this photo of Lt. Bond was taken as he stood with Col. Hall by his B-17's No. 1 engine, his crew clustered on the wing and by the engine. Sadly, this reprieve from death or injury was only delayed by 15 days, as the bulk of the crew were KIA over Eschwege on 19 April.

GD-B "Carolina Queen" is photographed after the belly-landing on 8 April '44. Her service at Ridgewell was comparatively short. Assigned on 25 March, she was one of six lost over Berlin with Lt. Wardencki's crew on 24 May.

to German airspace, from where the population could witness the RAF's destruction first hand!

A very lengthy route into SE Germany was planned for 24 April. An air-storage depot at Erding 20 miles NE of Munich was bombed by 31 aircraft comprising the CBW Lead and headed by Col. Shackley. Although the Lead bomber was PFF-equipped, the perfect visibility stretching 30 miles rendered its H2X gear redundant. At least seven other targets were observed under equally effective assault. Erding quickly cast up dark palls of smoke visible for a long time during Group withdrawal. S/Sgt Merle Tolbert made the very pertinent comment that "It could have been a tough trip without our escorts"; the Luftwaffe could still manage to hand out wicked punishment whenever it got through to any uncovered units.

At this time the PFF bombers were not based at Ridgewell, but were concentrated over at Bassingbourn. After completing some missions in which their standards of navigation had attracted the attention of Col. Leber, Lt. John Howland's crew, along with that of Lt. Carl Clark, were asked if they wished to volunteer for this duty. They duly moved over to the 91BG base, but soon found there were several drawbacks to their revised role. For one thing, they were expected to fly over to Ridgewell or Nuthampstead. The transfer was usually during the late evening or even in the early hours preceding the mission. Their presence was rarely welcomed, since it usually indicated the crews could expect to be airborne for a considerable time. On the other hand, short-range or "milk-run" types of missions did not usually involve PFF crews.

Metz/Frescaty airfield was well over 200 miles into SE France, and so was no "milk-run." Sgt. Steve Gaspar (ROG) might have hoped for an easier last mission, as might his pilot on 42-39890 "Return Ticket," Lt. Emil Urban. They took off along with 27 other crews to encounter minimum flak both over the coast and the target, and with the few fighters contesting their progress kept at bay by P-47s. The 8/10 undercast broke up just short of the I.P., and a concentrated bomb-strike was made. However, problems were now beginning to accrue for Lt. Urban. No. 3 engine had "quit," and No. 4 had begun to give trouble, although continuing to function. The jettisoning of all available gear could not prevent the B-17 falling behind even as the bomb-run was in progress.

A full escort was available, but such was the bomber's ailing state that the possibility of having to "ditch" in the Channel loomed up. The decision was now taken to cast off the ball-turret (whether with a conscious view to "ditching" or just to lighten the aircraft appears uncertain), but the action of losing several hundred lbs. of dragging weight was dramatic. Not only did the pilots maintain height, but they also arrived back at base ahead of the others! Sgt. Gaspar later said "I was sweating out the mission, but I guess we had nothing to worry about. This is the third time she has come home on three engines, and she ought to be good at it by now!" No doubt this was a view shared by T/Sgt Glenn Holmes flying his 28th mission.

Despite the light opposition there was one crew MIA, which was Lt. Claytor (535BS) in 42-3511. Among his crew was the experienced S/Sgt Charlie Middleton, and much surprise was expressed at his inclusion within a team flying only its second mission. This stance reflected a similar reaction to Sgts Myers and Bang's inclusion within the equally untested crew of Lt. Zum during the previous September 3 mission.

The Metz run started a seven consecutive daily sequence of missions. Col. Leber was in charge on the 26th when a 10/

10 undercast led to Brunswick being bombed with H2X assistance. Moderate flak inflicted just one recorded casualty when Lt. Joe Scott, navigator to Lt. Haring, took shell fragments in his back. It was back to France (27th) with Lt. Putek on his final mission sharing the Lead B-17 with Maj. Jones in an attack on La Glacerie on the Cherbourg Peninsula; Putek's tail-gunner, Sgt. Vinovich, was also finishing-up. Flak damaged a number of bombers, but caused no losses.

Today's mission was one of prime importance, because it marked the 100th completed mission for the 381BG, and achieving this milestone free of loss was a double cause for celebration. Ten months and five days had elapsed since the Group had entered combat. Both personnel and aircraft had endured the 1943 summer battles and the "Autumn Crisis" that had virtually stalled the Daylight Bombing Offensive and had lost the bulk of human and technical material in the process. The severe loss-rate had not materially diminished during the "Big Week" and "Big B" periods of operations, but the resolve to beat down the opposition had never wavered. Recent evidence of faltering Luftwaffe resistance must have been heartening, although this Force was still regarded as being some way from being totally broken.

The christening of USAAF aircraft was steadily expanded from 1944 onward. On 23 April '44 "Stage Door Canteen" was accorded this honor. A uniformed Mary Churchill, Laurence Olivier (center), and Alfred Lunt (hand before face) were present. Also seen behind Lunt is Brig. Gen. Fred Anderson.

12

SECOND CENTURY

The start of the Group's second century of missions was to an airfield in Northern France already visited on 5 Feb. – St. Avord. Group Lead was handed to Maj. Osce V Jones, who would share the cockpit of 42-38061 "Georgia Rebel II" with its regular pilot, Lt. Harold Henslin. It was Jones who had taken this B-17's named predecessor "Georgia Rebel" into a Swedish bog on 24 July 1943, and he was fated to make a second and almost lethal exit from combat today. Henslin's crew was one of the most experienced at Ridgewell, having started out in December. Henslin's navigator, Lt. Arthur Guertin, was another who had accompanied Jones to Sweden.

St. Avord was typical of the more lightly defended targets regarding flak, and the bomb-run was made with no difficulty. However, just after "bombs away" Sgt. Bill Blackmon (WG) sighted the first in a "tracking" quartet of shells building up from behind. He never completed the count, because either the third or fourth burst impacted around No. 2 engine and tore it completely off. Bill was thrown to the floor by the B-17's downward dip. In so doing he inadvertently crushed his fellow-gunner against the tailwheel cover, an act which in Bill's opinion rendered S/Sgt Williams helpless with pain. The doomed bomber gave the impression of alternately dipping and levelling off, and it was during one of the latter spells that Bill finally managed to claw his way to the open rear hatch and hurl himself into space.

A steady parachute descent deposited him right on the airfield perimeter. Armed with the knowledge that other Groups were still on their bomb run and that some ordnance already dropped was of the "delayed action" type he hurried over to a nearby bunker. Here he was confronted by two airmen who brandished their guns and yelled "Los, Los!" and other phrases at the uncomprehending American.

After the raid was over Bill was bundled onto a vehicle and taken to the main airfield complex. As he was being put through an initial form of interrogation a stretcher was brought in bearing Sgt Padgett (ENG.). Although his main injury was a bruised face, the engineer was moaning softly and clutching his chest as tightly as possible. The reason for his action was later revealed when he and Bill were left on their own for the first time. Padgett had earlier borrowed Bill's A2 jacket, the back of which was emblazoned with 16 bomb symbols and – even worse – two blood-dripping swastikas! Padgett had been fearful of receiving a rough reception had his captors noticed the jacket's design. He had therefore promptly removed the

A 381BG formation is seen as it joins the circuit after a mission in the Spring of 1944. Photo was one of several color shots taken by Lt. Van Buskirk, bombardier on Lt. Zapinski's 532BS crew.

jacket and thrust it against his chest in a desperate attempt at concealment. Now he was able to relieve himself of the offending garment by returning it to its rightful owner! (Bill never discovered whether or not the artwork ever came to the Germans' notice, and if so what was their reaction).

The sole other survivor from "Georgia Rebel II" was Maj. Jones, with all three men being extremely fortunate to come through. S/Sgt Tom O'Brien (BT) was a friend of Sgt Blackmon and a fellow 535BS gunner. At de-briefing he reported that the missing B-17, although falling out of formation, was initially intact and under apparent control. Then it had suddenly split into five or six sections. He also noted how the radio-room Perspex cover had flashed in the bright sunlight as its fuselage segment had tumbled over and over. Lt. Henslin and six of his crew had "struck out," and their final resting place would be among those for whom they had fought so valiantly to free from Nazi oppression.

The returning 27 B-17s did experience a brief skirmish with around 25 Fw190s and Me 109s a few minutes after bomb-release, but the attacks directed at the Low Sqdn. proved ineffectual. Bombing results were recorded as "good," and the single aircraft loss was the sole sour note. (The 535BS notes about this incident commenced with the terse statement "There are no easy missions")

"Big B" cropped up as a target choice directly following the St. Avord mission. Passage inwards towards the Nazi Capital for Col. Kunkel and 27 crews was quite smooth with little interference from flak. Few fighters were seen, and the handful

This Group formation picture was taken in 1944 before CBW color markings were introduced during July. In foreground is "Lucky Me!" (533BS), which was MIA on 25 Sept. Directly above is "Schnozzle," a 534BS bomber which was to be involved in a fatal mid-air collision with "Egg Haid" (535BS) over the base on 21 Jan '45.

The value of flak helmets and helmet liners is more than amply demonstrated by Sgt. Nick Rotz, a 535BS gunner. He is holding the shard of metal from a flak shell which caused the tears in his head gear, and which would almost certainly have taken his life had he been wearing just the standard leather helmet.

that came close enough to the Group for some gunners to engage shot past to take on an adjacent B-24 Group. There was an 8/10 undercast, but the assigned target was struck squarely in the face of what was for Berlin a "moderate" flak barrage. However, what seemed a steady-paced mission for both the 381BG and 1CBW was not the experience for other units and Wings. The Luftwaffe had formed specially commissioned forces known as Sturmgruppen, which were equipped with heavily armed and armored Fw190s. These were intended to exploit those segments of the bomber-stream where escort cover was thin or absent. They would generally descend from behind on the unfortunate Group in the hope of tearing it to pieces, or scattering its aircraft so thoroughly that they were then easy individual prey for the Fw190s or their Me109 high cover. This new and shocking tactic among a diminishing "bag of tricks" for the Luftwaffe was used this day especially against the 3BD, which lost 38 B-27s. It was small wonder that the 8USAAF's overall loss factor on this particular mission stood at 63 – the highest figure for a single April mission.

One 533BS bomber flown by Lt. Ned Renick and named "Big Mike" (42-39997) suffered damage to its hydraulic system and the loss of one engine prior to bombing, and completed its bomb-run with another group. On landing back at Ridgewell the bomber drifted off the runway-end into a ditch. Apart from one crewmember wounded by flak, all the others on board came through the incident unscathed. "Big Mike" was originally assessed as a "Category E" case, but M/Sgt Barbier persuaded his superiors that the B-17 could be brought back to full operational condition. This was a task that was spread over a period of weeks, whose successful outcome resulted not only in a restored aircraft, but also a change of name, which was now "Frenchy's Folly!"

The increased pace of missions being flown was reflected by many of the bombers' crews. For Lt. John Williams (534BS) the Berlin run was his team's seventh in seven days, and the eighth day was to provide no respite, since they were required to fly a practice mission! Lt. Phil Gnatzig (535BS) and his crew were equally battle-tested with six over the same number of days. Flying the Berlin mission in 42-31067 "Phyliss," a replacement for their regular B-17 42-97511 "Egg Haid," Gnatzig lost an engine supercharger and bombed on three engines. A second failed about 45 minutes from the enemy coast, but the struggling B-17 was picked up by a fighter and escorted home. The day before the crew had almost been wiped out when the pilot was forced to stand his aircraft on its head in order to avoid colliding with the stricken "Georgia Rebel II."

One of the six Fortresses MIA on 24 May '44 was 42-31968 (535BS) flown by Lt. Clarence Wainwright. The wrecked tail section of the B-17G, which impacted close to Gruental NE of Berlin, is being inspected by two German women. Picture was supplied by a relative of the women (Ulrich Lange), who was then a teenager and who currently resides in America.

Reassigned on the 29th was Lt. Earl Duarte, who became the third member of his crew to evade capture after his B-17 had to be abandoned over Southern France on 31 Dec. The 535BS records also noted that Sgt. Nassam Abraham (radar specialist) won one of the boxing matches at the 1BD Championships held in Cambridge. Nassam was a broad-shouldered man whose gentle nature concealed a tremendous aptitude and enthusiasm for the Noble Art.

Bron airfield, which was close to Lyons and deep into Central France, was the 1BD planners' target choice with which to round off April. Group records indicate that only 12 bombers actually unloaded, but their pairs of 2000-lb bombs went down on the MPI. Virtually no opposition was encountered, which was a bonus, given the lengthy duration over enemy territory for the formations.

There was to be no respite as May was entered, with no less than 19 successful missions being flown by the 381BG, which was easily the highest monthly total to date. On the 1st marshalling yards at Troyes came in for attention from the Group that was flying as part of the 1BD's second mission launched during the afternoon. Lt. Dale McCrory (532BS) led the formation, and the general impression of the crews was one of marginal interference from fighters and flak only encountered over the French coast. Bombing results were good despite 5/10-cloud cover.

Over the ensuing five days just one mission was completed to the undoubted relief of all. A briefing for Berlin on the 4th, which involved only the 1BD, was sent out. However, a "recall" signal was subsequently issued as the Dutch coast was being crossed and, apart from some 40 crews from other groups, was acted upon. Capt Winters (532B) was not one of the participants, but may well have wished he had been by the day's end. A local flight, along with three other Group personnel in 42-97315, turned into a survival exercise when Nos. 3 and 4 engines suddenly caught fire. The B-17G quickly lost height, leaving the pilots with little option but to slide the bomber into a field near Halstead. Those on board suffered no serious injuries, but the aircraft was totally burnt out.

On the 2BD mission to Sottevast in the Pas de Calais (5th), the first use of the British radar equipment G-H was made by the 93BG; this was a refinement of the original GEE navigational aid which promised much more precise "bombing through cloud" results. Such was the confidence of the Allied authorities concerning G-H's accuracy that its use over what were normally prohibited regions was now indulged in. The equipment was again in use next day (6th) when the 1BD joined

Capt. Doug Winters (532BS) was making a local flight with a skeleton crew of three on 5 May '44. The successive loss of two engines forced him into a hurried crash-landing close to Halstead, Essex. The B-17G caught fire and burnt out, but not before the quartet of airmen got out safely. British civilian firemen can be seen rummaging through the remains of the left wing.

with the 2BD in attacking the V-1 sites. However, whereas the B-24s went ahead with their bomb-runs over the totally "socked-in" area, the absence of G-H among the B-17 Groups forced all to abort their bombing runs.

Flying their maiden mission within the 1CBW was the 398BG based at Nuthampstead, but its strength was spread around the Division's units due to a series of planning misfortunes culminating in an incomplete Group formation. The fact that the CBW was again operating with three Groups was regarded as a distinct bonus at Ridgewell. Over the past six months the CBW Composite Group formed out of two outfits with likely variations in formation flying techniques was a situation which never rested easily with the 381BG crews, at least not according to Group records. Henceforward, they could concentrate on their own formation structure without having to hive off elements for a Composite Group.

The major mishap experienced by the 398BG was fortunately not in evidence next day, which was just as well, since the bomber force was headed for Berlin. An almost complete undercast over the industrial sites selected for attack meant that Targets of Opportunity came in for attention with PFF guidance. This particular mission for the 381BG was the sixth in an eventual run of ten during which no aircraft losses or crew fatalities were to be borne. Although "Big B" could still hand out rough treatment, it was the opinion of the Ridgewell veteran fliers that it was becoming just one more target. Future missions would enforce a much more realistic appraisal of the opposition to be encountered over Germany's Capital! Berlin cropped up again next day when it was swiftly substituted for a "scrubbed" mission to Oldenburg. Once again the solid undercast found the formations having no recourse but to release their ordnance under PFF guidance. M/Sgt Stormer (535BS) was a navigator who had been wounded on a past Berlin mission, and today signalled his return to combat. He had recently been fitted up with G.I. glasses, which in his words "Look and feel like Hell but keep me flying!"

St. Dizier felt the weight of the Group's bomb loads on the 9th, but the true event of the day involved no less than 15 combat crewmen who were finishing up. Returning from detached duty at Nuthampstead were Maj. Lord, Capt Marquam, and Lt. Bannon, who had assisted with the Operations Office, Ordnance, and Mess-Hall aspects during the 398BG's working-up period. Today was also the occasion on which a sequence of Pre-Invasion missions to French targets commenced. However, missions were to continue to be dispatched to locations further afield; in this way little clue as to the short-range missions' significance was likely to slip through to the Nazi High Command. For example, on the 11th the 1BD and 3BD were assigned a variety of targets spread between Germany, Belgium, and Luxembourg, while the 2BD was continuing the "softening-up" process over France. As for the 381BG, it was forced by bad weather conditions to divert from its Primary, with loads being dropped on marshalling yards at Bettembourg and Thionville.

Big Brass visit. Gen. Kepner (CG of 8th Fighter Command) strokes his chin as Brig. Gen. Williams (extreme right) converses with other officers. Col. Gross (1CBW CO) is in center of the group. B-17E in background was originally "Peggy D" (41-9043) of the 97BG, which had participated in the first ever "heavy" mission on 17 August '42. Assigned to Ridgewell, she was stripped of camouflage and re-named "Little Rock-ette" (Little Rock, Ark. was Col. Hall's home).

Lutzkendorf's oil refineries came in for treatment from 100-lb M47 incendiaries on the 12th. The Group was leading the CBW, with Maj. Halsey flying in a PFF bomber whose specialist gear proved to be necessary; records stated "results believed to be good" – a clear indication of a blind drop. More oil targets, this time even further afield in western Poland, were briefed next day. Poor weather forced the 1BD to seek targets of opportunity along the Baltic coast. The 381BG dropped its bombs on Stettin and Stralsund through hazy cloud and with unobserved results. Fighter opposition appeared to have been primarily directed at the 2BD, which lost ten of the 12 "heavies" lost by the 8USAAF. Ridgewell's contingent came through unscathed with at least one Fw 190 "destroyed" credited to S/Sgts Richard Brown and Formby (532BS).

Three missions to Orly airfield (15th and 16th) and Rotenburg (17th) were all "scrubbed" at some stage prior to take-off. Among the combat personnel finished-up and ready to return home was T/Sgt Lifford French, the proud holder of the second DSC to be awarded a 381BG airman. It was at this time that the 532BS diarist recorded that a physical-fitness test had been conducted, which involved pull-ups, sit-ups, and a 300-yard dash – but the results were never disclosed!

On the 19th the 2BD went to Brunswick while the other two Divisions headed for out Berlin. Heavy cloud impeded vision and made PFF assistance mandatory. The 381BG's run-up and release over railroad yards was conducted in the face of flak variously described as "meager" or "intense and accurate." The latter assessment may well have been more accurate, since two bombers were MIA.

Lt. Earl Sharp was flying his 17th mission. He had been temporarily "grounded" during March with sinus problems, and on returning to operations had found his co-pilot and navigator promoted to airplane commander and Lead navigator. One mission with a totally new crew left Earl stating that he would rather face a court-martial if he were placed in such a position again, whereupon he was assigned a team of experienced fliers! Today's mission was to prove fortuitous for his navigator, Lt. Farrell, who was currently grounded with facial boils that apart from their discomfort also prevented his wearing an oxygen mask. Lt. Hardwick, who was his stand-in, was making his first mission.

Sharp was flying as 533BS Lead, and during the bomb-run suffered a flak strike to No. 2 engine, which resulted in an oil-pressure drop and a propeller that refused to "feather." He could see flames below the wing, but the fire did not seem to be intensifying. The bombs were scarcely released when the superchargers went out on Nos. 3 and 4 engines. At this stage the landing gear was lowered as an indication that the B-17 was dropping out, while thought was also given to the possibility of heading North for Sweden. All too soon this latter prospect became doomed when the entire electrical system failed and the fire increased in intensity. Earl had sensed he was beginning to succumb to hypoxia during the past few minutes, a fact confirmed when he noted a gash in his oxygen-hose. Clamping his hand over the gash, he continued to steer the B-17. It seemed to take an eternity before his "bale-out" order could be physically passed around, but finally all eight crewmen were out and apparently safely away. Tragically, there was one casualty; Lt. Hardwick's chute failed to open properly, and his body was later seen by Lt. Britenbaker (B).

Before jumping Earl remembered to reverse his grip on the parachute-pack rip-cord; should he lose consciousness before pulling it (given that the B-17 was flying at 22000 ft.), the natural action of his arm falling away would fulfil the task.

T/Sgt Floyd Hanson (a 535BS ROG) is assisted to the ambulance on 21 May '44. One of the Orderlies holds a dressing to the airman's left side. This was where a flak fragment struck him at the gap where his flak suit front and rear sections linked up! Hanson returned to combat duties soon after and completed his run of missions.

Fighting a path through the flames to the bomb bay, he dropped out but had no recollection of deploying his chute. He passed out several times on the way down, and was in this state when he impacted with the ground. Upon coming to he experienced dreadful agony in his abdomen and groin and discovered he was unable to move below his waistline. Taken in a cart with others of his crew to a hospital, he had no memory that Sgt Bratton (TG) had assisted him into a Medical Center until informed of the fact at a 381BG Reunion in 1985. Here the doctors' examination confirmed he had suffered a fractured pelvis. The civilian hospital was to be Earl's home for many weeks while the laborious and very uncomfortable healing process was complete. Then it was off to Dulag Luft for the standard interrogation spell, after which he ended up at Stalag Luft III, Sagan.

The sole other loss of the same mission was 42-32088 piloted by Lt. Blog, flying as Group Deputy Lead. The bomber had been set on fire in No. 3 engine just before Lt. Sharp's B-17 was struck, and quickly fell away with up to eight parachutes appearing. The aircraft came down near Mehrin airfield, and seven of its crew were swiftly rounded up. However, Lts. Blog and George Dennis (CP) were to be at liberty for a full 48 hours before they were finally apprehended.

One of the crewmen returning to Ridgewell could regard himself as both lucky and unlucky. T/Sgt Floyd Hanson (535BS) had been wearing a flak suit, but the metal fragment, which created the wound in his side, had passed through the slight gap between the front and back sections! Happily, its force must have been largely spent, otherwise the outcome could easily have been fatal. As it was, Hanson was able to walk to an ambulance with the assistance of two Medical Orderlies.

Lt. Van Buskirk is pictured in confident pose under the chin-turret of his B-17G. His A-2 jacket bears the 532BS insignia, which is a flying Trojan Horse.

A pre-Invasion target was featured the next day when Villacoubley airfield, outside Paris, was the focus for attack, although only a sparse force of 13 bombers led by Maj. Shackley shared in the 1BD effort. The 21st of the month would prove to be the final respite for the Group during May. What was an intense operational spell commenced with a run to Kiel when Maj. Briggs (534BS CO) took the lead. Patchy cloud persisting all the way across the North Sea did not prevent the bombardiers from delivering their ordnance directly onto a factory within the port area. An aircraft factory in eastern France was next on the list, but this time around a persistent undercast prevented the Primary from assault. Col. Leber accordingly diverted his force to the Secondary, a marshalling yard at Saarbrucken, where a convenient hole in the cloud allowed visual sighting and release to be effected.

The following morning the briefing map outlined Berlin as target city for the fourth time in May. The previous three missions, although strenuous, had seen fighter opposition in particular greatly reduced in comparison to the March and April series of runs to "Big B." They had also proved relatively inexpensive, with just the duo of losses on the 19th. Outward passage this day, although uncontested by the Luftwaffe, had proved difficult if not dangerous. This was due to thick cloud and haze adversely affecting visibility, which was compromised further by the lingering contrail patterns from preceding Groups. Flak was meager, and a partial lightening of the clouds over Berlin gave the bombardiers a visual target sighting. Up to this point the mission appeared to be evolving into no more than a tedious exercise in formation flying, but a dramatic turn was to occur just as the bomb-run was being completed.

The 381BG had completed its run in the Lead and High Group elements of the 1CBW (the 398BG were not operating this day, which probably explained this sub-division of the Ridgewell force). The crews were turning off left for the Rally Point when a large formation of Fw190s and Me 109s swept in to the attack from both frontal and rear angles. (At the Group de-briefing, some crewmen asserted the assaults occurred before the target was bombed, but the majority of reports cited a post-target time-spell). Regardless of this disparity in time, the result of the action was to prove a disaster for no less than six B-17s and their crews.

Lt. Higgins (535BS), flying within the Lead Group's High Sqdn. in 42-31878 "Spamcan" was said to have blown up with

Hospitality, English style. The support personnel had greater opportunity to cement relations with the local population. In this picture S/Sgt Ray Ater, Engineering Section (on right) and T/Sgt Gilbert Staatz (Photo Section) are making one of their regular visits to Mr. and Mrs. Warren, residents of Ridgewell village.

no parachutes sighted. In fact, four men survived – all officers, other than Higgins and T/Sgt Baird (Eng.). Lt. Burns (CP) recalled that the order to bale out had been given by Higgins, who appeared uninjured, whereupon the four others up front had promptly gone out the nose hatch. The B-17 crashed between Melchow and Biesenthal, and the six dead crewmen were buried in the area. (Higgins and three of the others among those lost had already served a tour of duty with the 15USAAF in Italy and had been flying between their seventh and tenth mission with the 381BG.)

A second 535BS crew flying within the same Sqdn. as Lt. Higgins was also taken down. Sgt. Harris (WG) in 42-31990 "Stage Door Canteen" saw Lt. Dasso in 42-39890 "Return Ticket" start to slide out to the right and almost strike his (Harris's) B-17. A few seconds later the right wing outboard of No. 1 engine became detached, upon which the B-17 rolled right and suffered a similar detachment to the left wing before the fuselage exploded. At least five of the nine crewmen were killed at this point, with several believed trapped inside when the bomber disintegrated. Lt. Isom (B) was picked up on the ground with just the parachute shroud-lines attached to his harness. A large hole in his head was thought to have been caused by his impacting with the Bendix turret gyro gun-sight when the unfortunate airman was pitched through the nose Plexiglas.

Lt. Ezzell was leading a Sqdn. in 42-38010 and was observed with a smoking No. 1 engine with a similar condition quickly developing in No. 3. He made a slow let-down with at least three crewmen being seen to bale out. In fact, only Sgts. Beninga (BT) and Schaaf (TG) were not clear of the doomed bomber when it finally went out of control. Schaaf had reported that he had been wounded, and the surviving crew thought that Beninga had gone to his assistance, with both men being trapped by centrifugal force. The 532BS aircraft came down near Wilmensdorf.

The 534BS suffered the loss of two crews, the first of which was led by Lt. Gardon flying 42-31291. Flying as No. 6 in the Lead Group, Lead Sqdn. Gardon's B-17 suffered an attack from 11 o'clock, which set the No. 3 engine and the surrounding wing area on fire. Two eye-witnesses stated the aircraft blew up a matter of seconds later, while a third said that another B-17 settled back down through the formation before lowering itself onto Gardon's B-17. On board Sgt. Neal (TG) had heard Lt. Moseley (B) call in "dogfight ahead," following which the bomber's nose was struck hard and fire took hold. The aircraft sagged and levelled off three times before O'Neal jumped, leaving it to crash near Wilmensdorf. Eight of the crew survived, with their pilot being the sole fatality. The other 534BS bomber to be taken down belonged to Lt. Wardencki. This was 42-97214 "Carolina Queen," which had been involved in a dramatic crash-landing on 8 April at the hands of the now deceased Lt. Leslie Bond (KIA 18 April). The B-17 was reported as being shot down in quick succession to Lt. Gardon when it blew up as a result of the initial fighter thrust, leaving no survivors among the nine-man crew.

Sgt. Dick Schneider (TG) was flying in a 533BS bomber, which was adjacent to the fellow-Sqdn. crew of Lt. Wainwright

Lt Williams (right) stands with his 534BS crew in the framework of "Joanne's" left elevator. His co-pilot, Lt. Paul Lear, heads the line with Lt. Parke Tamplin (B) third from left. Heat from the explosion of two Group bombers through which the B-17G flew on 24 May '44 has buckled the fin center-section surface, as well as burning off all control-surface fabric. Sgt. Ross (TG) baled out over Germany.

flying 42-31698. Dick had become friendly with this crew's tail-gunner, Sgt. Nalley. A short time before the fighters struck he had made visual contact with Nalley by moving his guns as a signal. Dick's next sight of Wainwright's B-17 was as a flame-wreathed mass after being involved in a collision with a bomber which had dived into it. Burning trails of gasoline enveloped Dick's B-17, and the heat effect started to roast him. Hearing no response to his calls from the pilots, and believing the bomber was doomed, he prepared to bale out. Fortunately, the pilot called in with a positive report on the B-17's state just as he was about to jettison his hatch and he resumed his position.

There should have been a seventh loss which involved Lt. Williams (534BS) flying 42-97174 "Joanne." The B-17 was second element leader in the same Sqdn. as Lt. Gardon and had flown directly into the fire-ball created by the pair of colliding bombers. The natural-metal-finished bomber emerged from the pall of flame and smoke in a parlous condition. Its nose and cockpit Plexiglas was fire-blackened, and all the fabric had been burnt off the control surfaces. In addition, the crew was minus Sgt. Ross (TG), who had baled out on the not unnatural assumption that he was sitting in a doomed aircraft! Williams, along with Lt. Paul Lear (CP), skilfully kept his charge aloft and in formation by using nothing more than the sets of trim-tabs! Since forward visibility was virtually nil as a result of the smeared windshield, the landing back at Ridgewell must have been fraught with risk. In spite of this severe limitation, Lts. Williams and Lear brought off a perfect approach and touchdown. "Joanne" was wheeled away for a thorough inspection and refurbishment to combat status, but a return visit to Berlin on 21 June would sadly prove lethal.

A second crew rode their luck when cannon shells started a fire in their B-17's nose compartment. The resultant blaze in 42-40017 "Me and my Gal" was tackled energetically and successfully by T/Sgt Paul Vanderzee (Togglier). The crippled aircraft was brought back by Lt. Yates (535BS). A mere six days later both airmen were to be presented with a similar situation.

Good fortune also attended 42-31990 "Stage Door Canteen" bearing Lt. Arthur Bailey's 533BS crew. The hydraulic system had been rendered inoperable, and five shells had knocked out No.3 engine, the radio compass, and the oxygen system in the rear compartments. The "windmilling" propeller on No. 3 could not be "feathered," and its vibration severely shook the entire airframe. Lt. John Anderson (CP) was also shaken when a stream of red fluid shot up and streaked the navigator's astrodome. His fear that it was blood from a badly wounded or dead navigator or bombardier proved unfounded; in fact, a hydraulic pipe had burst and sprayed out its contents!

Unable to maintain formation, Lt. Bailey was forced to utilise the heavy cloud in order to avoid any marauding fighters. However, his erratic course was tending to interfere with his navigator's course plotting. Conformation of this problem was duly made when the lone B-17 found itself over-flying Bremen with its formidable flak concentration, which now put more holes in the aircraft than were inflicted over Berlin! As much surplus equipment as possible was jettisoned as the coast was being approached, while the waist, ball, and tail-gunners were having to exist on no more than three emergency oxygen bottles. The braking system was "out," and so Lt. Bailey hit upon the alternative of parachutes. S/Sgt. Paoli (TG), along with S/Sgt. Highsmith (RW) were ordered to secure their packs and "pop" them out of the jettisoned rear and tail hatches just after landing. The resultant retarding effect of the twin canopies successfully halted "Stage Door Canteen" about three-quarters of the way along the main runway. (This crew would feature in a second dramatic incident on 21 June when their landing would be made – in Sweden!)

Blissfully aware of the carnage over Berlin was Lt. "Zip" Zapinski (532BS). During Group Assembly he had lost a propeller governor unit, but "feathering" the affected engine could not prevent a steady drift back through the formation even after the bomb load had been jettisoned. Having finally "aborted" and while on course back to Ridgewell, T/Sgt Webb (ROG) picked up a distress signal from another B-17 about to "ditch." The downed bomber was eventually located, and a vessel seen in the immediate area was flashed the necessary co-ordinates for the crash-site. What would have been a long mission in normal circumstances now turned into an even more protracted

The full extent of fire damage to 42-97174 "Joanne" from the 24 May '44 Berlin mission is depicted in this post-mission shot. The fabric surfaces on ailerons, rudder, and elevators were virtually burnt away.

effort as the "impromptu" Air-sea Rescue duty was finally completed after eleven hours. It was a particularly bone-tired team that tumbled out of their B-17 that evening, although the nine airmen must have felt a sense of satisfaction in respect of their "mercy" mission.

The loss of eight B-17s within six days must have acted as a sobering reminder to the combat crews. If any among their ranks had still harboured thoughts that the going was becoming progressively easier during May, then the last two visits to the Reich Capital would have firmly quashed such an illusion. There was a long path still to tread before the Nazis' military forces and their civilian industrial support machine were to be vanquished, and in fact, the German nation would "fight to the death." (It is an open question whether the agreed Allied policy of "unconditional surrender" announced at the Casablanca Conference was to prove counter-productive. Under the Declaration's stark terms, all Germans – whether Nazi or otherwise – were to be treated the same under the stark conditions of that policy. Since there was nothing with which to negotiate, the entire nation was arguably welded together in a common feeling of "sticking it out" right up to the final, if inevitable, outcome on 8 May 1945.)

No less than 21 airfields, marshalling yards, and coastal gun batteries throughout France and Belgium were attacked on 25 May. The specific target allotted the 1CBW was Nancy/Essey airfield, and in the lead was Col. Leber, who was to depart for the Rest Home upon his return. The 75 bombers were split among the 91BG and 381BG, with the 398BG the sole 1BD Group not called upon to operate. The 8USAAF remained on the ground next day, but there was still an event of note at Ridgewell. A ceremony was laid on which for once related solely to the ground personnel. A number of crew chiefs were awarded the Bronze Star (the latest decoration to be granted Presidential authorisation). The qualification for the medal required an assigned bomber having completed 30 missions without incurring an "abort." No less than five chiefs – M/Sgts Fitzgerald, Gerberding, Helmer, Shanahan, and "Mouse" Davis – were from the 535BS. There was a twist to the occasion, because the actual medals were still not on hand, despite Group records indicating that the orders had been received at the end of the Official chain!

A chain of marshalling yards across the Central and Southern regions came in for attention on the 27th, with Mannheim and Ludwigshafen specifically allocated to the 1BD, whose bombers dropped over 600 tons. Only 14 out of the 318 B-17s were MIA, but among this figure was Lt. Stuart (532BS) flying 42-107023. His bomber had suffered loss of power in one engine, which he was confident would not prevent him holding position in the formation. However, when the climb to bombing altitude occurred at a point well inside the Continent Stuart announced he was dropping into the CBW's Low Group; shortly after this he turned back for England. As the isolated bomber was coming up through France it was intercepted by fighters whose gunfire landed fatally crippling strikes and forced the pilots to bring off a heavy crash-landing at Champfleury. Only one crewman was killed – Lt. Blyth (N) – although Lt. Eisen suffered a leg injury and had to be freed from the now burning aircraft by other crewmen. After the eight survivors assembled away from the wreck they naturally assumed that Lt. Blyth had also got out and run away into a nearby forest. It later transpired that his body was discovered pinned under the left wing. It was likely that he had been pitched out

The full extent of fire damage to 42-97174 "Joanne" from the 24 May '44 Berlin mission is depicted in this post-mission shot. The fabric surfaces on ailerons, rudder, and elevators were virtually burnt away.

through a section of the forward fuselage that had fractured under what was a severe impact with the ground. Lt. Stuart and four of his crew soon ended up as POWs, but Sgts. Glen, Jones, and Kaplan managed to clear the area and were still in friendly French hands when the region was liberated during September.

One of the crews setting out for Dessau next day was that of Lt. Beackley (535BS) for what was only his second mission. The major portion of the Group ended up bombing the Secondary, an aviation plant at Leipzig, while the remainder dropped on a marshalling yard at Frankfurt. Beackley's problems began over Leipzig when he lost two engines and was forced to drop down to minimum altitude. Although several P-38s had followed the B-17 down and then attempted to draw ground-fire away from their charge, fuel shortage finally forced their pilots to head for home and leave the B-17 still deep inside enemy territory. Crewmembers later reported they were flying so low that they could see Germans firing their rifles or scurrying for cover. Given their combat inexperience – all but the pilot were on their first mission – it was to their credit that they brought 42-97267 "Tomahawk Warrior" safely back to Ridgewell. (Beackley would face another daunting experience during his tour of duty, but would win through in the end.)

Yet another wearying flight was in prospect on the 29th when more aircraft production facilities at Posen in Western Poland were attacked. This severe type of physical pressure was maintained the next day. Lt. "Zip" Zapinski's crew had matured fast since their baptism on 9 April. Not only had they flown 20 missions, but several times had returned with disabled engines and "windmilling" propellers, as well as heavy damage to fuselage and wings. During one landing the No. 2 propeller had flown off and belted the artwork on "Silver Lady" in a strategic position! In fact, "Zip" had piled up so many incidents that he was strongly inclined to name his regular B-17 "So What?," but there is no absolute confirmation that he did so.

The 30 May run to the Junkers production plant at Dessau was probably regarded as just one more notch on the path home, no more and no less. The Group was in the CBW Lead position with Col. Gross (1CBW CO) up front, along with a 533BS crew. The weather conditions were stable, and the chance of a visual strike on the target was in prospect, but the same conditions allowed the Luftwaffe fighters to home in on the bomber stream. On return Gross was to report that when around 40 miles distant from Dessau fighters were sighted in numbers of between 40 and 50, constituting a force sufficient to inflict severe casualties among the B-17s. Their contrails were describing an ominous pattern as the pilots manoeuvered for the classic "twelve o'clock high" approach. Sure enough, as the bombers settled down on a NE heading for the bomb-run, an element of ten Me 109s stormed into the apprehensive sight of the crews, carrying out what was the first of three head-on thrusts to which was added sniping attacks from the flanks. When the battle was over the 532BS was short one B-17 and the 533BS two.

The latter pair of crews were those of Lt. Merrill Burton in 42-102672 and Lt. John Monohan in 42-38188. Burton was flying No. 2 in the Lead Sqdn's second element. His B-17 was struck and set on fire between the Nos. 3 and 4 engines, and the B-17 peeled off and down to the right. It then completed almost a half circle before being reported as levelling off and then blowing up. Both pilots were killed, along with S/Sgt Powell (BT) and T/Sgt John Eylens (Eng.). The latter named crewman had saved his B-17 when it had caught fire during the 16 March mission to Munich. Eylens was last observed fighting the flames engulfing the bomb bay with a fire extinguisher, but his chute pack was not attached to his harness. One of the surviving crewmen recalled the nose hatch being stuck, followed by a frantic call from Burton to "get the hell out"; as this airman baled out he was struck by the right wing as it folded up, but fortunately was only slightly injured.

Sgt. Bob Hittel (TG) had just returned from the Base hospital where he had recovered from a frozen foot condition and was flying this mission as a "spare." He responded promptly to the bale-out bell, but was still scrambling for his escape hatch when an explosion blew him out into mid-air. As he floated down and approached the ground he spilled air from his chute in order to avoid landing in a lake. Once on the ground he was surrounded by a group of farmers wielding various implements, but he was escorted to a nearby village without any physical punishment. Here he was joined by S/Sgt Hammond (WG), who had also been blown out of the bomber. As they sat under a tree and pondered the probability of their being mis-treated by the civilians surrounding them, a passing woman bearing a basket of apples handed each an apple; this simple and unexpected act greatly alleviated the airmen's fears.

A large Mercedes then drove up, into which they were bundled to be driven to a local Luftwaffe base. At the door of his cell Bob was asked to chalk his name on a board. He had written HIT when the guard swung at him with his rifle butt, under which Bob ducked. The German had evidently thought his captive was in the process of writing HITLER! Happily,

Bob then induced the guard to look at his dog tags, and the situation was resolved. At a later stage in his interrogation Bob was to wryly recall the words of his German-born grandfather. As a child, whenever he would show distaste at a particular food item on the table the old man would growl "Du ist noch Stroh, mein Kleiner" (You'll eat straw yet). What his words were suggesting was that one day Bob would find himself so hungry that he would be only too glad to do so. This memory from the past now came to Bob, who was experiencing extreme hunger pangs as he was sitting in his cell with its floor littered with straw!

Lt. Burton's B-17 had crashed between Piethen and Cattau, SE of Kothen, where the Luftwaffe base was located, and the four dead crewmen were extricated from the wreckage and buried in the town cemetery. A post-war witness whose father was on leave from the Russian front hurried behind him to the crash-site near Gnetsch. Coming across several SA members firing up at the descending American parachutists, the father drew his pistol, placed it against the chest of the ring-leader, and said "One more shot and I will kill this man." This drastic threat had the desired effect, and the shooting abruptly ceased. (It was never clear whether any fatalities occurred among the parachuting airmen, although records show that those buried were found without their chutes in or around the wreckage). This crew was a very experienced team, with individual members having flown between 25 and 27 missions, which proved once again that the "Grim Reaper" did not discriminate in selecting his victims.

Capt. George Porter (right) was part of the S-2 Intelligence section. He is seen with another officer preparing documents for next day's mission – a momentous one in this instance, as the photograph was taken on the Eve of D-day.

In Lt. Monohan's B-17, instant carnage resulted from the fusillade of shells. T/Sgt Hoyle (Togglier) was killed instantly in his seat, and it was believed that S/Sgt Catter (Eng.) was a second victim. The No. 2 engine was disabled, and the bomber now drifted back and out of the formation. The bale-out order was quickly given, but Lt. Monohan did not survive, being seen by Lt. Cea (CP) with a spilled chute at the nose hatch. The fourth fatality was S/Sgt Emanualsen (WG), who was last sighted at the rear hatch. The bomber finally impacted about 8 kilometers east of Kothen. Monohan's crew were similar veteran contemporaries of Lt. Burton, being at least halfway through their combat tour.

The third B-17 downed was 44-6025 flown by Lt. Zapinski. Lt. Bob VanBuskirk (B) was peering forward when he picked up the incoming wave of Me 109s. He had the responsibility for operating the Bendix chin-turret, but had never hitherto had the opportunity – here was his chance, at last! He did his best to zero-in on the fighters, but with little or no discernible effect in the split seconds allowed for him to fire. In years to come he would acidly sum up the action; "I didn't get them, but they sure as hell got us!" Although the badly damaged bomber was headed in a NW direction, the eventual ignition of No. 3 gas-tank forced Zapinski to ring the bale-out bell. The abandoned B-17 was seen to circle menacingly over Karow, a small village NE of Burg bei Magdeburg. It finally swooped in over the rooftops to impact in a field scant yards away from the houses.

All the crew, bar Lt. VanBuskirk, were captured in this area. Bob had been the first out and had delayed opening his chute until close to the ground and a large forest. Once down, he got out his compass and started in what was an indicated Westward direction. All through the remainder of the long day and into the ensuing night he trudged on. However, when the dawn light came he was dismayed to find himself virtually back at his starting-point! Not long afterwards his bid for freedom was ended when he was apprehended. The days of three-engine landing for Zapinski and Bob's use of his cine-camera were now closed out. (Amazingly, Bob's mixture of colour and monochrome film survived both official and unofficial scrutiny to get back to his family in California!)

The B-17 flown by Lt. Yates (535BS) was reduced to three engines after the initial attack, and for the next 30 minutes the pilots were engaged in a desperate solo battle for survival against the fighters. At some stage during the series of twisting, rolling, and zoom manoeuvers Lt. Klutho (CP) and S/Sgt Dixon (Eng.) baled out. T/Sgt Paul Vanderzee (Togglier) took over the right-hand cockpit seat in order to assist Lt. Yates. A

"Stage Door Canteen" suffered this serious damage during her century of missions. The "runaway" propeller on No.1 finally became detached and smashed into its neighbouring engine, knocking it partially out of its mounting. It required a fine act of airmanship by the pilots to bring the B-17G home in this condition.

second engine was disabled, but this potentially lethal loss of power was thankfully countered by the belated arrival of escorts, which drove away the Luftwaffe and left the B-17 to continue home alone. Yates and Vanderzee were recommended for the Silver Star, with the latter airman's citation making reference to his heroism on the 24 May Berlin mission. In the event, the awards were reduced to DFCs.

Col. Gross later recalled the ferocity of the Luftwaffe pilots. Two Me109s shot past his B-17 with one barely skimming over, and one barely under, the same wing. The resultant air pressure created by their action was felt throughout the bomber's entire airframe. A strike on the aircraft's batteries in the nose compartment filled it with smoke, and Gross called up to see if the occupants were still there. He need not have worried about Capts. Brunning (N) and Bill Johnson (B). Despite the fighters, flak, and smoke, they were setting up for what would be a successful bomb-run, and for which they would both be awarded the DFC. Gross said; "They were there to get bombs on target, and that is precisely what they did, in spite of the hell that was going on around them"

The mission on the 31st was in stark contrast to the mayhem experienced over Dessau. Twenty-five aircraft unloaded onto Florennes airfield in France, although the heavy cloud obscured confirmation of the result. With pressure building up for D-Day the normal rule of not blind-bombing a target in a Nazi-occupied country was again waived. The strategic and tactical watershed due to be created in six days by the Invasion of Europe was naturally still unknown to the combat crews. The benefits for the "Big Friends" arising from the steady rolling back of the Germans in France and Belgium would only start to materialise around September. From this point onwards the crews would often find themselves spending less time over enemy territory. However, there would be a reverse problem looming in the shape of the German Flak. This would increase in inverse proportion to the shrinking boundaries of the dying Nazi Empire. So it would be that targets such as the oil refinery complex at Merseburg/Leuna were to become the flak equivalents of Schweinfurt and Oschersleben.

The groundcrew's at Ridgewell were continuing to add their contribution to the truly excellent operational record of the Group within the 1BD, as the following statistical comparison for the month of May confirmed:

	381BG	1BD
Percentage of operational aircraft	84%	76%
Percentage of Early Returns	0.4%	4.8%
Average number of aircraft dispatched	25	19
Average number of aircraft bombing	24	16

13

D-DAY

During the first part of June '44 the 381BG, in common with most of the 8USAAF, would send its bombers to French and Belgian targets as an essential part of the D-Day plan. The full significance of this operational switch was perhaps realised by the crews, but the pace of operations would be seen more as a means to a speedier end of their combat tours. The first of seven consecutive daily missions went out on the 2nd with a double run to France. At 0915 some 24 aircraft carried out a PFF attack on gun batteries near Boulogne, and at 1730 half this number led the 1CBW to marshalling yards at Palisseaux/Massy, close to Villacoubley. The combination of broken cloud and a partial overcast prevented any sight of the bombing, even though the briefed altitude of 22000 ft was lowered to 19000 ft.

The morning mission was no. 4 for Lt. John Doyle, Jr. (532BS). He and his crew had already had a rougher induction into combat than most. Posen (29 May) had seen their B-17 lagging behind and calling for emergency landing facilities while jettisoning all excess gear. At one point a "ditching" seemed likely, and the crew took up position in the radio-room. Fortunately, the B-17 made it in over the East Anglian coast, but even then the pilots were forced into a "dead-stick" landing when their last fully functioning engine failed on final approach. As if this were not enough pressure, next day over Dessau an engine caught fire and forced the aircraft to drop out and down to around 5000 ft before the flames were extinguished. Today's easy-paced experience must have left the crews hoping for a regular recurrence, but the realities of combat would only indulge such hopes for a further 17 days. Boulogne's gun batteries cropped up again next day, but only six crews from the 534BS took part. It was very different on the 4th when 49 aircraft under Maj. Halsey formed up to strike at the same type of defensive structure at Taillville in the Pas de Calais.

Crews were used to being awakened in the early hours of the morning, especially during the summer; for example, on the 5th the Charge of Quarters (CQ) came around at 0430. Therefore, their exhortations to "Up and at 'em!" at 0100 on the 6th brought only the normal reaction of verbal abuse and no more. The drowsy personnel assembled in the briefing-room

Maintenance of aircraft spanned 24 hours, as evidenced by this night-time shot. Camera had caught 42-39997 in the hangar. Originally titled "Big Mike," the B-17G was crash-landed by Lt. Renick and initially declared Category E. Then M/Sgt Charles Barbier persuaded his superiors the bomber was worth saving, and over a protracted period resurrected his charge to combat status. And the new name for the 533BS bomber? – "Frenchys Folly!"

were likely anticipating yet another short run across the Channel. Their wishes were duly indulged when the target was announced as gun emplacements in Normandy. What shook them out of their torpor was the added announcement that they would be bombing ten minutes in advance of the Allied Invasion Fleet poised off-shore to dis-gorge tanks, artillery, and infantry onto the five designated beach-heads! D-Day was here, with all the promise for a successful launch and consolidation, which would ultimately return Peace to Europe. The 535BS diary tersely stated "This is what we came over here for last June and what every Bomb Group in the ETO has been paving the way for."

The guard around the base had been doubled, the groundcrews were already armed, and pistols were now issued to the combat crews for use should they come down in enemy territory. Some officers regarded the arming of the former body of personnel with trepidation, but no incidents of mis-use were recorded during this momentous day. Weather conditions were generally none too good for visual bombing, but all available aircraft totalling 34 were dispatched and split between two formations. Locations at Vers-sur-Mer and Courselles-sur-Mer were unloaded upon without sight of the results, which created something of an anti-climatic feeling among those taking part. A second smaller force of 12 bombers went out later in the day to a target near the strategic city of Caen just East of the Landing Zone.

It was off to the NW French coast on the 7th when 35 crews led by Capt. Armstead (535BS) struck Kerlin/Bastard airfield, close to the infamous U-boat base at Lorient. An unfortunate malfunction of the Lead B-17's bomb-sight caused eight B-17s to release early, but the remaining bombardiers contributed to a good bomb pattern. Flak was moderate but sufficient to put one burst into Lt. John Martyniak's No. 4 engine on 42-97258 "Our Captain," which resulted in oil and gas spewing forth. Full boost was applied to the other three engines, but was insufficient to keep the crippled B-17 either in formation or at a constant altitude.

Further power-loss and a troublesome No. 3 culminated in the pilot calling for fighter escort as the aircraft slumped downwards at around 500 ft a minute. Believing that a long glide could still see his B-17 making it all the way North to SW England, Martyniak called for all equipment to be jettisoned to assist in this bid. Lt. Jim Manion (N) gave the aircraft's position to T/Sgt Paul Stewart (ROG), who made contact with Air-Sea Rescue. No. 267 Sqdn. RAF was stationed at Portreath and was equipped with the Vickers Warwick, an adaptation of the famous Wellington bomber; these mounted motorised life-boats underneath to be parachuted down to "ditched" crews. It was this unit's aircraft which now responded to the call to assist the American bomber, whose hopes of gaining friendly soil were dashed by the time it was abreast of the Channel Islands. Lt. Dick Kellum (CP) worked with Martyniak, while the other seven men filed into the radio-room for the ever hazardous duty of putting the B-17 down into the sea.

The pilot kept calling out his altitude as a means of keeping in touch with the ASR Service. Some seven miles off the Nazi-occupied Islands the bomber was skilfully slid tail-first into the mercifully calm waters to leave the crew intact, apart from two minor injuries. The sea immediately swirled in through the camera-well, and the radio-room was half submerged by the time the last crewman clambered out. Both dinghies were thankfully intact and were released from their compartments, inflated, and gotten into – which was none too soon, since the aircraft sank within two minutes of touchdown! Two Spitfires arrived within a few minutes and circled as the Americans vainly scanned the horizon for signs of the Invasion Fleet. They were probably unaware that the Channel Islands were not included in operation "Overlord," and indeed would not be liberated until May 1945.

Several more fighters arrived and hovered above until what was described as a "Wellington" came lumbering into sight an hour later. A further 30 minutes elapsed while the RAF crew calculated the wind and drift-angle in order to ensure a precise drop. Coming in at 300 ft the Warwick released its life-boat. Martyniak reported "These parachutes supported the boat un-

Lt. Art Bailey stands on the left along with his 532BS crew sometime in mid-1944. Officer in center holds the crew mascot, which was a Manchester Terrier – small in size, but ferocious in temperament! Behind them is the former "Big Mike" (42-39997), now re-titled "Frenchys Folly" after major refurbishment and return to the Group's combat strength.

til touch-down when small explosive charges blew them clear. It was beautifully carried out." The men paddled over and climbed aboard, but experienced difficulty in starting up the motors. One did splutter into life, but its propeller blades were fouled by the dinghy-line. Better luck was had with the second motor, and the boat limped along over a mile before an ASR launch manned by RAF personnel hove into sight. The nine men thankfully transferred over again, but a further element of farce attended efforts to secure the lifeboat to its larger companion's stern. Sgt Jackson stated "Soon after we started for home the same thing happened to the launch motor as to our boat – the tow-line tangled in the propeller, and its motor quit!" Fortunately, the launch was twin-motored, and the functioning unit brought its crew and their American Allies back to a SW seaport. There the airmen were given hot food, dry clothing, and medical attention. Next day they were transported back to base in "Yankee Eagle." To complete a "ditching" without incurring serious injury or death was a true bonus for any crew so afflicted; the action was one which could scarcely be practised beforehand, and many crews were not as fortunate as Lt. Martyniak's team.

As part of the interdiction effort to deny vital supplies to the Germans within the Normandy beach-head a railroad bridge at La Frillerie near Tours was taken out by 35 of the 36 bombers dispatched. The 36th had failed to make Group Assembly and attached itself to another Group; however, this "orphan" crew brought their bombs back in company with all the others when the bomb-run was cancelled. On this day S/Sgt Bill Palmisano was awarded the Silver Star for his gallantry over Eschwege on 19 April; despite wounds to his chest and left arm, he had crawled back to his gun and manned it until all enemy fighter activity was ended.

Behind the combat crews were the groundcrews, who received minimal publicity. Behind both bodies were these Sections, who were generally even more disregarded but whose work was just as vital, as in the case of the cooks. Often maligned, they worked around the clock and never refused any request for their services.

Armorers trundle lines of 500 lb bombs out of trucks and along crude "rail-lines" into the bomb dump. Initially, such ordnance was generally inert without the insertion of fuses. However, with the advent of the far more volatile RDX explosive content it was possible for spontaneous detonation of fuse-less bombs if, for example, these were kicked out of trucks onto the ground!

Coastal batteries at Hardelot in the Pas de Calais received a battering from the twin 2000 lb bombs carried by each of the 22 Group B-17s despite 10/10 cloud preventing a sight of the target. The four-hour duration of the mission was one of the shortest on record for some time. Beaumont/Le Roger airfield was hit on the 11th, with Lille/Nord airfield targeted next day. This trio of short-range strikes caused a 535BS diarist to note "Soon we won't be able to make sarcastic remarks about what the Liberator boys do for a living!"

A "scrubbed" mission to Emmerich, West of the Ruhr (13th), and a completed attack upon Melun/Villeroche airfield next day was followed by a mission whose duration raised wry reflections regarding the recent series of short-time operations – at least double the average time was passed in hitting Bordeaux/Merignac airfield down on France's SW coast. The 48 crews formed into two groups, with the larger led by Maj. Fitzgerald and the smaller by Col. Kunkel. An accurate flak barrage at the target seriously damaged B-17G 42-38009 flown by Lt. Kelley (534BS). The bomber dropped out with a smoking No. 3 engine but still under apparent control; up to four chutes were reported out before the aircraft disappeared. (A book written by the Group Chaplain states the crew returned to

Ridgewell, while official records for Group aircraft MIA do not include Kelley's B-17!).

A duo of daily "scrubbed" missions permitted a welcome release from combat, which was as well, since the target called up on the 18th was Hamburg. The break would be even more appreciated over the next eight days because, in spite of 8USAAF commitment to tactical bombing, five of these consecutive daily missions would be deep-penetration ones. Three sub-units were formed out of the 52 bombers, with Maj. Shackley in overall command. Flak was intense over what was Germany's second largest industrial city, as well as its major seaport. Oil refineries at Hamburg and Nisburg were partially cloud-covered, and a diversion to port docks (Secondary) was made despite the presence of a PFF B-17. (Only a fraction of the 467 bombers from the 1BD hit their assigned targets, with the rest of the Division striking their Secondaries).

On the 19th a Hamburg briefing was quickly switched to one for Bordeaux/Merignac. Among the 51 crews heading South was Lt. Doyle in 42-107088 and flying his 13th mission. His was the crew with bad experiences over Posen and Dessau during late May, and their B-17 was the same one that had brought them through both missions. Col. Hall led the main force and Lt. Reese the remainder. Of the 49 aircraft making

Capt. Winters drives a party of 532BS Lead Crew out to the dispersal. They are (L-R) Lts. Normand Klare and Jack McGregor (Pilots), Jim Schomberg (Co-pilot), John Krc (Navigator), and Bruce Rivett (Pilot). In background is one of the huts built by groundcrew, which doubled as living quarters.

the bomb-run only 32 dropped on the Primary, and the rest, including Lt. Doyle, headed for the Secondary.

Post-mission descriptions of this latter strike as being a "milk-run" were not applicable to the Lt's hapless crew. Apparently, two bomb-runs were made, both at the same altitude, speed, and heading – a risky action even when flak was of the "light" intensity. At 0914 while on the run-up 42-107088 received a direct hit on the right wing-root, which totally separated wing from fuselage, as well as blowing the ROG out of his radio-room. The bomber then half-rolled with bombs tumbling out of the open bay. F/O Dick Richards (N), Lt. Bernard Leavitt (B), and Sgt Bob Matthews (TG) scrambled out of the nose and tail hatches, but the remaining six men were held by centrifugal forces until their B-17 smashed into the ground. (Richards also failed to survive, although the reason for his demise remains unclear). Mission No. 13 was always faced with concern; the associated ill luck had been borne out in its full harshness as regards the Doyle crew.

Hamburg was again visited on the 20th by 41 aircraft split into two segments, the second of which was led by Capt. Franek and formed up not with its own CBW but with the 40CBW. All assigned Primaries were hit by the Division, but there was a contradiction between Group records stating that the weather conditions were CAVU and the 535BS record referring to cloud-cover being met for most of the mission. That cover seemed to have been absent over Hamburg at least, because the MPI was recorded as being very tight. There was certainly no disagreement about the flak being "intense"; apart from causing injury to several crewmen it was responsible for one B-17 MIA. Lt. Mark Dunkel (533BS) was flying in the 43-37612 "Old Iron Gut," a 532BS bomber. It was seen to absorb strikes in the bomb bay and then develop a spin from which it never recovered. Four chutes were sighted, but only three men were later confirmed as POWs – Lt. Frank Kelley (N) and Sgts Schmitt and Beaman. Among those who returned injured was Lt. Lessenger flying another 533BS B-17G "Railroader." Hit in one knee, he slumped over the controls, leaving Lt. Wetzel (CP) to not only hold him back, but also fly home most of the route on his own. Lt. Ira Zipperman was struck in the left eye and was so badly injured that he was rendered blind on that side. A third injured airman was a 535BS navigator, Lt. Jim Chisholm.

Berlin was still a prime target for the 8USAAF, which made its latest foray to the city on 21 June. The Group mustered 38 aircraft, with Maj. Halsey in charge and riding in Lt. Jim Tyson's PFF B-17, but with Lt. Reese leading a Composite Group from among the overall figure. Weather was good, but the Luftwaffe

M/Sgt Jim Brewster (534BS) supervises his groundcrew as they carry out repairs to 42-102968 "Via Panola Express" following her eleventh mission. Aircraft was assigned in late May '44 and was salvaged after a forced-landing on the Continent on 10 November.

duly obliged by turning up in force. Between 60 and 80 Fw190s, Me109s, and Me 410s made savage lunges, which included rockets fired from the latter twin-engine type. Group gunners were to state they had never had so easy a time knocking down Jerries, and backed this confidence with claims for 39-17-14! These figures were very optimistic, because 8th Air Force Command allowed an overall maximum of 20 fighters "destroyed" and scaled the Group figures down to 3-8-3!

Flak took over as the bomb-run commenced. One B-17 had already been claimed by the Luftwaffe – 42-31980 flown by Lt. Dassault. The bomber took strikes in the right wing that appeared to induce an explosion. The chin-turret was on fire as the aircraft went down under partial control, and one man was sighted squeezing out of the nose hatch, although up to three chutes were separately reported. In fact, two men, Sgts Elmer Meier (Eng.) and Howard Corum (BT), were later confirmed KIA. This crew had been assigned on 15 May, the same day as Lt. Doyle, and had shared his crew's fate within 48 hours.

The 533BS' 42-38194 "Baboon McGoon" was still in formation, although having suffered numerous cannon shell strikes which had left her with half power. Reports of a large hole behind No.3 engine and a wing on fire proved exaggerated, although bomber and crew were in deep trouble. Strikes from an Me 410 now so damaged the B-17 that Lt. Arthur Bailey called Lt. Lloyd Peterson (N) for a course to Sweden. A second attack resulted in a bale-out order being issued; Lts. Peterson and Erwin Brown (B) responded promptly, but sadly their action proved very precipitate. Whereas they ended up in POW camp, the other seven were destined to become guests of the Swedish Government, as the crippled bomber remained in the air and safely negotiated the Baltic Sea!

An extremely delayed drop saw Lloyd's chute opening bare seconds before he landed near to a forest of tall pines. Bereft of his escape kit, which had slipped out of his shirt after bale-out, he used the Sun as a rough guide for a Northward course in the hope of getting as far as a Baltic seaport and stowing away on a neutral vessel. Having walked all afternoon and well into the evening, he now decided to exchange the fields and woods for the open road. This was an unwise act, because he soon ran into a cyclist coming in the opposite direction. The initial reaction of the German was to momentarily keep on going, before reversing his direction and cycling past Lloyd. He then halted, pulled out a pistol, and motioned the airman towards him – and that was the end of the evasion path and stage one on the route to Stalag Luft III for Lloyd!

Machine-gun maintenance was an absolute priority. This quartet of gunners are working inside a B-17. T/Sgt Art Andrzejewski (left) later changed his name to Tatera. The others are (L-R) T/Sgt McQuire, S/Sgt David Gildin, and S/Sgt Bob Helmer. All are 535BS, with the exception of McQuire, who belongs to the 532BS.

Lt. Roy Pendergist (534BS) was guiding 42-97174 "Joanne" between the flak clusters as much as was possible. He was to recollect that he anticipated a burst on one side by swinging slightly the other way, but guessed wrongly and ended up being hit! With the B-17 on fire he rang the bale-out bell, and was barely out of the bomber himself when it exploded. Seven men survived, but there would be no "Kriegie" status for S/Sgt Hal Lehman or S/Sgt Byron King, and the fate of King remains uncertain to this day.

Berlin flak gunners were rightly regarded as post-graduates at their lethal art, and up to 27 bombers received varying degrees of damage. Maj. Halsey's B-17 had its control cables shot out and the nose chewed up, while the Maj. was struck in his pants by shell fragments. Lt. Ken Cagwin (B) was preparing to unload when a razor-sharp shell splinter measuring 6 x 1 inches sliced through his bomb-sight and dealt a numbing blow to his hand. The splinter then proceeded to slam into the chest of Lt. Chuck Gilpin (N), knocking him unconscious. This was the fifth time Gilpin had been so afflicted in the course of 29 missions – always struck on the chest, and always saved by his flak-vest! Lt. Winters' bombardier, Lt. Pete Kowalski, was hit on the jaw, but managed to complete the bomb-run and close the bomb-doors before passing out. His devotion to duty earned him one of the 22 Silver Stars to be awarded Group personnel. A second Silver Star was won this day by a ball-turret gunner, Sgt Wczolek, who stuck to his post although also badly wounded.

On board 43-37704 "Button Nose" (535BS) a flak burst several minutes after bombs were released demolished the hydraulic system and started a fierce fire in the cockpit. Lt. Oscar Myerscough (P) was sprayed with burning hydraulic fluid. As he leapt from his seat he was dragged down by S/Sgt Clarence Rolla (Eng.), who smothered the pilot's blazing clothing with his hands and body before extinguishing the fire. Meanwhile, Lt. Bob Long (CP) took over the controls until Myerscough (who was very lucky to escape with a singed forehead) was

Fourteen mission symbols adorn the silver-finished nose of "Our Captain" from the 534BS. Eight days after the caption-date this B-17G was "ditched" off the Channel Islands by Lt. Martyniak, all of whose crew survived the experience.

Two 532BS B-17Gs are having their gas tanks replenished from the massive trucks positioned in front of each bomber. Camoflaged aircraft is "Mizpah," and the silver-finished example in background is "Flak Magnet." Both had long combat careers and survived through to VE-Day. Absence of red CBW color markings indicate picture taken prior to July 1944 when these were first applied.

again able to take charge. Total loss of braking power forced Myerscough to have a pair of chute-packs secured at the left waist window and the tail. Their release just after landing proved effective in halting the B-17. "Marsha Sue" was a second bomber making similar use of chutes due to hydraulic failure. Lt. John Winter also utilised chutes in this manner, but after his aircraft's momentum was spent he swung off the runway onto the grass; waiting on hand was an ambulance crew, who hastily drew out the injured bombardier, Lt. Kowalski, and rushed him to the Base Hospital. Despite the loss of three bombers the crews were jubilant at what they regarded as the biggest pasting Berlin had endured, with nearly 1100 tons dropped at a cost of just 16 of the 456 1BD B-17s actually attacking.

The Invasion Front was not being overlooked, and next day 1100 "heavies" struck at industrial locations and airfields in NW France. In addition, over 300 B-17s and B-24s from all three Divisions carried out a separate assault on "Noball" sites in the Pas de Calais. Three 12-plane formations comprised the 381BG contribution. Light but accurate flak was being steadily pumped up as the Group tracked over the target without releasing its bombs. During the run-up 42-97084 flown by Lt. Samuel Peak (534BS) and one of the formation leaders, Lt. Petroski, was hit and caught fire. A few seconds later one wing detached, and the B-17 nosed up above the formation before sliding down to the left and blowing apart; only S/Sgt Oberlin (ROG) was reported as a POW.

This particular loss was hardly an auspicious way with which to celebrate the start of the Group's second year in combat. On a more positive note, compared to the travails of 1943 the 8USAAF was now getting through to its targets while suffering a greatly reduced loss-rate in bombers and crews. In addition, the 381BG was typical of all Groups in the enhanced figures of aircraft dispatched. Whereas the average mission strength up to the year-end had rarely exceeded 20, it was currently not uncommon for double that number to be assembled.

A "Noball" site at Bachimont was struck by a relatively small force of 19 aircraft, and the British G-H blind-bombing system first introduced in May by the 2BD was employed as the crews skirted the meager and inaccurate flak barrage. This was the second of four daily runs to France. A railroad bridge at Tours/La Riche (24th) bore the brunt of 36 bomb-loads, and although a slight but persistent haze made the bombardiers' task none too easy, a good strike was still registered. On the debit side, another B-17 and crew were shorn from Group ranks. Lt. Victor Romasco (534BS) was High Group Lead, and his 42-102585 took a strike in the radio-room that killed S/Sgt Cosandier at his post. The pilots held position for about four minutes before their bomber fell away on fire; shortly afterwards the tail became detached, and the main portion exploded on the ground. Romasco, F/O Chandler (N), Sgt Ernie Waldow (TG), and Sgt Elbert Giddens (Eng) somehow managed to bale out into captivity, but much more fortunate was Lt. Ray Stewart (B), who evaded and ultimately returned to Ridgewell. On the other hand, luck had finally run out for Lt Richard Kellum (CP), who had been on board "Our Captain" when it was "ditched" on 7 June.

The current loss-pattern of six crews in nine days was an unpleasant reminder there was no easy or swift method of beating the Nazis other than to fight them to an utter standstill on the ground, as well as in the air. An airfield at Toulouse/

"Baboon McGoon" has all her armament removed as she sits alongside another B-17 in Sweden. She was flown into that neutral land by Lt. Arthur Bailey (533BS) after suffering severe damage en route to Berlin during the 21 June '44 mission. She had completed 32 missions at this point.

"Happy Bottom's" pristine condition is evident in this photograph. The 532BS bomber is not parked with her Sqdn. around the North Hangar (visible behind the bomber's tail), but is positioned across the field within the 535BS dispersals and close to the control tower. She is probably awaiting the christening ceremony involving Edward G Robinson, which took place on 5 July. "Tomahawk Warrior," seen on the right, caught fire and exploded after landing on 26 April '45.

Francazal (25th) and a bridge at Fismes, also in France (28th), completed June's mission tally. The former target was way down on the Mediterranean coast and could be expected to throw up some opposition, but there was none of consequence. CAVU conditions over Fismes permitted a good strike, but cost the life of Sgt Bill Burens, whose jugular vein was severed by a shell splinter. In contrast to his ill-luck, Capt. Seth Armstead, Lts. Joe Scott, Buchsbaum, Liddle, Watson, Fayard, and F/O Haring, all from the 535BS, were heading home on completion of their combat tours.

June '44 had witnessed the highest monthly missions total flown to date (22), with the next highest being May when 19 were completed. Several of the current month's figure involved short-range runs being associated with D-Day or elimination of the latent (but real from 13 June) threat of the V-1 "buzz-bomb." This was a contrast with May when the bulk of missions were deep-penetration in nature. The noticeable increase in the pace of missions was benefiting many crewmen, since they were now completing their tours of between 25 and 30 missions in a more compressed time-scale, compared to their predecessors from the early months of the Group's presence overseas. Over this period the average time taken to finish-up was six months; now it was not unusual for this time-factor to be cut virtually in half. For example, Sgt Warren Walker (533BS) had commenced on 18 April and flew his 30th by 19 June! Lt. Zapinski's crew had started out on 9 April and was downed while flying their 21st on 30 May. Sometimes even a Lead Crew status could accelerate the mission-rate; Lt. Armor

Col. Leber leans nonchalantly against one of the propellers on "Stage Door Canteen" as actor Edward G Robinson talks to the assembled personnel. During his visit on 5 July '44 he would christen 42-102664 "Happy Bottom" (532BS), but a mere 11 days later this B-17G would be "ditched" by Lt. Jack McGregor!

Edward G Robinson *"does the honors" by smashing a bottle of undisclosed liquid over "Happy Bottom"'s chin-guns. NCO leaning out of the cockpit is believed to be T/Sgt Joe Hudrick, one of the 532BS crew chiefs.*

Edward G Robinson stands by "Happy Bottom," along with (L-R) Maj. Halsey (535BS CO), Col. Leber, Col. Reed, Capt. John Silva (532BS Engineering Officer), and Maj. Fitzgerald (532BS CO).

Bowen (532BS) completed his 25 in marginally over three months.

With the advent of several blind-bombing devices whose efficiency-rating ranged from very approximate (H2X) to very precise (G-H), the 8USAAF felt able to complete missions that would hitherto have been "aborted" as regards bombing. However, the weather over Britain and the Continent was still a factor in causing mission-abortion during the stages of take-off, Assembly, and dispatch into Europe. The experience of the 381BG was again typical of all Groups; whereas the first 100 fully executed missions spanned a ten month period (22 June '43 to 27 April '44), the next 100 would be tucked away by 9 Oct. Not many of the "original" combat crew were around to witness these advances, but two worthy exceptions were Col. Conway Hall and Maj. George Shackley (533BS CO). Both would see out their time at Ridgewell, as well as surviving through to VE-Day. Other senior "originals" were Dave Kunkel (534BS CO), Maj. Bill Fullick (Group Bombardier), and Maj. Jim Delano (Group Navigator), all of whom would experience similar good fortune.

July 1944

As July was entered the strategic bomber forces were still being called upon to provide direct support to the Allied Armies in Normandy. Wehrmacht resistance was very determined despite a vast numerical inferiority, particularly in respect of armored units. The small and heavily hedged fields in the region leant themselves to defensive purposes, and the Anglo-American Armies were advancing at a painful and costly rate. However, the primary function of the Lancasters, Halifaxes, B-17s, and B-24s in pursuing the dislocation of German industry was to be steadily restored even in the course of July. Ridgewell records tended to support this trend, with fully two-thirds of launched missions being to German targets.

It was the 4th before the Group again got off the ground to participate in a 1BD assault on airfields and bridges East of the battlefield, whose intention was to impede Wehrmacht or Luftwaffe reinforcements. However, bad weather thwarted the bombing of the 381BG's target at Tours, and the B-17 flown by Lt. Bob Bobrow (535BS) was MIA. About 20 minutes away from bombing and with his no. 2 propeller "feathered" he called

The triangle L insignia on the wing is the sole indication this is the 534BS B-17G which over-ran into the railroad cutting South of Ridgewell on 13 July '44. Fire and Rescue crews stand on the embankment but can only damp down the wreckage. Only Lts. Houston (P) and Scruggs (CP) escaped before part of the bomb load exploded, killing the other seven crewmen.

Col. Nazzaro returned to Ridgewell on 27 July '44, the first time since he relinquished Group Command and departed for USSTAF HQ. Seen here are (L-R) Col. Leber, Maj. Kidd (S-2), Maj. Kurner (S-4), Capt. Hawkins (Photo Section), Col. Kunkel (534BS CO), Nazzaro, Maj. Goodrum (Group HQ), and Col. Reed (Ground Executive). All were "original" staff, with the exception of Col. Leber.

up to say he could not hold formation in 42-38117 "Touch the Button Nell II." The bomb-load was salvoed, and the B-17 turned back covered by two P-38s. Despite further lightening of the bomber by dumping gear the pilots could not halt the descent, and the crew started to bale out as the aircraft went into a spin around 10000 ft. Sgt Clinton Word (ROG) was one of the first out, and noted how the spin was corrected and the B-17 nearly pulled out of its dive. Much closer to the ground Sgts Ken Hitchcock (WG), Polski (BT), and Synder (TG) decided to jump, but only the former had time to pull his ripcord. Three of the four officers and probably the engineer were still on board and died in the crash, while the fourth officer who followed Word out cruelly got 'hung upon a propeller blade and also perished.

A return to the "Rocket Coast" (Group diarists' title for the Pas de Calais) on the 6th saw the involvement of the entire 1BD in plastering V-1 sites. This mission was to signal a four-day combat spell, with two further short-range and one long-range sortie. An aircraft plant at Leipzig/Mockau (7th) was visited by 36 crews headed by Col. Leber. Moderate to intense flak did not prevent the MPI from being smothered in the bursts from all three CBW Groups. Only a handful of fighters were seen, none of which attacked the 381BG. The next day two 12 plane formations went after V-1 sites at Rely and Coubronne. The Primary was cloud-covered on the 9th, but a 4/10 to 6/10 undercast allowed a visual strike on St. Omer airfield, which was currently housing one of the elements of JG 26.

The Bavarian city of Munich was a major industrial center, which for three days commencing 11 July became the single focal point for the 8USAAF. With this prime target situated in SE Germany the bomber crews were facing a long and wearying day's work each time. Visual conditions were consistently poor, and all attacks were completed with H2X radar assistance.

Upwards of 100 crews took part in the trio of missions, and all returned safely to Ridgewell. However, this record was sadly marred on the 13th. The 534BS B-17 flown by Lt. John Houston was barely off the runway in the early morning murk when power was lost in two engines. Lts. Houston and Bill Scruggs made at least two attempts to line up with the runway in the face of an inexorable loss of height, but this proved impossible in the extremely limited visibility. The third time around the B-17 barely cleared the Southern edges of the base

A visiting B-17F from the "Bloody One Hundredth" based at Thorpe Abbotts is parked outside one of the hangars. In front of the B-17 is the Piper Cub used as a "hack" machine, and to the right is a fully armed P-47 from an un-identified Group. Photo was taken no later than mid-June '44 when the B-17 returned States-side.

This silver-finished B-17G was one of three PFF bombers assigned to the 533BS. The radar equipment is housed in a retractable "dust-bin," which displaces the ball-turret. Bomber was first assigned to the 533BS during Sept '44 and was lost on 22 March '45 when Lt. Fawcett and nine other crewmen were KIA.

before being set down smoothly in a wheat-field. Fortune now intervened to convert a miraculous bid into a disaster. The bomber's momentum was almost spent when it slid at right-angles into a gully through which the local railroad line ran.

The fuel tanks ruptured, and the aircraft went up in flames, but it was several minutes later that three of the 500 lb bombs exploded. In that all-too-brief period the pilots forced their way out of the cockpit side-windows. Lt. Houston was slightly burnt, but was able to run clear of the crash-site. Lt. Scruggs was less lucky, since he was hampered by a broken leg as well as being seriously burnt as he worked his way up over the blazing wing. He had barely managed to crawl up over the lip of the gully when the explosion occurred, and it is possible that he was further burnt by sprays of burning gas as he lay helpless. None of the other seven crewmen ever succeeded in getting clear. It was possible they had been knocked out or even affected by a form of mental paralysis known as "negative panic," where the mind blanks out to leave a sense of lassitude. Whatever the reason, they had become the latest victims of combat flying at Ridgewell. It seemed an eternity before the ambulance could negotiate the twisting English roads to get through to the crash, and even when achieved the medics had to return to the Base Hospital to fetch a supply of morphine with which to dull the co-pilot's agony. He was on the Critical List for some time, but eventually recovered, as did his physically lesser affected pilot, Lt. Houston

On the 5th the base received a VIP of some note when Edward G. Robinson arrived. The reputation he had earned on the cinema screen for playing gangsters with an excess of muscle and a corresponding lack of brains was not evident, because here was a man of much cultural background. His presence centered around the christening of a silver-finished B-17G of the 532BS (42-102664) with the name "Happy Bottom." Far from remaining in the company of the Senior Staff, the actor circulated among the various ground echelons, which included those on KP duty in the kitchens. He was escorted up onto the flight line for the ceremony, where he delivered a superb impromptu speech, which particularly emphasised the need for continued links between America and Great Britain. Then he was gone, leaving his "baby" to face her next mission on the morrow.

Despite the fact it was mid-summer, weather conditions remained very indifferent on the 16th when Munich and Augsburg were attacked. Flak formed the main defensive barrier and was intense as PFF techniques were resorted to for bombing. "Happy Bottom" was participating and was being

Aerial view of the Southern hangar with the Photo laboratory and Motor pool tucked in behind. Two "Hangar Queens" from the 532BS and 533BS are reduced to fuselages and inner-wing sections, the detached parts being cannibalised for use on other bombers.

flown by her regular pilot, Lt. Jack McGregor. His combat career with the 532BS would progress to a happy conclusion, whereas his B-17 was now fated to fall after only a handful of missions. Damage to the bomber caused by flak proved so severe that the pilots were forced into a "ditching" off the Essex coast, from which all nine men emerged safely.

Two days later a mission dispatched the 8USAAF bombers to the experimental rocket-center at Peenemunde on the Baltic coast. So far the ten July missions had cost just two B-17s, but a third was about to be added, though in much more favorable circumstances for its crew. Lt. O'Black (533BS) flying in 42-102663 was forced by flak damage to divert Northward into Sweden, where the entire crew was interned. This was the second Sqdn and third (and final) Group bomber to seek neutral sanctuary.

Crewmen were trained to react to every possible situation, regardless of when an emergency might arise. Sometimes such reactions could be counter-productive to the extent of bringing death or injury. This scenario arose in the darkness of the 19th as the bombers were taking off for Lechfeld. S/Sgt Paul Stewart, a 534BS radio-operator who on 7 June had "ditched" in "Our Captain," responded to the bale-out bell and threw himself out of the rear door, despite the gunner's efforts to restrain him. The delay in pulling his rip-cord almost proved fatal, because the B-17 was still low over the countryside. As it was, the braking effect of the canopy did not prevent him from slamming into the ground with dreadful force.

As if this were not bad enough, the injured airman's experience was to span a period of at least eight hours. Firstly, although his absence was radioed back, his pilot had little idea where Stewart had come down other than along the take-off path. Secondly, the winding English roads and small fields made the task of location doubly difficult. It was mid-morning before Col. Leber had an aircraft sent up to spot the Sgt., but the pilot's efforts were spread over a protracted period before he eventually picked out the spilled chute canopy. What now proved equally difficult was to direct those on the ground to the position. As the aircraft circled its pilot tried to guide the rescue vehicles, but it was well after mid-day before Stewart was finally reached. He had suffered fractures to his back and both ankles, and would spend many weeks in a plaster-cast at the 121st Hospital, Braintree. While this dramatic individual recovery was running its course, the Group bombers were plastering the depot and training base at Lechfeld at no cost in aircraft or crews – a basic situation holding true until 31 July.

This might not have been the case next day had the Group been in the CBW Low Group slot instead of the 91BG. The Bassingbourn crews were literally at the tail-end of the bomber-stream, and worse still had become detached just as what was probably a Sturmgruppe caught the B-17s and handed out summary punishment to the tune of eight. Instead, no fighters were seen as the 381BG delivered a good strike in perfect weather conditions to an aircraft plant at Dessau. (This was a distinct improvement compared to the previous Group run to this tar-

Smoke marker bombs were released by Lead B-17s at "bombs away" in order to provide an additional indication for bombardiers or toggleers to follow suit. This example is mounted under the wing just outboard of the fuselage/wing joint.

get on 30 May.) A much more familiar name was called up on the 21st when Schweinfurt's ball-bearing plants were chosen. This was the Group's fifth visit, and the contrast between the first on 17 Aug '43 could not have been more striking. A good bomb-run in the face of heavy flak ended with an equally sound release, and all aircraft returned.

The American 1st Army was gathering its strength for a break-out at St. Lo, and the 8USAAF was called upon on both 24 and 25 July to blitz the German defence lines prior to armor and infantry advancing. The Group provided 54 out of the nearly 1600 B-17s and B-24s sent out the first day, but more than 500 were prevented from dropping due to ground haze. Two less crews headed out next day to repeat the task of helping to put over 3000 tons of bombs down on the hapless enemy. Bombing was conducted from a relatively low 14000-ft altitude, but errors in target-approach and in the use of ground marker flares caused a degree of short bombing which killed Gen. Leslie McNair and more than 100 soldiers.

Oil refineries were given priority by 1BD and 3BD Groups on the 28th and 29th, with the infamous complex at Merseberg/ Leuna being struck by over 1200 bombers in this 48 hour period. On each occasion PFF methods were used for the drop as moderate to heavy flak tracked the formations, but fighters left the 1CBW alone. The Presidential Citation for the Oschersleben mission on 11 Jan. '44 was announced on the 29th. This was the Group's second Distinguished Unit Citation award in WWII, the first being for Bremen on 8 Oct '43.

A 24-hour stand-down preceded the last monthly mission when the 381BG attacked the BMW aero-engine plant at Allach, NW of Munich. Cloud piling up to 27000 ft did hamper the operation all the way in, but several clear patches over Allach permitted a quick switch from PFF to visual bombing, whose results were assessed as "good." For Lt. Pearson's crew in their 533BS bomber (42-102423) the result was far from good. Their B-17 was last sighted after "bombs away" with two engines knocked out and on a Southerly heading. No chutes were seen, but all nine men did survive a crash-landing at Biberach/Kies in Wurttemburg Province to become POWs.

14

OIL - THE NAZI ACHILLES HEEL

It was now almost two months since "That Mighty and Noble Venture" talked about by Winston Churchill had commenced its course on 6 June. After a period of consolidation and steady advance, the Allied Armies were on the threshold of a decisive break-out which would push the Wehrmacht back towards Eastern France and up into Belgium by the end of August.

For the strategic bomber forces it would mean a release from commitment to the battlefield and a wholesale return to their primary duty of hammering Nazi industrial resources.

Top of the list of industries to be concentrated upon was that linked with oil production. Gen. Spaatz had been credited with pointing out the vulnerability to bombing of this vital industry and of introducing a concerted Campaign against its refineries and synthetic plants from May onwards. Up to now consideration towards Tactical Support on and after D-Day had had priority. However, with the medium bomber and tactical fighter strength of the 9USAAF and the RAF 2nd Tactical Air Force (2TAF) in full flow, there arguably was not the same call for the "heavies" to be so involved in Support operations.

The switch away from Tactical operations was clear from the middle of August. The 381BG's experience was typical of the 8USAAF in that 11 of the 18 missions flown in the month were to German targets. Weather conditions were still very indifferent for what was High Summer. For example, an early morning scheduled take-off (6am) on the 1st was stalled five hours by mist and heavy drizzle. Only then did 37 bombers get off to bomb French airfields at Meulan/Villaroche and Etampes.

A nonchalant Col. Leber with pipe in mouth poses by the side of the Group's L-4, one of several "hack" machines at Ridgewell. Picture taken in mid-1944 to judge by the full foliage on the trees.

T/Sgt Gilbert Staats (Photo Section) stands in reflective pose within a newly reaped and stacked wheat field. The unusually brilliant summer weather provides not the slightest hint of the pressures of War affecting the English countryside.

On 26 May '44 the 533BS received this B-17G. Aircraft 44-6095 quickly became "Fort Worth Gal," whose artwork was based on one of the superbly creative Varga females. Bomber lasted until 10 Sept. when Lt. Germano failed to return from Gaggenau.

This picture of a Group formation returning from a mission depicts the classic pattern for landing. The bomber peeling off to the left will be followed at well-spaced intervals by those other aircraft within its sub-formation.

A similar set of weather conditions 24 hours later put a total clamp on operations, but on the 3rd a similar force coursed over marshalling yards at Mulhouse in Eastern France to drop through 8/10 cloud with unobserved effect. Flak was negligible, but still contributed to the loss of one B-17 and nine men. Just after crossing the coast on the way in, Lt. Wilcock in 42-32049 called up to say he had lost an engine. Shortly after his element leader, Lt. Don Soale (also 534BS), saw him peel off for home, but the bomber never made it. Wilcock's body

The second 533BS bomber and the last of three Group aircraft to divert into Sweden was "Yardbird." Almost one month after "Baboon McGoon" landed at Rinkoby Lt. O'Black touched down at Bulltofta on 18 July, due to heavy flak damage. Armament still has to be removed, but the national insignia is already painted over.

Lt. Sam Whitehead (P) shakes hands with Lt. Saleeby (N) as Lt. Fine (CP) looks on. Gash was caused by a runaway propeller which detached from the No. 3 engine, fortunately without harming Lt. Fine or fatally damaging the bomber. Crew belong to the 534BS.

The tall figure of Lt Whitehead (fourth from right) leads his crew away from their B-17G after completing another mission. This crew's combat tour commenced in April 1944 and was successfully completed by August. Mechanic attending to No. 3 engine has a bucket slung under the mounting; the Wright Cyclone was notorious for exuding oil.

was plucked out of the North Sea by a British ASR launch next day, but his eight fellow-crew still rest somewhere in that turbulent stretch of sea.

A second sortie to the experimental center at Peenemunde went out next day, and all of the 36 attacking crews came home. There should have been one more B-17 taking part, but it ended up a smashed wreck not far from Ridgewell. This was the assigned Deputy Lead, which was a 533BS aircraft (42-97594) flown by Lt. Cupernall and Capt. Moore. Also on board was Capt. Francis Hawkins (Photo Section Officer), getting in one of an ultimate total of six missions. It was shortly after take-off that the B-17 caught fire and finally had to be abandoned. Only S/Sgt Norris (TG) failed to jump, and was found at his post when the bomber's remains were examined at the crash-site close to the A-20 base at Wethersfield.

Underground oil-storage tanks at Nienburg, just West of Dessau, were the assigned target on the 5th. On the way in and over the NW German coast Lt. Melomo, flying as right wingman to the CBW Lead B-17 in 42-97771, was struck by flak based at Cuxhaven and Wilhelmshaven. Lt. Freeman (N) was killed, and the bomber was forced to drop into the Low Sqdn. Even this position proved untenable to hold, so bombs were salvoed and Melomo turned for home. Nos. 3 and 4 en-

Bright morning sunlight and dark-outlined clouds form a breath-taking but somber backcloth to the start of a mission in mid-1944. Embankment at rear forms part of the firing-range and identifies this area of the airfield as that assigned to the 535BS.

gines had been disabled, and when fire took hold some 50 to 70 miles out from the coast a bale-out into the hostile North Sea was forced upon the crew; the Fortress exploded just as the last men jumped. By great good luck, German patrol boats were in the immediate vicinity and picked up five of the crew, some of whom had been immersed for upward of two hours and were terribly weakened as a result. Lt. Melomo and Sgt Gilbertson (Eng.), along with Sgts Hill and Vaughn, were never found. The engineer had been wounded in one shoulder, and the survivors conjectured he had failed to release his harness on entering the water and was drowned. The mission itself was judged a success, with thick clouds of black smoke billowing forth.

While the B-24s of the 2BD punished oil refineries on the 6th, the 1BD went for munitions and machine-assembly plants at Brandenburg. As the target was being cleared flak smacked into 44-6020 "Underground Farmer" (532BS). No. 3 propeller was knocked off and the engine ignited, while No. 4 suffered a "windmilling" propeller. This drastic power loss on one side left the pilots fighting the B-17's asymmetric flight path. The nose Plexiglas was blown off, and both Lt Gomez (B) and an un-named Sgt acting as nose-gunner were either blown out or baled out. The bale-out bell was jammed in the "off" position, but the bomber's critical condition dictated the need for the remaining crew to jump. This they did, coming to ground in the Northern suburbs of Lubeck, while their aircraft crashed in the Baltic. Only S/Sgt Patrick was unaccounted for until a German crash-boat pulled his body out of the sea.

Oil again featured in the first of two days concentration on French targets when 51 aircraft blitzed oil-storage facilities at St. Florentine and Marlotte. Then it was a return to direct support of the British/Canadian Armies, who were seeking to break-out SE of Caen. Persistent tracking flak peppered the

Superb artwork adorns "Smashin' Time!" of the 534BS, which is being christened by Pvt. Cynthia Burfield of the British ATS. Col. Reed's attention appears to have been caught by some other object! This B-17G was salvaged after a forced-landing in SE France on 21 Jan. '45.

"heavies" as they unloaded from just 14000 ft. Over 2400 tons of ordnance pummelled the German troops at a cost of just seven bombers. Flying Group Deputy Lead in 43-37704 "Button Nose" was Capt. Tom Barnicle (535BS). As the bomb-run was in progress a flak strike ignited the bomb-bay, but thankfully did not set off the bomb-load. T/Sgt Glover (Eng.) attempted to combat the flames with a fire extinguisher, but this was suddenly pulled from his grasp.

Pulling the doomed B-17 off to one side, Barnicle headed for the nearby Allied lines as the flames spread inexorably to one wing. When satisfied he was over friendly soil he rang the bale-out bell and followed his crew out; the deserted and dying bomber was left to smash into a school located within the Canadian Army's sector of the Front, which was fortunately unoccupied.

At least two derelict farmhouses within the airfield perimeter were left intact when Ridgewell was constructed. This is the example close to the control tower; it has been utilised as the 535BS Operations building.

Although shaken up and bruised, all the crew were safe. Lt. Jim Long (B) got hung up in a tree, but a British or Canadian private climbed up and helped him out of his harness. The majority of the men assembled at a C-47 base during the day, where they spent the night before being flown back to England. During this brief stay Capt. Barnicle indulged in a crap-game, where he won 700 French francs – an act which ensured he would not quickly be welcomed back!

The regular dispatch of large numbers of bombers could not be maintained forever, and was a prime reason why Groups were granted "stand-down" spells in order to bring their strength back to normal establishment. On the 9th (The seventh consecutive daily mission) the 535BS notes state "This is the first

"Flak Magnet" of the 532BS is photographed in the company of two other B-17Gs of the 535BS. By this stage of the War (Post-July 1944 to judge by the CBW color markings) camouflage had been deleted from all Fortresses.

time in nine missions that the Group has failed to put up CBW strength in aircraft" when only 27 B-17s led by Col. Kunkel went out to attack Saarbrücken's marshalling-yards. Flak was heavy, and although inflicting no aircraft losses inevitably added to the increasing scale of maintenance problems. (The day before no less than 24 bombers had received major damage, of which only ten were available for Saarbrücken). On the 10th a stand-down was finally announced. It was naturally welcomed by the combat crews, but not by the mechanics of the 448th Sub-Depot, who were duly restricted to base in order to bring all aircraft up to operational condition.

Summer weather returned on the 11th with clear skies, and 36 crews bombed fortifications at Brest on the Brittany Peninsula; these were held by the Wehrmacht, which was still resisting all American Army efforts to capture the seaport city. A day's break, and then it was back to action, this time making interdiction assaults on the German Seventh Army snared within the Falaise Pocket; Capt. Sandman (533BS) led 36 B-17s, whose bomb-loads hit an important road junction near Rouen. The 535BS sustained one fatal casualty – its first in many weeks – when Lt. Sweetland's navigator, Lt. Haines, bled to death after a flak fragment took off one leg and nearly severed the other. What was to prove the last mission to a French target for almost two months followed on the 14th, but the 398BG was absent from the 1CBW. Flying in VACU conditions and uninterrupted by flak or fighters, the bombs were deposited squarely on Metz/Frescaty airfield.

Fighter opposition was totally absent in respect of Group operations on the 15th and 16th when Ostheim airfield, South of Cologne, and an aircraft assembly plant at Halle were re-

On 3 Oct. '44 this B-17G of the 532BS over-shot the runway and ended up in a hedge with a collapsed left landing gear. The second frontal view reveals how the No. 2 engine nacelle is badly twisted, and the center of the wing at the fuselage joint has buckled. Aircraft was salvaged two days later.

"Pella Tulip"'s distinctive artwork is well displayed against the B-17G's natural metal finish. The 532BS bomber was one of 200 from the 55-BO production block and arrived at Ridgewell on 22 May '44.

spectively hit. However, Halle proved costly for the 91BG, who near Eisenach lost six within a minute to the Luftwaffe. (The 533BS records state four or five bombers were lost from the succeeding CBW, but no mention of the 91BG losses was made.) While engaged in attacking Ostheim the crews reported seeing RAF Halifaxes and Lancasters striking at similar aviation facilities in Belgium and Holland.

The fine spell of weather deteriorated once again into cloud and rain, and apart from the 18th proved instrumental in grounding the 8USAAF. Capt. Sandman was promoted to Major on the 21st, having assumed command of the 533BS. Three days later he headed 36 crews to hit a factory at Weimar believed to be producing V-1 components. Foul weather at take-off cleared for most of the outward stretch, but a huge cloudbank during target-approach threatened the chance of a visual drop. Fortunately, the bombardiers were left with enough ground-sight to render a solid strike.

The days of short-run missions were over for the immediate future. A Focke-Wulf assembly factory at Neubrandenburg (25th) preceded a trip into "Happy Valley" (the Ruhr) when Gelsenkirchen was attacked. Bombing on the 25th was reported as "not concentrated around the MPI," while bombardiers salvoed into the smoke of the preceding formation's strike on an oil refinery at Gelsenkirchen. A Berlin run on the 27th was "aborted" in favor of Emden, where a blind drop on its port facilities was made.

The playing of "Taps" last thing in the evening was generally taken to indicate a mission on the morrow. Although heard on the 28th and 29th, nothing transpired first time around. Lowering cloud on the 30th suggested non-action, but around 11am a briefing was conducted, and ninety minutes later the B-17s

"Pella Tulip" (42-102703) of the 532BS is seen at Debach, home for the B-17s of the 493BG. On 15 Oct '44 a flak shell inflicted this damage around the cockpit, which seriously wounded Lt Reseigh (P) and knocked out most of the flight and navigational instrumentation. The frontal shot of the B-17G reveals how the damage extended to the top-turret. Salvage action was ordered next day.

were lifting off into 10/10 cloud on the way to Kiel. Weather was no better there, and bombs were released under PFF direction. The moderate flak wrought major damage on a 533BS bomber, 44-6095 "Fort Worth Gal." Throttle and propeller control-cables were severed, and the forward oxygen system knocked out. The B-17 dropped around 6000 ft before Lt. Rolin regained control. Having no way of regulating their speed due to the throttle cables' failure, the pilots were faced with a major problem. It was then that S/Sgt Greathouse (Eng.) made his contribution. He crawled into the nose and grasped the severed cables at a point under the pilots' position. He then reacted perfectly to the instructions fed to him over the intercomm as the B-17 crept home at around 130 mph. Lt. Rolin commented on his engineer's work; "To demonstrate the tremendous job Sgt Greathouse did, we still beat the formation back home!"

September 1944

In September the 1BD did not open its account until the 3rd when a major synthetic-oil plant at Ludwigshafen received over 1000 tons of high explosive and incendiary. This dosage was repeated on the 8th with virtually the same bomber force, and therefore a similar tonnage. On the first Ludwigshafen strike Lt. Fulton (534BS) flying in 42-31569 lost one engine as the Group were at bombing altitude. He lost a second as the I.P. was looming up, whereupon he salvoed his bombs and trailed the formation as it turned for home. Some 30 miles SE of Rheims he called up to say he was altering course towards the Paris region in the hope of gaining the Allied lines. In fact, the B-17 got as far as St. March, south of Dijon, where it was bellied-in after a third engine went "out." All crew survived, despite the fact that the bottom was torn out of the bomber on landing.

In between these two missions lay a period of operational inactivity caused primarily by the weather (although the Group was excluded from operations on the 5th). Another social event of note took place on the 2nd. Actor and singer Bing Crosby was the star performer heading a troupe of entertainers who provided a two-hour show in No. 1 Hangar. They played before an audience comprised of American and British Service personnel and local civilians. The show was the first in a program of activities tying in with the ARC Aeroclub's anniversary and the "Home stretch" in the Victory Squadron War-bond drive. That same evening a mammoth dance was held in Great Yeldham, during which a "Beauty Queen" was selected from among the British Servicewomen. The winner was an ATS, Pvt. Cynthia Burfield, whose "prize" was to christen a new 534BS B-17G "Smashin' Time" the following afternoon. This was also the final day for the 8USAAF War Bond drive, and the 533BS won within the 381BG by purchasing Bonds totalling $32000, which was well above the established "goal" of $20000. The 535BS records on the 4th noted that as part of an overall USSTAF plan to reduce Sqdn combat crew strength to 22, a cadre of men with varying degrees of duty-tour time were being transferred to 12 RCD.

There was no doubt that the B-17 was a responsive bomber in terms of its overall ability to withstand the tremendous air pressures that could build up on its control surfaces. This aspect of performance was more than amply demonstrated on 3 Sept by Lt. Art Bailey (532BS). Directly after "bombs away" the Group made a diving turn to the left through some broken cloud. It appeared the Lt.'s B-17 was in danger of colliding with a fellow Fortress, and he tightened his turn a little more sharply while simultaneously running into turbulence from the preceding Group. The result was that the bomber went over on its back and began a series of vicious spiral turns lasting through several thousand feet.

The pilots managed to correct the spin, but still found their combined strength insufficient to pull their charge out of what was virtually a vertical dive. With the airspeed recording beyond the red "danger" line it looked odds on that only a break-up of the airframe could permit any chance of salvation for the crew. In a final desperate measure Lt. Bailey commenced rotating the elevator trim-tab ever so gradually. Amazingly (albeit painfully slowly), the B-17 eased itself back into level flight

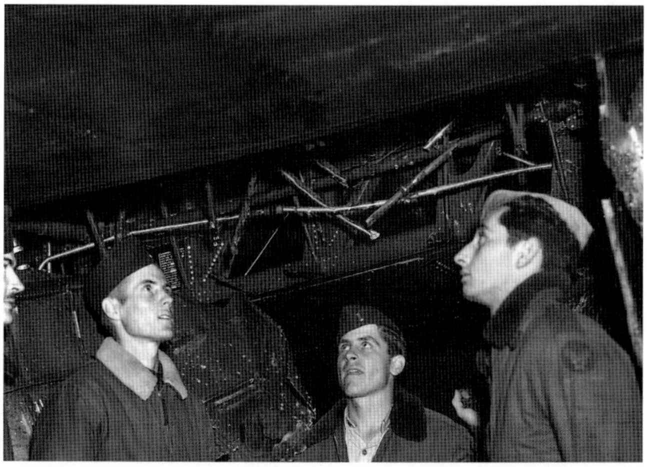

The officer complement on Lt. O'Connors' 535BS crew gaze reflectively at their B-17's severely damaged bomb bay. Flak was responsible for this in addition to disabling one engine. As if this were not enough, the pilots then had to evade the attentions of two Me 163 rocket-jets for several minutes, losing a second engine to their gunfire, as well as having the propeller feathering-control knocked out. B-17G was "Los Angeles City Limits" and date was 7 Oct '44.

"Green Hornet 2nd" took the place of her 534BS predecessor "Green Hornet" when the latter was MIA on 11 Jan '44. She had completed 28 missions when this summer shot was taken and added a number more up to 17 Oct. Then, on return from Cologne, Lt. John Rice was forced to crash-land her in Belgium after baling out his crew, and the badly damaged bomber was declared "Category E."

as the pilots silently prayed the wings would not fracture under the inordinate strain. Art recollected it was a very subdued crew which cruised back to England! (Whenever Art gets a chance to inspect one of the preserved Fortresses, he acknowledges the frisson of fear coursing up his spine at the thought of how such minute flying surfaces as the elevator trim-tabs could have fulfilled the task that the elevators manifestly could not!)

A marshalling yard at Mannheim was hit with PFF assistance on the 9th, and next day it was the turn of a transport-assembly factory in Gaggenau to receive attention. Bombing results were excellent and flak assessed as "meager," at least up to "bombs away." Lt. Germano was flying 44-6095 "Fort Worth Gal," which had recently been brought home despite having severed throttle and propeller control-cables. This time around it was not so lucky when flak strikes left the inboard engines smoking. The B-17 was seen to peel off right, then reverse course on a heading for France with six chutes reported. There were eight survivors, with S/Sgt Siders (TG) the sole fatality. Several crewmembers claimed to have seen a blood-stained helmet and scarf (The latter item definitely belonging to the gunner) which was shown them by a woman; it was the general consensus that Siders had been attacked and killed by civilians. However, a separate report stated Siders had suffered a broken neck after landing in a tree. In addition, the B-17 exploded in mid-air, so it was possible he had failed to get out alive. Whatever the reason, the young airman had forfeited his life.

The extremes of fortune in combat were again highlighted the same day when S/Sgt Yancek (533BS) was reassigned. He had made a premature bale-out over France when the Group was returning on 16 March. T/Sgt Eylens had fought and extinguished the fire started around his top-turret area that had threatened to destroy the B-17 out of which Yancek had baled out, and Lts. Duncan and Franek brought it safely home. It was likely Yancek had got into the hands of the Resistance and was sheltered until the region was liberated in late August.

Oil was still the basic objective for the Allied bombing campaign, and the bombers were directed to Merseburg (11th) and Brux, Czechoslovakia (12th). The German High Command was now fully aware of this trend, and over these two days a strong Luftwaffe presence was felt as the 75 bombers MIA confirmed. However, it appears that these losses were borne by specific parts of the bomber stream, because the 1CBW suffered just one loss in this time. The 381BG were not called on next day, and for the ensuing 72 hours there was no call at all upon the 8USAAF.

The resumption of operations on the 17th was connected to Operation "Market/Garden." The plan involved a drive up through Eindhoven, Grave, and Nijmegen to the vital location at Arnhem, whose bridge spanned the Lower Rhine. Up this corridor, whose length was to be secured by the American 82nd and 101st Airborne Divisions and at Arnhem by the British 1st Airborne Division, would come the British 2nd Army; this force would then sweep around and into the Ruhr – industrial heartland of Germany. In this way it was envisaged the War could be over by the year-end, since the Ruhr's seizure would cut the economic heart out of the Nazi Empire.

Nearly 900 B-17s hammered the enemy defences in Holland during the 17th, and the 381BG added its weight to the assault by attacking gun emplacements around Eindhoven. This was to be the sole departure for the "heavies" from their strategic function during September, apart from next day when B-24s dropped reinforcement supplies to the Parachute Armies. (The 13 CBW of the 3BD also went to Warsaw to drop supplies to the beleaguered Polish Resistance fighters in that stricken city.) Maj. Shackley returned from States-side furlough to resume his 533BS command, which had been assumed by Maj. Sandman during his absence.

Marshalling yards were priority for the 1BD on the 19th and 21st, with Hamm and Mainz the main focal points. The important Hentschel armored vehicle plant at Kassel received 1700 tons from a combined 1BD and 2BD force on the 22nd, but a bad weather spell spanning 72 hours then curtailed operations. The 381BG took part in all three missions, as well as four of the remaining five monthly missions. Two further marshalling yards at Frankfurt (25th) and at Osnabruck (26th) were

The smashed nose compartment on 42-97265 "Hells Angel" of the 535BS bears mute testimony to a tragic accident on 10 Nov '44. Three 110 lb bombs released from another Group B-17 struck the bomber; two knocked off the Plexiglas, and the third lodged inside after killing Lt. Leroy Drummond (B) instantly.

hit with the latter target recorded as the first visual strike within the previous five. Cologne (27th) was a failure for the 1BD in terms of a Primary strike, because almost the entire Division had to divert to Secondary options; the Group records state, "PFF bombing – possibly of marshalling-yards in the city." A Madgeburg run next day also resulted in a PFF attack, which was adjudged to be on the Primary. A comment in the 533BS records says "Flak met at target – but the Luftwaffe appears to be absent!" This was a rather generous comment, especially when considering that 34 bombers in all were MIA.

The bicycle was the primary form of transport, both around the base and whenever the airmen had a few hours to themselves with which to explore the countryside. On one occasion Lt. Art Bailey and several of his 532BS fellow officers visited a Fair about ten miles distant, and the following account is worthy of a first-hand quote:

"The ride was mainly downhill on a narrow road that wandered through the beautiful English countryside, and proved a refreshing change from our normal routine which we found really exhilarating. The Fair was in session, with one big crowd gathered around a platform on which one gentleman from among the local dignitaries was pleasantly haranguing the folk to bid for the prize he held – a single orange. We did not enter the bidding, but I can still recollect the conflict of emotions. As Americans we felt it was good citizenship to join in and express our gratitude towards our Allies. However, by doing so we ran the risk of offending by seeming to flaunt our comparative wealth.

Later in the day Ed, the other crew's bombardier, rushed up to say he had won first prize in a skittles competition, which he proudly said was a pig – a live, grunting, squealing pig. We went over with him to the pen expecting to see a nice little piglet, but were shocked at the sight of a 60-lb beast! Our immediate reaction was that it had been fun and this would provide a good story for our grandchildren – but Hell, it was getting late, so forget the pig and let's get back to base before dark. Ed was adamant we not abandon our prize, and after some discussion the challenge was accepted with misgivings.

It was one thing to win the prize, but quite another to take possession. We drew quite a crowd as a burlap bag was got and we entered the pen. On one side were five Officers in full Class A uniform, on the other a grimy and very agitated pig. The subsequent sounds of battle now consisted of encouraging yells from the five, mad squealing of the bemused porker, and jeers of the crowd. The pig was finally sacked, but by now the victors were grimy and agitated individuals. This was only the beginning, and the real challenge lay in transporting our prize ten miles up-hill to base – on bicycles!

The largest crowd for any event that day gathered around as we realised that none of us was capable of pedalling away with the sack. A discussion resulted in an outcome of pure Yankee ingenuity. We got a pole some six or seven feet long to which the sack was tied, and a cyclist would take each end. The bombardiers volunteered for the initial effort, which was a total failure due to Ed and Bob not being able to co-ordinate a standing-start launch. Stan and I then tried, but still failed. By now we noticed that Hal, the other crew's navigator, had melted into the crowd as though disavowing he ever knew us! The crowd was now several deep and gathered around in an arc just like a marathon start.

We needed momentum that only a flying start could guarantee. With Ed and Bob mounted up, Stan and I held the pole and backed off twenty feet. The pair charged towards us but Ed arrived fractionally ahead of Bob, and the pig got bounced. A second try was a humiliating failure as Stan held his pole-end too low and jammed Bob's wheel to pitch him off; he duly picked himself up and dusted off as the crowd howled with delight at the spectacle. The third attempt ended with a beautifully executed launch, and we were shakily on our way. The pole's greater than expected flexibility, coupled with the bicycles' erratic motion, caused the burlap bag to make contact with the ground on more than one occasion, which upset our future roast pork!

The trip home was a long, grueling nightmare. It was dark, and the totality of the Blackout had to be experienced to be believed. Twice we were literally forced off the road by oncoming trucks, which we could hear but not see due to their dim lights until they were almost on top of us. A warning would be yelled, and the two unfortunate pig "escorts" had no choice but to veer off into an invisible ditch. How we managed to start up again in the darkness I will never know.

We arrived back exhausted and mentally numbed, but soon recovered. Hell, we had performed our most challenging mission of WWII. The pig was well subdued by now, and this situation led to another inspiration. The other crew's co-pilot had a well-deserved reputation for a less than discriminating taste in female company, and would often return from the Club absolutely blotto. His bunk was in a corner by the door, so we tied the pig under the blankets before turning off the lights.

A string of incendiary bombs cascade down from this veteran B-17G of the 534BS sometime after July '44. Presence of a solid undercast almost certainly means PFF methods of aiming were being used. GD: F came to the Group on 22 May '44 and returned home after VE-Day.

Then we waited, all the while trying to stifle our giggles. Sure enough, around midnight the door burst open and a body ricocheted off a wall and staggered over to the bunk. We were quickly rewarded by the pig's squeals and a cursing co-pilot thrashing about in the dark. It was a moment to be savoured forever!

Next day we scavenged two bedsprings and built a pen outside our hut. We fed the pig for several days until his odour resulted in an order for him to go. A local farmer with whom we regularly traded cigarettes for eggs agreed to raise him upon the understanding that when we completed our final mission it would be on hand for a roast feast. However, on completion of our tour of duty our single obsessive thought was to get home. As a result, the pig was simply forgotten, so his posthumous presence at our celebrations never occurred!"

15

HOME FOR XMAS?

Despite the failure of Operation Market/Garden, there still remained a possibility that the Germans might be induced to surrender before the end of 1944. The Allied bomber fleets were determined to add to the inexorable pressure being exerted upon their adversary, but only a physical occupation of Germany could ensure a final and victorious outcome to the conflict.

October commenced with a SNAFU for the Group in general, and the 533BS in particular. It was all too easy when taxiing along the perimeter track for a B-17 to get too close to the one in front. This happened when Lts. Schinz and Bigham came together to render their B-17s inoperable and reduce their Sqdn. cadre to seven in the process. The ordnance plant at Kassel was cloud-covered, and so the city itself was bombed. On the way back the Lead radar-navigator brought the formations across the Ruhr Valley, whose flak batteries ensured a warm reception.

A rest day on the 3rd and bad weather next day preceded the Group's second October mission to Cologne, a city that would be regularly visited during the month. Cologne had been briefed the day before, and this time a solid cloud-base prevented a sight of the bomb-strike that was directed at the city center. The next run was up onto the Baltic coast and Politz's synthetic-oil refineries, but this too was a total failure in its

Practice formation picture picks out two 533BS B-17Gs. "Dreambaby's" artwork is in the center of an impressive tally of mission symbols, which would continue to grow up to VE-Day. By contrast, "Lucky Me!," although marking up a large mission score, would be MIA with Lt. Gills' crew on 25 Sept. '44. Both bombers bear full 1CBW color markings, which dates the picture after July '44.

A Summer ground mist partially shrouds the B-17Gs of the 535BS. Poor visibility was often a contributory factor in causing flying accidents. Earth mound on the right is the gun-firing range.

The Group Headquarters complex consisted of three Nissen huts fronting a larger, flat-roofed structure and a similar small building at one side. This location was down from the Southern hangar. In common with most of Ridgewell's buildings, this site has been cleared and now has a small plot of private houses.

"Chug-A-Lug IV" of the 535BS eases its way past the 532BS dispersals clustered 'round the North Hangar and onto the main runway sometime during the Summer of 1944. Repetition of the aircraft letter on fuselage was not a standard feature of this Sqdn. Bomber was finally MIA with Lt. Levitoff's crew on 6 Nov.

primary intention. Instead the Group bombed a power station located at Stralsund after P-51 Weather Scouts recommended abandonment of the briefed target due to adverse weather.

A worrying development for the Allies was the advent of both jet and rocket-propelled fighters, with the latter represented by the high-speed but short flight-durability Me 163 Komet. During the bomb-run over Zwickau on the 7th 42-107018 "Los Angeles City Limits," flown by Lt. O'Connor (535BS), had the bulk of its bomb-doors torn off by flak, which also disabled two engines. While straggling back on its own the B-17 was suddenly faced by no less than three of these lethal gadflies. It was great good luck that the Luftwaffe pilots did not make a concerted attack while the bomber's pilots managed enough evasive action to put off the aim of their adversaries. Just a few minutes into the unequal contest several P-51s fortuitously intervened and drove the Me 163s away to leave the Fortress staggering its way back to Ridgewell.

The latest entertainer to visit the base on the 8th was the English comedian Tommy Trinder, who gave a two-hour show in No. 2 Hangar. His sense of humor was apparently not in tune with those attending, according to the 535BS diarist, who wrote waspishly: "Last night a buzz-bomb landed near Great Yeldham. I missed both events, but the bomb supposedly outdid Trinder – we will have to develop a taste for English music-hall humor, I guess!"

A B-17G of the 534BS has an unusual formation off its left side; instead of B-17s they are C-47s of the 9USAAF. On 17 Sept '44 Gen. Louis Brereton (CG Parachute Armies) flew from Ridgewell to observe his transports forming up at the commencement of Operation MARKET GARDEN. It is likely that this B-17 was the mount for his observations.

This is a view of the 533BS dispersals looking Eastward. The lead bomber is turning onto the short NE/SW runway. At top right is one of the other derelict farmhouses on the airfield. Nearest dispersal on left was the location for the fatal bomb-loading explosion on 23 June '43. Picture taken after addition of CBW color markings in July '44.

"Century Note" of the 532BS bears just a handful of mission symbols along its nose after being assigned in April '44. By VE-Day this figure would rise to three figures. Last three numbers of aircraft serial gave rise to the 100-dollar Bill artwork.

The Group's sixth visit to Schweinfurt on the 9th was also mission No. 200. The crews met little or no opposition from fighters or flak. Gen. Williams refused to sanction a beer party to celebrate this milestone, and probably based his decision on the over-reaction at two similar base events, where one murder and one suicide were recorded! Instead, separate dances at the Officers Club and the Yeldham Hangar were to be arranged. Another social event involving a single crew took place on the 13th. Lt. Fred Davison took his 535BS crew up to London, along with M/Sgt Clarence Bankston's support team. They comprised the combat and groundcrew, respectively, for the 535BS's "Stage Door Canteen," and their visit was to the famous hostelry after which the B-17 was named. Texan Senator Maury Maverick appeared on the 12th to christen another 535BS bomber (44-8228 "The Alamo") whose crew-chief was T/Sgt John Shanahan. Although not destined to achieve the same mission tally as "STC," this new B-17G would share her good fortune in making it through to VE-Day.

Cologne was briefed for the 12th and 13th, but weather intervened both days. However, no such interruption happened on the 14th when elements of all three Bomb Divisions were dispatched to hammer the numerous marshalling yard complexes located within the city's sprawling boundaries. The 533BS was up front, leading a five Group task force, and the bombing of the yards at Geroen was conducted through 7/10 cloud with fairly accurate effect. Cologne's yards at Nippes

"No Comment Needed" was assigned to the 534BS on 6 Aug. Three calendar months later she went down over Hamburg, along with "Chug-A-Lug IV" from the 535BS. All nine of Lt. Dudley Brummett's crew baled out successfully. Simple artwork design is blunt, but relates perfectly to the words applied above!

All four Wright Cyclones have been detached from "Tomahawk Warrior" of the 535BS for major maintenance work. Although this is a B-17G, she bears the center-fin section from a B-17F (42-30613), which was recorded as transferred out on 12 April '44 to 2 SAD (Strategic Air Depot) following a take-off accident.

Senator Maury Maverick from Texas does the honors at the christening of "The Alamo" (44-4228) of the 535BS on 11 Oct '44. The officer on the left with closed eyes appears to be Col. Leber who, if this is correct, is now minus his distinctive moustache!

Lt. Fred Davison's 535BS crew are photographed with staff-members of the Stage Door Canteen in London during a publicity visit in 1944. This crew's regular B-17G bore the name of the famous hostelry. Davison stands on the right, and Lt. Leroy Drummond (B) hugs one of the girls (Drummond was tragically KIA in November by a bomb from another B-17 which penetrated his bomber's nose compartment.)

were picked out for attack by the entire 8USAAF next day. A moderate flak barrage nipped at the flanks of the bomber stream, but succeeded in culling just four bombers from the 1BD ranks.

There should have been a fifth when a heavy caliber shell impacted against the cockpit and nose of 42-102703 "Pella Tulip" (532BS). The Fortress slumped away with a shattered windshield and shredded nose, as well as a large hole torn around the right side of the cockpit. Lt. Rautio (CP) was injured, but nothing like as seriously as his pilot Lt Reseigh. Almost every engine and flight instrument was non-functioning, and the oxygen supplies were knocked out. His helmet, oxygen mask, and goggles had been whipped away in the icy blast, and so Lt. Rautio had little option but to keep dropping down in the hope of levelling off at normal breathing altitude, a task not helped by a severed left elevator.

T/Sgt Nushy (Eng.) fought a fire caused by fluid from broken hydraulic lines to his turret and assisted the pilot down into the nose for medical attention from the bombardier. He then joined Rautio at the controls as a decision was taken to head for England, despite the closer proximity of Allied bases in Belgium. The landing gear had descended, and the energy-sapping task of cranking it back into position was shared by Sgts Kaplan (ROG), Penner (BT), and Erling Anderson (WG).

The danger of frostbite affecting Lt. Rautio's face and hands was partially countered through regular massage by Sgt Nushy. Meanwhile, the flaps were found to be jammed half-way down, and the propeller governors on the rightside engines were damaged. Adding yet more to the B-17's potentially lethal condition was the No. 4 engine on which the propeller "ran away," while No.3 ultimately faded away altogether. Lt. Winicki (N) faced an equally daunting task with the radio equipment "out." He salvaged a flak-map and a magnetic compass blown forward from the flight deck. Using these and with occasional glimpses of the ground he managed to skirt all flak concentrations and made all directional signals to Rautio via his lid-less astrodome.

"Sweet N' Lovely" bears 27 mission symbols and 16 triangles denoting Cycle-relay flights on behalf of the 65th Fighter Wing. The 533BS badge is painted below the symbols. Lt. Charles Bordner (P) kneels on the right as he signs the Flight report. The crewman directly below the artwork is Sgt. Warren Walker.

Two non-operational aircraft are photographed outside one of the Group hangars. In the foreground is a UC-64 Norseman. Behind this is a A-35B Vultee Vengeance, which joined the Group strength around Oct '44. The Norseman was not similarly recorded and was probably just visiting Ridgewell.

The well-worn and oil-stained wing surfaces on "Princess Pat" (533BS) confirm this B-17G's veteran status. Bomber was assigned on 13 Jan '44 and was ultimately salvaged following a non-operational crash on 27 March '45. Red outline to the national insignia was officially displaced by blue in Sept '43, and its presence in this post-July '44 shot suggests outer wing section is a replacement.

With the North Sea safely traversed the numbed co-pilot made a cautious circuit of the first available field in East Anglia (Debach, home for the 493BG). He knew that with two engines "out" on the same side and with no brakes he had just the one approach and landing attempt on hand. Parachutes stationed at the waist windows and radio hatch helped to solve the latter deficiency, but the asymmetric power balance inexorably swung the ailing Fortress off to the left of the runway and directly towards a dispersal housing another B-17. A scant few feet away from a potentially fatal collision, "Pella Tulip" hit soft soil which mired-in the wheels and jolted her to a halt.

The pilot was able to walk to the ambulance despite bad wounds to his left arm and leg. Lt. Rautio suffered slight facial frostbite, and Sgt Nushy's face was cut by Plexiglas splinters from his turret. However, Lady Luck had played no small part in the overall incident. Lt. Winicki had been standing up minus his flak helmet in the astrodome and was promptly told to put this vital head protection on. Sgt Nushy had been stooping down to correct a minor fault in his oxygen system. It was literally one second after this that the flak shell exploded!

In the second half of October the 8USAAF continued to attack a mix of rail and oil-related targets. The results in terms of striking the Primaries proved variable. For example, on the 19th only 75 out of 945 crews achieved this object, with a further 474 striking Secondary sources and the remainder dropping on Targets of Opportunity. This contrasted with the 22nd, where all but 49 of the 1073 B-17s and B-24s got through to their Primaries.

Lts. Dave Morgan (right) and Larry Weston – pilot and navigator, respectively – display their class A uniforms, with the single variation being the two forms of hat-wear. This duo and their crew flew combat from June until 29 November '44.

The Morgan crew's faces show the mounting strain of combat as they pose by "Sleepy Time Gal," in which they flew several missions. Standing (L-R) are Lts. Dave Morgan (P), Jacques Mousseau (CP), Larry Weston (N), and Bob Dewhurst (B). In the front row at center is T/Sgt Jack Mackay (ROG).

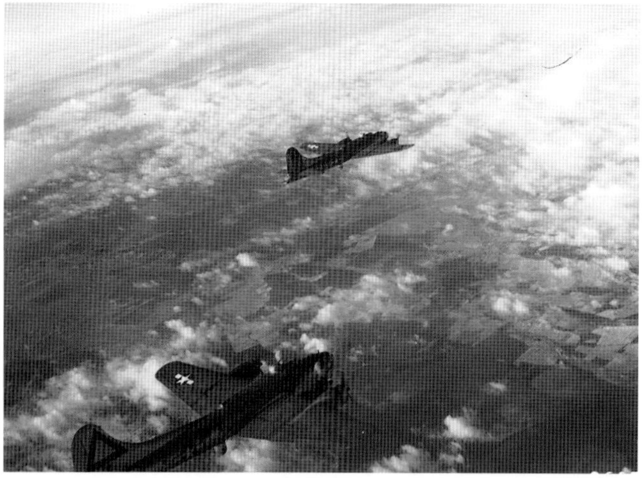

Two PFF B-17Gs are identified by the retractable H2X pods extending down from the ball-turret aperture. Bomber at the lower left belongs to the 401BG from Deenethorpe. Group records indicate the use of other Groups' PFF aircraft, even after a full establishment of these specialist bombers was made at Ridgewell.

The 381BG participated in six of these eight missions starting on the 17th with a fourth sortie against Cologne's marshalling yards. A Kiel mission next day was "scrubbed" at Ridgewell, although the 1BD sent out over 300 bombers. The onset of autumn with its indifferent weather patterns was reflected by the now regular occasions on which PFF bombing methods were employed. Mannheim (19th) was one such mission, with only a small fraction of the 1BD actually bombing the assigned armored vehicle factory, and the others releasing over the city in general.

The Cologne mission on the 17th signalled a rough introduction to combat for Lt. John Rice's 534BS crew. First of all, assembly in the dawn light left the bomber flying too far to the South of the Sqdn. Assembly point. Then, turbo-booster problems left their B-17 hopelessly trailing the Group. On the bomb-run the No.1 engine "ran away," and its propeller was "feathered." The bombs were scarcely released when flak damaged No. 3 engine, and the B-17 plummeted down to around 8000 ft. before full recovery was made. All loose gear was jettisoned, and a call for fighter cover brought in a single P-51. The ailing No. 3 engine finally failed halfway back towards the frontlines, and a mere 1800 ft was left as the bale-out order was given.

Lt. George Kaluger (B) recalled diving out and counting to three before "ripping." He barely missed the pointed roof of a farmhouse and several fruit trees before slamming into the ground on his back to leave a large indent in the soil. Two Belgian women emerged from the house, but were soon joined by a patrol of three Canadian soldiers with guns raised. The latter were soon convinced of George's friendly status, and he was quickly on his way to a reunion with his crew in Brussels. His pilot had been forced to crash-land after his chute "spilled" in the cockpit. Although damage to 42-31550 "Green Hornet II" was severe enough to merit her being salvaged, Lt. Rice was unhurt.

This crew's second mission to Münster (28th) was nearly as rough. No. 3 engine ran rough on the way back, and at one point the crew prepared for a possible bale-out, since the "run-away" propeller was inducing severe vibration. The propeller shaft thankfully broke cleanly, and the B-17 landed in good order. Return to Ridgewell was made alone, as the disabled B-

"Rotherhithes Revenge" has found a soft spot in the runway through which its right landing gear has penetrated. Bomber has been brought back to level configuration by the use of inflatable air-bags and will then be towed out and back to its 533BS dispersal.

17 could not sustain the climb-out ordered by the Group Leader to clear a weather front over the North Sea.

Over the ensuing five days the bombers completed just one mission (22nd) in which the 381BG did not take part, but was called on for an attack on Hamburg oil refineries (25th) and rail bridges at Bielefeld next day. The Ridgewell and Nuthampstead elements of the 1CBW went to Münster for a drop on marshalling yards along with just three other 1CBW Groups. (It is interesting to note that the 200 bombers put up by this quintet were equal to the strength of between eight and ten Groups during 1943. It is also a pertinent reminder of the 8USAAF's enormous expansion since those parlous days). Hamm's marshalling-yards turned into a Secondary for the bulk of the 1BD on the 30th when the weather intervened to block a planned attack on oil-refining facilities located at Gelsenkirchen.

November 1944

The bombing campaign against Germany's oil industry was emphasised in November when fully eleven of the 18 missions were devoted to this resource. A marginal return to tactical bombing occurred in mid-month as the Allied Armies executed Offensives in the Northern and Central sectors of the front-line. There were also four occasions when the 1BD dispatched just the 41CBW with one other Group in order to carry out bombing by Gee-H method.

The 381BG would operate eleven times in November, and it was not until the 4th that the first call came with a mission to strike oil-refineries at Hamburg/Harburg. The Group led the 1BD in a PFF-directed drop through heavy, but surprisingly inaccurate, flak. The same tactic was due to be employed over Frankfurt's marshalling yards next day, but a hole in the other-wise solid undercast permitted all but the leading Division elements to gain credit for a "visual assist" drop.

It was back to Harburg's oil refineries on the 6th, and this time flak was much more accurate in downing two Group bombers, one each from the 534BS and 535BS. (The latter loss was that Sqdn's first over 65 missions). Lt. Julius Levitoff was flying M/Sgt "Mouse" Davis' 42-97330 "Chug-A-Lug IV" when it sustained a strike on No. 3 engine during the bomb-run. The pilot's reaction in salvoing his bombs was misinterpreted by those bombardiers in the Group's rear elements, and their bomb loads dropped well short of the intended MPI. The stricken bomber was seen to be going down under control as it disappeared out of sight.

Its 534BS companion in distress was 43-38114 "No Comment Needed" with Lt. Dudley Brummett's crew. All nine men baled out, but Lt. Bill Barker (B) received an ankle wound which resulted in his receiving a Post-war disability pension. Two incidents involving Bill occurred during the initial hours after capture. He was incarcerated in a hut before being instructed by his guard to transfer to another building some dis-

Resplendent in natural metal-finish, "Los Angeles City Limits" (42-107018) flares out some 50 feet above the main runway-end. She was assigned to the 535BS on 25 March '44 and completed regular missions up to the end of the Bombing Campaign on 25 April 1945.

tance away. His wound had rendered him quite unable to walk – so the guard slung Bill along with his rifle and "piggy-backed" him to the new location. Later on, several soldiers appeared and started to goad Bill physically. He finally reacted to one such probe by striking out at his tormentor, whereupon the others cocked their rifles and pointed the barrels directly at him. Suddenly (and perhaps fortuitously) an officer strode up and berated the men after ordering them to "shoulder arms." It appeared that the lecture was made not for threatening to shoot their prisoner, but for daring as enlisted men to strike an officer!

The Group now enjoyed a two day spell of non-operations. This did not mean that all flying activity was suspended, and on the 8th the CBW held a big practice flight which browned off everybody. (The 398BG was absent on mission duty, and so was spared the torment!). Making his third flight from Bovingdon on Detached Duty to the 15USAAF in Italy was M/Sgt Edgar Dutton (535BS). The regular interchange of servicing personnel between the two Strategic Air Forces was one of the lesser-known aspects of the War in the Air. In this instance 1BD HQ had put in a specific request for Dutton as a result of the excellent work-reports submitted by the 15USAAF authorities. The M/Sgt's reaction was nothing close to enthusiastic, but his top-grade standard of efficiency had seen him "hoist with his own petard!"

The month's first tactical mission took place on the 9th when support was given to Patton's 3rd Army. Ouvres/Chesay (Nord) airfield was bombed using a combination of PFF and "visual assist" methods. Seven days later the second such mission was completed. This time the emphasis shifted North to backing for Gen. Simpson's 9th Army and Gen. Hodges 1st Army around Aachen. The 1BD bombed gun positions around Eschweiler, just East of Aachen. In between these two missions came one to Cologne/Ostheim airfield (10th). One of the risks inherent in maintaining a tight formation was that of accidentally "bombing" another B-17. This was to be the fate of Lt. Metts (535BS) flying 42-97265 "Hells Angels." Just after the bomb-run was completed, three 110-lb bombs, which had jammed in a higher-flying B-17's bomb bay, came free. These struck the nose compartment, two of which knocked off the Plexiglas, with the third smashing into the interior and killing Lt. Leroy Drummond (B) outright. The surviving crew then had the unnerving task of attempting to jettison the ordnance, which was only fulfilled by way of the nose hatch after 45 minutes had elapsed. Such was the traumatic effect upon the men that on return they were hospitalised overnight.

Apart from the 26th the remaining five November sorties for the Group all involved oil-related targets. The first two were scheduled to strike Merseburg, but only the second (25th) saw the bulk of the 1BD attaining the Primary. On the first (21st) barely half of the force did likewise, and 381BG records, for example, show the town of Friedburg North of Frankfurt as a Target of Opportunity. Disappointment awaited the crews on the 26th as they took off in the morning sunshine to hit a railroad bridge at Altenbecken, NE of Paderborn. They discovered a fat cloud formation sitting right over the target and had to resort to PFF-guided bombing. As Maj. Bill Fullick (Group Bombardier) tersely remarked on return, "I think we hit a field." The 532BS crew of Lt. Kyle Smith in 42-106994 'Little Guy' was MIA following this mission.

The Group led the 1BD to Misburg three days later and had a touch of good fortune on the bomb-run when the flak barrage lightened in intensity, only to resume in ferocity as the succeeding CBW came in to bomb behind the 1CBW. Maj. Taylor (535BS CO) was in charge on the 30th, but had to "abort" with a blown engine manifold-head some 15 minutes short of

This mobile Air-Traffic Control trailer has been rigged with the discarded nose from a B-17. The bombardier's optical flat has been removed to afford the operator a clear sight for his signal-lamp. Trailer is painted in the standard black and white chequered design.

the oil storage facilities at Zeitz, East of Merseburg. No aircraft were lost, but Lt. Guise (533BS) rode his luck when "aborting." His landing effort was so heavy that the right landing gear strut broke and a stream of gas from ruptured tanks shot down the runway, accompanied by the bomb-load as the B-17 smacked into the runway. Thankfully, the bomber did not catch fire, and the crew were left shaken but alive.

Although no aircraft were actually shot down on the 29th, the Group lost a veteran B-17G, 42-31614 "Minnie the Mermaid." Lt. Nelson was flying the 533BS bomber, which suffered damage from the strong flak barrage put up over the oil refinery complex. This was sufficiently severe for the pilots to divert into an airfield on the Continent where their B-17 languished until 27 January when it was struck off charge. The 29th was a milestone for yet another fortunate crew, when Lt. Dave Morgan (532BS) touched down off the Misburg mission where he had acted as Group Lead. It was his and the crew's 30th and final mission; this completed a combat tour which had begun the previous 26 June, during which they had had their share of good fortune on several occasions. Dave recalled one of the more mundane yet potentially dangerous incidents. The soporific effect of four 1200hp Wright Cyclones could and did induce a barbiturate effect upon the senses of what were already stressed crewmen. It was Dave's practice for each pilot to fly the B-17 while the other kept a formation watch with the surrounding aircraft. The controls had been taken over by Lt. Mousseau (CP) for the standard 15-minute spell. A few minutes into this time-spell Dave noticed the B-17 was edging dangerously close to another bomber. Looking across to his fellow-pilot, he found him with his head slumped down and virtually asleep!

The Enlisted Mens' Club was sparsely decorated compared to the Officers Club, but did have one notable piece of artwork. This took the form of a Fortress interior looking back towards the waist-guns. The gunner would have been in mortal danger of falling out if the real bomber's waist-gate sills were as low as the examples recorded in the painting!

16

DECEMBER CRISIS

By the final month of 1944 the general impression of a beaten Wehrmacht, whose defensive efforts would all too soon be swept away, remained foremost in the minds of the Allied High Command. This heady optimism was to be badly blunted by December-end following the German counter-attack in the Ardennes. The initial success of Von Rundstedt's brilliant plan owed no small measure to the shocking weather which intervened to badly hamper air operations over the first eight days of the Offensive. In spite of this severe negative factor, the 8USAAF took to the air in moderate or large-scale strength for 12 days out of the 16 available during the second half of the month. Nine missions were also flown up to the 16th when the Germans commenced their Offensive. The general emphasis of assault during December was switched from oil to rail transportation.

The first full-scale involvement of all three Divisions took place on the 4th when a number of marshalling yards came under attack. The 1BD went to Kassel and Soest, with the latter being the focus for the 1CBW. Bombing was conducted through the use of Gee-H. (This British-developed beam radar was equally effective for navigation or blind bombing. The equipment consisted of a transmitter sending signals back to two ground beacons, which provided a very accurate ground-plot. It was susceptible to jamming and was limited in range by the Earth's curvature, but did guarantee a good degree of accuracy.) Flak and fighters were absent, and the general im-

On 9 Dec '44 "Boulder Buf" of the 535BS was forced to make an emergency landing on the Continent after suffering flak damage, which also wounded five men in Lt. Clark's crew, several of them seriously. One of the men is seen being taken away by stretcher after his removal via the nose hatch. Aircraft was salvaged 13 days later.

The officers Club is well patronised in this picture taken on 23 Dec '44. Maj. Ed Kurner (S-4 Supply CO) is sitting on the right, and Maj. Fitzgerald's unmistakable frame is next to a rather bemused-looking RAF officer.

On 23 Dec '44 a children's Xmas party was laid on. Upwards of 400 local youngsters were present, some of whom are being given presents by the first of two personnel putting on the robes of Santa Claus – the first being so exhausted he had to be replaced!

One of the Mess-halls has been fully decorated for the forthcoming 1944 Xmas celebration. Mural on the wall has a map of the States on one side and one of Europe on the other. Parachute canopies on the ceiling add a gentle touch to the basically stark interior layout.

pression gained was that of a "milk-run." The Group was left off the operational schedule next day when munitions and tank works in Berlin were struck by a reduced force of B-17s from each Division. Instead, the crews were sent off up the English coast for a gunnery practice exercise spanning between five and six hours – no doubt the gunners were regarded as rusty, especially when the virtual absence of the Luftwaffe over the past month or two was considered!

Stuttgart (9th) provided no answer to this exercise because hardly any enemy fighters were seen by the bombers, and even the fighter escorts only managed to down one of the Luftwaffe. Flak described as "moderate but accurate" wounded six crewmen, four of whom were on board 42-32060 "Boulder Buf." The 535BS bomber was damaged to the extent that Lt. Clark was forced to break rank and divert towards France. He finally came down near Melun, but over-shot and ran the B-17's nose into an obstacle. Lt. Murphy (CP) and S/Sgts Sladek, Hallstrom, and Murphy – the latter already holding one Purple Heart – were taken to hospital; all other crewmen were flown back to Ridgewell three days later. Hallstrom subsequently had one leg amputated in a Paris hospital and was rotated States-side in January. The B-17 was declared salvaged on the 22nd. One of the other two men wounded off the mission (T/Sgt Rafael Larsen) was less fortunate since he died two days later.

The Sgt's sad fate was paralleled on the same day when the Group headed out to Mannheim and shared a Gee-H directed drop onto a railroad bridge with the 41CBW. Flak was no more than meager, but still took down a 532BS bomber (43-38780) flown by Lt. Belskis. A burst on No. 2 engine tore it loose, and flames extended back as far as the waist. The entire left wing then fell off, and the B-17's remnants rolled over into a vicious spin. One man was seen to come out of the waist, and a further two apparently without chutes were spotted be-

The Black-out is totally compromised – albeit in the most positive manner – by this Xmas tree, which the 533BS erected in 1944. Board at base of the tree bears a number of reindeer-drawn sleighs, along with a Santa Claus. Words read THE 533BS EXTENDS SEASONS GREETINGS.

The enterprising ball-turret gunner on Lt. Don Smith's 532BS crew snapped this Group formation from his spherical position. Only one of the B-17Gs is camoflaged, which is a clear indication of its removal from production-line bombers from early 1944 onwards. Bomber in right foreground returned home after VE-Day.

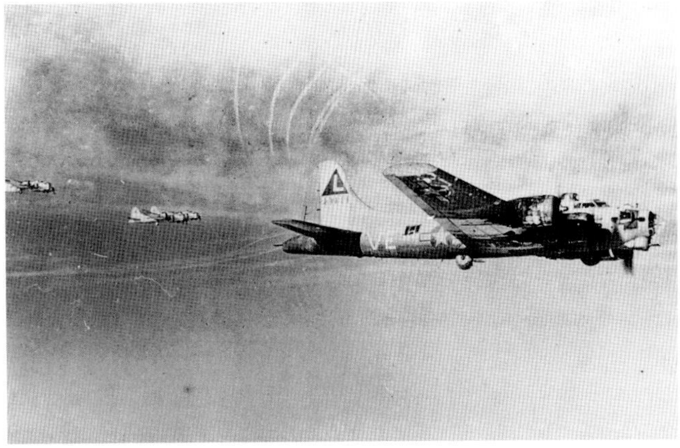

"Old Iron Gut" was a B-17G from the 20-DL production batch, which came to the 532BS on 23 Dec '43. In this picture the operationally-tested and well-stained bomber is seen bearing the original "wedge" tail-gun shape.

fore the bomber exploded. Only two enlisted men (T/Sgt McCoy and S/Sgt Suggs) reached the ground alive, where they were swiftly rounded up.

Merseburg came in for another pounding from the 1BD next day when the flak gunners destroyed just one B-17 out of the 337 making effective sorties – a remarkably minimal figure for such a heavily protected target. Marshalling yards at Kassel were on the Group's target list three days later, and this mission was to be the first of a trio spread over nine days. In fact, bad weather had scuppered operations over the previous 48 hours and was the major cause of restricted action right up to Xmas Eve.

The 1BD did take off on the 16th, but abandoned the mission while it was still forming up over England. The German surprise and initially successful strike through the Ardennes – with the object of capturing Antwerp and splitting the Allied Armies – was two days into its course before the 8USAAF again got off the ground. This time the bombing of selected rail and road communications was a tactical measure designed to impede the flow of reinforcements. This process was repeated on the 19th and 23rd, but without 381BG participation.

In spite of the critical developments on the Continent, the planned Xmas Party for local British children went ahead on the 22nd and was held in the American Red Cross Club. More than 300 youngsters of all ages (the eldest not much younger than some of their American hosts) were treated to movies and given oranges, ice-cream, and gifts from not one but two Santas – the first being "burnt out" after 60 exhausting minutes, and gratefully replaced by Cpl. Tom Terriri! About 50 officers and enlisted men helped with the proceedings, and were in the words of one Sqdn. record-keeper "wishing only to have some of the only Xmas cheer we are likely to have around this bog!" (The

"Dee Marie" (42-97076) of the 534BS has a collapsed left landing gear and has come to rest away from the runway. Incident occurred on 31 Dec '44, and the B-17G was soon repaired for return to combat duty. It arrived at Ridgewell in March '44 and flew home with the Group in May '45.

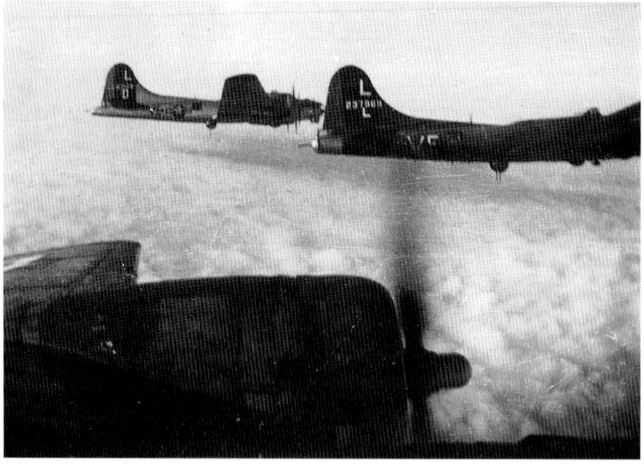

A later picture of "Old Iron Gut" shows her with a Cheyenne tail-turret, whose silver finish stands out against the overall camouflage scheme. It is probable this Field Modification was carried out as a result of battle damage. Aircraft survived more than sixteen months of combat, but was dispatched to 2SAD on 31 May '45 where it was salvaged.

same airman, gloomily anticipating a protracted Conflict resulting from the German advance, conjectured how the 1945 Xmas Party would stack up against today's!)

The enforced lull in operations permitted 13 bombers whose engines had suffered burn-outs as a result of over-boosting on the Cologne mission (18th) to be "slow-timed" – a duty completed inside a mere two hours. This addition to overall aircraft strength was very opportune, because all would be needed on the morrow. The fog-bound Ardennes region was on the verge of clearing under the influence of a high-pressure zone extending across Western Europe, and a maximum-effort mission was in the planning stage that very evening.

The combat crews were duly called to a briefing in the early hours, at which Col. Leber stated "We are going to give our ground troops the best Xmas present they will never forget." In fact, more than 2000 B-17s and B-24s were going over, which was more than the combined total making the previous three missions. (Many of the Liberator Groups even included their stripped-down and garishly painted Formation Ships, such was the will to assist the sorely-pressed G.I.s) Ridgewell organised 51 bombers which were split between two formations. One formation made up part of the "A" CBW leading the 1BD, and Col. Leber headed the other formation leading the 1CBW. Airfields and communication centers extending into Central Germany were the briefed targets, and CAVU conditions permitted most of these Primaries to be plastered. Landing grounds – airfields without runways and temporary facilities – at Ettinghausen and Kirchgons felt the weight of the Group's ordnance. Lt. Kelley, a 535BS navigator, was looking out on the bomb-run when he was horrified to sight a B-24 Group approaching head-on. The two units miraculously weaved past each other without incident, but the Lt. saw one B-24 explode as the Group flew away.

The perfect weather over the Continent was not reflected back in England as fog started to roll in, particularly over the largely Midland bases of the 1BD. Ridgewell was the furthest East within the Division and not affected. Therefore, it was hardly surprising that its personnel got ready to receive a further 75 B-17s from fog-affected units, a total which included the 398BG. Somehow, this massive inflation in aircraft numbers was handled all right, with the subsidiary runways utilised as temporary dispersals. The cooks did a sterling job in feeding an extra 600 to 700 combat crewmen for whom bedding was made available.

The stage was set for a full-scale return to operations, and missions were completed by the 8USAAF on every remaining day of December. (However, no element of the 1BD got off over the next 48 hours, and the 1CBW was not called upon until the 28th.) A "White Xmas" in the form of thick frost greeted the personnel at Ridgewell as a mission to Schwerte was briefed and then "scrubbed." A comprehensive Xmas dinner was provided which would have satisfied even the most gluttonous individual!

The significance of the Ludendorff rail bridge at Remagen on the Rhine meant nothing more to the crews than any other target as they were briefed to take it out. Lt. Col. Briggs (Group Operations Officer) was in charge, along with Capt. Demagalski (535BS). Good clear weather provided a perfect backcloth for a successful attack, but the result was disappointing if not surprising – an accurate strike on such a narrow objective was always tricky. It is a supreme irony of history that leaving the bridge standing at this time was to work to Allied advantage during early March when the 9th Armored Division seized the structure intact!

One of the more unusual visitors to Ridgewell was this P-51D from the Debden-based 4FG. It has been converted to twin-seat configuration, and the canopy is split into two sliding sections. In right background can be seen a UC-64 Norseman, along with an single-engine Proctor, which was an RAF communications aircraft.

Pressure on road and rail communications was maintained on the last two days of December. A marshalling yard at Mainz and communications center at Prom, which was directly behind the Ardennes Front, were the respective Group targets. After de-briefing of the latter mission the crews wound down with dances at the Officers Club and G.I. Theater, while the PX "Grog Shop" was opened for sales. Just to complete the illusion of Peace, a light snow bedecked the base during the evening.

Unknown to all but a handful of 534BS personnel was the critical medical condition affecting Lt. Waynant. Earlier on the 31st he was being checked out for an airplane commander slot by Lt. Troy Jones. An indifferent landing attempt resulted in the landing gear folding up. Worse was to follow, for No. 2 propeller shattered and one blade sliced into the pilot's compartment to totally excise the Lt's. left leg above the knee. Cpl. Jeronimo Casaz was on duty near the control tower when the B-17 cracked-up. Rushing to the bomber, the young medical orderly clambered inside and promptly applied tourniquets to Waynant's legs. Then he ordered the ambulance driver to prepare a litter outside the forward hatch before removing the barely conscious pilot from his seat and lowering him skilfully through the hatch. All this work was achieved in a matter of minutes. As the airman was being transported to the Base Hospital Casaz prepared blood plasma solutions, which the Flight Surgeon now administered on the way. After temporary patching-up Waynant was transferred to the Braintree Military Hospital, where he subsequently made a full recovery. (In the minutes before Casaz's arrival the Lt. managed to successfully staunch the heavy flow of blood by applying pressure to his truncated thigh. As it was, severe shock soon overcame him, and it was touch and go over the next few days whether or not he would pull through).

"Railroader" (533BS) has sustained severe damage to its rudder and tail-gun position. Picture was taken after July '44 when red CBW color markings were applied on the fin center-sections.

On 15 Nov '44 a Mk III Short Stirling (LK437) from No. 1657 Heavy Conversion Unit (HCU) lost power during a forced landing and crashed short of the SE/NW runway. It was fortunate that the pilot, Fl/Lt. Henderson, managed to avoid impacting with Tilbury church, seen in the background.

"Pair of Queens, Gee and Bee" of the 535BS is part of a Group formation tracking over a heavy undercast. She was assigned in July '44 and came through many missions between then and VE-Day. The practice of repeating aircraft letters on the fuselage was only adopted by the 535BS from mid-1944 onwards.

Sgt Fred Kreuger (Weather Section) is 5 ft 8 ins. tall, but is here dwarfed by his working colleague Joe Warren Brown – all of 6 ft. 7 in. – as they pose in the snow. Long-Johns were an absolutely essential item of clothing in the East Anglian atmosphere, which was extremely damp, often freezing, and rarely even moderately warm!

The harsh contrast between Peace and War is epitomised by this picture. An ancient but well-tended country dwelling has its Centuries-old tranquillity disturbed by a B-17's engines. These are straining at maximum power to bear their load of men and ordnance off the airfield and up into the atmosphere for yet one more thrust at a fiercely defended Nazi target.

Two veteran 532BS B-17Gs are captured in close-up profile by the camera. The nearest aircraft is "Flak Magnet," which was assigned on 10 June '44. She belied her title by remaining intact and returning States-side in May '45. "Sleepy Time Gal" was assigned to Ridgewell on 6 April '44 and regained American shores at the same time as "Flak Magnet."

The same two 532BS B-17Gs are seen from below, with a third aircraft completing the formation element. The latter is 42-106994 "Little Guy" of the 533BS, which was not so lucky as "Sleepy Time Gal" or "Flak Magnet." On 26 Nov '44 she was lost along with three of Lt. Kyle Smith's crew

"Little Rock-ette" displays her distinctive color scheme in this winter shot. The former 97BG B-17E (then named "Peggy D" and one of the twelve bombers completing the inaugural 8USAAF mission on 17 Aug '42) now has all camouflage removed along with the gun turrets. Dark stripes on nose and outer engine cowlings and aircraft name on fuselage are red. Group insignia on fin is enclosed by a simple triangle outline.

Two officers are photographed sitting by the fireplace in the Officers Club. The wall above is decorated with details of Group missions conducted during its first two months in combat. Also on display is the Group badge, as well as a painted practice bomb.

17

BOMBERS CRESCENDO

New Years Day 1945 witnessed no let-up in the pace of air operations. The Ardennes Front was almost stabilised, but it would take most of January before the "Bulge" was squeezed out at a continuing cost to Allied ground forces, although the task of harrying the Wehrmacht from the skies could be left to the 9USAAF's tactical aircraft. A measure of support was still provided by its "Bigger Brother," with the 2AD going for rail bridges while the other two Air Divisions turned to oil installations as their goal. (The term Air Division had supplanted the existing Bomb Division nomenclature from 1 Jan '45). The assigned target this day was at Madgeburg. On the way over and while flying between two cloud-layers, Maj. Taylor elected to climb the 37 aircraft to gain clearer air-space. When this was achieved it resulted in a well-scattered formation whose re-assembly was effected far too late for it to assume its correct position in the Divisional formation-stream.

Bad weather thwarted the first two bomb-runs, and as the third was being completed 43-37553 lost both rightside engines. (The 533BS records state the High and Low Sqdns. became separated and Lt. Renick assumed command to make a PFF attack on Kassel, while the Lead Sqdn. also abandoned runs on the Primary and headed West to make a drop on Cologne). Lts. Peters and Nelson (535BS) strove to keep their B-17 aloft, but all their attempts at level flight induced a spinning tendency due to the asymmetric power-balance. The alternative was a shallow glide which sustained the bomber and its

The occupants of a house located just outside the airfield boundary were fortunate to escape injury from this complete stabiliser laying outside one of the doors. It came either from 42-97511 "Egg Haid" or 42-40011 "Schnozzel," which collided in the circuit on 21 Jan '45. Lts. Smith and Tauro (532BS) and sixteen other crewmen were all killed.

A second shot of the aftermath from the 21 Jan '45 collision. The only recognisable part of a once mighty B-17G is the skeletal frame of the rudder seen in the background to the left of the smoke-pall.

This picture of "Me and my Gal" (535BS) was taken in Belgium on 14 Feb '45. After baling out his crew Lt. Wulf brought off a very risky belly-landing on a short, sloping piece of ground. So severe was the impact that the lower part of the fuselage was ground away and all four engines wrenched from their mountings.

anxious crew over the next 50 minutes; this proved sufficient to gain the Allied Lines near Metz in France. By now the B-17 was down to 1500 ft. and was not going to make it to the intended Brussels location.

Peters ordered the crew out, and one of the last to jump was Lt. Kelley, who had been witness to a Group near-collision with B-24s on 24 Dec. He came out through the bomb-bay, and despite having to make a double somersault on landing escaped with just a sprained thumb. Two rifle-bearing G.I.s approached and ordered him to put his hands up. They had been alerted to a possible parachute attack in the wake of Operation "Bodenplatte," a massive Luftwaffe attack upon Bel-

The early evening light catches part of one Sqdn. as it breaks into the circuit preparatory to landing, while the remainder of the Group hold station above.

An unidentified 535BS B-17G is receiving the "carved turkey" treatment. The No.1 engine has been detached, and the No. 2 engine is un-cowled for examination. The greater proportion of bomber servicing was conducted in the open, hangar space being reserved for major work.

Group personnel gather 'round the bulk of an auxiliary gas-tank. These were inserted into the bomb-bay whenever an extended-range mission was being set up. However, their presence meant that only one side of the bomb-bay could be used for ordnance, which further restricted the B-17's already modest bomb-load.

Senator Canfield was another visitor performing a christening ceremony, in this instance 44-6163 "Passaic Warrior" of the 533BS. Col. Shackley (Sqdn. CO) is on the Senator's left, with Col. Reed (Ground Executive) on right and Lt. Saul Schwartz (PRO) between Reed and Shackley.

gian and Dutch airfields earlier that day. Kelley indicated his fast-disappearing B-17, and this fact coupled with his American accent convinced his "captors" he was friendly. The Lt. was transported to an MP Station where he was reunited with three others from his crew; all nine were later accounted for. Sgt. Giannacoupolis had broken a leg and was subsequently sent home. Sgt Bolin was extracted from a minefield, and Sgt Knaus was fired upon by GIs in a moving truck, whose aim was fortunately in inverse proportion to their enthusiasm! Four of Kelley's crew were to be involved in another B-17's loss on 30 March with much more tragic consequences. One was Lt. Nelson, who swore he would never bale-out again, come what may.

Lt. Peters put "Feather Merchant II," which had completed many missions since original assignment on 27 May, down in Belgium, where she was salvaged. A further two 535BS crews – Lt. Smith in 43-38998 and Lt. Clark in 42-97267 "Tomahawk Warrior" – also diverted to Belgium, but did return to Ridgewell. The weariness associated with combat flying was surely enhanced after this mission thanks to an official SNAFU. The previous evening combat crews attending the regular Officers' party had been assured by a Brigadier Gen. that a "stand down" was definitely in force for the morrow. Those who had over-celebrated and were listed for the mission were only brought back to a state approaching normal by liberal mixtures of coffee and oxygen! In fact, only five crews returned direct to base, with the remainder scattered throughout the Continent.

Lt. Rice (534BS) was experiencing more problems on this mission. During the bomb-run the forward oxygen-lines were

Capt. Ewing Watson arrived at Ridgewell during December '43. He was assigned to the 533BS and flew 47 missions over the next 16 months. In addition, he assumed command of the Sqdn. in early 1945. After WWII he was a successful lawyer.

This quartet of Group "original" officers are examining a number of photographs. Maj. Linn Kidd (left) was the S2 Section leader. The other three men are (L-R) Maj. Jim Delano (Group Navigator), Col. Dave Kunkel (534BS CO), and Col. George Shackley, who served as CO of the 535BS and 533BS before assuming the post of Group Air Executive. All of the three combat personnel survived the War.

The original caption states, "A formation of the 381BG on its way to bomb Germany." In fact, the picture is one in a series of publicity shots taken in August '44. The 1CBW color markings contrast well with the bombers' natural metal finish.

knocked out, and minutes later the pilot received a flak strike in one shoulder. Sgt Rauslin (Eng.) took care of Rice after he was moved into the nose, and Lt. Kaluger (B) assisted Lt. Stow to fly the B-17. Lt. Stow's oxygen system then failed, and the bomber had to be dropped to normal breathing altitude. Lt. Rice recovered sufficiently to resume his position, and the bomber returned to base.

A marshalling yard at Gerolstein was bombed on the 2nd by what was now a regular Group complement of 37 aircraft, one or more of which were surely PFF machines. This "blind" form of release guidance was now often in demand, as evidenced next day when Cologne's Hermulheim marshalling yard was hit through solid cloud. Capt. Watson (533BS) was Group Lead, but was forced to "abort" with engine problems; his place was taken by Capt. Ackerman (534BS), who was currently on his second combat tour. Rail-related targets were continuing to feature on the Group's list, with facilities at Heimbach hit on the 5th, followed by rail bridges in Cologne next day. Another rail bridge at Alzey was allotted the Group on the 8th, but again the results were unobserved. For Lt. Williamson (535BS) in his Sqdn's 43-38127 "Pair of Queens, Gee and Bee" the mission's end was far from normal. His No. 1 engine was "out," and No. 2 started to falter as an emergency landing was in progress at Earls Colne. He managed to land all right, but could

A second shot from the same publicity sequence picks out a P-51B of the Steeple Morden-based 355FG. Escorts flying this close to the bombers could provide little measure of protection. In addition, no self-respecting fighter pilot would risk approaching so near – most bomber gunners fired first and identified after!

"Railroader" suffered a more serious accident on 13 Jan '45. Battle damage from the Germersheim mission caused Lt. Fawcett to force-land on the Continent. The replacement tail-gun position is sprayed Olive Drab, and the original silver-finish rudder has given way to a camoflaged unit with a natural-metal trim-tab. Bomber was later salvaged.

This 534BS Fortress suffered a collapsed right landing gear, but was soon put back into service. Aircraft force-landed abroad on 21 Jan '45, but returned to Ridgewell nine days later. It had been assigned on 21 Feb '44 and was from the final Douglas production-black (30-DL) to bear camouflage.

not prevent an over-shoot into thick mud; the crew later travelled the few miles between there and Ridgewell in a truck.

Snow was falling two days later as the bombers under Col. Shackley's command took off for Cologne/Ostheim airfield. The mission was well under way when Shackley was forced to "abort" due to two engines failing on his B-17. What transpired next is related by Lt. Marks (B): "At this point we were getting into serious trouble as we headed back towards the Belgian coast to jettison our bombs. There was total cloud cover below, and I had to use radar in order to maintain our land position. We still lost altitude after bomb-release, and now we had to find a friendly airfield in Belgium. We were flying through heavy snow which had obliterated all ground reference, and were only about 1000 ft. up as Capt. Stone (N) and I worked hard to find some small field to land on.

Shackley spotted what looked like a field through the gloom, which he circled and then made an abortive pass. He called me to say 'We are at 900 ft, so get the men in the rear into a crash-landing position. I will make one more try, and if the ship doesn't make it we will have to bale out.' I looked out and saw a church steeple go by – that made me realise we were too low to jump. Seconds later we could feel the left wing dip and slide towards the ground. Just before touch-down Shackley straightened out and slid the bomber in for a perfect belly-land-

In early 1945 Official orders were issued for specific turrets to be deleted from the B-17s. In Ridgewell's case this applied to the ball-turrets on 534BS bombers, an example of which is seen on the aircraft in the foreground.

Nearside trio of B-17s are from the 534BS, and all conform with the order for removal of ball-turrets. Maximum speed was marginally improved due to the reduced weight and drag factors. In practice, this could be of little or no benefit when in formation, which had to be flown according to the pace of the other Group bombers who still suffered from the drag effect of their ball-turrets.

ing on an ice and snow-covered runway, along whose full length we progressed! WE WERE ONE HAPPY CREW. Who can be happy under these conditions? WE CAN!"

The Col's 533BS was in Group Lead position, but after his departure this was passed over to the High Sqdn. and the mission went ahead. Becoming separated over the target, Lt. Rouse in a 303BG B-17 equipped with Gee-H led the 533BS in a bomb-run executed through moderate to intense flak. One burst badly damaged this bomber around the tail and severed one of S/Sgt Hafner's legs. The oxygen supplies and all communications were rendered useless as Rouse signalled he was dropping out by lowering his landing gear. The control surfaces, and the rudder in particular, were destroyed or jammed, and Rouse, along with his co-pilot, Lt. Crouse, found it almost impossible to correct the aircraft's heading, which was due East! It was only through juggling with the engines' RPMs that a tortuously gradual swing to the right was achieved with much air-space and gas consumed in the process. Sgt Hafner was given several morphine shots as the errant B-17 flew a roughly rectangular path, which ended in a landing approach to a Belgian airfield.

Lt. Marks, from Shackley's crew, recollected that about two hours after their own touch-down he and the others sighted a B-17 coming in which as it got closer was identified as a 1AD bomber. The aircraft over-shot the runway and landed up in a cabbage patch with barbed wire wrapped round the propellers. When they reached the stranded machine they were astonished to discover it was the one flown by Lt. Rouse – to whom Shackley had handed over the Group Lead! Sgt Hafner was rushed to a hospital at which his life was saved, and the two crews were transported back to Ridgewell minus their aircraft.

Bridges at Germersheim (13th) and Cologne (14th) were attacked; solid cloud over the former target meant Gee-H had to be employed, but CAVU conditions over Cologne/

During early 1945 Lancaster PO;S of 467 (RAAF) Sqdn. made a tour of 8USAAF bases. Her crew stand below the very impressive "scoreboard," whose tally rose to 137 before VE-Day. Hermann Goering's empty boast made as far back as 1940 is also recorded. This bomber still exists today as a key exhibit in the RAF Museum at Hendon in North London.

Maj. Jim Delano (seated on left) conducts a briefing of Group navigators. Alongside him is Lt. Donald Hamm, one of the four survivors from the mid-air explosion of "Red Hot Riding Hood" (533BS) on 14 July '43.

The frost-covered grass has a shallow trench scored into its surface by the ball-turret on "Ice Col' Katy" of the 534BS. No. 2 engine has been wrenched from its mounting after the left landing gear collapsed. Bomber still carries the original pattern tail turret, which has an Olive Drab anti-dazzle surface. Incident occurred on 8 Jan '45.

Rodenkirchen resulted in a good bomb-pattern. Flak hit 42-97313 flown by Lt. Robuck (535BS) as the front-line was crossed, and Sgts Shott, LaValle, and Leiner baled out to be reported MIA during de-briefing. All three later returned to Ridgewell, but Sgt LaValle actually landed behind enemy lines. The other two took to their chutes directly over the front-lines and were fired on without effect by German troops.

Actress Mary Bryan arrived at the base on the 15th to christen 43-38983 "Fort Lansing Emancipator" of the 534BS. Jack Parker, a Fort Lansing radio-station announcer, also attended with a BBC sound-recorder truck to interview Bryan and those members of the B-17's crew from the Michigan town. Fog rolled in next day to curtail operations, but there was no similar weather impediment 24 hours later when 37 crews headed out to blitz Paderborn's marshalling yards. No opposition was encountered, and the same non-reaction by German defences occurred over Mannheim on the 20th where a rail bridge was clobbered.

The first eleven January missions had caused no MIA losses in aircraft or personnel, although three B-17s had been salvaged and one crewman severely injured. However, the greatly diminished scale of enemy resistance did not mean the crews could relax their concentration for a split second. This was particularly the case when flying in close formation, often over lengthy periods of time and in indifferent or poor weather. The danger posed by a mid-air collision was always present in those circumstances.

Col. Harry P Leber was completing his tour on the 21st and was leading the Group as it made a run over cloud on a marshalling yard at Aschaffenburg. On return he was presented with the Silver Star by Brig./Gen. Gross, the 1CBW Commander. The pleasure of the occasion must have been somewhat dampened by the tragic accident occurring as the bomb-

Lt. Rouse (532BS) inspects the very severe damage inflicted on his B-17G after a forced landing in Belgium on 10 Jan '45. Aircraft is a PFF machine carrying the Red triangle and Group letter C of the 303BG (Molesworth), from whom it was detached for use by the 381BG.

The Rouse crew are snapped without their tail-gunner Sgt Hafner, who was severely injured and subsequently had one leg amputated. The pilot is second from left with Lt. Crouse (CP), while Lt. Stuart Newman (N) is on the right. Standing on the left is Sgt Irving Schlom (Eng.).

ers came over into the landing pattern. Lts. Tauro and Smith (both 532BS) had collided as one lifted up into the other's path. B-17Gs 42-97511 "Egg Haid" and 42-40011 "Schnozzle" plummeted into fields just off the airfield perimeter. The formation was just a few hundred feet up at this point, and none of the 18 crew had much chance to bale–out. (One of the tail-gunners did survive within the crumpled remains of his bomber's tail section, but expired a short time after). Sgt Strong in Lt. Godwin's 532BS crew had just emerged from his ball-turret when he was thrown about as his pilot banked sharp left to avoid being involved in the collision. A fellow crewmember later claimed their right wing had bounced off the No. 1 engine nacelle on one of the doomed B-17s!

The Group was already one crew short on return. "Smashin' Time" (43-38158) had returned from the 448 Sub-Depot the previous afternoon. Her crewchief had told Lt. Coates prior to today's mission that his team had worked on the bomber until well into the night. Over France the No. 1 began to malfunction, and its propeller refused to "feather." The crew kept pressing on until No.3 began to play up, and Lt. Coates decided to turn back; at this stage the navigator was unsure whether they were over friendly soil.

Shortly after banking for home the situation altered drastically when No. 4 went out. With an inoperable airspeed indicator, full bomb-load, and iced-up windshield the crew were in mortal trouble as their B-17 sank into the undercast. The pilot waited until he estimated his height at around 1000 feet, and was about to instruct the crew to jump when he broke out into the clear. Bombs were ordered to be released on "safe" just in case they were back over Allied territory, and the geography was scanned for a suitable landing site. This turned up in the form of a potato field, into which the sagging bomber was neatly deposited in wheels-up attitude.

A mixed group of French civilians and U.S. soldiers mill around "Smashin' Time!" of the 534BS. Bomber was crash-landed by Lt. Bob Coates on 21 Jan '45 and was salvaged the following month.

Caption date of 5 Feb '45 for this picture of two 532BS B-17Gs evading flak on the bomb-run is incorrect; bomber on left was MIA two days previous with Lt. Anderson's crew. "Century Note" was much more fortunate and lived up to her name, since she reportedly completed 100 missions by VE-Day. Her serial is extended onto the rudder, a common feature on B-17s with seven-figure serials.

Gunfire could be heard in the distance, and a decision was taken for evasive action should the crash-landing have been in enemy-held country. This possibility was heightened by the appearance of a group of civilians wielding farming implements. The crew's natural apprehension at this sight thankfully diminished when a U.S. truck rolled into view. However, the feeling swiftly resurrected itself when the driver yelled out "Don't move, fellas – you're in a mine-field!"

The crew was guided out to the road by the truck-driver, who loaded them into his vehicle for transport in the direction of Luneville. The crash-landing had been NNW of Strasbourg, and as the truck passed through Saverne Lt. Coates spotted a sign "700 Ordnance Coy," in which unit he knew his brother was serving. Signalling his driver to halt, he jumped out and made his way to the outfit where he had a memorable reunion with his kin! Next morning he continued on to Luneville and rejoined his crew for eventual repatriation to Ridgewell.

A prolonged spell of bad weather restricted operations to one of the next six days, and it was the 28th before the bombers went out in force again. Marshalling yards and road bridges in the much-battered city of Cologne were the briefed Primaries, but in the 381BG's case its crews had to resort to a Target of Opportunity at Gütersloh airfield. Meager and inaccurate

A fox clasping a foaming beer glass adorns the side of a 534BS B-17G. The name refers to one of the many hostelries around Ridgewell. This aircraft survived over eight months in combat prior to the St. Valentines Day mission in 1945. Battle damage finally forced it to be abandoned by Lt. Dean Anderson's crew near Dellen, Luxembourg.

M/Sgt Clarence Bankston accepts a huge slice of cake from the cake held between him and British actress Anna Neagle. This was to celebrate the 100th mission flown by the crew chief's B-17G "Stage Door Canteen." The current crew's co-pilot, Lt. J. O'Neal, is standing behind Bankston.

flak was met over Niederlahnstein, to the South of Cologne, next day when a marshalling yard was hit through 10/10 cloud using Gee-H.

Col. Leber's departure would normally have witnessed an outside appointment to the Group Commander post. On this occasion the regulations were to be relaxed, and the third and final 381BG Supremo in WWII would come from its ranks. Lt. Col. Conway Hall had been with the Group since its creation at Pyote, and this experienced airman and administrator was now assuming full command. He had provided excellent support to Cols. Nazzaro and Leber in his capacities as Group Operations Officer and Air Executive, and no better choice for the top post could possibly have been envisaged. Another veteran airman was assigned to take Hall's place as Air Executive. This was Lt. Col. George Shackley, who relinquished his charge of the 533BS in favour of Maj. Ewing Watson.

February 1945

As the Anglo-American Armies prepared for the Operation that would culminate in the crossing of the Rhine – Germany's final Western barrier to penetration of its hinterland – the 8USAAF was going about its business with minimal interference from the Luftwaffe, linked to noticeably varying degrees of opposition posed by flak. Despite the tremendous advances in technological equipment used to aid accurate bombing, there were still occasions when either Secondary or Target of Opportunity locations had to suffice. In Feb. '45, out of the 16 Group missions flown no less than two and six were to fall into these respective categories.

Marshalling yards at Mannheim opened the month's operational account. The veteran B-17G 42-32102 "Julie Linda" flown by Lt. Kuhns "aborted," and after the bombs had been dumped in the North Sea came in to land down-wind with just one engine functioning. The bomber swung off the runway and smashed into several 533BS groundcrew huts, breaking her back in so doing. She had served since early March '44 but this was her final mission, as the degree of damage inflicted did not warrant her repair and she was duly salvaged. (The Lt. was returned to a co-pilot status.)

On the 3rd came the Group's first visit for over seven months to "Big B" – Berlin. Despite Tempelhof's marshalling yards being the briefed target, the overall weight of attack was borne by the city's central districts. The 381BG did bomb the Primary, flying through flak pitched at a moderate but very accurate level and which claimed two bombers – 43-38898 flown by Lt. Pucylowski (534BS) and 42-102873 with Lt. Anderson's 532BS crew.

Sitting in the latter B-17's ball-turret was S/Sgt Mike Medzie. A former member of Lt. Ed Miller's Lead crew, he was behind his buddies in missions flown and was "filling in" as a way of making up the deficit. He would normally not have worn a chute-pack within the cramped confines of his turret, but had taken up this action after his third mission when his B-17 was badly shot-up. Over Berlin one of the left wing gas tanks took a strike (it had been emptied but then refilled from the other wing's tanks). With flames spreading across No. 2 nacelle and bale-out signalled, all Mike did was to release the turret door and flip out backwards.

A long delayed drop from 27000 to 13000 ft. was followed by a pleasant chute descent – that is, until he tangled with a single-limbed tree, leaving him dangling 50 ft above the ground and too high to release his harness! Using his initiative, Mike burnt off the canopy cords, tied a bunch together, and weighted the end to create a crude form of "bolas." This was utilised to get a purchase on the tree-trunk. Then, in order to get out of his harness he adopted a head-down angle before releasing his straps.

Once on the ground he ran off into the forest and settled beneath a tree. As he did so he heard a noise behind, which came from two armed soldiers belonging to a tank-destroyer outfit. He was marched into the nearby village of Ebenswalde where, despite his captors' presence, he was set upon by civilians before being locked up in a box-room for the next three days. Then transported by mule-drawn cart to Tempelhof, he spent a further two weeks in a dungeon full of Allied aircrew. Moved again to Wetzlar, he was reunited with his crew, which sadly was minus Lt. Anderson (P), the single fatality. During the last weeks of the War and while on a forced-march to Nuremburg the POW column of which Mike was a member got caught out in the open and was strafed by P-47s attacking a nearby railroad yard; this tragic action resulted in a number of deaths. His odyssey ended at Mooseberg POW compound, which was liberated in late April by Gen. Patton's tanks.

On the 6th three crews were assigned to the 535BS, one of which was headed by Lt. Turner Brashear. Only four of the 23 missions this crew was to fly by VE-Day would be linked to 44-6883 "RAFAAF," but these would involve two incidents – on 24 March and especially 11 April – which would test them both to the limit. Turner's men were typical of the third generation of 8USAAF combat crew who would see the Conflict through to its bloody conclusion.

The oil targets scheduled for attack this day were almost totally protected by poor weather conditions, forcing the vast bulk of the bombers to strike Targets of Opportunity. For the 381BG this meant unloading on Ohrsdruf, an effort about which Group records acidly stated: "The target was considered nothing more than a wide spot in a second-class road, and the less said about this one the better!"

A mission to Essen (7th) was launched, but was cancelled by weather while Assembly was being made over England. The 8USAAF split each Air Division's strength (on the 9th) between bombing oil-refineries with a Main Force and rail yards and viaducts with a smaller Force. The 381BG was involved in the latter function, and contributed to a strike on a rail viaduct at Arnsburg with unobserved result. St. Valentin's Day was the next major mission, with the target being the sizeable marshalling yards at Dresden. The majority of the 1AD attacked the Primary. This was a follow-up to the previous night's raid by the RAF that had devastated so much of the city center. However, the 1CBW went off course on the way in and lost its place in the bomber-stream. The other two Groups ultimately bombed the Czech City of Prague, while the 381BG was forced to seek a Target of Opportunity at Brux, also in Czechoslovakia.

Lt. Frank Palenik (Lead Bombardier) picked out an industrial complex, which was later identified as a large synthetic oil-fractionating plant NW of the town. The Low Sqdn. failed to drop, and its 12 aircraft subsequently struck the Skoda works at Pilsen. There was post-mission concern that the crews might have strayed too far east and intruded upon Russian-occupied territory, but the doubts were allayed by confirmation of the plant's location behind German lines. Weather conditions were particularly poor, and at least 18 crews landed either on the Continent or on other English airfields. The 535BS's experience in this respect was typical. Lt. Beine crash-landed near Alconbury in 44-6975, while Lt. Greenspan in 44-6809 "PFCs Ltd" and Lt. Rojohn in 43-38998 landed abroad due to fuel shortage.

Lt. Wulf (also 535BS) was in charge of B-17G 42-40017 "Me And My Gal." (She had originally been christened

A second picture of the SDC celebration shows her current pilot, Lt. Malleus (extreme left), alongside Lt. Lyons (N), who is next to Phyliss Calvert. Her fellow-actress looking left is Anna Neagle, and Pat Roc completes the British actress trio. Kneeling on the left is S/Sgt Charles Majors.

"Assend" until Col. Leber spotted this title during a practice mission and demanded it be changed!). The veteran bomber had survived upwards of 14 months combat, but today was to be her operational swan-song. Strikes to an engine and one of the fuel tanks over the target were followed by further punishment inflicted close to the Belgian border. By this stage the aircraft was down to one sound engine. The engineer suggested this be switched off, as fuel was pouring out of the right-inner wing directly behind the functioning engine, but Wulf decided to retain what power he had until the last possible moment. He finally engaged the autopilot and rang the bale-out bell, but was unable to locate his chute-pack. Lt. Dahlgren (N) suggested he stay on board to assist the pilot, but the request was refused; he jumped at what was a very low altitude and landed in a mine-field.

Disengaging the auto-pilot, Wulf desperately sought a suitable crash-site among the thickly wooded area. Suddenly, an open space sloping away in front came into view; the pilot settled in for a landing, lowering the landing gear at the last moment to cushion the impact. The space was littered with rocks and sloped upwards at the far end, so it was a miracle the B-17 did not over-turn. As it was, the main wheels and engines were ripped asunder, and the fuselage subsided several feet into the ground as the lower section caved in. Wulf was unhurt apart from facial bruising when falling against the control column. A group of G.I.s appeared and assisted him up the far slope to await further medical attention. All other eight crewmen had landed safely, and the complete crew was taken to Brussels, from where it was flown home on the 20th.

The 534BS's "The Fox" (43-37657) was a second Group veteran ending her combat career. Lt. Anderson's aircraft lost an engine on the way over and suffered the loss of a second to

On 1 Feb '45 Lt. Kuhns (535BS) "aborted" the mission and jettisoned his bombs in the North Sea. He swung badly on landing and careered off the runway into several 533BS huts, wrecking the veteran 42-32102 "Julie Linda" in the process. The scattered remnants of one hut are directly behind the B-17's tail. Camoflaged rudder is probably a replacement unit.

target flak. Forced to return alone and at low altitude, the cripple came in for intermittent punishment, culminating in No. 3 catching fire. The bale-out order was passed and promptly executed by those in the rear. A stuck nose hatch delayed those up front, but it was finally forced free. This potentially lethal delay proved very fortuitous, because the crewmen who had already jumped floated down into enemy hands, unlike their buddies who came down on the right side of the Front-lines! Lt. Anderson managed to bring the bomber into an Allied airfield, where it languished until declared Category E on 4 March.

More trouble was in store for Lt. Rice (534BS) this day. Flak on the bomb-run badly damaged the left wing, and Sgt Aman (BT) reported that he could see gas pouring out. The pilots now tilted their bomber 30 degrees down to the right to stop the flow and were forced to fly in this attitude all the way back to Ridgewell. After taxiing the bomber back into its dispersal Sgt. Keeney (crewchief) set up a ladder under the hole and climbed up to inspect the damage. On stepping down he expressed the opinion that any violent manoeuvering would have buckled the wing! Despite the severe damage the B-17 was repaired and put back into commission.

The 14 February mission was the first of twelve the Group would fly before the month-end, and the first of 50 before the Bombing Campaign ran its final course on 25 April. Both these statistics were symptomatic of the manner in which the 8USAAF was more than able to function at a sustained pace and peak capacity. Oil was back on the target-list over the next five days, but this key industry remained at least partially unaffected. The persistently adverse weather caused Dresden to take most of the ordnance intended for Ruhland (15th), and the 1AD did not even clear home territory before being recalled on the 17th. In between these dates three plants were bombed by the majority of the Division's 349 B-17s making effective sorties. In the case of the 381BG it sought out a Target of Opportunity described as "an oil plant and fuel dump" at Langendreer. The quartet of missions was completed on the 19th, but even then just over half the Division actually dropped on Dortmund and Bochum, with the remainder striking the marshalling yard Secondary at Münster.

The 16 Feb. mission was the first for Lt. Brashear's crew, and the diary notes of S/Sgt Jack Prillaman (TG) are a good summary of a new crew's reactions; "Went on our first mission to the Ruhr, or 'Happy Valley.' It was the Group's roughest for some time – we surmised that much when the flak came up, but were uncertain due to our newness. Got up at 5.30 and took off at 9.45 – crossed the enemy coast over Holland at

12.30. Crossed out over Northern France and crossed the English coast at 4.00 PM. Bombed from 26000 ft. and had moderate/intense flak for some 20 minutes. Joe (Sgt Newell) in the ball turret passed out during the bomb-run, but came 'round with the help of Red (T/Sgt Edwards, Eng.). Harry (Sgt. Durham, ROG) was throwing out 'chaff' while Red and I kept look-out for fighters and sweated out the flak; we had no escort. At times the flak seemed to march alongside from about 100 yds. On return encountered fog and flew at 100 ft., but finally found the base. Got out on good, solid ground. Two holes in the ship – one just outside No. 1, the other in the right elevator. Kept a flak piece for a souvenir. Wrote letter – did not say much, as I am still keyed-up."

Nuremburg endured a blitz over the next two days which was centered on its railroad station and marshalling yards. Then came Operation CLARION, an all-out assault by the Anglo-American "heavies" on rail and road communications which was spread over 48 hours. Briefed to bomb a marshalling yard at Gardelegen, the Group were thrown off their bomb-run by another Group cutting across their path; two Sqdns. diverted to bomb an over-pass at Kobbelitz, and the third to a similar road layout at Klotze. Sgt Prillaman's notes of this 22 Feb mission reflect the "bare-knuckle" aspect of strategic bombing: "We flew our first low-level mission. Bombed from 9000 ft and practically destroyed a whole town of several thousand people. Visual bombing, so could not miss. Fighters attacked in groups – no flak. Saw a P-51 go down on an Me 410 and blow it up over the target. Saw a big dogfight take place. Could see cars on the ground – we did a horrible amount of damage. Also saw P-51s strafe a train and a factory, which blew up in the biggest sheet of flame I ever saw – at least 1000 ft high, with white smoke up to about 7000 ft. (I found out later it was a chemical works)." Cloud cover prevented the yards at Hof from being clobbered on the 23rd. Instead, 23 crews struck yards at Meiningen with good results, while 12 other crews achieved what was adjudged a fair result at Adelsberg.

The dispatch of between 1000 and 1300 bombers was a standard feature of operations, as was instanced over the last five days of February when approximately 5500 sorties were flown; a reduced total of 745 on the 27th was the exception to the rule. The Luftwaffe was almost beaten out of sight, and the main danger posed to crews was from flak, although this was often pitched at "light to moderate" levels and often reported as inaccurate. A good example of this was experienced over Hamburg on the 24th. The mission was recorded as "a piece of cake," with the gunners throwing up a meager and inaccurate response – changed days from just a matter of months back when a mention of the city's name would have sent a thrill of apprehension up any combat crewman's back!

The same could now be said for another well-remembered city – Munich – although the mission on the following day did experience a moderate level of flak; even this intensity was not achieved until the Group had already bombed. The smoke screen intended to conceal the marshalling yards was blown away by wind, and bombardiers had ample time to zero-in for a concentrated strike. Only Lt. Schlesser in 42-97265 "Hells

The surplus gas in "Julie Linda"'s tanks are being emptied off into the tanker standing in the background. Bomber was declared "surplus to requirements" on 2 Feb.

A light dusting of snow covers the runway as a B-17G with 1CBW red wingtips lifts off with landing gear already retracted. The wind-angle is not directly down the runway and has pushed the bomber off to one side as it clears the airfield perimeter. Picture taken during the winter of 1944/45.

Angel" did not return to base, having diverted into a Belgian airfield with no reported casualties.

Back at Ridgewell M/Sgt Clarence Bankston was posed by official USSTAF and British newspaper photographers as preparing to consume a monster mouthful of cake wielded by the British actress Anna Neagle. The occasion was a celebration of the crewchief's B-17G having flown its 100th mission (By this date she had completed a further five). The bomber was "Stage Door Canteen," which was originally christened by Mary Churchill in April '44. Also present were Miss Neagle's fellow actresses Phyliss Calvert and Patricia Roc.

Berlin was still a priority target, which on the 26th received over 1000 bomb loads. The "Spot Jammer" gear carried by a number of bombers was calculated to be having an adverse effect on the flak-gunners' ability to direct accurate barrages via their radar predictor apparatus. Capt. Doug Winters, a veteran 543BS pilot and last Wartime CO of the 534BS, described the mission as a "milk-run." Of all targets meriting such a summary, the last one to come to mind in 1943/44 would have been "Big B!" An exception to this was Leipzig (27th), whose heavy flak barrage still brought down none of the 1AD.

18

THE BATTLE IS WON

By 1 March 1945 the German national territory was still intact East of the Rhine, but the Russians were across the Polish/German border and advancing steadily in the direction of Berlin. Operation VARSITY – code-name for the projected Rhine crossing – was well into the planning stage. Transportation was to feature prominently in the month's mission tally, with the presumed intention of blunting any attempt at reinforcement after the operation had been initiated. The Wehrmacht was a spent defensive force as the rapid deployment from the Rhine bridge-heads was to confirm; however, a "worst case" scenario of dogged resistance had to be catered for, given the experience of the Ardennes Offensive.

An anticipated visual attack on marshalling yards at Neckarsulm on the 1st gradually faded away as cloud increased from 1/10 to 7/10 and Gee-H was brought into operation. On the way home No. 4 engine on 43-37675 "Flak Magnet" caught fire, and Lt. Price (532BS) alerted his crew to prepare for a bale-out. On seeing the co-pilot vacating his seat, Sgt Hawkins (Eng.) took this as conformation to jump and went out through the nose hatch. His canopy was not seen to deploy before he

Bombers rarely saw the inside of a hangar unless long-term inspection or severe battle damage was involved. MS;Y of the 535BS appears to be intact and has probably been taken under cover for the former stated reason. Photo dated 1 March '45.

Sgt Fred Kreuger (Weather Section) flew on a practice mission during which he shot several pictures. This example catches "The Alamo" with its silver finish and Cheyenne tail turret, along with the camoflaged veteran "Phyliss" which bears the original "wedge" tail-gun shape. Both are 535BS aircraft. Top B-17G is the equally battle-tested "Rotherhithes Revenge" of the 533BS. Only "The Alamo" did not return States-side in May 1945. Instead, it was transferred to the 306BG and salvaged in Germany the following year.

This 533BS B-17G (44-8544) burns fiercely following a non-operational crash on 14 March '45. Top-turret frame with its twin machine-guns pointing forlornly upwards is outlined by the fire-truck's lights. Next morning scattered oxygen-bottles are seen among the wreckage, while all that remains of the left wing are its propeller-less engines. Aircraft was one of two Sqdn. bombers equipped with Gee-H blind-bombing/navigational gear.

disappeared into the undercast, but he did succeed in pulling his ripcord and drifting down for a landing near Arras, France. His action was perhaps natural, but precipitate, because the fire was extinguished and the B-17 brought down safely onto a French airfield!

Next day only a small proportion of the Division made visual strikes on the assigned synthetic–oil plant at Böhlen and a refinery at Rositz. The majority of the force went for the Secondary at the city of Chemnitz. One rest day, and the Group were back over Germany to hit railroad facilities at Ulm (4th) and attempting to bomb Ruhland's oil plant (5th). Compared

Capt. Graham (Equipment Safety Officer) shakes hands with one of seven fellow airmen from the 535BS. All wear the Sqdn. badge, apart from the officer second from left, who sports the Group emblem. The 105-mission veteran "Stage Door Canteen" appears to carry no tally of symbols to denote her pre-eminent combat status.

to the 2nd, an even smaller proportion struck the Primary, whereas 166 crews again added to Chemnitz's destruction. Ridgewell's Lead Sqdn. progressed further down the scale to bomb a Target of Opportunity at Plauen. Hüls in the Ruhr contained a benzol plant among its multifarious industries, and this was given full attention on the 8th, although 10/10 cloud meant the result of the Gee-H assisted drop was not seen.

Lt. Charles "Hotrock" Carpenter should have been part of the force sent out this day. He had "aborted" the mission just after take-off, but then transferred over to a 535BS B-17. Setting off again, he made a bee-line for where he thought the Group might be intercepted. Eventually a host of black fly-like shapes loomed up on the horizon – but the expected B-17s evolved into RAF Lancasters on their way to bomb Cologne! Nothing daunted, Carpenter joined the throng to add his bombs to those of his "adopted" formation. After turning for home the lone Fortress was spotted by the Lancaster crews who commenced exchanging signals, and in two instances closed up to formate with their American Ally. Upon landing back at base Carpenter was to claim that he noticed his B-17's name – "RAFAAF." Asked for his reason in joining up with the Lancasters, he retorted "Daylight bombing is our forte, and I could not allow the RAF to think it could do better!"

It had been several weeks and upwards of 20 missions during which period Death had taken a welcome holiday, but the Grim Reaper was always hovering around, and on 9 March he struck. A rail depot and repair-shop at Kassel was visually attacked as the B-17s tracked their way through fairly accurate flak. One shell impacted with No.3 engine on 43-39012 flown by Lt. Scherman (532BS). Fire took rapid hold and streamed

Numerous visiting aircraft were to be seen at Ridgewell. In this case the CY codes identify the fighter as a P-51D from the 55FG based at Wormingford. Reduction of the D-Day stripes to an area below the rear fuselage indicates picture was taken from late 1944 onwards.

back along the fuselage as the doomed B-17 sagged and plunged through 10000 ft. before exploding; only two chutes were seen to open, and these bore the sole survivors. The aircraft's wreckage came down at Fritzlar, SW of Kassel.

Six days later Death struck again, but this time at just one airman. Lt. Carpenter (533BS) – he of the solo run to Cologne on the 8th – was on his way back from Oranienburg's rail yards when a tremendous flak burst nearly tore 43-37561 in half. The main impact was centered around the radio-room, which was totally destroyed, but it was S/Sgt Walter Ahl (WG) who was killed instantly. A fifteen foot gash was torn along the right fuselage side, and rudder and stabiliser controls were jammed solid. The chute-packs for Ahl and the ball turret gunner were shredded, while the tail-gunner and "spare" packs were blown out of the bomber, so negating the chances of all crewmen seeking salvation by bale-out. The pilots flew their maimed B-17 back to the massive Emergency Landing Field at Woodbridge, Suffolk. Here their frantic attempts to touch-down safely ended up with the landing gear collapsing, the rear fuselage detaching, and two engines catching fire as the bomber slithered to a stop. Fire-tenders were immediately on hand to put out the blaze, and once the survivors had clambered out Carpenter (who was flying his 34th mission) coolly held a crew-muster!

A relaxed party of "original" senior staff sit on the wing of "Little Rock-ette" during March '45. Col. Hall (Group CO) and Col. Shackley (Air Executive) are on the left. Extreme right is Capt. Francis Hawkins, in charge of the Photo Section, and alongside him is Maj. Ed Kurner (S-4 Supply).

This B-17G is jacked-up in the hangar and the right wing detached. Bomber was struck by a bomb from another B-17 and was lucky to survive, given the point of impact was close to the wing main-spar. Incident reportedly occurred on 25 Feb '45.

A very happy Lt. John Rice is taxiing his B-17G "Patsy Ann" (42-97285) back into her dispersal for the last time. His 534BS crew had survived several harrowing incidents. First came a forced-landing on the Continent on 17 Oct '44 when "Green Hornet II" (42-31550) was "written off." Then on 14 Feb '45 a huge hole was torn in "Patsy Ann"'s left wing by flak, and the B-17 was flown home tilted at a 30 degree angle to prevent any further loss of gas from the ruptured tanks!

The four missions between these fatal incidents were all routine, but only the one was visually carried out when a railroad bridge at Vlotho was hit. The other three – Sinsen's railroad center (10th), U-boat yards at Bremen (11th), and a second rail center at Dillenburg (12th) – were cloud covered. Although Böhlen's refineries were briefed for the 17th, only one Sqdn. released there, the other two Sqdns. going on for the Zeiss-Jena factory. The Group's 24th mission to Berlin (18th) proved nothing out of the ordinary, although the flak gunners did resort to their expected level of intensity. A variation in target-type presented itself next day when Böhlen's flak sites were down to be given a taste of their own medicine. In fact, the Group was again forced to seek out the secondary, a chemical plant at Plauen, which was bombed using H2X.

The emphasis now temporarily shifted from industrial to military targets. A whole series of airfields, especially those believed to be housing the Me 262 jet fighter, were nominated for attack on the 21st, and the Group contributed to the 180 bomb loads put down visually onto Rheine/Salzbergen. Next day it was the turn of military encampments located at Dorsten

Lt. Brashear's crew are photographed after completing the 22 March '45 mission. Trio of officers on right are (L-R) Lts. Horn (CP), Greenlee (B), and Leyton (N). Brashear is fourth from left and is flanked by Sgts. Edwards (Eng.) and Durham (ROG), with Sgt Joe Newell (BT) in between Durham and Horn. S/Sgt Jack Prillaman (TG) is on the left, alongside Sgt Norcom (WG).

On 24 March '45 "RAFAAF" received a strike on her No. 3 engine, resulting in a "runaway" propeller which finally came free, fortunately without hitting the fuselage. Lt. Brashear (P) and T/Sgt "Red" Edwards (Eng.) survey the damaged cowling. Numerous flak holes resulted in the B-17G being hangared for repair and later return to combat.

In common with most Groups, the 381BG possessed a number of supplementary, or "hack" aircraft. Cols. Hall and Reed stand with several enlisted men in front of an L-4 Piper Cub. It was said Col. Hall liked to fly through the hangars in this diminutive machine, and that some unkind soul suggested closing the doors at the far end whenever this act was indulged in!

Senior and Support Officer line-up taken in early 1945. Cols. Hall and Reed at left rear accompany (L-R) Majs. Sandman (Operations), Greenlee (Adjutant), Wilcox (S-1), Lt. Thayer (Communications), Capt. Tyson (Asst. Operations Officer), and Capt. Eichenbaum (Ordnance). In the front row Capt. Porter (S-2 Section) is second left, with Lt. Olsen (Weather) and Capt. Platz (Armament) on Porter's left. Capt. Hawkins (Photo Section) is on the right

and Feldhausen to feel the weight of Group ordnance from among the large 1AD force.

Capt. George Stone was a veteran 533BS navigator well into his second combat tour. On the 22nd he was part of the Lead Crew headed by Lt. Fawcett and bearing Capt. Gotthardt as the Group Leader. Another veteran flier was Lt. Pete Kowalski (B), the proud holder of the Silver Star. The B-17 was a radar-equipped ship, with the experienced Lt. Hiller as "Mickey" operator. The crew contained no less than seven officers out of the ten men on board.

The first scattered flak bursts were encountered prior to the bomb-run, and gradually built up to an intense and accurate level just before "bombs away" was signalled. It was now that the Lead B-17 took a strike between No. 3 engine and the fuselage that ignited the gas tank.

A slow spin developed, and after only a few gyrations the tail section broke off. Upward of six chutes were reported, but official USAAF records from the following August still listed all ten men as MIA. The loss of any crew was a sobering event, but today the shock waves felt at losing such an experienced team radiated throughout the entire Group. Capt. Gotthardt, for instance, held a high reputation among the personnel, which paralleled that of Capt. Edwin Manchester (535BS), whose loss way back on 8 Oct. '43 had engendered a similar sense of bereavement around the base. The incident once again reinforced the fact that nobody was safe from the moment of approach to

A clear sky during the Winter of 1944/45 catches four B-17Gs lined up on the runway with a fifth moving along the perimeter track. Closest to the camera is 42-102590 "In Like Errol" of the 535BS, which is paired with a 534BS ship. Directly behind "Errol" is another 535BS bomber, 42-31067 "Phyliss."

"Miss Florala" of the 534BS would be the Group's last combat loss on 8 April '45. Only two Sgts survived out of Lt. Adelmeyer's eight-man crew. This Sqdn. had removed the ball-turrets from its aircraft, which probably explains why the standard crew complement of nine was reduced by one.

On 11 April '45 Lt. Greenspan's B-17G collided with Lt. Brashear on the route home from Freihan. Three of the former crew inspect the badly twisted aileron on their bomber (44-8826). Both crews were from the 535BS

a bomber until leaving its presence on return. Taking over Group Lead after 44-8175 went down was Capt. Ackerman (534BS). He was also on his second tour, and not only had one calendar month left of his life, but was fated to die in cruelly inappropriate circumstances.

A visual and well-concentrated strike on a marshalling yard at Münster occupied 37 crews' attention on the 23rd. Over on the Continent the Anglo-American Armies were standing-to for a Rhine crossing North and South of the Ruhr to be spearheaded by airborne troops. Early on the 24th the crews were roused and briefed for the second of three missions to be dispatched by the 1AD out of an 8USAAF total of eight. The day started badly when a 534BS aircraft caught fire. Sgt Downey responded by leaping out onto the night-shrouded dispersal with a fire extinguisher; seconds later he was dead, having run straight into one of the aircraft's whirling propellers. Take-off was at 0615, with return six hours later. The airfield at Fürstenau/Vechta was in the clear and provided excellent bombing results. However, a price was paid as a very accurate flak barrage peppered the sky.

The 533BS crew of Lt. Jankowiak flying 44-6478 suffered the loss of No. 4 engine, which was torn from its mounting. Lt. Levenson (B) salvoed his load, and the pilots pushed the B-17 into a gentle dive in an attempt to extinguish the resultant fire, which defied all such efforts and increased in intensity. The bale-out order was finally given as a slow spiral began to develop and the blazing outer-wing section was beginning to fold up.

Satisfied that all crew up front were gone and hearing nothing from the rear, Lt. Jankowiak now struggled against the mounting centrifugal force as he worked his chute-pack out from under his seat and headed for the nose hatch. As he emerged into the slipstream with his right hand clasped to the ripcord he was smacked against the fuselage. The force of impact caused him to involuntarily pull the ripcord, and the canopy tumbled back over the left stabiliser and anchored itself in place. It appeared there would be no salvation from an ugly death for the Lt. Suddenly, there was a big explosion and the tail section broke off, leaving the canopy to pull providentially clear, although with large tears in its fabric. A very hard landing left Jankowiak with a badly broken left leg, thereby rendering impossible any attempt by him to conceal himself in a nearby forest. He was soon apprehended and off on the first stage of a

Lt Brashear's "RAFAAF" lost its entire right stabiliser in the collision, but he and Lt. Horn still managed to correct the flat spin into which their B-17G was pitched, and even brought off a normal landing back at Ridgewell. In this shot taken directly afterwards 535BS personnel inspect the bare remnants of the excised stabiliser. T/Sgt "Red" Edwards (Eng.) is walking away past the tail-turret, and S/Sgt Harry Durham (ROG) faces the camera on the left.

Lt. Turner Brashear has a wistful facial expression as he stands by "RAFAAF" and points to the vacant space once occupied by the inner edge of the 18-ft. stabiliser, now reduced to a few metal shards and the shorn end of the rear spar. Lt. Bob Horn is the other officer, and on the left is the crew chief, M/Sgt Harry Gerberding.

journey to Stalag Luft 1 at Barth. Lt. Roche (CP) and Sgts Moberg (ROG) and Berger (WG) were not so lucky, and were later confirmed KIA. The B-17's remnants crashed down onto Quakenbrück airfield.

A flak fragment cutting through the thin skin of Lt. Bennett's 535BS bomber took the life of Sgt Bob Bolin (Mickey operator). On 1 Jan. he had baled out, only to land inside a minefield from which he was extracted; this time around Luck had deserted him. Another 535BS aircraft flown by Lt. Brashear took a heavy beating, including a thoroughly shot-up No. 3 on which the propeller refused to "feather." Worse still, it kept moving forward and back on its shaft and threatened to spin off into the fuselage, with likely disastrous effect on both bomber and crew. Happily, when it did at last detach the whirling disc sailed clear over the aircraft. Back at Ridgewell the count of holes was abandoned after 200, and 44-6883 "RAFAAF" was trundled off into the hangar for repair and an eventful reunion with the Brashear crew. By contrast, the second 24 March mission was uneventful. The target was Twente/Enschede in Holland, which was also well plastered. Only one Sqdn. took part, along with Sqdns. from the 91BG and 398BG.

A total recall of both the 1AD and 3AD after take-off for Zeitz was made on the 25th due to bad weather. Twenty-four hours later Zeitz and its synthetic-oil plant were back on the briefing-boards. A combination of lousy weather, particularly over the Primary, and an inoperable bombsight in the Lead B-17 resulted in just the Low Sqdn. making what transpired as a failed run at the target. The other two Sqdns. bombed a mill at Plauen with marginal results. The Group's final visit to "Big B" came two days after when H2X was utilised for the attack. The meager flak barrage came up through the heavy undercast as the ordnance fell upon tank and armament factories.

"In Like Errol" (42-102590) was a long-standing feature on the 535BS dispersals. The silver-finished B-17G had arrived in late May '44 and had piled up an impressive number of missions. She was currently looked after by S/Sgt Dave Martin's team of mechanics. Lt. Bennett's crew was on board as she lifted off for Bremen's U-boat construction yards on 30 March. With Bennett were Lt. Alex Nelson (CP), T/Sgt Chester Slomczenski, and Sgts. Cal Hockley (BT) and Chuck Knaus (TG). All four had baled out of Lt. Peter's B-17 on 1 January, an experience Lt. Nelson had sworn never to repeat.

Although the city's flak defences were quite heavy, the 427 attacking B-17s of the 1AD got their bombs off while suffering just twelve crewmen killed or MIA. Sadly, most of this human cost came from Ridgewell's veteran bomber. The standard nine-man crew had been added to by the presence of a radar/radio signals "jammer," Sgt Charlie Majors. Crippled by flak that had knocked out two engines during the bomb-run, "In Like Errol" descended in an initially controlled fashion, and the call for fighter cover soon materialised in the form of four P-51s. Minutes after stark tragedy arose as the ailing B-17 sustained a slashing fighter attack from head-on, which sent her into a terminal plunge.

To this day there is great debate among the survivors as to whether the assassin was an Me 262 or one of their P-51 "escorts." The suspicion that the latter aircraft might have been a captured example put back into commission by the Luftwaffe

RAFAAF did not return to combat duty after her dramatic survival. In this picture her Bendix chin-turret has been detached and the aperture plated over, while the cheek-gun frame is replaced by a flat sheet of Plexiglas.

still persists in their minds. Of course, to a tension-laden gunner, a P-51 with drop-tanks in position could so easily assume the same basic outline as the Me 262. A better explanation for the confusion could lie in the post-mission comments of S/Sgt. Majors and S/Sgt Hockley (BT). They both sighted a P-51 boring in from the left at right angles to their B-17. It is likely the pilot was trying to cut off the Me 262 from delivering its attack. However, to those crewmen who were unaware of the Me 262's presence, their "executioner" could easily have been regarded as the P-51!

Whatever the explanation on this subject, there was barely time for the three enlisted men to scramble for the exits and parachute safely. Lt Nelson's body was reportedly found in the wreckage, with his fellow airmen later being shown some of the Lt's personal articles by his captors; it would never be known whether the co-pilot had been unable to clear the bomber or had indeed elected to ride her down. Sgt Knaus was later alleged to have fallen victim to civilians who stoned him to death. In fact, Sgt. Majors, after his prompt capture on landing, was escorted over to the tail-gunner's body and was able to confirm his death as due to a failed chute-opening. Sgt Slomczenski's Polish ancestry had previously led him to assert he would try to pass himself off as a forced-labourer should he ever be shot down. He was still officially "missing in action" after the War, and another nine years would elapse before the cruel news of his body's discovery emerged during 1954.

Although the target list was to shrink as rapidly as the Anglo-American forces advanced into Germany, the 8USAAF would still put up large numbers of bombers in the few weeks remaining for the Bombing Campaign to run its course. Over 1300 bombers headed out on the 31st for synthetic-oil plants, but the 1AD had to be satisfied with punishing its allotted Secondary – Halle's marshalling yards – thanks to 10/10 cloud intruding at Merseburg.

April 1945

The combat crews were by now soberly confident that the end of the European Conflict was rapidly approaching. However, such confidence was surely balanced by the needling thought that none of them was guaranteed a passage to unlimited life until the final shots had been fired. Death still roamed the skies, albeit in greatly reduced form, but that was no consolation for those unlucky exceptions on whom it would descend. At Ridgewell there were around 40 personnel, both combat and groundcrew, who would never live to see the shores of their native Land.

A total of 15 missions during April would close off the Group's combat career, but the month started with a mission (2nd) to Denmark which was "scrubbed" when the bombers were almost across the North Sea. Despite having progressed so far, no mission credit was granted the crews. The first completed run for the whole 1AD was two days later with several airfields in the Bremen/Münster region the focus for attack. In the case of the 381BG its crews settled for bombing the Secondary at Hoya. When the B-17s droned into the circuit, red flares which indicated "casualties aboard" shot up from a 532BS aircraft. But all the medics had to do when the propellers stopped rotating was to stretcher out the body of F/O Ralph Thomas, from which life was fast ebbing – the first of the final human cull from Group ranks as the Bombing Campaign drew to a close.

Next day's attack upon an ordnance factory at Grafenwöhr was conducted through 8/10 cloud, but the crews were confident their loads of 500 lb and 1000 lb bombs had struck squarely. Capt Cronin (a former 534BS pilot and newly appointed 535BS CO) was up front on his 48th mission, which was to Kohlenbissen airfield. The Lead Bombardier this day (7th) was another veteran from the winter of 1943/44. Capt. Frank Palenik (535BS) displayed his skill by identifying the airfield despite both a ground haze and heavy broken cloud.

Next day it was an oil dump at Derben and an airfield at Scharfstadt, towards which over 300 Division bombers wended their way. The majority turned to attack Secondaries when weather intervened. Even so, the strike result for the Group at Stendal's rail yards was reported as a "miss." To compound the sense of frustration, one crew was MIA. Lt. Adelmeyer

The natural metal finish on 44-6950, a B-17G assigned to the 532BS, provides a superb background to a neat piece of female artwork. Photographed after assignment on 1 Feb '45, the bomber went on to VE-Day and returned Stateside during May.

(534 BS) had headed out unaware of the fate awaiting him and most of his crew. Flak damage suffered over the target blossomed into a fire as the formation skirted 'round Kassel. A controlled dive to extinguish the blazing No. 3 engine only resulted in spreading the flames to the bomb bay. Then "Miss Florala" (44-6173) fell into a spin after one wing separated, and the bomber was finally seen to smash into a building. Three chutes were spotted, with one being fired on by soldiers. A few days later Sgts Hayden and Houser arrived back at base to confirm that the other six crewmen were dead. (The absence of a ninth man on board was probably due to the 534BS having been ordered in January to remove ball turrets from their aircraft). Aerial combat had claimed its last victims from Ridgewell.

An early 0600 briefing on the 9th was not followed up by take-off until noon thanks to slowly dispersing fog. The latest airfield to be struck was Oberpfaffenhofen, near Munich, where a wholesale destruction of the main East/West runway justified the "1-1" message. An ordnance depot at Oranienburg was hit next day. It was here that the crews for the first time in weeks got a sight of the Luftwaffe in the form of 30 Me109s and Fw190s, along with six Me 262s. They were generally too taken up with their own survival to present any real threat to the "Big Friends." However, a pair of Me109s did whip through the group during the bomb-run, but did not open fire. Then, as the Lead and Low Sqdns. were turning for the Rally Point, the greater menace in the form of an Me 262 appeared. It was being ineffectually pursued by P-51s, but again there was no exchange of gun-fire – the jet was much too fast for the gunners' .50s to focus upon it, and the German pilot was probably more interested in "ditching" his Mustang tormentors!

The Munich region was again over-flown on the 11th. when an oil depot at Freihan was struck by 300 bombers. A large smoke pall covered the target when the 381BG came in to bomb and the bombardiers released into this. A perfect fighter escort was provided, and the clear weather on the way in persisted as the Group headed back. One of the prime dangers ever present when flying formation was that of collision. The Post-war Hollywood impression of a mass of B-17s or B-24s flying ruler-straight lines was a world away from the real experience. Apart from those at the front, all other pilots were struggling against the accumulative air turbulence created by the preceding bombers. It was no wonder that the average pilot lost weight during his combat tour. This was as much from the physical effort of controlling what was a swaying, lurching, aircraft, as it was from the mental stress of combat itself. The experience of 21 January over Ridgewell had demonstrated how the collision factor was present even during the final stages of a mission.

Flying as 535BS Lead in Lt. Greenspan's B-17 was Capt. Garrett on his last mission. Below and to their left was Lt. Brashear, back in command of "RAFAAF." While heading up past Ludwigshafen on the way home 44-8826 suffered a vicious down-drop, probably induced by an air pocket. Sgts Prillaman (TG) and Norcom (WG) had seen the Leader sagging down upon their B-17, and so urgently called for their pilot to "drop it," but the warnings were delivered too late. Lt Greenspan's left wing-tip smacked into RAFAAF's right stabiliser and excised it completely from the fuselage.

Damage to the Lead B-17 was serious with the aileron bent up and backward along its outer edge, but the bomber proved quite manageable and was carefully husbanded back for a safe landing at Ridgewell. The situation for "RAFAAF" proved much more serious. The loss of a complete control surface threw the B-17 into a flat spin, and centrifugal force at once exerted its malign influence on the crew. Sgt Prillaman was thrown around his position with ammunition, chute-pack, and other items strewn around. He managed to grab and clip on the pack, and kicked out the escape hatch just as Lts. Brashear and Horn were succeeding in pulling out about 7000 ft below the formation. Both pilots had had their legs thrust up against the instrument panel, while Sgts. Edwards (Eng.) and Durham (ROG) were literally pinned to the top of the turret and radio-room, respectively.

Lt Brashear was to recall how he had literally pulled himself down onto his seat using the control column as a "lever." He had quickly cut the throttles back, but found that one aerodynamic problem had been exchanged for another; now the

This fire-blackened, shattered fuselage belongs to B-17G 43-38856 of the 534BS. On 23 April '45 she smacked into the highest point on the Isle of Man in the Irish Sea. All 31 crew and personnel proceeding to Northern Ireland on Rest and Relaxation were killed.

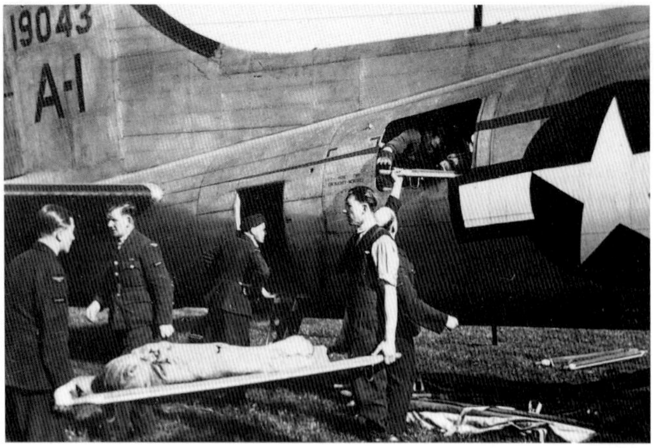

The wrapped corpses from the Isle of Man disaster are being stretchered by RAF personnel in through the waist-window on the Group "hack" ship, B-17E "Little Rock-Ette."

errant B-17 was adopting an incipient climbing attitude! Within a few minutes the physical effort of forcing the bomber along a level path was rapidly tiring both pilots, who were endeavouring to drop their charge down to below oxygen mask altitude. With the prospect of holding the aircraft aloft for several hundreds of miles fast fading, Lt Brashear posed the question of baling out for the other crewmen, but none took up the option.

It was at this stage that Brashear hit upon the idea of utilising a length of the severed control cables hanging down in the waist area. Calling upon T/Sgt Edwards to go back and extract around 6 ft of cable, he then had the engineer knock out a pair of dials mounted in the instrument panel. The cable was passed through the apertures and fed back around the control column yoke, making two loops. A square knot was formed, and a machine gun part was produced to form a crude turnbuckle. Rotation of the machine gun part allowed Brashear to tighten or loosen the cable. This action provided basic control of the remaining left-hand elevator. However, the resultant strain on the cable was so great that the instrument panel was bowed outward. In any event, it withstood the tremendous pressure as the B-17 was headed homeward.

The measure of lateral and vertical control over "RAFAAF" permitted her pilots to avoid over-flying known flak concentrations, and the total absence of the Luftwaffe added to the firm prospect of regaining friendly shores. Once over the Allied front-line, the question of baling out was again raised, but was just as quickly turned down. (Unknown to all but Lt. Horn was the fact that Lt. Brashear would almost certainly be unable to evacuate the bomber, because it would snap into a spin immediately when the controls were released).

As the Channel was being traversed a Spitfire drew up in a bid to escort the crippled bomber. Ironically, his efforts were not appreciated, since he flew a weaving course so close in front that Brashear was half in mind to have his engineer fire a burst near, or even at, the "Little Friend!" Just over four hours after the collision occurred, "RAFAAF" eased into the Ridgewell circuit as the last remnants of the Group formation were completing their landing circuits. A further 20 minutes passed until all were down and Lts Brashear and Horn could concentrate on making a possible landing.

The sight of the aircraft without one stabiliser must have jolted the memory of those ground observers at Ridgewell who 13 months previous had watched the equally incredible spectacle of "Whodat" and wondered how it had remained airborne, as "RAFAAF" was now doing. Col. Hall was one of those who were observing the parlous state of the circling B-17. An order from the Col. was duly passed via the control tower for Brashear to follow the advice given to the pilots of "Whodat" to bale out the crew and then to abandon the B-17 over the coastline. However, the 534BS bomber had been too mortally wounded to risk a landing, whereas "RAFAAF" was still in a reasonably manoeuvrable condition. In addition, this was the B-17 in which Brashear's crew had flown their 13th mission when they were badly shot-up on 24 March; today was only the fourth time the crew had taken her up, but a kind of emotional attachment to the aircraft had already developed in their minds.

For the third time, the bale-out option was refused, and preparations made for what was a hazardous, if not potentially lethal, landing approach. With the bomber displaying a tendency to stall at anything lower than 140 mph, the pilots had no choice but to make a long approach. The crew was braced in position within the radio-room as the final left-hand turn was made. Over the ensuing few, and extremely fraught, minutes, Lt Horn made minute, reducing movements of the engine throttles as Brashear similarly adjusted the turnbuckle contraption around the control column. With no chance of over-shooting for a second landing approach, "RAFAAF" shot in over the runway threshold, with Horn dropping full flap and chopping the throttles as ordered. In spite of the high landing speed the pilots managed to bring the B-17 to a halt without over-shooting the runway.

For the second time "RAFAAF" had delivered her crew from a combat incident, which could well have merited them taking to their chutes. Few better examples of both the inherent structural stamina and sound flight characteristics of

"Boeing's Best" were to be found during WWII than with "RAFAAF." The Freihan mission spelled the end of the combat road for the aircraft. She was repaired and used as a "hack" machine by the 9USAAF in Germany before being salvaged in Dec. '45. (After the 11 April incident a scurrilous tale was circulated among the personnel at Ridgewell. This concerned one senior Group officer who went to the runway-end with a cine-camera, hoping to film a spectacular crash!)

By now the USSTAF authorities must have been scratching around for targets, since Nazi-held territory had shrunk to a minuscule geographic area. After bombing a marshalling yard at Neumünster with good results (13th), the Group was then part of a 1AD force going out for the second day to unload on German strong-points around Bordeaux in SW France. The mission on the 16th proved a rather frustrating experience for the 37 crews, since the bomb-pattern was well short of the rail yards at Regensburg. Next day was no better, despite a visual sighting, because the strike again fell short of the Dresden engine-sheds.

A very variable result came out of the run to Elsterwalde (19th). It was later considered that the Lead bombardier had not allowed for the maximum 30 degrees correction for wind-drift the Norden bombsight could accommodate. Following "bombs away" the Low and High Sqdn's bombs went well astray from their intended marshalling yard target. Those two sub-units then stood off as the Lead Sqdn, which for some reason had not dropped, flew around in search of an alternative. This turned up in the form of a rail junction at Falkenburg, onto which their tonnage was precisely aimed. An immediate repercussion of this semi-farce was that Col. Hall ordered all senior combat personnel, apart from Col. Shackley and Capt. Cronin (535BS CO), to fly next day. With Hall in the Lead B-17 there was no repetition, and the rail junction and engine-shops at Brandenburg were perfectly patterned!

Cols. Hall and Shackley appear in a relaxed frame of mind in this picture. In fact, their mood was very somber as the location was the Isle of Man, to which they had flown following the loss of Capt. Ackerman and his party.

Col. Shackley was up and in command on the 21st when the recurring 10/10 cloud made observation of a strike at Munich's marshalling yards impossible. The bombing of Germany by the 8USAAF was over, and only one more mission to Czechoslovakia was scheduled for its crews. However, in between these two missions there occurred a tragic incident which was to leave its mark throughout the ranks of the 381BG.

Capt. Charles Ackerman was a 534BS pilot well into his second combat tour and with every chance of "coming through" and going home. On the 23rd he climbed aboard his Sqdn's 43-38856 with a skeleton crew comprising a co-pilot, navigator, engineer, and radio-operator, and 26 other officers and enlisted men. The party was headed for a Rest and Relaxation visit to Belfast, Northern Ireland. Due to a general run-down in the intensity of combat operations it had been decreed that a specific number of selected personnel could enjoy this visit.

The B-17's route was out over the Irish sea, in the middle of which stands the Isle of Man. The weather conditions were reported clear when it took-off and headed towards the West. Less than 90 minutes later it was a fire-blackened carcass straddling the upper slopes of the Isle's highest point, from which not one of the men escaped alive. The previous mass tragedy to strike the 381BG had been on its second day in combat. Now, by grim coincidence, today's calamity had happened just two days before the 8USAAF was to complete its brief. The 23 June '43 incident had solely concerned the 533BS, but the Isle of Man incident spread shock waves through most of the Group's sections. The 535BS records, for example, cited the Sqdn members' stunned reaction at the loss of Sgt Mata, an experienced gunner; Sgt Max Martinez, an "original" in the Pay Section and the father of two children, "One of whom he had never seen"; PFC "Chollie" Quagliarello (Parachute Section); and Cpl. Gupton (Ordnance), who was another "original" from Pyote and a family man.

The task of bringing the bodies down from the hillside was complicated by a general lack of roads or even paths, and it was a day or so before the grisly duty of carriage and identification was made. Meanwhile, Cols. Hall and Shackley flew over in the Group "hack" B-17E 41-9043 "Little Rockette," into which the wrapped corpses were gently packed for return to Ridgewell. Finally, on 27 April, in a Service at Madingley conducted by Capt. Brown and attended by large numbers of personnel, the 31 luckless airmen were laid to their eternal rest – the last in a far too long line of 381BG fatalities.

The briefing-room beckoned the combat crews on 25 April for what was expected to be yet another long haul over enemy territory. What could not be known this day was the fact that the sortie was destined to be the 8USAAF's final thrust. The Czech city of Pilsen housed one of the largest armament factories in Europe, and the Skoda plant and the nearby Pilsen airfield were assigned to the 1AD. Weather was terrible, and in the case of the Group only two of its 37 contingent dropped their bombs (without authority), the others withholding on the grounds this was a Nazi-occupied country whose citizens were our Allies. The last flak barrage ever to be faced was recorded as "heavy and accurate," but caused no Group losses, although bringing down six B-17s from other units. And so, as the Fortresses circled into the landing pattern at Ridgewell and other bases, the curtain was finally lowered upon one of the most intensive and savagely contested Battles in the history of Mankind.

In the remaining days of April the 8USAAF was still at combat readiness and crews held on top-line ready for the call to arms. On the 26th 42-97267 "Tomahawk Warrior" of the 535BS was taken aloft by Lt. Cotea on a practice flight, along with a full bomb-load of twenty 250-lb bombs. The right wing caught fire upon landing, and the B-17 was quickly taxied off the runway and onto the perimeter track, where she was abandoned to turn into a fiery mass. Fifteen minutes later the entire load exploded, blowing the 97-mission veteran to pieces and scoring a shallow crater into the track surface.

Lt. Martin Matyas and T/Sgt Herb Kwart, members of Lt. Marelius' 534BS crew, are seen in happier times. Herb came through his combat tour, but Martin was one of the ill-fated passengers involved in the Isle of Man crash on 23 April '45.

19

"IT'S OVER, OVER THERE"

VE-Day arrived on 8 May, and in the interval between the final bombing mission on 25 April and this momentous day the sole use of the USAAF heavy bombers had been in a peaceful mode. Several 3AD Groups, along with RAF Lancasters of No. 3 Group, had participated in Operation "Manna/ Chowhound." This involved the dropping of urgently needed supplies to the starving population in the still-occupied Northern regions of Holland.

With thousands of Allied POWs piled up within various places of captivity there was an urgent call for aircraft to transport them back to Britain and France. Stalag Luft I, Barth, on the Baltic coast was one of the largest camps for Allied airmen, and Lubeck airfield proved another destination for the Lancasters and B-17s sent over. Lt. Wilbur Larsen was a 533BS pilot, and the notes made by Lt. Rau (CP) and Sgt Hayes (ROG) on his crew are worth reproducing:

Rau 10 May '45 Lubeck-Rheine-Royce 9.45 hours.

"Today is very interesting. We went into Germany and brought out 25 POWs. They were so happy to leave. We flew over Holland, and the tulips are out in bloom and are very beautiful. Each field has a separate color, and the array of color was hard to believe.

Rau 11 May '45 Lubeck-Luneberg-Rheine 7.10 hours

Went for POWs again. We didn't get any for reasons unknown. I guess we are taking them out faster than they can be processed. It's very interesting to fly at low altitude over Germany; we wander around and look at things of interest. Hamburg is more of a wreck than I thought anything could be. There is little left standing. When we got back and landed the ball-turret had become un-stowed. The guns were vertical and broke

Capt. Brown (Group chaplain) addresses Group personnel from the control tower. Slight figure with hands behind his back is Col. Hall (Group CO), who stands alongside Col. Reed (Ground Executive). Occasion was believed to have been a Service of Commemoration following the death of President Roosevelt.

off. Mac (Sgt McCarthy, engineer) will probably catch hell for it.

Hayes 13 May '45 Barth-Laon (France) 9.30 hours

Seeing as how I was still Lead radio I flew with the Col. (Hall) to Barth so he could oversee the evacuation. RHIP (Rank had its privileges!), and so his B-17's bomb-bay was gutted, and a table with a sort of portable mess-hall installed. We were on the ground for a while, so were advised that the Russians saluted any rank of Sgt and above – and to be specially careful to return the salute! They were happy; most had bad teeth, their uniforms were baggy, and they all seemed to carry sub-machine guns. We were also warned not to touch anything that might be booby-trapped. One G.I. with a memory problem slid the canopy back on a German fighter parked on the field and had his hand blown off.

Rau (no date)

We went on another trip to bring POWs back. This time we got all Air Corps, and they were sure happy to be on their way. I really feel good going on these flights. I feel it is constructive, and even though we don't get back until 8 pm I do not mind. These boys were liberated by the Russians and told us many good stories. Most of them had been captured over a year ago. They said the Germans treated them rather well. I guess I will go again tomorrow."

This latter diary entry indicates the respect of those combat crew who came through their tours for their buddies, who though fortunate to escape with their lives had to endure the shadowy existence of "Kriegydom"; they had borne the uncertainties, and in some cases the privations of an indefinite prison sentence. The remarks about the destruction wreaked upon Germany's cities would be echoed by thousands of groundcrew in the weeks immediately following the cessation of hostilities. They became aerial witnesses carried in their Groups' B-17s and B-24s for "sight-seeing" flights over the Continent (known as "Trolley mission") in order to confirm the important contribution they had made to the winning of the Air War in Europe.

A number of the POWs evacuated out of Barth came from the 381BG, and it is worth reflecting at this point on the very different experiences facing the American "Kriegies" in the period leading up to their liberation. Those incarcerated at Barth were freed "on site," as it were, when the Russians occupied the region during late April, although final evacuation would not occur until after VE-Day. Typical of those personnel held here was Lt. Pax Sherwood (535BS), who had been held since April '44.

It was a different situation for those held in camps further to the East. As the Russian Armies advanced inexorably upon the Third Reich, the Germans cleared out the Air Force Stalags. In the case of Stalag Luft III at Sagan, such a move could not have come at a worse time – in the dead of one of the severest winters to strike the Continent. The evacuation was begun in the early hours of 28 Jan. and signalled the start of an eleven day ordeal. A series of forced-marches covering anything up to 20 kilometers a day in sub-zero temperatures and drifting snow was made more critical by minimum food supplies. In addition, many of the over-night stops were in buildings too small to accommodate everyone's need for proper rest. The men, already under-nourished and therefore easily exhausted, were further worn down by what were apparently unnecessary route-

MS:W of the 535BS is pictured with the happiest "crew" she would ever take into the air. The location is an airfield at Barth, which was adjacent to Stalag Luft 1, and these men are USAAF "Kriegies" who are about to be flown back to Britain or France after their release.

alterations. So it was with great relief that the majority who had survived staggered into a prison compound at Moosberg, close to Munich. (Some of the men had been loaded into box-cars around Feb. 4 and had travelled the remainder of the distance to Moosberg) There they were to remain until freed by the tanks of the 3rd U.S. Army under the volatile command of Gen. Patton. Among their ranks were Lts. Lloyd Peterson (533BS), Bob Van Buskirk, and Dave Fuller (532BS).

A similar series of forced-marches faced the enlisted men located at Krems (Stalag XVIIB) in Austria. This march was not commenced until 7 April, but the weather conditions were no better, with snowfalls as heavy as that afflicting the Sagan contingent in January. It was not until the beginning of May that contact was initially made with elements of the 3rd U.S. Army. Among those from Ridgewell who shared this wonderful experience were Sgts. Bill Blackmon (535BS) and Bob Geraghty (534BS).

The previous Summer a similar transfer of personnel involving Allied fliers held at Stalag Luft VI, Heydekrug, in the Baltic State of Lithuania proved much shorter, but was arguably even more traumatic. Sgts John Crawbuck (534BS) and Lowell Slayton (533BS) were two of the personnel taken down to the port of Memel, where they were loaded on board a cargo vessel normally used for the transport of coal. Much worse was to follow, as the airmen were ordered down into the holds, which were then battened over, to leave a virtually air-tight zone. The situation was exacerbated by the fact that the transfer was taking place in the middle of a heat wave.

There was no room to lay down, and constant pleas for water to relieve the physical torment were initially rejected. Eventually their captors relented and allowed buckets to be lowered into the holds, while small groups of men were permitted to come up on deck. One man went berserk during this all-too-brief period of relief and jumped over the side into the sea, where he was summarily dispatched by the guards' rifle-fire. After two or three days the protracted and extremely primeval voyage ended in the port of Swinemunde. To the sheer discomfort of the voyage had been added the ever-present risk of torpedo attack from one of the numerous Russian submarines, with death by drowning as the almost certain outcome for the Allied airmen.

The "Kriegies'" travails were far from over, however. Their supervisory party of Naval cadets was led by a Hauptmann Pichardt and an N.C.O. nick-named "Big Stoop." The airmen were shackled in pairs, after which commenced a forced march up to their new Lager located at Kiefheide. Prodded and stabbed at by their guards' bayonets, they were hustled along an uphill path lined with machine-gun pits – the clear inference being that the slightest hint of anybody making a break would be met with a fusillade of bullets. Countless items of precious gear were being discarded as the men shuffled along with the stronger assisting those less well able to cope with the physical strain. It was a miracle nobody was actually killed during the horrendous incident, although it is likely that many of the men developed Post-war problems arising out of their harsh treatment this day. (When the RAF contingent from Heydekrug subsequently marched up along the same route and witnessed the scattered mass of abandoned gear they could not imagine what had happened to create this situation).

Already held at Kiefheide was S/Sgt Tom LaMore (532BS), whose B-17 had collided with another Group B-17 and staggered back as far as the Pas de Calais, where Lt. Rickerson crash-landed. Tom was badly injured, but still managed to get into French hands. However, he was not passed down the escape lines, nor did he accept passive sheltering by his Allies until the area was liberated. Instead, being an expert in explosives handling, he elected to fight alongside the Resistance – an act which technically placed him outside the rules of Warfare as defined under the Geneva Convention.

He now participated in several acts of sabotage over the month of May. However, towards the month-end it was arranged that he be taken into Lille to begin the bid to get through to Spain. Met by two men who escorted him to a car for the journey, the vehicle's ultimate destination turned out to be a German Security building; he and his fellow-evader, Sgt. Durward Williams, had been betrayed!

Sgts Jack Prillaman (TG) and Harry Durham (ROG) are squatting on the stabiliser of an abandoned Ju 88G nightfighter. Picture was taken at Barth on the Baltic coast during the Group's involvement with evacuating Allied Air Force POWs out of Stalag Luft 1 in early May '45.

Constant interrogation culminated in one session where he was totally stripped of all clothing and stood in front of a table behind which was seated a joint Wehrmacht/SS officer team. One of Tom's answers was so much to his guard's dislike that he slugged him full in the face with his rifle-butt. The resultant mangling of his mouth forced a halt to the session, but Tom then had to endure the insertion of internal stitches without the benefit of anaesthetic. He was finally sentenced to death by firing squad and spent his last night in the company of a young Frenchman facing the same fate. Their cell was below ground level, and through the narrow window they could see the courtyard and its wall pitted with bullet-marks.

Sure enough, at dawn the guards came and escorted the Frenchman away to his doom, and all too soon Tom heard the crackle of gunfire signalling this frightful act. A full half hour later into the cell came an SS Sturmbannführer, who sneeringly said: "We are going to let you live, since you have already told us all we need to know." Tom's bitter reaction was to say that he didn't care whether he was shot or not.

While en route to the Allied POW camp at Kiefheide the train containing Tom and his two guards was attacked by Allied aircraft. As the trio scrambled out of their carriage to seek shelter by the track side one of the guards was killed by the fusillade of fire which engulfed the area. Once incarcerated in the Stalag, that would normally have been the end of Tom's movements until the camp was evacuated in the early Spring of 1945. However, his odyssey was to continue. During the final weeks of the War, a successful escape attempt and flight towards the East saw him and his companion meet up with forward elements of one of the Russian Armies. It was with this unit that Tom now fought alongside, all the way up to VE-Day and as far as Lübeck on the Baltic coast!

In common with the majority of its contemporary units, the 381BG wasted little time in its preparation to return to the United States. Equipment was packed ready for movement to the nearest available seaport, and the personnel similarly readied themselves for transportation home by the same means. However, a proportion of the groundcrew was to be much more fortunate in that they would cross the Atlantic in a matter of days, having been flown home in the Group's B-17s.

On the very day Chaplain Brown was ready to clear the base his Assistant, Sgt. Bob Nagle, rushed up to him to say, "Chaplain, we must not forget the Flag which has flown over Ridgewell since we first arrived here!" The proud National emblem was lowered from the flag-pole and neatly folded before being placed in Capt. Brown's B-4 bag. (Some 37 years later the very same flag would be flown on the occasion of the Memorial dedication ceremony at the base).

The final act. Lt. Brashear (standing, second right) and crew are making a stop-over in Gandar, Newfoundland, along with a party of enlisted men flying as passengers. The B-17's chin-guns are wrapped up against the elements.

The bulk of the Ground Echelon was transported back to the United States on the very same vessel, which had brought many of them to Britain virtually two years before. This was the Cunard liner "Queen Elizabeth," but the passage home was in marked and vastly more pleasant circumstances compared to 1943. Disembarkation in New York at the end of June saw the personnel make the short journey to Camp Kilmer, New Jersey. From here, and following a period of Rest and Relief, an element of the Echelon was transferred to Sioux Falls, SD. It was here, having served out its narrow Wartime function, that the final act of Group inactivation occurred on 28 Aug.

By the end of June an air of desolation hung over Ridgewell. Empty, oil-stained dispersals and closed-up hangars, coupled with silent briefing-rooms, Mess halls, barracks, and offices – this was the legacy the 8USAAF was leaving behind all over Eastern England. In the years ahead the countryside out of which the countless Wartime airfields had been carved would remorselessly take over to leave little of a practical memorial to the American airmen. They who had come from another country and distinctive culture had been regarded at the onset with reserve and even suspicion. Once their courageous endeavours were recognised they grew in their Ally's estimation, and "Those B….. Yanks" quickly became "Our boys" in the hearts and minds of all who lived around their airfields.

The American fliers, for all they were to accomplish, were just ordinary men, the vast majority of whom were citizen-soldiers, and all volunteers within this specific field of combat. They were very young on average, and those who sur-

"At the going down of the Sun, and in the morning, we will remember them." S/Sgt Jesse Powell (533BS) stands in quiet respect among the rows of headstones at Madingley Military Cemetery. Picture was taken during the 381BG Memorial Association's very first visit to England in 1982 when a Memorial at the main entrance to Ridgewell was dedicated.

Two lines of Group bombers line the runway in late May '45 as last minute preparations are made for the return States-side. Nearest B-17G is 44-8830 "South Boston Shillelagh" of the 535BS.

vived grew up extremely rapidly in the face of a fearsome array of dangers. Technical failure, weather conditions, anoxia, and frost-bite – to these were added the basic threat to life and limb posed by an inveterate, skilled, and (it has to be acknowledged) often courageous human opponent.

The magnificent American Military Cemetery at Madingley, with its serried rows of headstones facing out onto the rolling Cambridgeshire countryside, is a poignantly beautiful reminder of the sacrifice made by the Wartime youth of America. At the base of the flag-pole is inscribed a line from "In Flanders Field," a poem written by Capt. John McCrae during World War I – "The War to end all Wars." This says "To you from failing hands we throw the Torch; be Yours to hold it high." The priceless legacy of such a scale of sacrifice is a half-century of continuing Peace and Freedom for the populations of America and Britain. May this salient fact never be forgotten.

Although there are no airworthy examples of B-17s that flew with the 381BG, the Group does have the distinction of having the last aircraft delivered to Ridgewell (44-83624) as part of the USAF Museum, Dayton. In fact, it was on public display for many years until she was finally supplanted by the arrival of the 91BG's "Shoo Shoo Baby." The Gulf Coast Wing of the Confederate Air Force currently displays its airworthy B-17G in the markings of the 533BS veteran "Princess Pat." A second B-17G based in Michigan sports the markings for a 534BS machine.

In the field of literature, the Group Chaplain had made his mark with "The Mighty Men of the 381st; Heroes All." Similarly, John Comer's account of his crew's experiences ("Combat Crew") provides a precise and thought-provoking insight into the pressures of combat. Dave McCarthy, navigator on "Our Mom," provides a similar insight into the parlous days of the Group's initial presence at Ridgewell ("Fear no More").

Appendix A:

381BG ASSIGNED AIRCRAFT

Group activated 3 November 1942
AF Station Ridgewell 9 June 1943 (Air Echelon)
FOS 22 June 1943
LOS 25 April 1945

Markings AD Group letter – L. Original codes displayed but replaced after FOS as follows;
532BS No change from VE
533BS OQ replaced by VP
534BS JZ replaced by GD
535BS PL replaced by MS

41-9019 381
00 05 42 AI 00 06 42 AOS 11 06 43 G
10 07 43 92BG

41-9043 534 GD-A1 (Originally Peggy D with 97BG before being renamed LITTLE ROCKETTE)
00 05 42AI 00 06 42 AOS 00 07 43 G 92BG
21 08 43 2SAD RG 24 08 43 29 10 34 Altus Oklahoma.
See MACD 61 NASA B65817AC

41-24500 535 MS Y ANNIE FREEZE
21 07 42 AI 27 05 43AOS 15 06 43 G
18 07 43 AF Bovingdon CCRC
See; FREL 120

42-2978 534 GD SIS
535 MS V
00 07 42 AI 00 05 43AOS 19 11 43G 306BG 06 04 44 AFSC 01 05 44 ZOI

23033 533 VP U
534 GD U
00 07 42 AI 00 05 43 AOS 00 07 43 G 94BG
23 09 43 2SAD RG 09 11 43
16 11 43 2SAD RG 17 11 43
00 00 43?RG 23 11 43
09 01 44 2SAD CCRC

23048 (Short-stay) 533 VP
00 07 42 AI 00 05 43 AOS 22 08 43 G 305BG
26 08 43 379BG

23078 534 GD M WINSOME WINN//HILDA
15 01 43 AI 24 04 43 AOS 00 00 43 G 100BG
13 11 43 2SAD RG 15 11 43
07 01 44 FTR AA/Fighters Cr Saarbrucken, Germany 2Lt Arden D Wilson
–2 KIA 8 POW- MACR 1873
See; BISA 239 - MACD 21, 26 –NASA 65824AC, A 65893AC, 65924AC –WARB – WARF

23092 533 VP T STRATO SAM, THOUGHEST CREW THAT EVER FLEW
32 01 43 AI 24 04 43 AOS 00 04 43 G
17 08 43 FTR AA GF Cr. Pesch, Germany – F/O James C Hudson – 1 KIA, 9 POW – MACR 399
See; MACA 32 MACD 8 - NASA 65822AC

23100 532 VE A1
01 02 43 AI 01 05 43 AOS 20 07 43 G 95BG
30 07 43 FTR AA C/L Deelen, Holland – Maj Robert F Post – 1 KIA, 9 POW –MACR 129
See; BOWG 65 – FREJ 18 – MACB 11 – MACD 9

32101 533 VP
01 02 43 AI 01 05 43 AOS 21 07 43 G 95B
19 08 43 FTR GF CR Out-Rozenburg, Netherlands - Lt Orlando H Koenig – 4 KIA, 6 POW – MACR 662

23118 534 GD N GREEN HORNET
10 02 43 AI 16 04 43 AOS 06 07 43 G 96BG
27 09 43 AF Chelveston 28 09 43 AFSC RG?
00 00 43 AF Great Ashfield RG 27 10 43
30 10 43 3SAD RG?
11 01 44 FTR GF CR Goslar, Germany – 2Lt Austin G Larson – 1 KIA, 9 POW –MACR 1875
See; AFMA 148 – MACA 33 – NASA 65935AC, B 65818AC – SCUD 44

23123 535 MS Z RON-CHEE
11 02 43 AI 21 04 43 AOS 16 07 43 G 96BG
08 10 43 FTR GF CR Bremen, Germany – Lt Leslie A Kemp Jnr. – 10 KIA – MACR 1396
See; NASA B65822AC

23134
18 02 43 AI 21 04 43 AOS 06 03 43 G 8FC or 92BG
06 03 44 Communication A/C
12 05 44 RG?
17 07 44 487BG

23177 535 MS O THE HELLION
09 03 43 AI 17 04 43 AOS 15 07 43 G 96BG
21 01 44 RAF Sculthorpe 25 01 44 RAF or 22 02 44 RAF
See HAWA 76 – MACA 33 – NASA A 65922AC

23180 533 VP Y FORGET ME NOT II
10 03 43 AI 06 05 43 AOS 16 07 43 96BG
09 10 43 FTR GF DIT North Sea – Lt. Herbert Carqueville – 10 KIA – MACR 888
See; MACA 32 – NASA B65820AC , B65887AC – VALA 35

23211 535 MS O T.S.
23 03 43 AI 24 05 43 AOS 15 06 43 G
14 07 43 MID FW CL RAF Manston 15 07 43 Salvage
See; BROB 74 – MACA 36 – MACD 7

23215 533 VP S LINDA MARY
04 03 43 AI 28 05 43 AOS 00 04 43 G
00 00 43 ? RG 27 06 43
18 07 43 MU RG 20 07 43
26 08 43 SAD RG 02 09 43
06 03 44 FTR GF CR Magdeburg Germany – 2 Lt Richard W Coyle – 1 KIA, 9 POW – MACR 3000
See; MACA 28 – MACD 5,34 – MCDA 53 – NASA C65819AC, B65852AC.

23217 535 MS T GEORGIA REBEL
25 03 43 AI 24 05 43 AOS 00 04 43 G
14 07 43 RAF Manston RG 16 07 43
24 07 43 FTR/INT AA CT Vannacka, Sweden – Lt Osce V Jones – 10 INT –MACR 132
See; FRED 63 – MACD 14 – MACD 11 – OLAA 43 – WEGA 40-41.

23219 534 GD
26 03 43 AI 07 06 43 AOS 00 04 43 G 00 00 43 94BG

23220 535 MS M DAMFINO
01 04 43 AI 28 05 43 AOS 00 04 43 G
17 08 43 FTR GF CR Marksteinach, Germany – Lt Harry M Smith – 10 POW – MACR 384
See; BISA 195, 242

23221 534 JZ E/GD E WHALETAIL
01 04 43 AI 28 05 43 AOS 00 06 43 G 384BG
25 06 43 RAF Foulsham RG 04 07 43
29 07 43 C/L Thetford – Lt William Wroblicka – SAL. 04 08 43
See; MACK 11 – NASA 66192AC

23223 533 VP R RED HOT RIDING HOOD
01 04 43 AI 02 06 43 AOS 00 04 43 G
14 07 43 CR AF Rattlesden - 6 KIA, 4 Survivors (disintegrated during Group Assembly) SAL
See; MACD 9

23225 535 MS V CHUG-A-LUG-LULU
01 04 43 AI 06 06 43 AOS 00 04 43 G
17 08 43 FTR CGF CR Tongeron, Belgium – Lt Lorin L Disbrow – 4 EVD, 6 POW – E & E 224,320, 508, 1192 – MACR 378
See; MACD 8 – NASA C65817AC, C65817AC, 80585AC

23226 533 VP S
01 04 43 AI 24 05 43 AOS 00 04 43 G
22 06 43 CL North Foreland UK 01 07 43 SAL

23227 534 GD G
01 04 43 AI 26 05 43 AOS 00 04 43 G
17 08 43 FTR GF CR Meerland, Netherlands – Lt Hamden I Forkner – 4 EVD, 6 POW –
E & E 237, 330, 331, 2192 – MACR 661

23268 (Short-stay) 534 GD MESSIE BESSIE
15 04 43 AI 04 06 43 AOS 00 00 43 G
06 07 43 96BG (CAROL JANE)

23411 532 VE I
08 06 43 AI 21 09 43 AOS 21 09 43 G
15 10 43 2SAD RG?
17 12 43 AF Rougham RG?
00 00 44 8FC RG 12 05 44
19 05 44 AFSC 18 06 44 ZOI 10 05 44 Bush Field

23511 535 MS
15 07 43 AI 19 08 43 AOS 22 04 43 G
23 04 44 FTR AA Cr Pracy? – 2Lt Andrew G Claytor – 7 EVD – 3POW
E & E 1021,1022,1024,1026.2358 – MACR 4286

23514 535 VP V DINAH MITE II/DOLL BABY
16 07 43 AI 08 09 43 AOS 24 09 43 G
28 09 43 2SAD RG?
09 10 43 MRU RG 01 11 43
17 12 43 RG?
11 01 44 FTR GF CR Minden? – Lt Billy F Chason – 10 POW – MACR 1878

23522 533 VP L
19 07 43 AI 06 09 43 AOS 27 09 43 G 96BG
03 10 43 2SAD RG?
23 12 43 RG 03 03 44
19 05 44 AFSC 13 06 44 ZOI 08 01 46 Walnut Ridge, Arkansas
See; DAVA 38 – MACD 15 – NASA 65443AC

23525 534 GD C
20 07 43 AI 07 09 43 AOS 22 02 44 G 482BG
19 04 44 FTR CF CR Frettenrode? – 2Lt Leslie A bond – 7 KIA – 2 POW - MACR 4050

23540 535 MS N BACTA-th'-SAC
26 07 43 AI 05 09 43 AOS G
17 09 43 2SAD RG?
24 09 43 BAD1 RG 02 10 43
01 12 43 FTR GF CR Huy? – 2Lt Warren C Hess – 2 EVD, 1 KIA , 7 POW – E & E 665, 1893 –MACR 1660
See; NASA 65968AC –SCUC 35

23562 532 VE
02 08 43 AI 00 09 43 AOS 21 11 43 G 401BG
01 12 43 Martlesham Heath 02 12 43 2SAD RG 20 12 43
00 00 44? RG 28 01 44
20 02 44 FTR GF CR Leipzig – Lt Kirch J Cogswell – 1 KIA, 9 POW – MACR 2929

23563 535 MS N
10 08 43 AI 09 09 43 AOS 00 10 43 G
09 10 43 CL RAF Netterwing? 19 10 43 2SAD RG 12 12 43
20 12 43 FTR GF CR Oldenburg? -Lt Bernard F Hollenkamp – 5 KIA, 5 POW - MACR 1721

25725 532 VE C THIS IS IT!!/ FLAPPER
05 10 42 AI 20 01 43 AOS 22 08 43 G 305BG
29 03 44 2SAD RG 06 05 44
05 06 44 ZOI 31 07 46 Stillwater, Oklahoma
See; DAVA 23 – MACD 16 – NASA B65888AC, 66001AC, 66021AC, A66021AC

25747 (Short-stay) 535 MS HANGAR QUEEN
25 11 43 AI 11 03 43 AOS 22 08 43 G 305BG 05 10 43 384BG

25845 534 GD A WHALETAIL II
14 03 43 AI 24 05 43 AOS 00 04 43 G
29 08 43 2SAD RG 0209 43
07 09 43 AFSC RG 22 09 43
24 09 43MRU RG 16 10 43
20 12 43 FTR AA CR North Sea – 2LT Leo I Canelake – 10 KIA – MACR 1724
See; BELB 32 – FREH 126 – MACA 34 – MACB 12 – MACD 22 – NASA 4201AC – SCUC 16

25846 535 MS X TINKERTOY
15 03 43 AI 24 05 43 AOS 00 04 43 G
09 10 43 MRU RG?
17 12 43 Bassingbourn RG
20 12 43 FTR GF CR Bremen, Germany – 2Lt Dorman F Lane – 7 KIA, 3 POW – MACR 1723
Se; BROB 313, 567 – COMA 147 – FRED 75 – FREJ 4, 150 – LANB 38 – A65853AC , 65888AC, 65841AC, 80284AC

25847 532 VE T MARGIE MAE
16 03 43 AI 21 05 43 AOS 00 04 43 G
12 08 43 FTR AA CR Maastricht, the Netherlands – 2Lt Theodore L Moon – 10 POW – MACR 660
See; MACA 32, 35 – MACD 9 – NASA 65821AC, - VALA 42

25878 533 VP Q
10 04 43 AI 29 05 43 AOS 18 09 43 G 96BG
30 09 43 2SAD RG 03 10 43
17 11 43 2SAD RG?
23 11 43 2SAD RG 12 43
11 01 44 FTR MID GSE CR Minden, Germany – 2Lt Alfred R Perot – 9 KIA, 1 POW –
MACR 1874

229506 532 VE A FULL BOOST!!
21 12 42 AI 17 02 43 AOS 22 08 43 G 305BG
01 12 43 FTR AA CR Cassel, France – 2Lt Jason H Duncan – 6 KIA, 4 POW – MACR 1578
See; COMA 168 – MACA 29 – MACD 20 –NASA 65889AC

229570 532 VE B BIG TIME OPERATOR II
31 12 42 AI 03 04 43 AOS 07 09 43 G 303BG
11 09 43 2SAD RG 11 09 43
05 04 44 AFSC 26 04 44 ZOI 05 05 44 CON SAL
See; MACA 36 – MACD 19

229633
18 01 43 AI 03 03 43 AOS 11 09 43 G 305BG
26 09 43 G 379BG
229731 532 VE E OLE' SWAYBACK
06 02 43 AI 17 04 43 AOS 16 07 43 G 96BG
17 08 43 FTR GF CR Ebrach, Germany – Lt Leo I Jarvis – 10 POW – MACR 663

229735 532 VE
02 02 43 AI 17 04 43 AOS 16 07 43 G 96BG
17 08 43 FTR GF DIT North Sea – Lt George R Darrow – 10 RTD.

229751 534 GD D MIS ABORTION/STUFF
09 02 43 AI 19 04 43 AOS 07 12 43 G 96BG
31 03 44 (Stalled) CR 2SAD 01 04 44 SAL
See; AFMA 117 – BIRG 19 , 34 – BIRK 27 – MACD 38 – NASA B65 834AC, C65834AC, 66175AC – VALA 42

229755 533 VP Y GREMLIN'S DELITE/ LAST STRAW!
09 02 43 AI 19 04 43 AOS 14 07 43 G 96BG
05 11 43 North Mathing, UK? RG
00 00 43?RG 04 01 44
17 01 44 AF Hardwick RG 24 01 44
05 04 44 AFSC ZOI 09 10 45 Altus, Oklahoma

229761 533 VP W MARTHA THE II
10 02 43 AI 16 04 43 AOS 14 07 43 G 96BG
12 11 43 2SAD RG 13 11 43
00 00 44 2SAD RG 04 01 44
30 01 44 FTR GF CR Deurne, Belgium – 2Lt Henry D Steele – 4 KIA, 6 POW – MACR 2244
See; FREH 124 – FREL 149 – MACB 16 – NASA 65331AC, C65818AC, 65865AC, 80153AC, - WOOC 175

229765 533 VP R NIP N' TUCK
10 02 43 AI 17 04 43 AOS 14 07 43 G 96BG
08 10 43 FTR GF CR Bremen, Germany – 2Lt James W Hartje – 3 KIA, 7 POW –MACR883

229784 534 GD E/F SMILIN- THRU
13 02 43 AI 04 03 43 AOS 11 09 43 G 305BG
04 10 43 384BG
See; NASA 65912AC

229789 532 VE O BIG TIME OPERATOR
13 02 43 AI 24 05 43 AOS 00 04 43 G
21 08 43 2SAD RG?
03 09 43 FTR GF CR Provine, France – 2LT Benjamin J Zum – 1 KIA, 3 EVD, 6 POW – E & E 135, 195, 382 - MACR 473
See; NASA 52342AC?, 65844AC, A65890AC

229803 533 VP P
20 02 43 AI 07 04 43 AOS 11 09 43 G 305BG
14 10 43 FTR GF CR Schweinfurt, Germany – Lt Bernard M Yorba – 4 KIA, 6 POW – MACR 1037

229832 534 GD H OUR MOM
23 02 43 AI 24 04 43 AOS 22 08 43 G 305BG
15 10 43 2SAD RG 16 10 43
05 04 44 AFSC 29 05 44 ZOI 23 11 44 ARLEDGE FIELD
See; BISA 103

229854 532 VE B OLE FLAK SACK
24 02 43 AI 01 05 43 AOS 16 06 43 G
18 07 43 MU RG 20 07 43
09 08 43 RG?
08 10 43 FTR GF CR Diepholz, Germany – Lt Arthur M Sample – 8 KIA, 2 POW –MACR 1395
See; BISA 83 – MACA 35 – MACD 17

229867 535 MS LUCIFER II
26 02 43 AI 07 05 43 AOS 22 08 43 G
04 10 43 384BG (Short-stay)

229888 532 VE H THE JOKER
04 03 43 AI 24 05 43 AOS 00 00 43 G
21 08 43 2SAD RG 09 08 43
11 05 44 AFSC 22 11 44 Arledge Field
See; JCA 170 – MACD 10 ,12 - NASA 65819AC, 65890AC, 65931AC – VALA 40

229923 532 VE K THE LUCKY STRIKE
09 03 43 AI 24 04 43 AOS 11 09 43 G
10 10 43 AF Lavenham RG 12 10 43
05 01 44 2SAD 07 01 44 SAL
See; AKMA 36 – BIRG 5 – BISA 256 – CAMA 158 – CAMB 14 – DAVA 22 – MACA 33 – MACB 10 – MACD 21 -, 23 – NASA 65688AC, 65818AC, 65852AC, - VALA 63 - WARB

229928 533 VP
10 03 43 AI 05 04 43 AOS 23 06 43 G
26 06 43 Bovingdon RG 27 06 43
04 07 43 FTR GF CR Tours, France – Lt Olaf M Ballinger – 4 EVD, 4 KIA, 2 POW – E & E 64, 248, 328, 380 – MACR 161

229941 535 MS R TS TOO
15 03 43 AI 17 04 43 AOS 15 07 43 G 96BG
26 08 43 2SAD RG 29 08 43
08 10 43 FTR AA CR Talge,Germany – Capt Edwin R Manchester Jnr. – 6 KIA, 4 POW –
MACR 884 – See; MACD 1 – NASA A65823AC

229950 535 MS N FORGET ME NOT
25 03 43 AI 28 05 43 AOS 00 04 43 G
12 08 43 FTR GF CR Rheydt, Germany – F/O Fred G Evans – 5 KIA, 5 POW –MACR 385
See; MACD 8

229953 535 MS Q MANOWAR
16 03 43 AI 24 05 43 AOS 00 04 43 G
22 08 43 305BG
See; NASA 65823AC(?), 65839AC(?)

229954 534 GD D DEVIL'S ANGEL
15 03 43 AI 31 05 43 AOS 00 04 43 G
25 06 43 AF Bungay RG 28 06 43
12 08 43 FTR AA CR Koln, Germany – Lt William Wroblicka – 5 KIA, 5 POW - MACR 383
See; NASA B65880AC

229958 534 GD J BATTLIN' BOMBSPRAYER
16 03 43 AI 23 05 43 AOS 00 04 43 G
25 07 43 RAF Oulton 31 07 43 MU RG 0608 43
09 10 43 FTR GF CR Schonberg, Germany – Lt James L Loftin – 2 KIA, 8 POW – MACR 886
See; MACA 35 – NASA 65884AC (MACR 886)*

229976 532 VE Q SAD SACK
18 03 43 AI 24 05 43 AOS 00 04 43 G
25 07 43 FTR AA GF CR Hamburg, Germany – Lt Jack H Owen – 10 POW – MACR 128

229978 534 GD F HELL'S ANGEL
18 03 43 AI 31 05 43 AOS 00 04 43 G
17 08 43 FTR GF CR Bad Schawalbach, Germany – Lt Reinhardt M King – 10 POW – MACR 382
See; MACD 4 – NASA 65 812AC?, 65882AC, 66174AC

229983 533 VP
19 03 43 AI 23 04 43 AOS 17 06 43 G 96BG
17 08 43 FTR AA GF CR Kesseling, Germany – Lt Challen P Atkinson – 2 KIA, 8 POW – MACR 398
See;NASA C65821AC

229984 533 VP
30 03 43 AI 21 04 43 AOS 16 06 43 G
22 06 43 CL AF Framlingham SAL
See; MACD 5 – NASA 65821AC

229988 535 MS S LUCIFER JR.
20 03 43 AI 23 05 43 AOS 00 04 43 G
22 08 43 305BG
See; MACA 31 – NASA B65821AC, 65853AC, 65856AC, B65893AC

229992 535 OQ J/
27 03 43 AI 28 05 43 AOS 00 04 43 G
23 06 43 Ground (Deb) SAL
See; MACD 11

229999 533 VP Z FERTILE MYRTLE
23 03 43 AI 07 05 43 AOS 16 07 43 G 96BG
13 09 43 2SAD RG?
11 01 44 FTR GF CR Eichholz, Germany – 2Lt Matthew J McEvoy – 10 POW – MACR 1880
See; MACD 26 – NASA 1013AC/

230004 534 GD B JANICE
25 03 43 AI 25 05 43 AOS 15 06 43 G
22 08 43 395BG
See; NASA 65883AC

230009 532 VE G FEATHER MERCHANT
24 03 43 AI 24 05 43 AOS 00 04 43 G
25 06 43 AF Lavenham RG 28 06 43
00 00 43 ? RG 18 08 43
08 10 43 FTR GF CR Diepholz, Germany – Lt. Jack S Pry – 2 KIA, 8 POW – MACR 1397
See; NASA A 65822AC, C65826AC

230011 535 MS R WIDGET
27 03 43 AI 26 05 43 AOS 00 04 43 G
14 07 43 FTR GF CR Amiens, France – Lt Robert J Holdem – 10 KIA – MACR 133

230012 533 VP K
25 03 43 AI 24 05 43 AOS 00 04 43 G
28 06 43 RAF Portreath RG 25 07 43
09 10 43 FTR GF DIT North Sea – Major Landon C Hendricks – 10 KIA – MACR 887

230013 532 VE E LETHAL LADY
25 03 43 AI 21 05 43 AOS 00 04 43 G
25 07 43 FTR AA CR Hamburg, Germany – Lt. William R Moore – 4 KIA, 6 POW – MACR 130
See; SCUC 12 – THOA 10

230014 533 VP B
25 03 43 AI 28 05 43 AOS 00 04 43 G
29 01 44 RAF

230015 533 VP O
26 03 43 AI 24 05 43 AOS 00 04 43 G
22 08 43 305BG

230016 532 VE M IRONGUT GERT
26 03 43 AI 24 05 43 AOS 00 04 43 G
22 06 43 FTR AA CR Terneuzen, Netherlands – 2Lt Earl R Horr – 2 KIA, 8 POW –MACR 134

230017 535 MS W
00 03 43 AI 23 05 43 AOS 10 07 43 G
14 07 43 390BG

230018 532 VE L OLD COFFINS
26 03 43 AI 23 05 43 AOS 00 00 43 G
22 08 43 305BG
See; MACA 33 – MACD 8. 46 – NASA A65820AC, - SCUD 44 – THOA 10 – VALA45

230020 532 VE N SWEET ELOISE
26 03 43 AI 24 05 43 AOS 00 04 43 G
16 06 43 AFSC
See; BISA 61 – MACA 35 – MACD 7 – NASA 66185AC

2-30021 533 VP L
27 03 43 AI 28 05 43 AOS 00 04 43 G
22 06 43 FTR AA CR Westerschelde (Krabbendijke, Netherlands – 2Lt John J Martin – 9 KIA, 1 POW – MACR 160

230024 533 OQ A
26 03 43 AI 24 05 43 AOS 25 05 43 G
23 06 43 GROUND EX. SAL
See; MACA 30 – MACD 4 -5

230025 532 VE
27 03 43 AI RZOI 00 04 43 G
00 00 43 ZOI
See; NASA 65817AC, A65837AC – THOA 10

230026 534 GD BATTLE WAGON
27 03 43AI 24 05 43AOS 00 04 4 G
29 05 43 384 BG
230027 533 VP E
27 03 43 AI 24 05 43AOS 00 04 43 G
25 05 43 FTR AA GF CR Bengerseil – Lt Robert K Schrader – 10 KIA – MACR162

230028 534 GD H SWEET LI' LANI
27 03 43 AI 25 05 43 AOS 00 04 43 G
17 08 43 FTR GF CR Düren Germany – 2/Lt Neil H Wright – 10 POW –MACR380
See; MACD12 – NASA 65880AC

230029 535 MS P CHAPS FLYING CIRCUS
28 03 43 AI 28 05 43 AOS 00 04 43 G
18 08 43 2SAD RG 21 08 43
30 01 44 FTR GF DIT North Sea – Lt Carl O Baer – 10 KIA – MACR2495
See; BROB 209 – MACA 33 – MACD 27 – NASA A65824AC, 65852AC

230032 532 VE
28 03 43 AI 06 06 43 AOS 00 00 43 G
00 00 43 384BG
See; MACD 1 – THOA 10

230034 532 VE NOBODYS BABY
28 03 43 AI 18 05 43 AOS 00 04 43 G 94BG
22 08 43 305BG
See; LANB 78 – MACA 32 – NASA C65823AC –SCUC 12

230114
10 04 43 AI 07 05 43 AOS 00 00 43 G
19 08 43 MU 95BG

230140 532 VE V KING MALFUNCTION II
14 04 43 AI28 05 43 AOS23 06 43 G
17 08 43 FTR GF CR Esch, Germany – Lt. Jack B Painter 2 EVD, 1 KIA, 7 POW –E & E 170, 171 –MACR 379

230151 532 VE J SPARE PARTS
16 04 43 AI 07 05 43 AOS 15 06 43 G
21 12 43 2SAD RG?
04 03 44 FTR MECH CR St. Omer France – 2Lt David D Keyes – 10 POW – MACR2910
See; MACD 11.

230152
15 04 43 AI 31 05 43 AOS 16 07 43 G 96BG
00 00 43 100BG

230153 532 VE
15 04 43 AI 08 05 43 AOS 16 07 43 G 96BG
25 07 43 FTR AA CR Sudmoor? – Capt Joe E Alexander – 10 POW – MACR131

230245 534 GD L LADY LUCK/LUCKY LADY II
30 04 43 AI 28 05 43 AOS 15 06 43 G
17 08 43 FTR GF CR Oostmalle, Belgium – Lt Weldon L Simpson – 1 EVD, 1 KIA, 8 POW –
E& E 1894 – MACR 381

230613 535 MS S
26 06 43 AI 05 08 43 AOS 28 02 44 G
09 04 44 2SAD 12 04 44 SAL
See; MACD39 – NASA 52104AC, 66 176AC

230676 532 VE E BABY DUMPLING
07 07 43 AI 24 08 43 AOS 19 09 43 G 482BG
25 10 43 2SAD RG?
05 01 44 FTR GF CR La Suze?, France – 2Lt Jack R Zeman – 3 EVD, 1 KIA, 6 POW –
E&E 368,417, 504 – MACR 1962

230721 533 VP T SWEET N' LOVELY
15 07 43 AI 30 08 43 AOS 20 09 43 G 482BG
24 09 43 MRU RG 05 11 43
09 11 43 2SAD RG 12 11 43
25 04 44 8FC RG?
See; BIRM 24 – CAMB 52 – FREH CP – NASB K2199A

230732 534 GD C BOBBY T
16 07 43 AI 30 08 43 AOS 20 09 43 G 482BG
25 09 43 2SAD RG 26 09 43
08 10 43 FTR GR CR Bremen, Germany – Capt Dexter Lishon – 10 POW –MACR 1398

230732 534 GD B PISTOL PACKIN' MAMA
17 07 43 AI 06 09 43 AOS 26 09 43 G
08 10 43 2SAD RG 09 10 43
05 02 44 SAL
See; BISA 261

230765 533 VP R CHUG-A-LUG
23 07 43 AI 03 09 43 AOS 20 09 43 G
03 10 43 2SAD RG?
29 12 4/3 30 12 432SAD SAL
See; BISA 93, 261 – MACB 12

230834 534 GD E MICKY FINN
31 07 43 AI 09 09 43 AOS 23 09 43 G
26 09 43 2SAD RG 27 09 43
04 02 44 CL 07 02 44 SAD
See; MACD 19

230852 535 MS Y BLOWIN' BESSIE
05 08 43 AI 11 09 43 AOS 24 09 43 G
00 00 43?RG 12 10 43
05 11 43 FTR CR Hollands Diep, Nr. Dordrecht, the Netherlands – 2Lt Donald K Hopp – 7 KIA, 3 POW – MACR 1399

230864 535 MS T
07 08 43 AI 08 09 43 AOS 19 09 43 G
30 09 43 2SAD RG 03 10 43
08 10 43 FTR AA CR Haupstedt, Germany – Lt William F Cormany Jnr. – 1 KIA, 9 POW –
MACR 885
See; MACD 1

231043
07 09 43 AI 10 10 43 AOS 19 10 43 G
03 03 44 379BG

231047 535 MS T WOLVERINE
08 09 43 AI 07 10 43 AOS 20 10 43 G
23 10 43 2SAD RG01 11 43
30 01 44 FTR GF CR Ottbergen, Germany – 2Lt Robert P Deering – 8 KIA, 2 POW - MACR 2243
See; MACD 27 – NASA 65818AC, 65918AC - WARF

231067 535 MS T BLACK WIDOW
PHYLISS
11 09 43 AI 07 10 43 AOS19 10 43 G
07 11 43 2SAD RG 09 11 43
21 03 44 2SAD RG 14 04 44
01 05 44 2SAD RG 22 05 44
26 03 45 BD 2SAD 28 03 45 RG 27 04 45
07 06 45 ZOI
See; AFMA 55 – CAMB 29 –NASA A65817AC, C65830AC – SCUD 51

231075 535 MS S THE REBEL
13 09 43 AI 07 10 43 AOS 19 10 43 G
00 00 43?RG 18 11 43
20 12 43 FTR GF CR Albstadt, Germany – Lt Waldo B Crossan – 3 KIA, 7 POW – MACR 1722

231097 535 MS MISSION BELLE
15 09 43 AI 01 11 43 AOS 21 11 43 G 401BG
01 12 43 FTR GF CR Niew Lekkerland, the Netherlands – F/O Harlan V Sunde – 3 KIA, 7 POW – MACR 1661 (MACR1661)

231099 532 VE TENABOVE
15 09 43 AI 25 10 43 AOS 21 11 43 G 401BG
11 02 44 FTR AA CR Amiens, France – 2Lt Robert V Laux – 7 EVD, 3 POW E7E 521,522, 523,524, 525, 1226, 2332 – MACR 2431
See; NASA B65840AC

231111 535 MS R FOUR ACES – PAT HAND
17 09 43 AI 09 10 43 AOS 19 10 43 G
02 11 43 2SAD RG 05 11 43
01 12 43 FTR AA CR Cologne, Germany – 2Lt Donald E Noxon – 10 KIA – MACR 1659
See; BISA 265 – MACB 12 – NASA 65834AC, 66035AC.

231129
20 09 43 AI 23 10 43 AOS 00 00 43 G
01 11 43 301BG
See; NASA C65836AC

231143
21 09 43 AI 13 10 43 AOS 00 05 45 G 306BG
00 05 45 ZOI 05 12 45 Kingman, Arizona

231197 533 VP Q SHACK RABBIT
27 09 43 AI 14 11 43 AOS 13 01 44 G
24 04 44 2SAD RG 10 05 44
19 05 44 AFSC 06 44 ZOI 14 09 48 Warner Robbins, Georgia.
See; MACB1 14 –MACD 44 – SCUD 50

231278 532 VE A
09 10 43 AI 15 11 43 AOS 20 12 43 G
04 01 44 SAL – Lt Cecil C Clore – 10 KIA
See; MACB 16 – MACD 24 – NASA 66202AC, A66202AC.

231291 533 VP F
12 10 43 AI 10 11 43 AOS 11 12 43 G
24 05 44 FTR MID CR Wilmersdorf, Germany – Lt Carl A Gardon – 2 KIA, 7 POW – MACR 5176

231357 535 MS N OUR DESIRE
22 10 43 AI 18 11 43 AOS 11 12 43 G
13 04 44 FTR AA CR Hunsruck, Germany – 2Lt James F Mullane – 9 POW – MACR 3865
See; MACD 39 – NASA 65839AC

231381 535 MS O JAYNEE B
22 10 43 AI 18 12 43 AOS 22 01 44 G
20 03 44 FTR AA DIT English Channel – Lt. George B McIntosh Jnr. – 10 POW – MACR 3315

231417 533 VP R PATCHES
28 10 43 AI 20 11 43 AOS 11 12 43 G
11 01 44 FTR GF CR Minden, Germany – Lt Ernest M Klein – 2 KIA, 8 POW – MACR 1879

231418
28 10 43 AI 08 12 44 AOS 00 05 45 G 306BG
30 05 45 91 BG

231443 532 VE M FRIDAY THE 13TH
01 11 43 AI 11 12 43 AOS 06 01 44 G
17 01 44 AF Hardwick RG ?
22 02 44 FTR GF CR Nr. Munster, Germany – Lt Francis J Flaherty – 6 KIA, 4 POW – MACR 2930
See; DAVA 41 – ETHB 1 – MACD 31 – WARF

231448 532 VE A HALF BREED
01 11 43 AI 09 12 43 AOS 06 01 44 G
06 03 44 FTR GF CR Julich, Germany – 2Lt Milton A Fastrup – 10 POW – MACR 3110

231490 532 VE K
06 11 43 AI 15 12 43 AOS 10 01 44 G
24 03 44 FTR MID 240008 CR Carvin, France (C/L) – 2Lt John A Rickerson – 4 EVD, 6 POW – E & E 1395, 1560, 1561, 2011 – MACR 3538
See; MACXD 41

231497 534 GD
08 11 43 AI 21 12 43 AOS 22 01 44 G
11 04 44 FTR AA CR Altteich, Germany – 2Lt Robert W Hesse – 9 POW – MACR 3821

231533 533 MS U
12 11 43 AI 19 12 43 AOS 05 01 44 G
22 02 44 FTR GF CR Wiedenbruck, Germany – 2Lt Charles H Downey – 7 KIA - 3 POW - MACR 2931
See; NASA 65946AC

231550 533 VP G GREEN HORNET 2ND
15 11 43 AI 31 12 44 AOS 13 01 44 G
17 10 44 FTR LOC 21 11 44 SAL
See; NASA C65831AC

231553 534 GD MYER'S FLAW
15 11 43 AI 23 01 44 AOS 19 02 44 G
06 03 44 FTR GF CR Wernsdorf, Germany – Lt Edward E Haushalter – 5 KIA, 5 POW – MACR 3241

231569 534 GD E SWEET PATOOTIE
17 11 43 AI 10 01 44 AOS 19 02 44 G
03 09 44 FTR LOC SAL RG?
05 05 45 SAL – E & E 2174, 2184, 2185, 2186, 2235, 2236, 2237, 2287
See; NASA 65925AC, 66075AC.

231570 533 VP W LUCKY ME!!
17 11 43 AI 29 12 43 AOS 02 02 44 G
25 09 44 FTR MECH CR St Goar, Germany – Lt Oscar W Gills – 9 POW – MACR 10203
See; FREH CP – MACB 15 – MACD 50, 53 – NASA 65837AC, B65870AC

231575 532 VE P MIZPAH
18 11 43 AI 06 02 44 AOS 20 02 44 G
00 05 45 ZOI
See; FRED 160 – NASA A65891AC

231614 533 VP L MINNIE THE MERMAID
23 11 43 AI 05 01 44 AOS 21 01 44 G
29 11 44 FTR LOC 26 11 44 SAL 27 01 45 SAL
See; MACB 17 – MACD 46 – NASA 65830AC, A65858AC, 65913AC – VALA 44

231696 535 MS
03 12 43 AI 23 01 44 AOS 20 02 44 G
22 02 44 FTR GF CR Detmold, Germany– 2Lt Henry Hustedt – 2 KIA, 8 POW – MACR 2932

231698 535 MS N
03 12 43 AI 15 02 44 AOS 23 02 44 G
24 05 44 FTR MID CR Melchow, Germany – Lt. Clarence D Wainwright – 7 KIA, 2 POW –
MACR 5319

231761 533 VP O ROTHERHITHES REVENGE
10 12 43 AI 16 01 44 AOS 31 01 44 G
00 05 45 ZOI
See; BROB 368 – FREJ 82 – MACD 30-31 – NASA 50083AC, A658828AC, 65997AC, 66155AC, 66156AC, 66177AC – WOOC 159

231878 535 MS SPAMCAN
27 12 43 AI 09 02 44 AOS 20 02 44 G
24 05 44 FTR GF CR Melchow/Biesenthal, Germany – 2Lt Walter K Higgins – 6 KIA, 4 POW – MACR 5177
See; NASA A65832AC

231969
07 01 44 AI 05 02 44 AOS 00 00 44 G
22 02 44 306BG

231980 532 VE J
10 01 44 AI 05 02 44 AOS 26 05 44 G
21 06 44 FTR GF CR Prenzlau, Germany – Lt Roger L Dussault – 2 KIA, 7 POW – MACR 5990

231990 535 MS R STAGE DOOR CANTEEN
10 01 44 AI 00 02 44 AOS 06 04 44 G
00 05 45 ZOI 26 02 46 Kingman, Arizona
See; AFMA 42 – BROB 566 – CAMB 29 – FRED 138 – FREJ 224, 449 – FREP 157 – MACD 63 – NASA 51869AC, 65857AC, 66145AC, 66148AC, 66208AC – VALA 69 –WOOA 144, 145 – WOOC 160

232007 533 VP
11 01 44 AI 20 02 44 AOS 00 00 44 G
01 03 44 384BG

232025 533 VP P DREAM BABY
13 01 44 AI 10 02 44 AOS 25 02 44 G
21 04 45 2SAD RG?
00 05 45 ZOI 20 12 45 Kingman, Arizona
See; FREH CP – MACD 53 – NASA A65830AC – VALA 103

232049 534 GD D YANKEE REBEL
15 01 44 AI 21 03 44 AOS 06 04 44 G
03 08 44 FTR AA CR Terneuzen, the Netherlands – 2Lt John C Wilcock – 9 KIA – MACR 7883

232060 535 MS V BOULDER BUF
18 01 44 AI 21 03 44 AOS 06 04 44 G
09 12 44 FTR LOC 22 12 44 SAL
See; NASA C65829AC, 65859AC

232088 532 VE M DRY GULCHER
20 01 44 AI 13 02 44 AOS 06 04 44 G
19 05 44 FTR AA CR Mehrin, Germany – Lt Harold C Blog – 9 POW – MACR 5030

232102 535 MS O JULIE LINDA
21 01 44 AI 02 03 44 AOS 23 05 44 G
01 02 45 BD 02 02 45 2SAD SAL
See; MACD 62 – NASA B65832AC, A65872AC, B65891AC

237719 533 VP X HELLCAT
10 08 43 AI 08 09 43 AOS 08 10 43 G
11 01 44 FTR AA DIT Zuiderzee, the Netherlands – 2Lt Donald E Nason – 9 KIA, 1 POW – MACR 1881
See; NASA C65833AC, 73060AC (?)

237721 534 GD L SUGAR
10 08 43AI 09 09 43 AOS 00 10 43 G
19 05 44 AFSC 02 06 45 SAL
See; MACB 13 – NASA A65834AC, 66023AC – SCUD 91

237730 533 VP U
10 08 43 AI 07 09 43 AOS 20 09 43 G
24 09 43 2SAD RG 25 09 43
11 01 44 FTR AA CR Minden, Germany – Lt Gordon W Crozier – 1 KIA, 9 POW – MACR 1887

237733 535 MS N PATCHES N' PRAYERS
10 08 43 AI 11 09 43 AOS 22 02 44 482BG
18 04 44 FTR AA CR Kidens, Germany – Lt Harlan D Soeder – 9 POW – MACR 4051

237754 534 GD I WHO DAT DING BAT
16 08 43 AI 04 09 43 AOS 20 09 43 G
28 03 44 CR English Channel
See; FREJ 211 – MACD 34-35

237760 532 VE F AVENGER
18 08 43 AI 09 09 43 AOS 20 09 43 G
02 10 43 BAD1 RG 18 10 43
00 00 44? RG 10 01 44
19 05 44 AFSC 489BG

237786 532 VE B
27 08 43 AI 01 11 43 AOS 21 11 43 G 401BG
25 02 44 FTR MECH CR Willmandingen, Germany – 2Lt Donald G Henderson – 6 KIA, 4 POW – MACR 2933
See; BELB 53 – FREJ 188 – MACD 31 – NASA 65331AC, 65974AC, 65981AC, 66019AC

237884 534 GD J
01 10 43 AI 14 11 43 AOS 20 12 43 G
29 01 44 FTR GF CR Mannheim, Germany – Lt Laurance W Mickow – 5 KIA, 5 POW –
MACR 2241

237933 535 MS R SUPERSTITIOUS ALOYISUS
19 10 43 AI 25 11 43 AOS 00 01 44 G
28 03 44 CR Kent, England 29 03 44 2SAD SAL

237962 532 VE L BETTY LOU
28 10 43 AI 23 11 43 AOS 20 12 43 G
11 01 44 FTR AA CR Gallenbeck, Germany – 2Lt Robert V Saur – 8 KIA, 2 POW - MACR 1878
See; NASA 4206AC, 65944AC

237969 532 VE L OLD IRON GUT
29 10 43 AI 18 11 43 AOS 23 12 43 G
12 01 44 2SAD RG?
15 03 44 2SAD RG/
30 05 44 2SAD RG/
20 01 45 FTR LOC RG/
23 04 45 2SAD 31 05 45 SAL

237983 532 VE N
04 11 43 AI 09 12 43 AOS 22 01 44 G
06 03 44 FTR DIT English Channel
See; BISA 118 – MACD 34

2-37986 534 GD K
05 11 43 AI 03 11 43 AOS 15 01 44 G
03 03 44 FTR MID CR Itzehoe, Germany – 2Lt Robert H Rogers – 10 POW - MACR 4737

238004 534 GD A
12 11 43 AI 07 12 43 AOS 06 01 44 G
19 04 44 FTR GF CR Rohrberg, Germany – Lt Robert W Rayburn – 3 KIA, 6 POW - MACR 4052
See; MACD 45 – NASA 65919AC – STEA 110

238009 534 GD N
13 11 43 AI 20 12 43 AOS 08 01 44 G
21 03 44 2SAD RG 24 04 44
15 06 44 FTR AA CR Bazas, France –2Lt Charles H Kelly – 9 EVD – E 7E 1032, 1033, 1191, 1192. 1218, 1953, 2296, 2297, 2298 - MACR 5799

238010 532 VE J
15 11 43 AI 15 12 43 AOS 13 01 44 G
24 05 44 FTR GF AA Berlin, Germany – Lt Clarence W Ezzell – 2 KIA, 7 POW – MACR 5178

238029 532 VE M
19 11 43 AI 25 12 43AOS 01 03 44 G
08 03 44 FTR GF CR Lettele, the Netherlands – 2Lt Thomas A Pirtle – 10 POW – MACR 3002

238045 534 GD C
24 11 43 AI 21 12 43 AOS 22 01 44 G
29 01 44 FTR GF CR Frankfurt, Germany – 2Lt Robert W Mohnacky – 5 KIA, 5 POW – MACR 2242

238061 535 MS P GEORGIA REBEL II
01 12 43 AI 08 01 44 AOS 02 02 44 G
28 04 44 FTR AA CR Avord A/F, France – Lt Harold F Henslin – 7 KIA, 3 POW – MACR 4241
See; JABA 164 – NASA A65841AC, A65846AC.

238079 532 VE R CARNIVAL QUEEN
06 12 43 AI 05 02 44 AOS 02 02 44 G
24 02 44 2SAD RG 14 04 44
22 09 44 FTR LOC RG?
21 04 45 ? 16 05 45 SAL

238102 532 VE A
14 12 43 AI 22 01 44 AOS 12 03 44 G 457BG
24 03 44 SAL

238103 532 VE B OUR BOARDING HOUSE
15 12 43 AI 04 01 44 AOS 12 03 44 G 457
30 05 44 2SAD RG 11 06 44
09 04 45 CL SAL
See; NASA A65860AC, C65827AC – VALA 46

238117 535 MS T TOUCH THE BUTTON NELL II
18 12 43 AI 13 02 44 AOS 26 02 44 G
04 07 44 FTR MECH CR Amboise, France – 2Lt Bob B Bobrof – 2 EVD, 7 KIA – E & E 920, 921 – MACR 6773
See; NASA 65841AC, 66032AC – VALA 53

238148
30 12 43 AI 08 02 44 AOS 00 05 45 G 306BG
03 12 45 Kingman, Arizona

238159 534 GD Q
01 01 44 AI 05 02 44 AOS 21 06 44 G
21 11 44 FTR LOC RG?
21 01 45 FTR LOC 30 01 45 SAL RG?
30 05 45 91BG

238188 533 VP K
12 01 44 AI 08 05 44 AOS 06 04 44 G
30 05 44 FTR GF CR Koethen, Germany – 2Lt John J Monohan – 4 KIA, 5 POW – MACR 5234

2-38194 533 VP V BABOON MCGOON
12 01 44 AI 17 02 44 AOS 25 03 44 G
21 06 44 FTR GF INT Rinkoby, Sweden – Lt Arthur J Bailey – 7 INT, 2 POW – MACR 5992
00 00 45 RG 14 12 45 Kingman, Arizona

239797 535 MS NANCY M
02 09 43 AI 30 11 43 AOS 21 01 44 G 384BG
04 02 44 12 02 44 2SAD SAL
See; NASA C65840AC, 65866AC

239798 535 MS L BUCKET O' BOLTS
02 09 43 AI 29 12 43 AOS 23 01 44 G
17 07 44 487BG

239808 534 GD F
06 09 43 AI 05 10 43 AOS 19 10 43 G
22 10 43 2SAD RG 23 10 43
25 10 43 2SAD RG?
01 12 43 C/L Kent, England 02 12 43 2SAD SAL

239890 535 MS Y RETURN TICKET
30 09 43 AI 24 11 43 AOS 22 12 43 G
24 05 44 FTR GF CR Melchow, Germany – 2Lt Carl M Dasso – 5 KIA, 4 POW – MACR 5179
See; MACD 43 – NASA B65864AC, 66201AC, 66261AC

239891 533 VP V
30 09 43 AI 17 11 43 AOS 13 01 44 G
02 03 44 FTR CR Arlon, Belgium – Lt Eugene Schultz – 1 EVD, 9 POW – E & E 2179 – MACR 2738

239895 535 MS S BERMONDSAY BATTLER
01 10 43 AI 14 11 43 AOS 22 12 43 G
22 02 44 FTR GF CR Hiddesen, Germany – Lt Lee W Smith – 10 KIA – MACR 2935
See; MACD 27 – NASA A65833AC, B65865AC, 65967AC

239906 535 MS X SQUAT N' DROPIT
05 10 43 AI 10 11 43 AOS 20 12 43 G
04 01 44 2SAD RG?
15 04 44 LAND CF 17 04 44 2SAD SAL
See; MACD 31, 43 – NASA 66122AC, A66122AC, B66122AC, 66201AC

239910 535 MS
06 10 43 AI 24 11 43 AOS 20 12 43 G
31 12 43 FTR GF CR Toulouse, France – 2Lt Earl B Duarte – 2 EVD, 8 POW – E & E 416 – MACR 1978

239933
12 10 43 AI 24 11 44 AOS 20 12 43 G
00 00 44 452BG

239946 533 VP
14 10 43 AI 13 12 43 AOS 22 01 44 G
22 02 44 FTR AA CR Leopoldshohe, Germany – Lt. Hal E Roling – 5 KIA, 5 POW – MACR 2936

239997 533 VP R BIG MIKE/FRENCHY'S FOLLY
29 10 43 AI 14 12 43 AOS 13 01 44 G
02 05 44 2SAD 24 05 45 ZOI 28 11 45 Kingman, Arizona

240007 533 VP M HONEY
01 11 43 AI 30 11 43 AOS 22 01 44 G
13 09 44 FTR LOC RG 16 09 44
25 11 44 FTR LOC 13 12 44 SAL
See; NASA 65833AC

240008 532 VE E
01 11 43 AI 02 12 43AOS 08 01 44 G
24 03 44 FTR MID 231490 CR Neustaft, Germany – Lt. Thomas P Tompson – 10 KIA –
MACR 3539

240011 534 GD O SCHNOZLE
03 11 43 AI 30 11 43 AOS 22 01 44 G
27 11 44 RG?
21 01 45 CDA MID 297511 – Lt James E Smith – 9 KIA
See; AFMA 171, 252 – BIRG 5 – BIRM 24 – CAMB 19 – MACD 57 – NASA C65837AC – NASB K2198 – VALA 100

240017 535 MS W ASSEND
ME AND MY GAL
03 11 43 AI 15 11 43 AOS 05 01 44 G
21 01 45 2SAD RG?
14 02 45 FTR LOC (C/L) 14 03 45 SAL
See; MACD 62 –USAS UC 230308

240025 535 MS TOUCH THE BUTTON NELL
06 11 43 AI 08 12 43 AOS 06 01 44 G
06 02 44 CL Dunkeswell, England – 3 crew baled out over France – E & E 533, 546, 1226.
07 02 44 2SAD SAL

297059 533 VP S MARSHA SUE
24 01 44 AI 14 02 44 AOS 15 03 44 G 457BG
12 12 44 FTR LOC 05 01 45 SAL

297076 534 GD K DEE MARIE
26 01 44 AI 02 03 44 AOS 17 03 44 G
06 06 45 ZOI 25 11 45 Kingman, Arizona
See; FREC 1 – MACD 57 – NASA B65838AC, 65872AC

297084 534 GD H SPARE CHARLIE
26 01 44 AI 12 03 44 AOS 06 04 44 G
22 06 44 FTR AA CR Nr. Calais, France – Lt Samuel E Peak – 8 KIA, 1 POW – MACR 5918
See; NASA B64830AC

297127 535 MS P
31 01 44 AI 14 02 44 AOS 00 00 44 G
07 03 44 100BG

297174 534 GD P JOANNE
04 02 44 AI 21 03 44 AOS 07 04 44 G
21 06 44 FTR AA CR Berlin, Germany – Lt Roy H Pendergist – 2 KIA, 7 POW – MACR 5993
See; MACD 47 – NASA C65828AC, C65830AC, 66076AC

297214 534 GD B CAROLINA QUEEN
09 02 44 AI 11 03 44 AOS 25 03 44 G
24 05 44 FTR MID CR Gratze, Germany – Lt John A Wardencki – 9 KIA – MACR 5181
See; NASA 66028AC (?)

297238 534 GD I OUR CAPTAIN
12 02 44 AI 22 03 44 AOS 06 04 44 G
07 06 44 DIT – Lt John Martyniak – 9 RTD.
See; NASA B53246AC,65829AC

297265 535 MS P HELLS ANGEL
14 02 44 AI 21 04 44 AOS 27 04 44 G 398BG
25 02 45 FTR LOC SAL 08 03 45 RG?
07 06 45 ZOI 28 11 45 Kingman, Arizona
See; NASA A65819AC, 65829AC, 66174AC – VALA 17 – WOOA 166

297267 535 MS X TOMAHAWK WARRIOR
14 02 44 AI 19 04 44 AOS 27 04 44 G 398BG
16 05 44 2SAD RG?
01 01 44 FTR LOC CF France RG 28 03 45
26 04 45 CF EX Ridgewell 26 04 45 SAL
See; MACD 51 – NASA 52101AC, 65831AC, 65846AC, 65874AC, 66022AC.

297285 534 GD C PATSY ANN
16 04 44 AI 30 04 44 AOS 21 05 44 G 398BG
06 06 45 ZOI 01 12 45 Kingman. Arizona

297313 535 MS N THE COLUMBUS MISS
18 02 44 AI 21 04 44 AOS 05 05 44 G 398BG
14 01 45 FTR LOC – MACR 11763
See; CAMB 15 – NASA B65831AC

297315 532 VE N
18 02 44 AI 20 03 44 AOS 06 04 44 G 398BG
05 05 44 CL CF Halstead, England 2SAD SAL
See; KAPA 193 – MACD 42 – NASA 66199AC, 66200AC

297323
19 02 44 AI 21 04 44 AOS 00 05 45 306BG
06 12 45 Kingman, Arizona

297330 535 MS S CHUG-A-LUG IV
21 02 44 AI 08 04 44 AOS 24 04 44 G
06 11 44 FTR AA CR Rotenburg, Germany – 2Lt Julius Levifoff – 2 KIA, 7 POW – MACR 10154
See; MACD 56 – NASA C65917AC, 65858AC, 65873AC, 65923AC, 66045AC, 80284AC – WARF

297357 533 VP Z THE RAILROADER
23 02 44 AI 29 04 44 AOS 19 05 44 G 398BG
13 01 45 FTR LOC SAL

239397
26 02 44 AI 06 04 44 AOS 00 05 45 G 306BG
20 12 45 Kingman, Arizona

297442 532 VE Q
17 11 43 AI 14 01 44 AOS 21 02 44 G
01 10 44 CR Practice mission 03 10 44 2SAD SAL

297454 533 VP U
20 11 43 AI 13 12 43 AOS 13 01 44 G
19 05 44 FTR AA CR Berlin, Germany – Lt Earl Sharp – 1 KIA, 8 POW – MACR 4932

297471 532 VE N MALE CALL
26 11 43 AI 19 01 44 AOS 12 03 44 G 457BG
20 03 44 CL Ridgewell 2SAD 21 03 44

297474 533 VP Z HOMING PIGEON
26 11 43 AI 23 12 43 AOS 15 01 44 G
22 02 44 FTR GF CR Opherdicke? Germany – Lt Francis N Fridgen – 7 KIA, 3 POW – MACR 2934
See; PHIA 63-65

297503 533 VP X PRINCESS PAT
04 12 43 AI 24 12 43 AOS 13 01 44 G
26 03 45 CL Ridgewell 2SAD SAL
See ; ETHC 46 – FREP 122 – MACD 32 – NASB K-KE2337 – WARB

42-97505
06 12 43 AI 11 01 44 AOS 00 05 45 G 306BG
05 12 45 Kingman, Arizona

297511 535 MS K EGG HAID
08 12 43 AI 08 02 44 AOS 22 02 44 G
12 09 44 FTR LOC RG 14 11 44
21 01 44 CDA MID 240011 2SAD SAL – F/O Nicholas Tauro – 9 KIA
See; NASA A65832AC, A65835AC – BIRK 28 - WARF

297589 533 VP Y
31 12 43 AI 07 02 44 AOS 00 04 44 G
21 02 45 FTR LOC RG?
26 03 45 CL CF 28 03 45 SAL

297594 532 VE B DRY GULCHER
01 01 44 AI 05 03 44 AOS 28 06 44 G 91BG
04 08 44 CR CF 05 08 44 SAL

297625 535 MS I SUNKIST SPECIAL
10 01 44 AI 22 03 44 AOS 00 00 44 G
27 04 44 AF Bassingbourn RG 05 07 44
05 01 45 Bassingbourn RG 18 01 45
08 03 45 CL SAL
See NASA 62766(AC),[2] BG5860AC - VALA25

297661 534 GD L
21 01 44 AI 08 04 44 AOS 09 04 44 G 482BG

297714
05 02 44 AI 24 04 44 AOS 26 05 44 G
00 05 45 100 BG

297771 533 VP
05 02 44 AI 10 06 44 AOS 05 07 44 91BG
05 08 44 FTR AA CR North Sea - Lt. Salvatore J. Melomo - 5 KIA, 5 POW - MACR 7884

297828 535 MS Q QUEENIE
09 03 44 AI 03 04 44 AOS 28 05 44 G
09 02 45 FTR LOC 04 03 45 SAL
See; NASA 66251AC, 65829AC

297882 533 VP K
25 03 44 AI 29 05 44 AOS 04 06 44 G
14 06 45 SAL

297990 532 VE F
26 04 44 AI 09 07 44 AOS 06 08 44 G
10 01 45 FTR LOC 11 01 45 2SAD RG 23 02 45
01 07 49 Oberpfaffenhofen, Germany

2102423 533 VP Q
03 03 44 AI 30 04 44 AOS 21 05 44 G
31 07 44 FTR AA CR Stafflangen? – 2Lt Jack B Pearson – 9 POW – MACR 7742

2102512 534 GD
11 03 44 AI 21 04 44 AOS 00 05 45 G 306BG
07 06 45 ZOI 04 12 45 Kingman, Arizona

2102578
17 03 44 AI 30 04 44 AOS 00 05 34 G 306BG
07 06 45 ZOI 07 06 46 South Plains, Texas

2102585 534 GD A THE BETTY L
17 03 44 AI 10 04 44 AOS 24 04 44 G
24 06 44 FTR AA CR Tours, France –2Lt Victor R Ramasco – 1 EVD, 4 KIA, 4 POW – E & E 1744 – MACR 6534
See; NASA 65831AC

2102590 535 MS M IN LIKE ERROL
18 03 44 AI 02 05 44 AOS 22 05 44 G
30 03 45 FTR AA CR Syke, Germany – 2Lt Robert A Bennett – 3 KIA, 7 POW – MACR 13542
See; AFMA 136 – NASA 65827AC – WOOA 167

2102656 534 GD L CAROL LEIGH
24 03 44 AI 03 05 44 AOS 21 05 44 G
10 05 45 92BG

2102663 534 GD L YARDBIRD
24 03 44 AI 03 05 44 AOS 21 05 44 G
18 07 44 FTR INT MECH Bulltofta, Sweden – Lt Frank R O'Black – 9 INT – MACR 7552
13 07 45 ZOI 13 12 45 Kingman, Arizona

2102664 532 VE F HAPPY BOTTOM
24 03 44 AI 02 05 44 AOS 19 05 44 G
16 07 44 DIT English Channel
See; BROB 569 – BOWG 59 – MCDA 55 – MACD 51 – NASA 66022AC, 66084AC - VALA 37 – WARB – WOOC 169

2102672 533 VP
25 03 44 AI 02 05 44 AOS 21 05 44 G
30 05 44 FTR GF CR Piethen, Germany – Lt Merrill O Burton – 4 KIA, 5 POW – MACR 5233

2102703 532 VE M PELLA TULIP
28 03 44 AI 02 05 44 AOS 22 05 44 G
15 10 44 2SAD 16 10 44 SAL

2102873 532 VE H THE JOKER II
14 04 44 AI 11 05 44 AOS 22 05 44 G
03 02 45 FTR AA CR Nr. Berlin, Germany – 2Lt John b Anderson – 1 KIA, 8 POW – MACR 12096

2102966 534 GD F AVENGRESS II
24 04 44 AI 21 05 44 AOS 23 05 44 G
06 06 45 ZOI 18 12 45 Kingman, Arizona
See NASA 65951AC - SCUC 38(?)

2102968 534 GD N VIA PANOLA EXPRESS
24 04 44 AI 12 03 44 AOS 27 05 44 G
10 11 44 FTR LOC 11 11 44 SAL
See; NASA 65951AC, B65890AC, 65891AC

2106994 532 VE K LITTLE GUY
21 01 44 AI 12 03 44 AOS 03 04 44 G
26 11 44 FTR AA CR Appeldoorn, the Netherlands –2Lt Kyle S Smith – 3 KIA, 6 POW – MACR 11205
See; ETHC 28 – NASA A65827AC, A65871AC

2107018 535 MS U LOS ANGELES CITY LIMITS
01 02 44 AI 08 03 44 AOS 25 03 44 G
19 04 45 AF Nuthampstead RG 03 05 45
09 06 45 ZOI 09 12 45 Kingman, Arizona
See; BROB 493 – ETHE 37 – FREH 155 – MACD 54 – NASA 51499AC (?), 65819AC, C65830AC, C65835AC, A65844AC, B65855AC, 65921AC

2107023 532 VE
01 02 44 AI 06 03 44 AOS 25 03 44 G
27 05 44 FTR GF CR Champfleury, France – 2Lt Andrew H Stuart – 3 EVD, 1 KIA, 5 POW –
E & E 1475, 1476, 1562 – MACR 5182

2107088 532 VE E
16 02 44 AI 04 03 44 AOS 25 03 44 G
19 06 44 FTR AA CR Nr. Bordeaux, France – 2Lt John B Doyle – 7 KIA, 2 POW – MACR 5994

2107100 532 VE D CENTURY NOTE
21 02 44 AI 23 03 44 AOS 06 04 44 G
28 10 44 FTR LOC RG 16 12 44
24 05 45 ZOI 28 11 45 Kingman, Arizona

2107112 532 VE O SLEEPY TIME GAL
21 02 44 AI 24 03 44 AOS 06 04 44 G
30 03 45 FTR LOC RG?
30 05 45 ZOI 18 11 45 Kingman, Arizona
See; ETHC 28 – MACD 37, 49 – NASA B65856AC, A65863AC, B65875AC – VALA 18 – WOOA 177

337514 534 GD B MY SON BOB
26 04 44 AI 18 05 44 AOS 12 08 44 G
01 02 45 FTR LOC 2SAD RG?
28 03 45 FTR LOC SAL RG?
06 06 45 ZOI 04 11 45 Kingman, Arizona
See; FREP 152 – NASA B65826AC, B65873AC

337536 532 VE C FRENCH DRESSING
28 04 44 AI 27 05 44 AOS 12 06 44 G
18 06 45 ZOI 07 06 46 South Plains, Texas

337538 535 MS Z WILD BILL
28 04 44 AI 22 05 44 AOS 29 08 44 G
26 02 45 FTR LOC RG 23 03 45
07 06 45 ZOI 05 12 45 Kingman, Arizona

337543 VE I LIBERTY BELLE
28 04 44 AI 29 05 44 AOS 04 06 44 G
24 05 45 452BG

337549 534 GD
29 04 44 AI 29 05 44 AOS 00 05 45 G 306BG
07 06 45 ZOI 20 12 45 Kingman, Arizona

337553 535 MS Y FEATHER MERCHANT II
29 04 44 AI 21 05 44 AOS 27 05 44 G
01 01 45 FTR CR Continent SAL – Lt Vincent J Peters – 9 RTD
See; NASA C65826AC

337560 533 VP R
01 05 44 AI 29 05 44 AOS 03 06 44 G
07 10 44 FTR LOC 30 11 44 2SAD RG?
04 12 44 FTR LOC RG?
24 05 45 ZOI

337561 533 VP J
01 05 44 AI 29 05 44 AOS 12 06 44 G
15 03 45 CL Woodbridge. England – Lt Charles Carpenter – 1 KIA, 8 RTD SAL

337598
04 05 44 AI 29 06 44 AOS 00 05 45 G 306BG
07 06 45 ZOI 06 12 45 Kingman, Arizona

337611
06 05 44 AI 02 06 44 AOS 00 05 45 G 306BG
07 06 45 ZOI 14 12 45 Kingman, Arizona

337612 533 VP OLD IRON GUT
06 05 44 AI 02 06 44 AOS 18 06 44 G
20 06 44 FTR AA CR Hamburg, Germany – 2Lt Mark R Dunkel – 6 KIA, 3 POW – MACR 5991
See; NASA B65835AC

337616
06 05 44 AI 04 06 44 AOS 00 05 45 G 306BG
30 05 45 ZOI 10 12 45 Kingman. Arizona

337657 534 GD I THE FOX
11 05 44 AI 04 06 44 AOS 10 06 44 G
14 02 45 FTR LOC 04 03 45 SAL
See; MACD 50 – NASA B65827AC (?) – VALA 36

337675 532 VE N PATCHES
FLAK MAGNET
14 05 44 AI 01 06 44 AOS 10 06 44 G
01 03 45 FTR LOC RG?
24 05 45 ZOI 17 12 45 Kingman, Arizona
See; FREP 120 – MACD 37 – NASA 55429AC, B65836AC, A65864AC

337704 535 MS J BUTTON NOSE
16 05 44 AI 06 06 44 AOS 16 06 44 G
08 08 44 FTR AA CR Caen, France – Lt Beackley – 9 RTD
See; BOWM 112 – MACD cover – NASA 56634AC – NASB K2260

337737 SECOND YEAR
18 05 44 AI 02 06 44 AOS 10 06 44 G
24 06 44 2SAD SAL

337791 533 VP V
24 05 44 AI 18 06 44 AOS 28 06 44 G
18 12 44 FTR LOC 05 01 45 SAL
See; ETHC 46 – NASB K-KE2337

337852 534 GD A
31 05 44 AI 01 07 44 AOS 17 07 44 G
06 06 45 ZOI 28 11 45 Kingman, Arizona

337898 535 MS
05 06 44 AI 00 06 44 AOS 03 07 44 G
04 07 44 95BG

338114 534 GD NO COMMENT NEEDED
28 06 44 AI 27 07 44 AOS 06 08 44 G
06 11 44 FTR AA CR Wittmundhafen, Germany – 1Lt Dudley K Brummett – 9 POW – MACR 10153
See; NASA B65872AC

338127 535 MS Q PAIR OF QUEENS, GEE AND BEE
29 06 44 AI 25 07 44 AOS 28 07 44 G
23 02 45 FTR LOC RG?
06 06 45 ZOI 18 12 45 Kingman, Arizona
See; NASA 66250AC, 65828AC

338153
30 06 44 AI 20 07 44 AOS 00 05 45 306BG
07 06 45 ZOI 09 12 45 Kingman. Arizona

338158 534 GD D SMASHIN'-TIME!
03 07 44 AI 25 07 44 AOS 26 07 44 G
21 01 45 FTR CL Sauverne, France – 2Lt Robert Coates – 9 RTD
28 02 45 SAL
See; CAMB 75 – MACD 52 – NASA C65825AC, 66210AC – VALA 50

338376
29 07 44 AI 10 09 44 AOS 00 05 45 G 306BG
07 06 45 ZOI 09 12 45 Kingman, Arizona

338383
29 07 44 AI 01 09 44 AOS 02 09 44 G
03 09 44 100BG

338412 31 07 44 AI 01 09 44 AOS 00 05 45 G 306BG
07 06 45 ZOI 05 12 45 Kingman, Arizona

338497 532 VE Q THE JOKER III
12 08 44 AI 19 09 44 AOS 20 09 44 G
24 05 45 ZOI 07 06 46 Kingman, Arizona

338550 532 VE A DAISY MAE
18 08 44 AI 18 09 44 AOS 19 09 44 G
07 06 45 ZOI 08 12 45 Kingman, Arizona

338683
05 09 44 AI 25 09 44 AOS 00 05 45 G 306BG
07 06 45 ZOI 28 11 45 Kingman, Arizona

338711
09 09 44 AI 09 10 44 AOS 00 05 45 G 306BG
07 06 45 ZOI 28 11 45 Kingman, Arizona
See; MACD 58

338771 534 GD E
19 09 44 AI 18 10 44 AOS 06 11 44 G
21 02 45 BD SAL RG 18 03 45
07 06 45 ZOI 03 12 45 Kingman, Arizona

338780 532 VE J
19 09 44 AI 07 10 44 AOS 14 11 44 G
11 12 44 FTR AA CR Mannheim, Germany – Lt Leo Belskis – 7 KIA, 2 POW – MACR 11341

338802
24 09 44 AI 05 10 44 AOS 00 05 45 G 306BG
07 06 45 ZOI 04 12 45 Kingman, Arizona

338856 534 GD M
28 09 44 AI 18 10 44 AOS 19 10 44 G
14 02 45 FTR LOC RG?
23 04 45 CR Isle of Man – Capt Charles E Ackerman – 31 KIS
2SAD SAL

338898 534 GD G HITLERS HO DO (HOODOO?)
05 10 44 AI 16 10 44 AOS 14 11 44 G
03 02 45 FTR AA CR Tutow, Germany – 2Lt Paul C Pucylowski – 1 KIA, 8 POW – MACR12295

338907 534 GD I
09 10 44 AI 16 10 44 AOS 20 10 44 G
23 02 45 FTR LOC RG?
16 04 45 FTR LOC RG?
00 00 45 401BG

338908 535 MS L
07 10 44 AI 17 10 44 AOS 18 10 44 G
07 06 44 ZOI 05 12 45 Kingman, Arizona

338910 535 MS
07 10 44 AI 18 10 44 AOS 21 02 45 G
07 06 45 ZOI 09 12 45 Kingman, Arizona

338913 532 VE
09 10 44 AI 20 10 44 AOS 21 02 45 G 306BG
07 06 45 ZOI 06 12 45 Kingman, Arizona

338914
09 10 44 AI 19 10 44 AOS 24 05 45 G 306BG
07 06 45 ZOI 30 11 45 Kingman, Arizona

338916
09 10 44 AI 19 10 44 AOS 00 05 45 G 306BG
07 06 45 ZOI 09 12 45 Kingman, Arizona

338967 533 VP L
21 10 44 AI 01 11 44 AOS 19 12 44 G
26 03 45 BD 28 03 45 2SAD RG 03 05 45
24 05 45 ZOI 18 11 45 Kingman, Arizona

338977 532 VE H FRENCH DRESSING
26 10 44 AI 18 11 44 AOS 08 02 45 G
24 05 45 ZOI 20 11 45 Kingman, Arizona
See; NASA C65875AC – VALA35

338983 533 VP S FORT LANSING EMANCIPATOR
28 10 44 AI 18 11 44 AOS 19 12 44 G 100BG
24 05 45 ZOI 30 11 45 Kingman, Arizona
See; NASA B65824AC, 66165AC – WOOC 188

338986 533 VP M
28 10 44 AI 09 11 44 AOS 08 12 44 G
12 12 44 FTR LOC 02 01 45 SAL

338998 535 MS S CRACK-A-DAWN
31 10 44 AI 18 11 44 AOS 19 12 44 G
14 02 45 FTR LOC RG 23 03 45
07 06 45 ZOI 20 12 45 Kingman, Arizona

229012 532 VE J MISS FORTUNE
04 11 44 AI 18 11 44 AOS 08 02 45 G
14 02 45 FTR LOC RG?
09 03 45 FTR AA CR Fritzlar,Germany – 2Lt Paul J Scherman – 7 KIA, 2 POW – MACR 12960

339025 535 MS W BUCKEYE
09 11 44 AI 14 12 44 AOS 17 02 45 G
06 12 45 Kingman, Arizona
See; MACD 63

339059 532 VE S
18 11 44 AI 05 12 44 AOS 06 12 44 G
06 12 45 Kingman, Arizona

339156
20 12 44 AI 20 01 45AOS 21 01 45 G
22 01 45 351BG

339161 534 GD G SHOOT LUKE
21 12 44 AI 06 01 45 AOS 05 02 45 G
07 06 45 ZOI 04 12 45 Kingman, Arizona
See; NASA 32400AC (?), A65826AC

339167 534 GD D
23 12 44 AI 06 01 45 AOS 05 02 45 G
06 06 45 ZOI 07 12 45 Kingman, Arizona

339170 535 MS V
21 12 44 AI 20 01 45 AOS 21 02 45 G
07 06 45 ZOI 29 11 45 Kingman. Arizona

339172 532 VE K LITTLE LULU
21 12 44 AI 06 01 45 AOS 05 02 45 G
24 05 45 ZOI 25 11 45 Kingman, Arizona

339174
21 12 44 AI 20 01 45 AOS 00 05 45 G 306BG
07 06 45 ZOI 30 11 45 Kingman, Arizona

339300 533 VP X
01 02 45 AI 13 02 45 AOS 12 04 45 G
24 05 45 ZOI 14 11 45 Kingman, Arizona

339449
21 03 45 AI 04 03 45 AOS 12 05 45 G
28 05 45 ZOI 21 02 46 Kingman, Arizona

339452 533 VP Y
21 03 45 AI 31 03 45 AOS 11 04 45 G
24 05 45 ZOI 26 11 45 Kignman, Arizona

46012
05 04 44 AI 02 05 44 AOS 00 05 45 G 306BG
30 05 45 91BG

46020 532 VE X UNDERGROUND FARMER
06 04 44 AI 13 05 44 AOS 28 05 44 G
06 08 44 FTR AA DIT Baltic Sea – Lt. Allen W webb – 1 KIA, 8 POW – MACD 7882
See; MACD 53 – NASA B65828AC – VALA 54

46025 532 VE I SO WHAT?
09 04 44 AI 30 04 44 AOS 19 05 44 G
30 05 44 FTR GF CR Karow, Germany – Lt Leonard E Zapinski – 9 POW – MACR 5235

46095 533 VP N FORTH WORTH GAL
29 04 44 AI 22 05 44 AOS 26 05 44 G
10 09 44 FTR AA CR Neibsheim, Germany – 2Lt Ernest Germano – 1 KIA, 8 POW – MACR 8906
See; LOGA 41 – MACD 49 – NASA B65825AC – VALA 35 – WOOA 165

46115 534 GD Q ICE COL' KATY
06 05 44 AI 29 05 44 AOS 10 06 44 G
14 01 45 CL 2SADRG 09 02 45
29 11 45 Kingman, Arizona

46148 534 GD M SMASHIN' THRU
24 05 44 AI 02 06 44 AOS 16 06 44 G
13 07 44 CR Ridgewell – Lt John M Houston – 7 KIA, 2 INJURED – 2SAD SAL See NASA A66/36AC

46163 533 GD P PASSAIC WARRIOR
19 05 44 AI 10 06 44 AOS 28 06 44 G
28 11 45 Kingman, Arizona
See; FREP 121 – IWM EA74531, EA74532 – MOYB 153 – NASA 54025AC, 56873AC, B65892AC, 66077AC – WARF

46173 534 GD H MISS FLORALA
19 05 44 AI 10 06 44 AOS 28 06 44 G
08 04 45 FTR AA CR Gottingen, Germany – 2Lt Harvey E Adelmeyer – 6 KIA, 2 RTD – MACR 13873
See; NASA A65857AC, 65926AC – SCUC 39

46478 533 VP W
16 08 44 AI 08 09 44 AOS 29 09 44 G
14 02 45 FTR LOC RG?
24 03 45 FTR AA CR Greven, Germany – 2Lt Robert E Jankowiak – 4 KIA, 5 POW – MACR 13606

46515
26 08 44 AI 12 09 44 AOS 14 05 45 G 306BG
27 05 45 398BG

46563
09 09 44 AI 19 09 44 AOS 14 05 45 G 306BG
07 06 45 ZOI 01 12 45 Kingman, Arizona

46585 535 MS COMMANDO CHIEF
16 09 44 AI 13 10 44 AOS 00 05 45 306BG
07 06 45 ZOI 01 12 45 Kingman, Arizona

46604
21 09 44 AI 18 10 44 AOS 00 05 45 G 306BG
30 05 34 91BG

46625 534 GD N PEACEMAKER
27 09 44 AI 16 10 44 AOS 04 11 44 G
06 06 45 ZOI 30 11 45 Kingman, Arizona

46809 535 MS Y PFC's LTD
17 11 44 AI 03 12 44 AOS 04 01 45 G
10 06 45 ZOI 27 11 45 Kingman, Arizona
See NASA 65826AC

46814
17 11 44 AI 03 12 44 AOS 00 05 45 G 306BG
07 06 45 ZOI 14 01 46 Kingman, Arizona

66883 535 MS Q RAFAAF
09 12 44 AI 18 12 44 AOS 18 02 45 G
11 04 45 MID 48826 16 04 45 SAL 31 10 45 SAL 9AF
See; CAMB 26 – FRED 227 –MACD 59-60 – NASA 65894AC

46908 16 12 44 AI 130 12 44 AOS 00 05 45 G 306BG
07 06 45 ZOI 01 12 45 Kingman, Arizona

46950 532 VE M ALABAMA GAL
27 12 44 AI 14 01 45 AOS 01 02 45 G
14 02 45 FTR LOC RG?
24 05 45 ZOI 17 11 45 Kingman, Arizona

46951
28 12 44 AI 17 02 45 AOS 00 05 45 G 306BG
07 06 45 ZOI 27 11 45 Kingman, Arizona

46975 535 MS K
05 01 45AI 13 01 45 AOS 01 02 45 G
15 04 45 91BG

48010 532 VE J
10 05 44 AI 15 07 44 AOS 15 08 44 G
15 01 45 91BG

48024 534 GD O/J
16 05 44 AI 24 07 44 AOS 01 08 44 G
23 05 45 306BG

48036
19 05 44 AI 04 08 44 AOS 15 08 44 G
23 05 45 306BG

48098
10 06 44 AI 29 07 44 AOS 01 08 44 G
02 08 44 490BG

48172
28 06 44 AI 23 08 44 AOS 07 05 45 G 92BG
23 05 45 306BG

48175 532 VP N
30 06 44 AI 23 08 44 AOS 17 09 44 G
22 03 45 FTR AA CR Feldhausen, Germany – Lt. Robert Fawcett – 10 KIA – MACR 13605

48196 533 VP U
06 07 44 AI 12 09 44 AOS 15 10 44 G
14 02 45 FTR LOC RG?
29 03 45 CL Ridgewell 30 03 45 SAL

48203 533 VP
07 07 44 AI 01 09 44 AOS 00 05 45 G 306BG
07 06 45 ZOI 01 12 45 Kingman, Arizona

48228 535 MS L THE ALAMO
14 07 44 AI 18 09 44 AOS 03 10 44 G 100BG
23 05 45 306BG
10 05 46 Germany SAL
See; MACD 58 – NASA A65826AC, C65843AC, 66079AC – WOOC 162

48349 532 VE G
19 08 44 AI 18 10 44 AOS 02 11 44 G
00 05 44 305BG

48350
19 08 44 AI 18 10 44 AOS 20 10 44 G
00 10 44 306BG 23 05 46 Germany SAL

48402 535 MS N
07 09 44 AI 18 12 44 AOS 19 01 45 G
00 05 45 306BG 10 05 46 Germany SAL

48516
06 10 44 AI 18 10 44 AOS 23 05 45 G 306BG
07 06 45 ZOI 01 12 45 Kingman, Arizona

48520
09 10 44 AI 19 10 44 AOS 00 01 45 G
19 10 45 ZOI 05 01 46 Walnut Ridge, Arkansas

48526 533 VE Q ONE MEAT BALL
10 10 44 AI 24 10 44 AOS 01 12 44 G
24 05 45 ZOI 14 12 45 Kingman, Arizona

48544 533 VP V
17 10 44 AI 16 12 44 AOS 18 01 45 G
14 03 45 CL Great Yeldham , England CF SAL

48599 533 VP M
31 10 44 AI 05 12 44 AOS 04 01 45 G
24 05 45 ZOI 27 11 45 Kingman, Arizona

48693 535 MS O
29 11 44 AI 18 12 44 AOS 11 02 45 G
26 03 45 FTR CL France 03 04 45 SAL

48779 532 VE S EVEYLN ANN
26 12 44 AI 31 01 45 AOS 21 02 45 G
00 05 45 306BG

48826 535 MS P
09 01 45 AI 13 02 45 AOS 27 03 45 G
11 04 45 MID 46883
23 05 45 306BG
See; MACD 59

48827 534 GD B DUSTY GAY
09 01 45 AI 04 02 45 AOS 16 02 45 G
23 05 45 306BG

48830 535 MS S SOUTH BOSTON SHILLELAGH
09 01 45 AI 13 02 45 AOS 12 03 45 G
23 05 45 306BG
See; NASA A65862AC, 65863AC, 66144AC

48855 533 VP W
16 01 45 AI 19 02 45 AOS 21 02 45 G
00 05 45 306BG 23 05 46 Germany SAL

48866 533 VP N
19 01 45 AI 15 02 45 AOS 17 02 45 G
00 05 45 306BG 01 04 46 Germany SAL

48868 532 VE LON BOY
20 01 45 AI 25 02 45 AOS 27 03 45 G 303BG
23 05 45 306BG 06 11 46 Germany SAL

48950
17 02 45 AI 26 03 45 AOS 28 03 45 G
21 05 45 306BG 42 05 45 ZOI 21 02 46 Kingman, Arizona

483252 533 VP Z
14 01 45 AI 02 02 45 AOS 24 02 45 G
24 05 45 ZOI 13 12 45 Kingman, Arizona

483624 532 VE F
00 00 45 AI 00 00 45 AOS 00 04 45 G
00 00 45 ZOI

Appendix B:

381BG NAME INDEX

Serial No	Name
46950	Alabama Gal
124500	Annie-Freeze
240017	Assend
237760	Avenger
2102966	Avengress II
238194	Baboon McGoon
23540	Bacta-Th' Sac
230676	Baby Dumpling
230026	Battle Wagon
229958	Battlin' Bombsprayer
239895	Bermondsay Battler
17	Bermondsay Special
17	Betsy Ann
237963	Betty Lou
17F	Big Bust
239997	Big Mike
229789	Big Time Operator
229570	Big Time Operator II
17	Black Jack
338898	Blind Date
231067	Black Widow
230722	Bobby T
232060	Boulder Buf
239798	Bucket O' Bolts
339025	Buckeye
337704	Button Nose
238079	Carnival Queen
297214	Carolina Queen
2102656	Carol Leigh
2107100	Century Note
230029	Chaps Flying Circus
230765	ChugaLug
17	Chug-A-Lug II
17	Chug-A-Lug III
297330	Chug-A-Lug IV
238159	Colonel. Bubb
338998	Crack-O-Dawn
338550	Daisy Mae
23220	Damfino
232088	Dry Gulcher
297594	Dry Gulcher
297076	Dee Marie
229954	Devils Angel
23514	Dinah Mite II?
23514	Doll Baby
232025	Dream Baby
17	Dresden Doll
17G	Duckie
48827	Dusty Gay
297511	Egg Haid
48779	Evelyn Ann
17G	Exodus
17G	Express
230009	Feather Merchant
337553	Feather Merchant II
229999	Fertile Myrtle
230015	Flyin' Hobo
338983	Fort Lansing Emancipator
46095	Fort Worth Gal
337675	Flak Magnet
229950	Forget Me Not
23180	Forget Me Not II
231111	Four Aces – Pat Hand
337536	French Dressing
338977	French Dressing
239997	Frenchys Folly
231443	Friday the 13th
229505	Full Boost!
17	Germany's Regret
23118	Green Hornet

231550 Green Hornet II
23217 Georgia Rebel
238061 Georgia Rebel II
229755 Gremlins Delite
23522 Gremlins Delite

231448 Half Breed
2102664 Happy Bottom
237719 Hellcat
229978 Hells Angels
297265 Hells Angel
338898 Hitlers Hoe Doe (Hoo Doo?)
238010 Hit Parader
297474 Homing Pigeon
240007 Honey
230852 Hot Toddy

46115 Ice Col' Katy
2102590 In Like Errol
229983 Iris
230016 Iron Gut Gert

230004 Janice
231381 Jaynee B
297174 Joanne
17 Jo Mo
232102 Julie Linda
17 King Malfunction
230140 King Malfunction II
17 King Tut

229755 Last Straw?
230013 Lethal Lady
337543 Liberty Belle
23226 Little Chuck
2106994 Little Guy
339172 Little Lulu
19043 Little Rock-ette
23215 Linda Mary
48868 Lon Boy
229988 Lucifer Jr.
229867 Lucifer II
2107018 Los Angeles City Limits
17 Lucky
230245 Lady Luck
230245 Lucky Lady II
231570 Lucky Me!

297471 Male Call
229953 Man O War
25847 Margie Mae
297059 Marsha Sue
229761 Martha The II
240017 Me And My Gal
46950 Melancholy Baby
23268 Messie Bessie
230834 Micky Finn
17F Midway
231614 Minnie The Mermaid

229751 Mis Abortion
46173 Miss Florala
339012 Miss Fortune
231097 Mission Belle
17F Mixmaster
231575 Mizpah
17F Moore-Fidite
17 Mr Yank
17 Mr Yank II
231553 Myers Flaw
17G Myrt's Revenge
337514 My Son Bob

239797 Nancy M
229765 Nip N' Tuck
230034 Nobodys Baby
338114 No Comment Needed

229854 Ole Flak Sack
229731 Ole' Swayback
230018 Old Coffins
17 Old Faithful
17 Old Ironsides
237969 Old Iron Gut
337612 Old Iron Gut
238004 Ol' Man Tucker
17 Old Sahib
48526 One Meat Ball
238103 Our Boarding House
297238 Our Captain
231357 Our Desire
17F Our Gang
229832 Our Mom

338127 Pair Of Queens, Gee and Bee
46163 Passaic Warrior
231417 Patches
337675 Patches
237733 Patches N' Prayers
297285 Patsy Ann
46625 Peacemaker
2102703 Pella Tulip
46809 PFCs Ltd
231067 Phyliss
230732 Pistol Packin' Mama
297503 Princess Pat

297828 Queenie

46883 RAFAAF
17F Rat Poison
23223 Red Hot Riding Hood
239890 Return Ticket
23123 Ron Chee
231761 Rotherhithes Revenge
231497 Round Trip Jeannie

229976 Sad Sack
17 Sad Sack II

240011	Schnozzle
337737	Second Year
17	Seldom Pecks
17F	Shoo Shoo Baby
339161	Shoot Luke
231197	Shack Rabbit
17G	Silver Lady
22978	Sis
2107112	Sleepy Time Gal
46148	Smashin' Thru
338158	Smashin' Time
229784	Smilin' Thru
48830	South Boston Shillelagh
46025	So What?
231878	Spamcan
297084	Spare Charlie
230151	Spare Parts
239906	Squat N' Droppit
231990	Stage Door Canteen
23092	Strato Sam
229751	Stuff
237721	Sugar
297265	Sunkist Special
237933	Superstitious Aloysius
230028	Sweet Li' Lani
230721	Sweet N' Lovely
231569	Sweet Patootie
230020	Sweet Eloise
48228	The Alamo
2102585	The Betty L
297313	The Columbus Miss
337657	The Fox
23177	The Hellion
229888	The Joker
2102873	The Joker II
338497	The Joker III
229923	The Lucky Strike
297357	The Railroader
231075	The Rebel
231099	Tenabove
25725	This Is it!
25846	Tinkertoy
17	Tinkertoy II
17	Toggleer
240025	Touch The Button Nell
238117	Touch the Button Nell II
23211	T.S.
229941	T.S. Too
297267	Tomahawk Warrior
17F	Uncle Sammy
46020	Underground Farmer
2102968	Via Panola Express
17	Viking
23221	Whaletail
25845	Whaletail II
17G	Whirlaway
237754	Who Dat?
230011	Widget
337538	Wild Bill
23078	Winsome Winn/Hilda
231047	Wolverine
2102663	Yardbird
25397	Yankee Eagle
232049	Yankee Rebel

Appendix C:

ROLL OF HONOR

PO	Name	Rank	Status	Date	P-No/Sqdn.	M-No.	MACR
N	Anderson Robert F	2/Lt	POW	30/01/44	229761 62	2244	
	Anderson Robert H		KIA	29/06/43			
RW	Abernathy, Walter H	S/Sgt	POW	22/02/44	297474	70	2934
LW	Abramo, Nicholas J	S/Sgt	POW	02/03/44	239891	73	2738
P	Ackerman, Charles E	Capt	KIS	23/04/45	338856		
N	Adams, Donald K	2/Lt	POW	25/09/44	231570	192	10203
N	Adams, Edward R	FO	POW	24/05/44	238010	116	5178
P	Adelmeyer, Harvey E	2/Lt	KIA	08/04/45	46173	286	13873
WG	Ahl, Walter J	S/Sgt	KIA	15/03/45	337561	270	
P	Alexander, Joe E	Capt	POW	25/07/43	230153	12	131
LW	Alfaro, Ralph A	Sgt	POW	06/03/44	231553	76	3241
TG	Alford, Allen T	S/Sgt	KIA	09/10/43	229958	37	886
CP	Allchim, Harry Jnr.	2/Lt	KIA	01/12/43	229506	46	1578
TT	Allen, Earl R	T/Sgt	POW	17/08/43	230028	20	380
TT	Allen, John L	T/Sgt	POW	20/12/43	231075	51	1722
	Allen. Roger H	Sgt	KIS	23/06/43			
BT	Alsheimer, Wilbur	S/Sgt	POW	12/08/43	25847	17	660
	Ammerman, Earl G	Sgt	KIS	23/04/45	338856		
N	Anagnos,Anthony A	2/Lt	KIA	11/01/44	237719	59	1881
BT	Anderson,Charles	S/Sgt	KIA	24/05/44	297214	116	5181
N	Anderson, Everett S	2/Lt	KIA	20/12/43	25846	51	1723
TG	Anderson, Cornelius G	S/Sgt	POW	19/05/44	232088	112	5030
RW	Anderson, Walter J	S/Sgt	KIA	30/07/43	23100	16	129
BT	Arbiter, Jerome	S/Sgt	KIA	09/10/43	230012	37	887
B	Arning, Eugene	Lt	KIA	28/04/44	238061	101	4241
RW	Arnold, Thomas	Sgt	POW	26/11/44	2106994	217	11205
	Ashcroft, Robert N	Sgt	KIS	23/06/43			
LW	Asher, Clarence C	S/Sgt	POW	25/07/43	229976	12	128
P	Atkinson, Challon P	Lt	KIA	17/08/43	229983	20	398
B	Atkinson, Howard C	S/Sgt	POW	06/03/44	231448	76	3001
N	Austin, Russell D	F/O	POW	22/02/44	231443	70	2930
BT	Avrett, John V	S/Sgt	KIA	20/12/43	25845	51	1724
BT	Ayers, George	S/Sgt	KIA	29/01/44	237884	61	2241
	Babines, Michael C, jnr.	Sgt	KIS	08/03/44			
B	Bach, Leo S	2/Lt	POW	11/04/44	231497	91	3821
TT	Backelin, Warren H	T/Sgt	KIA	24/05/44	297214	116	5181

P	Baur, Carl O	Lt	KIA	30/01/44	230029	62	2495
TG	Bailes, Milton G	S/Sgt	POW	18/04/44	237733	93	4051
P	Bailey, Arthur J	Lt	INT	21/06/44	238194	140	5992
	Bailey, Edward G		KIS	23/04/45			
RW	Baird, Carl L	S/Sgt	POW	08/10/43	230009	36	1397
TT	Baird, John S	T/Sgt	POW	24/05/44	231989	116	5177
RO	Baker, Louis K	T/Sgt	POW	24/05/44	238010	116	5178
B	Baker, Robert J	2/Lt	POW	06/03/44	32315	76	3000
RO	Balentine, William L Jnr.	S/Sgt	POW	17/08/43	230140	20	379
BT	Ball. Philip M	Sgt	KIA	11/01/44	25878	59	1874
P	Ballinger, Olaf M	Lt	EVD	04/07/43	229928	7	161
TT	Ballou, Howard W	Sgt	KIA	08/10/43	229854	36	1395
RO	Balmore, George M	T/Sgt	KIA	11/01/44	237730	59	1877
RW	Bang, Charles F	S/Sgt	POW	03/09/43	229789	25	473
	Banotai, Charles G	2/Lt	KIA	22/03/45	48175	275	13605
	Barbour, Andrew R	Sgt	KIS	23/04/45	338856		
N	Barer, David	2/Lt	KIA	30/01/44	231047	62	2243
B	Barker, William G	2/Lt	POW	06/11/44	338114	211	10153
N	Barkett, Philip J	2/lt	POW	24/05/44	239890	116	5179
TG	Barr, Henry R	Sgt	POW	11/02/44	231099	67	2431
BT	Bartle, Garrett M	S/Sgt	POW	22/02/44	297474	70	2934
RW	Bartolo, Anthony J	S/Sgt	KIA	25/02/44	237786	72	2933
N	Bascon, Liston A	2/Lt	POW	25/07/43	229976	12	128
LW	Bassinger, Robin L	S/Sgt	POW	17/08/43	230245	20	381
TG	Batchelder, Robert K	Sgt	KIA	19/04/44	23525	94	4050
RW	Bauscher, Harry W	S/Sgt	KIA	04/07/43	4229928	7	161
TT	Beach, Perry E	S/Sgt	POW	30/01/44	229761	62	2244
TG	Beaman, Roger L	Sgt	POW	20/06/44	337612	139	5991
TG	Beasley, Chester J	S/Sgt	POW	17/08/43	230245	20	381
TT	Beck, Eugene N	T/Sgt	INT	18/07/44	2102663	155	7552
N	Beck, James A	2/Lt	POW	24/05/44	231989	116	5177
N	Becker, Jerome D	FO	POW	18/04/44	237733	93	4051
N	Beckerman, Hyman	2/Lt	POW	09/10/43	229958	37	886
BT	Beech, Frank M	S/Sgt	POW	17/08/43	232045	20	381
TG	Belgrasch, Francis N	Sgt	KIA	20/12/43	425845	51	1724
P	Belskis, Leo	Lt	KIA	11/11/44	338780	222	11341
CP	Bemis, Ralph Jnr.	2/Lt	KIA	24/03/44	238102	84	
TG	Beneke, Louis F	S/Sgt	POW	05.08/44	297771	167	7884
BT	Beninga, Harm R	S/Sgt	KIA	24/05/44	238010	116	5178
P	Bennett, Robert A	2/Lt	POW	30/03/45	2102590	281	13542
	Benward, Robert A	T/Sgt	KIA	13/07/44	46148	153	
RW	Berg, Robert J	T/Sgt	POW	29.01/44	238045	61	2242
RW	Berger, Paul L	Sgt	KIA	24/03/45	46478	277	13606
LW	Berk, Matthew	S/Sgt	POW	08/10/43	229941	36	884
N	Bernstein William	2/Lt	POW	05/08/44	297771	167	7884
N	Berry, Alvin C	2/Lt	POW	30/05/44	2102672	121	5233
TG	Beschta, Staley F	Sgt	POW	24/03/45	46478	277	13606
RW	Beus, Raymond C	Sgt	KIA	11/01/44	237719	59	1881
TT	Biglin, Joseph H	S/Sgt	KIA	22/03/45	48175	275	13605
LW	Bingenheimer, Ralph F	S/Sgt	POW	17/08/43	230028	20	380
WG	Biskop Stanley R	S/Sgt	KIA	22/03/45	48175	275	13605
B	Black, Robert C	Lt	KIA	08/10/43	230864	36	885
N	Blackfield, Willard I	2/Lt	KIA	24/05/44	297214	116	5181
LW	Blackmon, William B	Sgt	POW	28/04/44	238061	101	4241
LW	Blake, Harold L	S/Sgt	POW	17/08/43	23220	20	384
BT	Blanch, Bernard J	S/Sgt	POW	11/04/44	231497	91	3821
P	Blog, Harold C	Lt	POW	19/05/44	232088	112	5030
	Boatwright, Charles C	Sgt	KIA	22/03/45			
P	Bobrof Bob B	2/lt	KIA	04/07/44	238117	146	6779

CP	Bohan, William E	2/Lt	POW	25/07/43	229976	12	128
	Bohlander, Irwin	T/Sgt	KIS	23/06/43			
	Boland, George K	Sgt	KIS	23/06/43			
RO	Boland John J	S/Sgt	POW	18/04/44	237733	93	4051
	Bolan, Robert B	S/Sgt	KIA	24/03/45			277
RW	Bollinger Hubert S	S/Sgt	KIA	24/03/44	240008	84	3539
P	Bond, Leslie A	2/lt	KIA	19/04/44	23525	94	4050
	Bongiorno Henry	Sgt	KIS	23/06/43			
CP	Borrego William	2/Lt	POW	20/02/44	23562	68	2929
LW	Bosley Edwin B	S/Sgt	POW	11/01/44	25878	59	1874
N	Boston Jesse S Jnr.	2/Lt	KIA	20/12/43	25845	51	1724
CP	Bowen George A	2/Lt	KIA	24/03/44	4240008	84	3539
RO	Boyington William E	Sgt	POW	31/07/44	2102423	163	7742
BT	Boykin Clayton M	Sgt	KIA	08/10/43	229765	36	883
BT	Boylan Robert P	S/Sgt	KIA	14/10/43	229803	39	1037
B	Boyle Judson F	2/Lt	EVD	11/02/44	231099	67	2431
RO	Bozzette Salvatore	T/Sgt	KIA	04/01/44	231278	56	
TG	Brandt Martin D	S/Sgt	POW	09/10/43	230009	36	1397
TT	Brashear Charles F	S/Sgt	EVD	15/06/44	238009	136	5799
TG	Bratton Felis D	S/Sgt	POW	19/05/44	297454	112	4932
CP	Bredeson David L	2/Lt	KIA	30/05/44	2102672	121	5233
TT	Brennan Robert	T/Sgt	KIA	22/02/44	297474	70	2934
TT	Bright Notra J	T/Sgt	KIA	22/02/44	231442	70	2930
LW	Brinton Charles W	S/Sgt	KIA	25/06/43			
BT	Bristow John L	S/Sgt	POW	19/04/44	238004	94	4052
B	Britenbaker Francis W	2/Lt	POW	19/05/44	297454	112	4932
RO	Brogden John P	Sgt	KIA	11/01/44	237962	59	1876
RO	Brooks Howard C	S/Sgt	EVD	15/06/44	238009	136	5799
B	Brown Erwin M	Lt	POW	21/06/44	238194	140	5992
BT	Brown Oliver E	S/Sgt	INT	18/07/44	2102663	155	7552
RW	Brown Richard W	Sgt	KIA	20/012/43	25845	51	1724
N	Brumback Charles E	2/Lt	KIA	19/04/44	23525	94	4050
P	Brummett Dudley K	2/Lt	POW	06/11/44	238114	211	10153
TT	Bruzewski Otto F	T/Sgt	EVD	17/08/43	23225	20	378
TG	Bryan John B	Sgt	POW	30/05/44	238188	121	5234
N	Brzoska Walter	2/Lt	KIA	24/03/44	240008	84	3539
RW	Budzik Anthony L	S/Sgt	KIA	08/10/43	229941	36	884
LW	Bukowski Casimir L	S/Sgt	POW	22/02/44	231443	70	2930
CP	Bull Raymond A	2/Lt	KIA	22/02/44	239946	70	2936
TG	Bull William L	Sgt	POW	08/03/44	238029	77	3002
BT	Bulsok Steve F	S/Sgt	POW	20/12/43	231075	51	1722
TG	Bunworth John S	S/Sgt	POW	11/01/44	231417	59	1879
BT	Buran Walter J	S/Sgt	KIA	19/08/43	23101	21	662
RO	Burgess Boyd E	T/Sgt	KIA	25/02/44	237786	72	2933
N	Burke Edward J	Lt	POW	20/12/43	231075	51	1722
RW	Burke Philip F	S/Sgt	POW	01/12/43	23540	46	1660
CP	Burns Herbert W	2/Lt	POW	24/05/44	231989	116	5177
RO	Burrows Robert W	S/Sgt	POW	08/03/44	238029	77	3002
BT	Burt William C	S/Sgt	POW	06/08/44	46020	168	7882
P	Burton Merrill O	Lt	KIA	30/05/44	2102672	121	5233
N	Burwell Roger W	2/Lt	POW	08/10/43	230009	36	1397
TG	Butler Arthur N	S/Sgt	KIA	22/02/44	231443	70	2930
N	Byrnes Joseph M	2/Lt	KIA	06/11/44	297330	211	10154
CP	Byser Joseph J	2/Lt	KIA	11/01/44	237719	59	1881
CP	Call Glenn S	2/Lt	EVD	27/05/44	2107023	118	5182
RW	Campbell Alfred M	Sgt	EVD	15/06/44	238009	136	5799
	Campbell Ralph E	Sgt	KIA	21/01/45	240011	241	
TT	Campbell Charles E	T/Sgt	INT	21/06/44	238194	140	5992
P	Canelake Leo I	2/Lt	KIA	20/12/43	25845	51	1724

CP	Capobianco Frank	2/Lt	KIA	11/01/44	237962	59	1876
CP	Carah John M	2/Lt	EVD	04/07/43	229928	7	161
RO	Carano Claudio S	Sgt	POW	01/12/43	231097	46	1661
LW	Carini Adolph V	S/Sgt	POW	22/02/44	231533	70	2931
RO	Carmichael Leonard A	Sgt	POW	06/11/44	338114	211	10153
P	Carqueville Herbert	Lt	KIA	09/10/43	23180	37	888
RO	Carr Donald B	T/Sgt	KIA	31/03/44	229751		
CP	Carr Walter C	2/Lt	KIA	05/11/43	230852	42	1399
BT	Carson Garland C	S/Sgt	POW	22/03/44	231381	81	3415
TG	Casaly Alfred	2/Lt	POW	30/07/43	23100	16	129
BT	Caserta Anthony J	S/Sgt	KIA	19/04/44	23525	94	4050
BT	Casey Elbert R	S/Sgt	POW	03/03/44	237986	74	2737
TT	Cassody George W	S/Sgt	POW	08/03/44	238029	77	3002
RW	Cater Francis B	Sgt	POW	05/01/44	230676	57	1962
BT	Cates Carl E	S/Sgt	POW	06/11/44	297330	211	10154
TT	Catter Loebert G	S/Sgt	KIA	30/05/44	238188	121	5234
TG	Cavalieri Rinaldo	S/Sgt	POW	24/03/44	240008	84	3539
N	Cawley Paul T	F/O	POW	30/03/45	2102590	281	13542
N	Cayori Paul G	2/Lt	POW	03/02/44	2102873	245	12096
CP	Cea Kenneth C	2/lt	POW	30/05/44	238188	121	5234
TG	Cecil Walter R	S/Sgt	KIA	12/08/43	229954	17	383
N	Champ Frank A	F/O	EVD	15/06/44	238009	136	5799
CP	Champion John F Jnr.	2/Lt	KIA	06/11/44	297330	211	10154
B	Chanault Joe P Jnr.	2/Lt	POW	08/10/43	229765	36	883
N	Chandler James H	F/O	POW	26/06/44	2102585	142	6534
RO	Chandler Julian R	S/Sgt	POW	29/01/44	237884	61	2241
CP	Chapin Allen J	2/Lt	POW	17/08/43	23225	20	378
TT	Chaplin Glenn A	S/Sgt	POW	22/06/43	230016	1	134
P	Chason Billy F	Lt	POW	11/01/44	23514	59	1978
TT	Chauvin Milner P	S/Sgt	KIA	22/02/44	231533	70	2931
CP	Chelf Paul C	2/Lt	POW	11/01/44	231417	59	1879
LW	Chevraux Raymond F	Sgt	EVD	05/01/44	230676	57	1962
TT	Chew Lin F	S/Sgt	POW	17/08/43	23227	20	661
CP	Childers Gordon L	2/Lt	POW	14/10/43	229803	39	1037
N	Christiansen Roger G	2/Lt	POW	01/12/43	231097	46	1661
TG	Christofero Ferdinand	S/Sgt	POW	03/09/43	229789	25	473
B	Cisek Max N	2/Lt	KIA	20/12/43	25845	51	1724
RW	Clark Hubert R	S/Sgt	POW	22/06/43	230016	1	134
B	Clark Luther R	2/Lt	KIA	03/09/43	229789	25	473
P	Claytor Andrew C	2/Lt	EVD	25/04/44	23511	98	4286
TT	Clyman Neal V	S/Sgt	POW	19/04/44	23525	94	4050
RW	Cobb Robert E	Sgt	KIA	08/04/45	46173	286	13873
RW	Cobb Thomas R	S/Sgt	POW	11/01/44	23514	59	1978
P	Cogswell Kirch J	Lt	POW	20/02/44	23562	68	2929
TG	Colborn Robert L	S/Sgt	POW	17/08/43	23220	20	384
N	Cole Charles D	2/Lt	KIA	04/07/43	238117	146	6779
TT	Coleman William R	S/Sgt	KIA	14/07/43	230011	9	133
N	Collett James V	Lt	KIA	11/12/44	338780	222	11341
RW	Collister Franklin R	S/Sgt	KIA	24/05/44	231989	116	5177
RO	Colson Leslie F	Sgt	KIA	26/11/44	2106994	217	11205
RW	Connable Joseph M	Sgt	EVD	25/04/44	23511	98	4286
N	Connelly Joseph F	2/Lt	POW	07/01/44	23078	58	1873
BT	Contreras Gustavo E	Sgt	KIA	26/11/44	2106994	217	11205
BT	Cook Shelby W	Sgt	POW	25/09/44	231570	192	10203
B	Cooper Harry F	2/Lt	POW	08/03/44	238029	77	3002
BT	Copeland Milton B	Sgt	POW	11/01/44	23118	59	1943
LW	Copp Eugene F	S/Sgt	POW	20/03/44	231381	81	3415
P	Cormany William F Jnr.	Lt	POW	08/10/43	230864	36	885
CP	Cornall Chester E	2/Lt	POW	09/10/43	229958	37	886

TT	Cornell Kenneth H	T/Sgt	POW	24/05/44	231291	116	5176
BT	Corum Howard L	Sgt	KIA	21/06/44	231890	140	5990
RO	Cosandier Paul G	S/Sgt	KIA	24/06/44	2102585	142	6534
NG	Counce James D	S/Sgt	KIA	11/01/44	231417	59	1879
B	Counts James R Jnr.	2/Lt	KIA	24/05/44	231698	116	5319
P	Coyle Richard W	2/Lt	POW	06/03/44	23215	76	3000
B	Crabtree Paul O	2/Lt	POW	30/01/44	231047	62	2243
CP	Craft Maynard V	2/Lt	KIA	19/04/44	238004	94	4052
TG	Craig Clyde V	S/Sgt	POW	20/03/44	231381	81	3415
BT	Cramer Henry Jnr.	Sgt	KIA	20/12/43	25846	51	1723
RO	Craver William L	S/Sgt	KIA	14/07/43	230011	9	133
LW	Crawbuck John	S/Sgt	POW	11/01/44	23118	59	1943
CP	Crofts Val J	2/Lt	KIA	21/01/45	297511	241	
P	Crossan Waldo B	Lt	POW	20/12/43	231075	51	1722
CP	Crowley William C	2/Lt	POW	25/07/43	230153	12	131
P	Crozier Gordon W	Lt	POW	11/01/44	237730	59	1877
RW	Culver Charles J	Sgt	POW	01/12/43	231097	46	1661
TG	Cummins Robert L	S/Sgt	POW	25/07/43	229976	12	128
TG	Cunningham Thomas L	Lt	KIA	09/10/43	23180	37	888
B	Curran John J	2/Lt	POW	01/12/43	231075	46	1722
	Cusick William M		KIA	13/07/44			153
TT	Cusson Edmond P	S/Sgt	KIA	24/03/44	238102	84	
RW	Cutino Rudolph	Sgt	EVD	11/02/44	231099	67	2431
TT	Cutting William K	T/Sgt	KIA	25/06/43	230027	2	162
BT	Cyrek Eugenen E	S/Sgt	POW	09/10/43	229958	37	886
CP	Cytarcymski Edward A	2/Lt	POW	08/10/43	229954	36	1395
LW	Cyyz Edward	Sgt	KIA	08/10/43	229765	36	883
B	Cyarny Stanley J	2/Lt	POW	09/10/43	229958	37	886
TT	Dailey Richard L	T/Sgt	POW	08/04/45	46173	286	13873
N	Dall Martin M	2/Lt	POW	14/10/43	229803	39	1037
RO	Daniels O K	Sgt	KIA	11/01/44	25878	59	1874
RO	Darrington Lovenzo M	T/gt	KIA	08/10/43	229941	36	884
P	Darrow George R	Lt	RTD	17/08/43	229735	20	
P	Dasso Carl M	2/Lt	KIA	24/05/44	239890	116	5179
TG	Davis Charles E	Sgt	POW	04/03/44	230151	75	2910
LW	Day George W	Sgt	POW	22/02/44	239946	70	2936
TG	Day George M jnr.	Sgt	POW	05/01/44	230676	57	1962
P	Deering Robert P	2/Lt	KIA	30/01/44	231047	62	2243
RW	Defenbaugh Ross E	Sgt	KIA	11/01/44	23118	59	1943
TG	Delange Francis R	Sgt	POW	26/11/44	2106994	217	11205
RO	Delgado Eddie	T/Sgt	KIA	24/05/44	231989	116	5177
TT	Dell George W	T/Sgt	KIA	04/07/44	238117	146	6779
N	Dennis George W	F/O	POW	19/05/44	232088	112	5030
CP	Dernberger William A	F/O	KIA	21/01/45	240011	241	
B	DeRosa Nicholas J	2/Lt	POW	25/02/44	237786	72	2933
RW	Derrington A C	Sgt	KIA	19/04/44	23525	94	4050
CP	Devono George J	2/Lt	KIA	04/07/44	238117	146	6779
CP	Dill Frederik L	2/Lt	POW	19/05/44	232088	112	5030
B	Dille Marvin E	2/Lt	KIA	04/01/44	231278	56	
P	Disbrow Loren C	2/Lt	POW	17/08/43	23225	20	378
CP	Disbrow Robert C	2/Lt	EVD	15/06/44	238009	136	5799
B	Dittus Carl W	2/Lt	POW	20/03/44	231381	81	3415
TT	Dixon James E	S/Sgt	KIA	30/05/44	240017	121	5385
TT	Dodge Charles G	T/Sgt	KIA	12/08/43	229950	17	385
RO	Doherty Edward V Jnr.	S/Sgt	KIA	01/12/43	229506	46	1578
LW	Doll Stewart A	S/Sgt	POW	12/08/43	229950	17	385
RW	Donaldson Alexander	Sgt	POW	10/09/44	46095	185	8906
N	Dorn Harry T	2/Lt	KIA	24/05/44	231698	116	5319
P	Downey Charles H	2/Lt	KIA	22/02/44	231533	70	2913

	Downey Thomas	S/Sgt	KIA	24/02/45			277
TG	Doyle George A	S/Sgt	POW	17/08/43	23092	20	399
P	Doyle John G	2/Lt	KIA	19/06/44	2107088	138	5994
LW	Draa Clyde C	S/Sgt	KIA	24/03/44	240008	84	3539
N	Dreiseszun Philip P	2/Lt	POW	25/07/43	230013	12	130
N	Drohan Nicholas J Jnr.	F/O	KIA	09/03/45	339012	265	12960
B	Drummond Leroy	2/Lt	KIA	10/11/44	297265	213	
LW	Duffy Raymond V	S/Sgt	KIA	08/10/43	23123	36	1396
TG	Duggan William P	2/Lt	KIA	09/10/43	230012	37	887
TT	Dugger Charles D	Sgt	POW	06/11/44	338114	211	10153
B	Duke Lloyd L	2/Lt	POW	17/08/43	230140	20	379
CP	Dulberger Murray E	2/Lt	POW	17/08/43	229983	20	398
RW	Duncan Charles E	Sgt	KIA	20/02/44	23563	68	2929
RO	Duncan Jason H	T/Sgt	KIA	01/12/43	229506	46	1578
P	Duncan Rudolph G	F/O	RTD	16/03/44	297454	79	4878
P	Duarte Earl B	2/Lt	EVD	31/12/43	239910	55	1878
T	Durban Peter J	T/Sgt	KIA	21/01/45	240011	241	
BT	Durnan Joseph L	Sgt	POW	20/02/44	23562	68	2929
RW	Dwyer Jack E	Sgt	KIA	29/01/44	237884	61	2241
LW	Dwyer James J	S/Sgt	POW	08/10/43	230864	36	885
RW	Dwyer Robert E	S/Sgt	POW	17/08/43	229978	20	382
B	Dybicz Edward J	S/Sgt	KIA	08/04/45	46173	286	13873
RW	Easley Cliff W	S/Sgt	POW	11/01/44	237730	59	1877
RO	Eason Wilbert E	Sgt	KIA	30/01/44	229761	62	2244
RO	East Roy W	T/Sgt	KIA	05/11/43	230852	42	1399
TG	Eden Lawrence V	S/Sgt	KIA	22/02/44	239895	70	2935
RO	Edwards Robert L	S/Sgt	POW	17/08/43	230245	20	381
	Egan Michael J	S/Sgt	KIS	23/06/43			
TG	Eggert Robert D	Sgt	POW	22/02/44	239946	70	2936
BT	Egliski Paul J	S/Sgt	POW	17/08/43	230028	20	380
RW	Ehler Alonzo L	Sgt	POW	21/06/44	231980	140	5990
N	Ehmann Paul J	2/Lt	KIA	22/02/44	297474	70	2934
N	Eichhorn Edison	2/Lt	KIA	01/12/43	231111	46	1659
B	Eisen Charles K	2/Lt	POW	27/05/44	2107023	118	5182
TG	Elce Robert N	S/Sgt	KIA	20/12/43	231075	51	1722
RW	Elliot George L	S/Sgt	KIA	24/05/44	297214	116	5181
RW	Elsberry John V	S/Sgt	POW	17/08/43	23220	20	384
RW	Emanuelson Morris N	Sgt	KIA	30/05/44	238188	121	5234
TT	Embach John F	Sgt	POW	07/01/44	23078	58	1873
BT	Embardo James J Jnr.	S/sgt	KIA	09/10/43	23180	37	888
TT	England William P	S/Sgt	POW	01/12/43	231097	46	1661
B	English Leo K	Capt	KIA	09/10/43	230012	37	887
B	Espinoza Lorenzo	2/Lt	POW	20/02/44	23562	68	2929
LW	Estep James C Jnr.	S/Sgt	POW	08/03/44	238029	77	3002
RO	Estie Elmer L	Sgt	POW	06/03/44	'231448	76	3001
BT	Evans Charles R	Sgt	KIA	03/08/44	232049	165	7883
B	Evans Clifford	2/Lt	POW	20/06/44	337612	139	5991
P	Evans Fred G	F/O	KIA	12/08/43	229950	17	385
CP	Evans James C	2/Lt	KIA	22/02/44	231533	70	2931
CP	Evans Roland P	2/Lt	KIA	22/02/44	239895	70	2935
RW	Everett Arthur L	S/Sgt	KIA	19/08/43	23101	21	662
TT	Eylens John J	T/Sgt	KIA	30/05/44	2102672	121	5233
P	Ezzell Clarence W	Lt	KIA	24./05/44	238010	116	5178
BT	Fabiano Frank	S/Sgt	POW	30/07/43	23100	16	129
TG	Fabianski Joseph E	Sgt	KIA	29/01/44	237884	61	2241
P	Fawcett Robert D	Lt	KIA	22/03/45	48175	275	13605
RO	Fair John L	Sgt	POW	04/03/44	230151	75	2910
TG	Fall Richard J	Sgt	KIA	03/08/44	232049	165	7883
LW	Farly Shannon B	S/Sgt	INT	24/07/43	23217	11	132

RW	Farr John T	Sgt	EVD	02/03/44	239891	73	2738
B	Farrell William R	2/Lt	POW	22/02/44	231443	70	2930
P	Fastrup Milton A	2/Lt	POW	06/03/44	231448	76	3001
B	Falconer Adelbert Jnr.	2/Lt	KIA	11/01/44	25878	59	1874
RW	Fecho Joseph	S/Sgt	KIA	20/12/43	25846	51	1723
B	Fedak John P	Lt	KIS	23/04/45	338856		
	Feeley Charles A	Cpl	KIS	23/06/43			
RW	Feller Michael S	S/Sgt	KIA	14/10/43	229803	39	1037
RW	Ferens Walter F	Sgt	POW	25/07/43	230153	12	131
	Fiamma George	Cpl	KIS	23/06/43			
B	Fiery Charles D	2/Lt	KIA	11/01/44	237719	59	1881
TG	Fitzgerald Hugh D	Sgt	KIA	09/03/45	339012	265	12960
P	Flaherty Francis J	Lt	KIA	22/02/44	231443	70	2930
BT	Flam Kenneth M	Sgt	KIA	24/03/44	238102	84	
RO	Fleming Michael	T/Sgt	POW	12/08/43	25847	17	660
	Flinn Jack R	Cpl	KIA	03/12/43			
CP	Flood Joe	2/Lt	KIA	29/01/44	238045	61	2242
TT	Floura Cecil L	S/Sgt	POW	17/08/43	229978	20	382
	Foerstal Milton J	Cpl	KIS	23/06/43			
TT	Fontenot Dewell J	Sgt	POW	31/07/44	2102423	163	7742
LW	Forbes James R	S/Sgt	KIA	08/10/43	229854	36	1395
B	Forbes William H	Lt	POW	03/02/45	2102873	245	12096
BT	Forke Waldon W	S/Sgt	INT	21/06/44	238194	140	5992
P	Forkner Hamden L	Lt	EVD	17/08/43	23227	20	661
BT	Fornaro Leonard J	S/Sgt	KIA	22/06/43	230021	1	160
RW	Fortier William L	S/Sgt	POW	25/07/43	230013	12	130
LW	Fossan Kenneth L	S/Sgt	KIA	14/07/43	230011	9	133
RO	Founds Ronald E	S/Sgt	KIA	30/05/44	240017	121	5385
CP	Fournier Jack L	2/Lt	POW	25/02/44	237786	72	2933
CP	Fowler Robert J	2/Lt	POW	20/03/44	231381	81	3415
N	Fox Alfred	2/Lt	POW	06/11/44	338114	211	10153
LW	Fox Anthony J	S/Sgt	KIA	09/10/43	23180	37	888
CP	Fox Boyd C Jnr.	2/Lt	POW	06/11/44	338114	211	10153
CP	Frampton John N	2/Lt	KIA	08/04/45	46173	286	13873
RO	Frautschi Russell H	T/Sgt	POW	08/10/43	230009	36	1397
N	Freeman Charles S	2/Lt	KIA	05/08/44	297771	167	7884
N	Freiberger Fred	2/Lt	POW	17/08/43	229983	20	398
TG	Fridberg Bernard G	S/Sgt	INT	18/07/44	2102663	155	7552
P	Fridgen Francis N	Lt	POW	22/02/44	297474	70	2934
RO	Friel Robert F	Sgt	KIA	03/08/44	232049	165	7883
TG	Frisby Lewis E	Sgt	KIA	25/06/43	230027	3	162
N	Frost Edwin D Jnr.	Lt	POW	08/10/43	230864	36	885
N	Fuller David E	2/Lt	POW	30/05/44	46025	121	5235
LW	Gaby Oliver G	S/Sgt	KIA	22/02/44	297474	70	2934
TT	Gardella Albert J	T/Sgt	POW	01/12/43	23540	46	1660
P	Gardon Carl A	Lt	KIA	24/05/44	231291	116	5176
CP	Garner Dorance	2/Lt	POW	19/05/44	297454	112	4932
N	Garrett William D	2/Lt	POW	24/03/45	46478	277	13606
BT	Garvan Peter D	S/Sgt	POW	25/07/43	230153	12	131
RO	Gasparovitch George M	Sgt	KIA	09/03/45	339012	265	12960
CP	Gatewood Robert W	2/Lt	POW	11/04/44	231497	91	3821
B	Gaydos George	2/Lt	POW	17/08/43	23225	20	378
TG	Geary William	S/Sgt	KIA	22/06/43	230021	1	160
	Geist William E	T/Sgt	KIS	23/04/45	338856		
	Gelman Edward Z	M/Sgt	KIS	23/04/45	338856		
B	Gentile Americus J	2/Lt	POW	11/01/44	23514	59	1978
BT	Gentry Giles E	S/Sgt	KIA	08/10/43	23123	36	1396
TG	Genz Raymond A	S/Sgt	EVD	17/08/43	230140	20	379
BT	Geraghty Robert J	S/Sgt	POW	07/01/44	230789	58	1873

TG	Gerber Gerald	S/Sgt	POW	19/04/44	238004	94	4052
RO	Geroulo Vito J	T/Sgt	KIA	09/10/43	23180	37	888
	Gibbs Ralph L	S/Sgt	KIS	23/04/45	338856		
TT	Gibson Lee B	S/Sgt	KIA	20/12/43			
TT	Giddens Elbert F	Sgt	KIA	24/06/44	2102585	142	6534
LW	Giddens Gordon W	S/Sgt	POW	11/01/44	237730	59	1877
TT	Gilbertson William G	T/Sgt	KIA	05/08/44	297771	167	7884
B	Gill Louis H	Lt	POW	11/01/44	231417	59	1879
P	Gills Oscar W	Lt	POW	25/09/44	231570	192	10203
CP	Giovannini George E	2/Lt	KIA	01/12/43	231111	46	1659
TT	Girvin Alexander M	T/Sgt	POW	05/11/43	230852	42	1399
RO	Givon Burton A	S/Sgt	POW	05/01/44	230676	57	1962
TT	Glauer Raymond R	T/Sgt	POW	06/03/44	231448	76	3001
RW	Glawson Jesse J	S/Sgt	POW	20/12/43	231075	51	1722
LW	Glennan Thomas J	Sgt	EVD	11/02/44	231099	67	2431
N	Gluck Robert	Lt	POW	08/10/43	230732	36	1398
B	Gomez George	2/Lt	POW	06/08/44	46020	168	7882
RW	Gonzales Adolph M	S/Sgt	POW	06/08/44	46020	168	7882
TG	Good Henry L	Sgt	KIA	20/12 /43	23563	51	1721
B	Goodman Bernard	2/lt	KIA	04/07/44	238117	146	6779
BT	Goody Cloyde I	Sgt	POW	10/09/44	46095	185	9806
N	Gordon Sidney H	2/Lt	POW	31/07/44	2102423	163	7742
TT	Gorgone William	T/Sgt	KIA	14/10/43	229803	39	1037
LW	Goss Hubert A	S/Sgt	POW	17/08/43	229983	20	398
RO	Goswick Hugh R	Sgt	KIA	22/06/43	230021	1	160
CP	Gotthardt Robert J	Capt	KIA	22/03/45	48175	275	13605
RO	Gracey Edward R	S/Sgt	POW	14/10/43	229803	39	1037
	Gray Joseph L	T/Sgt	KIS	23/04/45	338856		
	Gray Virgil L	S/Sgt	KIA	21/01/45	240011	241	
RW	Grayson William H	S/Sgt	KIA	08/10/43	229954	36	1395
TG	Greco Anthony E	S/Sgt	KIA	07/01/44	23078	58	1873
RW	Green Earl E	S/Sgt	POW	03/02/45	338898	245	12295
RW	Greene Elburn L	S/Sgt	KIA	09/10/43	23180	37	888
LW	Greenwood Howard J	Sgt	POW	11/01/44	23514	59	1978
LW	Greer Julius F	S/Sgt	KIA	05/11/43	230852	42	1399
Bt	Greevey Edward J	Sgt	KIA	06/03/44	231553	76	3241
RW	Gregory Paul A	Sgt	POW	17/08/43	230245	20	381
CP	Grey James M	2/Lt	POW	10/09/44	46095	185	8906
N	Griffith George P	2/Lt	KIA	22/06/43	230016	1	134
TT	Grisham Lendon L	T/Sgt	POW	06/08/44	46020	168	7882
TT	Gronstal Byron J	T/Sgt	POW	04/07/43	229928	7	161
LW	Grossman Herman E	S/Sgt	POW	17/08/43	229731	20	663
N	Grossnickle Earl S	2/Lt	KIA	06/08/44	46020	168	7882
B	Grote George C	2/Lt	POW	18/04/44	237733	93	4051
BT	Grugan Joseph W	Sgt	POW	29/01/44	238045	61	2242
N	Geurtin Arthur L	2/Lt	INT	24/07/43	23217	9	132
N	Guertin Arthur L	2/Lt	KIA	28/04/44	231381	101	4241
B	Guidotti Alfred H	2/Lt	POW	31/07/44	2102423	163	7742
B	Gwinn Lloyd W	2/Lt	POW	17/08/43	23220	20	384
N	Haas Leland M	2/Lt	POW	30/05/44	238188	121	5234
TG	Hackett Kenneth L	S/Sgt	POW	12/08/43	229950	17	385
RO	Haga Warren K	S/Sgt	KIA	24/05/44	231698	116	5319
	Hagen Wesley M	T/Sgt	KIS	23/04/45	338856		
B	Haines William G Jr.	2/Lt	KIA	13/08/44			
CP	Hamer James J M	2/Lt	POW	12/08/43	25847	17	660
B	Harnes Leroy N	2/Lt	POW	30/07/43	23100	16	129
CP	Hamilton John Jr.	Capt	KIA	25/06/43	230027	3	162
BT	Hamilton Richard C	Sgt	EVD	11/02/44	231099	67	2431
B	Hammel Edward J	2/Lt	POW	24/03/44	231490	84	3538

NT	Hammond Robert J	S/Sgt	POW	30/05/44	2102672	121	5233
LW	Hanna Leslie J	Sgt	KIA	22/02/44	231696	70	2932
TT	Hanna Richard J	T/Sgt	POW	17/08/43	229983	20	398
N	Hannon George A	2/Lt	POW	11/01/44	237730	59	1877
N	Hardwick Wayne T	2/Lt	KIA	19/05/44	297454	112	4932
	Hargraves Irwin R	Sgt	KIS	23/04/45	338856		
RO	Harker Charles E	S/Sgt	KIA	19/06/44	2107088	138	5994
TG	Harness Donald A	S/Sgt	POW	30/05/44	46025	121	5235
RW	Harper Hamilton B	S/Sgt	POW	30/05/44	46025	121	5235
RO	Harrah Luster T	S/Sgt	KIA	11/01/44	237719	59	1881
CP	Harrer Donald G	2/Lt	POW	11/02/44	231099	67	2431
N	Harris David E Jnr.	2/Lt	POW	12/08/43	229954	17	383
TT	Harrison Frederick W	S/Sgt	POW	27/05/44	2107023	118	5182
	Hart Wayne W	Lt	KIS	23/04/45	338856		
P	Hartje James W	2/Lt	POW	09/10/43	229765	36	883
RW	Harvey Lloyd L	S/Sgt	POW	24/05/44	238010	116	5178
N	Harvey Robert L	2/Lt	POW	21/06/44	297174	140	5993
N	Hasseltine Robert E	2/Lt	POW	06/03/44	23215	76	3000
RW	Haugen Alfred E	Sgt	INT	24/07/43	23217	11	132
P	Haushalter Edward E	Lt	KIA	06/03/44	231553	76	3241
N	Haverkamp Clifford M	2/Lt	POW	17/08/43	230028	20	380
LW	Hawkins George E	S/Sgt	POW	07/01/44	23078	58	1873
CP	Hawkins Samuel J	2/Lt	POW	17/08/43	23220	20	384
RW	Hawkinson Alan L	S/Sgt	POW	18/04/44	237733	93	4051
RO	Hayden James H	T/Sgt	RTD	08/04/45	46173	286	13873
CP	Hayes John W	2/Lt	POW	06/08/44	46020	168	7882
P	Haynes Kenneth T Jnr	2/Lt	KIA	24/03/44	238102	84	
TT	Haynie James E	S/Sgt	INT	24/07/43	23217	11	132
B	Hazelton Richard M	2/Lt	POW	20/12/43	23563	51	1721
TG	Healy John F	Sgt	KIA	01/12/43	231097	46	1661
B	Hearn William D	2/Lt	POW	02/03/44	239891	73	2738
P	Hedin Charles E	2/Lt	KIA	14/07/43	23223	9	
RO	Heidebrink John W	T/Sgt	POW	19/04/44	232088	112	5030
CP	Heim William O	2/Lt	KIA	08/10/43	23123	36	1396
RO	Heintz Warren G	T/Sgt	KIA	08/10/43	229854	36	1395
LW	Heist James E	Sgt	POW	25/07/43	230153	12	131
RO	Helfgott Abe A	Sgt	EVD	11/02/44	231099	67	2431
B	Hellmann Harold	Lt	POW	25/0743	230151	12	131
RW	Hellman Robert J	Sgt	KIA	19/06/44	2107088	138	5994
P	Henderson Donald G	2/Lt	POW	25/02/44	237786	72	2933
P	Hendricks Landon C	Maj	KIA	09/10/43	230012	37	887
B	Heniff Eloy W	2/Lt	POW	21/06/44	297174	140	5993
CP	Hennessey William H	2/Lt	KIA	29/01/44	237884	61	2241
BT	Henry Charles R	2/Lt	POW	22/06/43	230016	1	134
CP	Hensley Herman N	2/Lt	POW	06/03/44	231553	76	3241
BT	Hensley John W	Sgt	POW	24/03/45	46478	277	13606
P	Henslin Harold F	Lt	KIA	28/04/44	238061	101	4241
CP	Herdlicka Donald E	2/Lt	KIA	22/02/44	231533	70	2931
RO	Hernandez Tony T	S/Sgt	KIA	20/12/43	25845	51	1724
B	Herrick John W	2/Lt	KIA	06/03/44	231553	76	3241
N	Hert Oral H	2/Lt	POW	22/02/44	231696	70	2932
P	Hess Warren C	2/Lt	POW	01/12/43	23540	46	1660
P	Hesse Robert W	2/Lt	POW	11/04/44	231497	91	3821
BT	Hickey Paul A	T/Sgt	KIA	24/03/44	240008	84	3539
RO	Hickman Clarence W	S/Sgt	KIA	30/12/43			
N	Hicks John D	2/Lt	KIA	22/02/44	231533	70	2931
B	Higginbotham Herbert	2/Lt	INT	18/07/44	2102663	155	7552
P	Higgins Walter K	2/Lt	KIA	24/05/44	231989	116	5177
RW	Highsmith Carol C	S/Sgt	INT	21/06/44	238194	140	5992

RW	Hill James R	S/Sgt	POW	17/08/43	230028	20	380	
TG	Hillard Bruce M	S/Sgt	POW	06/11/44	297330	211	10154	
	Hiller Elbert W	2/Lt	KIA	22/03/45	48175	275	13605	
B	Hilton Gerald O	2/Lt	KIA	19/04/44	23525	94	4050	
	Hinkel James M	Lt	KIS	23/04/45	338856			
RW	Hitchcock Kenneth F	S/Sgt	EVD	04/07/44	238117	146	6779	
TG	Hittel Robert	Sgt	POW	30/05/44	2102672	121	5233	
RW	Hylnsky Peter	Sgt	KIA	30/01/44	229761	62	2244	
B	Hoag Wallace W	2/Lt	KIA	22/06/43	230021	1	160	
B	Holcomb Ralph H	S/Sgt	POW	21/06/44	231980	140	5990	
P	Holdem Robert J	2/Lt	KIA	14/07/43	230011	9	133	
P	Hollenkamp Bernard F	Lt	KIA	20/12/43	25845	51	1721	
B	Holt Elbert H	S/Sgt	POW	30/03/45	2102590	281	13542	
TT	Holton John L	S/Sgt	POW	11/02/44	231099	67	2431	
LW	Holtz Harold A	Sgt	KIA	30/01/44	229761	62	2244	TT
TT	Holub Libor J	T/Sgt	KIA	24/03/44	240008	84	3539	
CP	Hoover Charles H	2/Lt	EVD	03/09/43	229789	25	473	
B	Hoover Chester L	2/Lt	POW	22/06/43	230016	1	134	
BT	Hoover Harold M	Sgt	POW	31/07/44	2102423	163	7742	
P	Hopp Donald K	Lt	POW	05/11/43	230852	42	1399	
TG	Horne Emory M	S/Sgt	KIA	09/10/43	23180	37	888	
TT	Horne Waddell H	S/Sgt	KIA	30/01/44	231047	62	2243	
P	Horr Earl R	Lt	POW	22/06/43	230016	1	134	
TG	Horsch Frank N Jnr.	Sgt	POW	06/11/44	338114	211	10153	
RW	Horton Harry H Jnr.	S/Sgt	EVD	17/08/43	23227	20	661	
B	Houck James M	2/Lt	KIA	25/07/43	230013	12	1308*	
RW	Houghton Herbert S Jnr.	Sgt	KIA	09/03/45	339012	265	12960	
TG	Houser Edward P	Sgt	RTD	08/04/45	46173	286	13873	
RW	Howard Lloyd A	S/Sgt	KIA	09/10/43	230012	37	887	
TG	Howell William C	S/Sgt	EVD	04/07/43	229928	7	161	
B	Hughes John N	2/Lt	POW	04/03/44	230151	75	2910	
B	Hughes Robert W	Lt	POW	24/05/44	231989	116	5177	
RW	Huhn Allen O	S/Sgt	POW	09/10/43	229958	37	886	
LW	Huitt Kenneth O	S/Sgt	KIA	14/10/43	229803	39	1037	
CP	Humason Guerdon W	Lt	POW	30/07/43	23100	16	129	
LW	Hunnicutt Thomas R	S/Sgt	KIA	25/02/44	237786	72	2933	
P	Hustedt Henry J	2/Lt	POW	22/02/44	231696	70	2932	
BT	Husvar Floyd S	Sgt	KIA	30/01/44	231047	62	2243	
RW	Hutchens Homer K	Sgt	KIA	20/12/43	23563	51	1721	
P	Ingenhutt William W	Maj	POW	08/10/43	230864	36	885*	
TG	Ingmire Richard E	S/Sgt	KIA	04/01/44	231278	56*		
B	Ingram William H	F/O	POW	11/01/44	229999	59	1880*	
CP	Irwin Robert H	2/Lt	INT	21/06/44	238194	140	5992	
B	Isom Norman B	2/Lt	KIA	24/05/44	239890	116	5179	
TT	Italiano Robert B	T/Sgt	POW	03/09/43	229789	25	473	
TT	Ivey John E	T/Sgt	POW	25/07/43	230013	12	130	
LW	Jackson Lloyd H	Sgt	KIA	30/01/44	231047	62	2243	
	Jackson Lloyd S	S/Sgt	KIA	13/07/44	46148	153		
N	Jackson Johns R Jnr.	2/Lt	KIA	22/02/44	239946	70	2936	
TG	Janis Charles G	Sgt	POW	31/07/44	2102423	163	7742	
P	Jankowiak Robert E	2/Lt	POW	24/03/45	46478	277	13606	
P	Jarvis Leo	Lt	POW	17/08/43	229731	20	663	
BT	Jeffers Leo D	S/Sgt	KIA	01/12/43	229506	46	1578	
RO	Jemiolo John	S/Sgt	POW	22/02/44	239946	70	2936	
TT	Jennette Arthur F	T/Sgt	KIA	08/10/43	23123	36	1396	
TT	Jerionoski John S	S/Sgt	KIA	11/01/44	25878	59	1874	
RW	Jemigan Cecil L	Sgt	POW	03/03/44	237986	74	2737	
CP	Jerome Joseph C	2/Lt	POW	08/10/43	229765	36	883	
LW	Johnson Alfred A	S/Sgt	KIA	08/10/43	230009	36	1397	

TT	Johnson Canute M	T/Sgt	POW	08/10/43	230732	36	1398
RO	Johnson Fred W	S/Sgt	POW	11/01/44	229999	59	1880
TG	Johnson George R	Sgt	POW	25/07/43	230153	12	131
CP	Johnson Harry B	F/O	KIA	20/12/43	25845	51	1724
TG	Johnson Johnnie N	S/Sgt	POW	14/10/43	229803	39	1037
TG	Johnston George R	S/Sgt	KIA	08/10/43	229854	36	1395
CP	Johnston John B	2/Lt	POW	20/12/43	25846	51	1723
B	Johnston William J	2/Lt	KIA	05/11/43	230852	42	1399
TG	Jones Arthur A	S/Sgt	POW	22/06/43	230016	1	134
RO	Jones Aurelius W	S/Sgt	EVD	27/05/44	2107023	118	5182
TG	Jones Charles L	S/Sgt	RTD	16/03/44	297454	79	4878
N	Jones David R	2/Lt	POW	17/08/43	23225	20	378
CP	Jones Dudley B	2/Lt	KIA	11/01/44	25878	59	1874
B	Jones Edward L	S/Sgt	KIA	21/01/45	297511		
TG	Jones Eldon R	Sgt	POW	06/03/44	231553	76	3241
CP	Jones George T	2/Lt	POW	20/12/43	23563	51	1721
TG	Jones James P	Sgt	KIA	11/01/44	237962	59	1876
P	Jones Osce V	Lt	INT	24/07/43	23217	11	132
CP	Jones Osce V	Capt	POW	28/04/44	238061	101	4241
LW	Jones Wilbert G	S/Sgt	KIA	19/08/43	23101	21	662
RO	Jones William R	S/Sgt	KIA	19/04/44	23525	94	4050
BT	Jonson Edwin M	S/Sgt	KIA	12/08/43	229954	17	383
LW	Josephine Carlton A	Sgt	POW	01/12/43	231097	46	1661
CP	Jukes Eldon D	Capt	KIA	08/10/43	229941	36	884
BT	Jupin John	S/Sgt	POW	17/08/43	23220	20	384
	Kakos Michael J Jnr	Sgt	KIS	23/04/45	338856		
LW	Kangas John V	Sgt	POW	20/02/44	23562	68	2929
WG	Kantor Robert L	Sgt	RTD	30/05/44	240017	121	5385
BT	Kaplan Herbert H	Sgt	EVD	27/05/44	2107023	118	5182
TT	Kapustka John P	T/Sgt	KIA	09/10/43	23180	37	888
CP	Karch Robert C	2/Lt	INT	18/07/44	2102663	155	7552
Tt	Karr Joe R	T/Sgt	KIA	28/04/44	238061	101	4241
TT	Kaseman Eugene W	S/Sgt	KIA	08/10./43	229765	36	883
RO	Kasha Stanley C Jnr.	T/Sgt	POW	7/08/43	229983	20	398
RW	Katsarelis Peter A	S/Sgt	POW	17/08/43	229983	20	398
B	Kaufman Harold W	2/Lt	KIA	22/02/44	239895	70	2935
N	Keays William J	2/Lt	POW	17/08/43	230140	20	379
TT	Kechel Aaron R	S/Sgt	KIA	20/06/44	337612	139	5991
RW	Keene Bermard M	Sgt	POW	11/01/44	237962	59	1876
N	Kelleher John E	2/Lt	KIA	03/02/45	338898	245	12295
TG	Kelleher Maurice M	S/Sgt	INT	24/07/43	23217	11	132
P	Kelley Charles H	2/Lt	EVD	15/06/44	238009	136	5799
BT	Kellogg Allen P	S/Sgt	POW	17/08/43	230140	20	379
CP	Kellum Richard L	2/Lt	KIA	24/06/44	2102585	139	6534
N	Kelly Frank L	2/Lt	KIA	20/06/44	337612	139	5991
CP	Kelly Joseph A	2/Lt	POW	17/08/43	23227	20	661
P	Kemp Leslie A Jnr.	Lt	KIA	08/10/43	23123	36	1396
TT	Kemper Harold C	T/Sgt	KIA	22/02/44	239895	70	2395
TT	Kempainnen Carl E	Sgt	POW	03/02/45	2102873	245	12096
TT	Kennedy Lowell D	S/Sgt	KIA	24/05/44	231698	116	5319
RO	Kern Herbert R	S/Sgt	KIA	12/08/43	229950	17	385
B	Kessler Robert G	2/Lt	KIA	01/12/43	229506	46	1578
RO	Kettlety Robert E	T/Sgt	POW	13/04/44	231357	92	3865
P	Keyes David D	2/Lt	POW	04/03/44	230151	75	2910
	King Bernard J	Sgt	KIA	22/03/45			
TG	King Byron E	S/Sgt	KIA	21/06/44	297174	140	5993
LW	King Ernest C	S/Sgt	POW	17/08/43	23225	20	378
	King James H		KIS	23/06/43			
N	King Martin P	2/lt	POW	06/03/44	231448	76	3001

P	King Reinhardt M	L	POW	17/08/43	229978	20	382
TG	Kiniklis William P	S/Sgt	EVD	17/08/43	23225	20	378
BT	Kinney William C	Sgt	POW	08/03/44	238029	77	3002
B	Kirby John J	2/Lt	POW	13/04/44	231357	92	3865
TT	Kithcart William H	Sgt	POW	30/07/43	23100	16	129
P	Klein Ernest M	Lt	POW	11/01/44	231417	59	1879
LW	Klima Norman J	S/Sgt	KIA	20/12/43	231075	51	1722
TG	Klinger Stephen J	S/Sgt	KIA	08/10/43	229832	36	
	Klinksiek Gottfried H	Capt	KIA	25/02/44			
CP	Klutho Robert J	2/Lt	POW	30/05/44	240017	121	5385
TG	Knaus Charles F	S/Sgt	KIA	30/03/45	2102590	281	13542
RO	Kochel Aaron R	S/Sgt	KIA	20/06/44	337612	139	5991
P	Koenig Orlando H	Lt	POW	19/08/43	23101	21	662
B	Kowalski Peter	Lt	KIA	22/03/45	48175	275	13605
BT	Korkuc Anthony J	S/Sgt	KIA	25/02/44	237786	72	2933
TT	Kowalski Matthew B	S/Sgt	POW	17/08/43	230140	20	379
LW	Kracium Eugene J	Sgt	POW	11/01/44	229999	59	1880
RW	Krainz Leo V	Sgt	POW	25/09/44	231570	192	10203
LW	Kralick Joseph G	S/Sgt	KIA	25/07/43	230013	12	130
LW	Kratzer John J	S/Sgt	KIA	12/08/43	229954	17	383
TT	Kreutz Alfred J	S/Sgt	POW	06/11/44	297330	211	10154
	Kristapovich Joseph J	Sgt	KIS	23/06/43			
RO	Kochel Aaron	S/Sgt	KIA	20/06/44	337612	139	5991
BT	Kruger Charles	Sgt	KIA	24/05/44	231698	116	5319
RO	Kucher Peter	S/Sgt	KIA	07/01/44	23078	58	1873
TG	Kudla Steve A	Sgt	POW	11/01/44	23514	59	1978
TG	Kulivinski John W	T/Sgt	POW	02/03/44	239891	73	2738
RW	Kuracino Vito R	Sgt	POW	22/02/44	231696	70	2932
RW	Kurnafil Stephen	Sgt	KIA	25/06/43	230027	3	162
TG	Kurtz Frank J	Sgt	KIA	28/03/44	237754	87	
TT	Kwoka Leon J	T/SGt	POW	09/10/43	229958	37	886
N	LaLuzerne Melvin A	F/O	POW	26/11/44	2106994	217	11205
TG	LaMore Thomas L	S/Sgt	POW	24/03/44	231490	84	3538
N	Lander John F	2/Lt	POW	12/08/43	229950	17	385
TG	Landes Robert M	Sgt	POW	03/02/45	338898	245	12295
B	Lane David W	Lt	POW	05/08/44	297771	167	7884
P	Lane Dorman F	2Lt	POW	20/12/43	25846	51	1723
RO	Lane John K	T/Sgt	POW	04/07/43	229928	7	161
	Langoff Christian	Sgt	KIA	28/03/44			
TT	Lantto James S	S/Sgt	KIA	22/06/43	230021	1	160
LW	Lantz John R	S/Sgt	POW	11/01/44	237719	59	1881
RO	LaPLace Gerald G	S/Sgt	POW	08/10/43	229765	36	883
TT	LaPointe Edward R	T/Sgt	POW	08/10/43	230009	36	1397
	Larsen Rafael C	T/Sgt	KIA	11/12/44			
P	Larsen Austin C	2/Lt	POW	11/01/44	23118	59	1943
BT	Larsen Burling	S/Sgt	KIA	22/02/44	231443	70	2930
BT	Larsen Lester P	S/Sgt	KIA	22/02/44	239895	70	2935
CP	Latton Howard W	2/Lt	POW	24/05/44	231698	116	5319
BT	Laurett Lynn J Jnr.	S/Sgt	KIA	11/12/44	338780	222	11341
P	Laux Robert V	2/Lt	EVD	11/02/44	231099	67	2431
RO	Lawing Wendell B	S/Sgt	POW	21/06/44	231980	140	5990
CP	Lawless Joseph W	F/O	POW	21/06/44	297771	140	5993
B	Leavitt Bernard S	2/Lt	POW	19/06/44	2107088	138	5994
TT	Leccese Raymond J	S/Sgt	POW	20/02/44	23562	68	2929
TT	Lee Harry E	S/Sgt	KIA	06/03/44	231553	76	3241
BT	Lee Harry F	T/Sgt		30/01/44	229761	62	2244
TG	Legg Raymond F	S/Sgt	KIA	06/03/44	23215	76	3000
RW	Lehman Harold M	S/Sgt	KIA	21/06/44	297174	140	5993
LW	Leidecker Theodore W	S/Sgt	KIA	25/06/43	230027	3	162

	Leiner Fred	Sgt	KIA	14/01/45			238
LW	Levandowski Henry F	S/Sgt	POW	04/03/44	230151	75	2910
B	Levenson Herbert H	2/Lt	KIA	24/03/45	46478	277	13606
P	Levitoff Julius	2/Lt	POW	06/11/44	297330	211	10154
B	Light James A	2/Lt	KIA	29/01/44	238045	61	2242
CP	Liming Max E	Lt	KIA	09/10/43		37	
TT	Lindenmeyer William E	T/Sgt	POW	25/07/43	229976	12	128
	Lintgen James J	S/Sgt	KIS	23/06/43			
N	Lipsky Henry I	2/Lt	POW	11/01/44	229999	59	1880
TT	Lischke Judd O	S/Sgt	POW	17/08/43	23220	20	384
P	Lishon Dexter	Capt	POW	08/10/43	230722	36	1398
B	Lockhart William D	2/Lt	POW	17/08/43	229731	20	663
TT	Loehrer Arthur T	S/Sgt	POW	11/01/44	229999	59	1880
P	Loftin James L	Lt	POW	09/10/43	229958	37	886
RO	Logan Avromonde R	T/Sgt	POW	17/08/43	229731	20	663
N	Long Harry R	2/Lt	POW	22/06/43	230021	1	160
CP	Long Carlton H	2/Lt	POW	08/10/43	230722	36	1398
TT	Loparco Harry C	S/Sgt	KIA	24/03/44	238102	84	
P	Lord Marvin D	Lt/Col	KIA	03/02/45	297632 (91BG)	245	12232
TG	Lorick Arnold B	Sgt	KIA	22/06/43	23223	1	
B	Lucas Norbert I	2/Lt	KIA	03/08/44	232049	165	7883
LW	Ludwig Allan G	S/Sgt	POW	01/12/43	32540	46	1660
TT	Ludwigsen Peter K	T/Sgt	KIA	01/12/43	231111	46	1659
BT	Lujan Alfredo	Sgt	POW	24/03/44	231490	84	3538
N	Lundberg John K	2/Lt	KIA	22/06/44	297084	141	5918
N	Lynch Ralph W	2/Lt	POW	04/03/44	230151	75	2910
TG	Lyons J R	S/Sgt	POW	17/08/43	229978	20	382
RW	Lyons Thomas J	S/Sgt	POW	06/11/44	338114	211	10153
BT	McDonald Stewart S	S/Sgt	KIA	14/07/43	23223		
N	MacKay Norman C	Capt	KIA	08/10/43	229854	36	1395
BT	Macklin William M	S/Sgt	POW	01/12/43	23540	46	1660
	Madden Elmer	Sgt	KIS	23/06/43			
RO	Madero Anthony P	S/Sgt	KIA	24/05/44	239890	116	65179
N	Magnabosco Valerio P	2/Lt	POW	21/06/44	231980	140	5990
B	McQuire Hugh E	2/Lt	POW	29/01/44	237884	61	2241
LW	McHaffey Donald B	Sgt	KIA	24/03/44	238102	84	
TG	Mahar John S	Sgt	POW	21/06/44	231980	140	5990
RW	Main Andrew R	S/Sgt	POW	19/04/44	238004	94	4052
SJ	Majors Charles L	S/Sgt	POW	30/03/45	2102590	281	13542
P	Manchester Edwin R	Capt	KIA	08/10/43	229941	36	884
CP	Mancinelli Eugene E	2/Lt	POW	17/08/43	229731	20	663
RO	Mandell Robert N	S/Sgt	POW	22/06/43	230016	1	134
	Manes Wayne K	S/Sgt	KIS	23/04/45	338856		
CP	Mann Edward C	2/Lt	POW	06/03/44	231448	76	3001
LW	Mann Julius D	S/Sgt	POW	17/08/43	229978	20	382
LW	Manning Andrew F	S/Sgt	KIA	22/02/44	239895	70	2935
RO	Marbry James E	S/Sgt	POW	30/05/44	2102672	121	5233
B	Marks Julian M	2/Lt	POW	17/08/43	229983	20	398
TG	Marques William J	S/Sgt	POW	08/10/43	230722	36	1398
N	Marsh Charles R	2/Lt	KIA	03/08/44	232049	165	7883
CP	Marsh Robert J	F/O	KIA	22/06/43	230021	1	160
P	Martin John J	2/Lt	KIA	22/06/43	230021	1	160
RW	Martin Othel L	Sgt	POW	22/02/44	239946	70	2936
BT	Martin Raymond W	Sgt	POW	11/01/44	23514	59	1978
	Martinez Jose M	Sgt	KIS	23/04/45	338856		
BT	Marushack Frank J	S/Sgt	POW	18/04/44	237733	93	4051
CP	Mason Wilber M	2/Lt	POW	19/04/44	23525	94	4050
WG	Mata Alfred M	S/Sgt	KIS	23/04/45	338856		
RW	Matcham Robert S	S/Sgt	POW	20/03/44	231381	81	3415

RO	Matheson Earl E	S/Sgt	POW	22/02/44	231553	70	2931
RW	Mattfield Paul A	S/Sgt	POW	12/08/43	25847	17	660
TG	Mattson Roy F	S/Sgt	POW	01/112/43	229506	46	1578
N	Matyas Martin M	2/Lt	KIS	23/04/45	338856		
CP	Mauzy Keith S	2/Lt	POW	22/02/44	231696	70	2932
	Maxwell Leslie H Jnr.	Sgt	KIS	23/04/45	338856		
CP	McCabe Glenn A	2/Lt	EVD	31/12/43	239910	55	1878
	McClain Albert	T/Sgt	KIA	31/03/45			
N	McConnell Paul H	2/Lt	EVD	04/07/43	229928	7	161
TG	McCook Wade	S/Sgt	POW	08/10/43	229941	36	884
RO	McCoy Elvis A	T/Sgt	POW	11/12/44	338780	222	11341
B	McCudden Bernard L	S/Sgt	KIA	21/01/45	240011	241	
	McCullough Walter A	T/Sgt	KIS	3/04/45	338856		
BT	McCutcheon Doyle C	Sgt	KIA	01/12/43	231097	46	1661
CP	McDonald Donald J	2/Lt	POW	07/01/44	23078	58	1873
TG	McDonald Frank H	Sgt	KIA	20/12/43	25846	51	1723
TT	McDonald Paul E	S/Sgt	KIA	20/12/43	25845	51	1724
	McDuffee Guy	Cpl	KIS	23/06/43			
P	McEvoy Matthew J	2/Lt	POW	11/01/44	229999	59	1880
RO	McFarlane Robert T	T/Sgt	POW	20/12/43	231075	51	1722
	McGhehey Laurence E	Lt	KIS	23/04/45	338856		
N	McGlynn Edward S	2/Lt	POW	17/08/43	229978	20	382
BT	McGoldrick James C	S/Sgt	KIA	17/08/43	229983	20	398
N	McGrath Francis R	2/Lt	POW	03/03/44	237986	74	2737
TT	McGrath James	S/Sgt	POW	24/03/45	46478	277	13606
TG	McGreevey Robert H	S/Sgt	POW	03/02/45	2102873	245	12096
CP	McGurk Donald F	2/Lt	POW	26/11/44	2106994	217	11205
CP	McIntosh George B Jnr.	2/Lt	INT	24/07/43	23217	11	132
P	McIntosh George B Jnr.	Lt	POW	20/03/44	231381	81	3415
BT	McLaughlin George B Jr.	S/Sgt	KIA	28/04/44	238061	101	4241
TT	McNeil Charles C	T/Sgt	KIA	09/10/43	230012	37	887
B	McNichol Bernard J	2/Lt	POW	12/08/43	25847	17	660
BT	Medzie Michael J	S/Sgt	POW	03/02/45	2102873	245	12095*
N	Mee William H	Lt	POW	17/08/43	230245	20	381
N	Meehan William R	2/Lt	POW	20/02/44	23562	68	2929
RO	MeHaffey Hubert G	T/Sgt	POW0	2/03/44	239891	73	2738
N	Meier Leonard P	2/Lt	KIA	22/02/44	239895	70	2935
N	Melvin Norman E	F/O	KIA	08/04/45	46173	286	13873
BT	Mendoza Daniel	Sgt	POW	06/03/44	23215	76	3000
RO	Menendez Gil H	S/Sgt	POW	06/11/44	297330	211	10154
BT	Mesler Walter V	S/Sgt	KIA	12/08/43	229950	17	385
TT	Meyer Russell E	S/Sgt	POW	03/03/44	237986	74	2737
LW	Meyer Russell A	Sgt	POW	29/01/44	238045	61	2242
CP	Mickelson Henry B	2/Lt	POW	11/01/44	23514	59	1978
P	Mickow Laurence W	Lt	POW	29/01/44	237884	61	2241
B	Middleton Charles D	S/Sgt	EVD	25/04/44	23511	98	4286
RW	Miller Charles C	S/Sgt	KIA	12/08/43	229950	17	385
TT	Miller Earl F	T/Sgt	POW	08/10/43	230864	36	885
N	Miller Phil R	2/Lt	KIA	11/01/44	237962	59	1876
B	Miller Henry E	F/O	POW	19/05/44	232088	112	5030
RO	Miller Robert E	S/Sgt	KIA	24/05/44	297214	116	5181
TG	Miller Wilfred L	Sgt	POW	20/02/44	23562	68	2929
CP	Mills Edgar J	2/Lt	POW	03/03/44	237986	74	2737
N	Mink John F	2/Lt	RTD	16/03/44	297454	79	4878
B	Miska Manny M	Lt	KIA	09/03/45	339012	265	12960
RW	Miskin John E	S/Sgt	POW	11/01/44	231417	59	1879
B	Mitchell Richard M	2/Lt	KIA	20/12/43	25846	51	1723
BT	Mitchell Stuart R	Sgt	POW	03/02/45	338898	245	12295
TG	Mizell James C	S/Sgt	POW	17/08/43	230140	20	379

LW	Mizer Frank S	Sgt	POW	31/07/44	2102423	163	7742
RO	Moberg Oscar J	S/Sgt	KIA	24/3/45	46478	277	13606
RW	Mogush Paul T	S/Sgt	KIA	01/12/43	231111	46	1659
P	Mohnacky Robert W	Lt	KIA	29/01/44	238045	61	2242
B	Monaco Albert F	2/Lt	POW	11/01/44	237730	59	1877
P	Monohan John J	2/Lt	KIA	30/05/44	238188	121	5234
CP	Mangerpan Joseph L	2/Lt	POW	19/08/43	23101	21	662
CP	Montgomery Otis A	2/Lt	POW	05/01/44	230676	57	1962
BT	Monzingo Garland W	Sgt	KIA	09/03/45	339012	265	12960
P	Moon Theodore I	2/Lt	POW	12/08/43	25847	17	660
RO	Moore Joseph F	T/Sgt	KIA	30/01/44	230029	62	2495
B	Moore Keith D	Lt	POW	08/10/43	229941	36	884
B	Moore Robert V	S/Sgt	KIA	08/10/43	229854	36	1395
RO	Moore Thomas R	T/Sgt	EVD	17/08/43	23225	20	378
P	Moore William R	Lt	POW	25/07/43	230013	12	130
BT	Moorhead James M	S/Sgt	POW	05/08/44	297771	167	7884
B	Morgan John B	2/LT	KIA	09/10/43		37	
TG	Mourning Harold A	Sgt	POW	25/09/44	231570	192	10203
N	Morse Loren C	2/Lt	POW	19/04/44	238004	94	4052
RO	Moses John	S/Sgt	POW	03/03/44	237986	74	2737
RW	Moulton John R	S/Sgt	POW	17/08/43	23225	20	378
LW	Mueller John E	S/Sgt	POW	06/03/44	23215	76	3000
CP	Mulhall Philip E	2/Lt	POW	18/04/44	237733	93	4051
P	Mullane James F	2/Lt	POW	13/04/44	231357	92	3865
RO	Mumper Robert H	T/Sgt	POW	30/03/45	2102590	281	13542
RO	Murkin Ralph K	S/Sgt	POW	06/08/44	46020	168	7882
	Murray Donald B	T/Sgt	KIA	13/07/44	46148	153	
P	Myers Connors C	Lt	KIS				
RO	Myers Edwin R	T/Sgt	EVD	03/09/43	229789	25	473
LW	Nadir Joseph C	T/Sgt	POW	09/10/43	229958	37	886
TG	Nalley Floyd M	Sgt	POW	24/05/44	231698	116	5319
TT	Nance James C	T/Sgt	POW	25/07/43	230153	12	131
	Neal Arthur		KIA	07/04/43			
	Neel Joseph L	Sgt	KIS	23/06/43			
N	Nelf Horace R	2/Lt	POW	11/01/44	23118	59	1943
RW	Nelson Alvin R	Sgt	POW	11/04/44	231497	91	3821
CP	Nelson Earl R	2/Lt	KIA	09/03/45	339012	265	12960
CP	Nelson Robert E	Lt	EVD	17/08/43	230140	20	379
B	Nelson Thomas B	2/L	KIA	08/10/43	23123	36	1396
CP	Nelson Alexander D Jnr.	2/Lt	KIA	30/03/45	2102590	281	13542
LW	Nersinger Raymond G	Sgt	POW	29/01/44	237884	61	2241
RO	Nessely George R	Sgt	POW	03/02/45	2102873	245	12096
B	Neville Edward J	2/Lt	KIA	24/03/44	240008	84	3539
B	Nevius Charles W	2/Lt	INT	24/07/43	23217	11	132
BT	Newcomb Charles W	S/Sgt	INT	24/07/43	23217	11	132
TT	Newman Walter R	T/Sgt	KIA	11/12/44	338780	222	11342
B	Nitikin Nicholas N	2/Lt	POW	11/01/44	229999	59	1880
RO	Nisbet Richard H	S/Sgt	KIA	06/03/44	231553	76	3241
WG	Norcom James F	S/Sgt	KIA	28/03/44	237754	87	
	Norris Harold F	S/Sgt	KIA	04/08/44			
N	Norton Edgar D	2/Lt	POW	08/10/43	229765	36	883
P	Noxon Donald E	2/Lt	KIA	01/12/43	231111	46	1659
CP	Nymeyer John L	2/Lt	POW	24/05/44	238010	116	5178
LW	O'Hara Ernest A	S/Sgt	KIA	09/10/43	230012	37	887
BT	O'Hara James J	S/Sgt	POW	08/10/43	230864	36	885
TG	O.Neal John S	S/Sgt	POW	24/05/44	231291	116	5176
P	O.Black Frank R	Lt	INT	18/07/44	2102663	155	7552
N	O.Phelan Patrick D	2/Lt	POW	13/04/44	231357	93	3865
RW	Oberlin Richard D	S/Sgt	POW	22/06/44	297084	141	5918

TT	Odium Clyde E	S/Sgt	POW	11/01/44	237730	59	1877
BT	Olsen Melvin J	S/Sgt	KIA	08/10/43	229854	36	1395
N	Oneschak Walter	F/O	EVD	24/03/44	231490	84	3538
CP	Opitz James R	2/Lt	KIA	20/12/43	231075	51	1722
RO	Orin George H	S/Sgt	POW	25/07/43	230153	12	131
TG	Osborn Edward F	S/Sgt	KIA	08/10/43	23123	36	1396
BT	Osborne Robert J	S/Sgt	POW	11/01/44	237730	59	1877
P	Owen Jack H	Lt	POW	25/07/43	229976	12	128
RW	Owens Francis E	S/Sgt	KIA	04/07/43	229928	7	161
RW	Owens Harry E	S/Sgt	KIA	24/06/44	2102585	143	6534
	Oxley Raymond		KIA	22/03/45			
RO	Padgett J W	T/Sgt	POW	28 /04/44	238061	101	4241
P	Painter Jack B	Lt	KIA	17/08/43	230140	20	379*
CP	Palmer Edwin W	Lt	POW	05/08/44	297771	167	7884
B	Palmer Philip	2/Lt	KIA	22/02/44	297474	70	2934
RO	Pannaccioni Gildo	S/Sgt	KIA	21/01/45	297511	241	
TG	Paoli Alfred	S/Sgt	INT	21/06/44	238194	140	5992
RO	Parker Albert L Jnr.	T/Sgt	POW	30/07/43	23100	16	129
TT	Parks Paul E	S/Sgt	POW	25/09/434	231570	192	10203
CP	Parsons Robert R	2/Lt	KIA	09/10/43	23180	37	888
N	Peterson Lloyd A	2/Lt	POW	21/06/44	238194	140	5992
LW	Patterson L T	Sgt	POW	11/01/44	237962	59	1876
P	Peak Samual E	Lt	KIA	22/06/44	297084	141	5918
TT	Peanoske John	S/Sgt	POW	20/12 43	25846	51	1723
P	Pearson Jack B	2/Lt	POW	31/07/44	2102423	163	7742
TT	Peck Wesley H	T/Sgt	POW	24/05/44	238010	116	5178
CP	Peeples Henry C	Lt	POW	17/08/43	229978	20	382
P	Pendergist Roy H	Lt	POW	21/06/44	297174	140	5993
BT	Pennybacker Merril L	S/Sgt	POW	19/05/44	297454	112	4932
TT	Perkins Leo I	T/Sgt	POW	19/08/43	23101	21	662
P	Perot Wilfred R	2/Lt	KIA	11/01/44	25878	59	1874
B	Perrin Ross W	2/Lt	KIA	11/12/44	338780	222	11341
BT	Persinger Charles L	S/Sgt	POW	17/08/43	229731	20	663
RO	Peterson Donald E	S/Sgt	KIA	19/04/44	238004	94	4052
B	Petrillo Francis A	Lt	POW	17/08/43	229978	20	382
RW	Phelan John C	Sgt	KIA	12/08/43	229954	17	383
RW	Phelps John	S/Sgt	EVD	24/03/44	231490	84	3538
LW	Philips Thomas W	Sgt	KIA	20/12/43	25846	51	1724
RW	Phillips Norman E	Sgt	POW	22/02/44	132553	70	2931
RO	Phillips Toby B Jnr.	T/Sgt	KIA	10/12 43	231111	46	1659
TT	Pearson Glendon B	S/Sgt	KIA	29/01/44	237884	61	2241
RW	Pillot Victor C	S/Sgt	POW	30/05/44	2102672	121	5233
BT	Pillotti John L	Sgt	KIA	20/06/44	337612	139	5991
TG	Pingel Robert C	Sgt	POW	22/02/44	231698	70	2932
RO	Pinsky David	T/Sgt	POW	17/08/43	23092	20	399
P	Pirtle Thomas A 2/Lt	POW		08/03/44	238029	77	3002
	Piter Andrew	T/Sgt	KIA	23/04/45	338856		
CP	Plemmons Howard M	2/Lt	POW	02/03/44	239891	73	2738
TG	Plows Arthur M	Sgt	KIA	24/03/44	238102	84	
LW	Poch Philip L	S/Sgt	POW	03/02/44	237986	74	2737
BT	Pollard Albert A	S/Sgt	POW	17/08/43	229978	20	382
BT	Poloski Stanley	S/Sgt	POW	19/05/44	232088	112	5030
BT	Poloski Edward F	Sgt	KIA	04/07/44	238117	147	6779
RO	Pope Howard A	T/Sgt	POW	11/01/44	231417	59	1879
TT	Poquette Howard R	T/Sgt	KIA	24/03/44	240008	84	3539
TT	Porter Robert K	Sgt	POW	26/11/44	2106994	217	11205
R	Post Robert F	Maj	POW	30/07/43	23100	16	129
BT	Powell Ralph J	S/Sgt	KIA	30/05/44	2102672	121	5233
CP	Prenatt Charles R	2/Lt	POW	25/09/44	231570	192	10203

BT	Prestwood Harold F	T/Sgt	KIA	11/01/44	237962	59	1876
TT	Prinz Alfred E	Sgt	KIA	03/08/44	232049	165	7883
N	Pritz Stephen J	2/Lt	POW	12/08/43	25847	17	660
CP	Proctor Joe L	2/Lt	POW	31/07/44	2102423	163	7742
CP	Prokopovitz Julian K	2/Lt	KIA	19/06/44	2107088	138	5994
LW	Provonsha William W	S/Sgt	POW	06/03/44	231448	76	3001
BT	Pruiett Cecil A	Sgt	KIA	25/06/43	230027	3	162
P	Pry Jack S	Lt	POW	08/10/43	230009	36	1397
P	Pucylowski Paul C	2/Lt	POW	03/02/45	338898	245	12295
TG	Purnell Walter R	S/Sgt	POW	11/01/44	237730	59	1877
TT	Purser William R	S/Sgt	POW	19/04/44	238004	94	4052
TG	Puryear Roy A	S/Sgt	POW	11/04/44	231497	91	3821
	Quarliariello Angelo	Sgt	KIS	23/04/45	338856		
CP	Quinley Cecil W	2/Lt	POW	08/10/43	230009	36	1397
N	Rabay Nicholas R	2/Lt	POW	20/03/44	231381	81	3415
P/OB	Ragan Everett B	2/Lt	POW	17/08/43	230140	20	379
P	Ramasco Victor R	2/Lt	KIA	24/06/44	2102585	143	6534
TT	Ramos Raoul B	T/Sgt	POW	25/02/44	237786	72	2933
RW	Ramsay John A	Sgt	KIA	03/08/44	232049	165	7883
	Ramsdell Richard B	Sgt	KIA	27/08/44		184	
	Ramsowr Merle L	Cpl	KIS	23/04/45	338856		
N	Randle David E	2/Lt	POW	01/12/43	23540	46	1660
P	Rayburn Robert W	2/Lt	KIA	19/04/44	238004	94	4052
TT	Rector Kenneth K	S/Sgt	POW	25/07/43	229976	12	128
B	Regan George T	2/Lt	POW	11/01/44	23118	59	1943
RO	Regan John F	T/Sgt	POW	01/12/43	23540	46	1660
RO	Reilly William J	T/Sgt	KIA	22/02/44	297474	70	2934
	Reinland Jack B	Lt	KIS	00/11/44			
CP	Remple Robert C	2/Lt	KIA	30/01/44	230029	62	2495
N	Reno Earl L	2/Lt	RTD	30/05/44	240017	121	5385
CP	Rice Roy J	2/Lt	EVD	25/04/44	23511	98	4286
RO	Rich Wesley K	S/Sgt	INT	18/07/44	2102663	155	7552
RW	Rich William	Sgt	INT	18/07/44	2102663	155	7552
BT	Richard Armand R	S/Sgt	KIA	05/11/43	320852	42	1399
N	Richards Richard H	F/O	KIA	19/06/44	2107088	138	5994
RO	Richards Walter L	S/Sgt	KIA	08/10/43	23123	36	1396
P	Rickerson John A	2/Lt	EVD	24/03/44	231490	84	3538
RO	Riddle Lloyd C	T/Sgt	POW	08/10/43	230722	36	1398
TT	Riemann George D	Sgt	POW	20/12/43	23563	51	1721
RW	Rigat James	S/Sgt	KIA	30/01/44	230029	62	2495
N	Riley Richard F	Lt	POW	17/08/43	229731	20	663
LW	Robbins Harold E	Sgt	POW	30/07/43	23100	16	129
CP	Robbins Joseph K	F/O	POW	12/08/43	229950	17	385
B	Roberson William G	2/Lt	POW	14/10/43	229803	39	1037
CP	Roberts William R	2/Lt	POW	22/06/43	230016	1	134
RW	Robinson Harold M	S/Sgt	KIA	04/01/44	231278	56	
CP	Roche Philip R	2/Lt	KIA	24/03/45	46478	277	13606
TG	Rockey Max L	S/Sgt	KIA	22/06/44	297084	141	5918
RO	Rodriguez Abelardo L	S/Sgt	KIA	22/02/44	231696	70	2932
RO	Roe John P	T/Sgt	POW	22/02/44	231443	70	2930
RO	Roeder Robert R	T/Sgt	POW	08/10/43	230864	36	885
TG	Roehl Eugene E	S/Sgt	POW	17/08/43	229731	20	663
CP	Rogers Jack W	2/Lt	POW	17/08/43	230028	20	380
P	Rogers Robert H	2/Lt	POW	03/03/44	237986	74	2737
TG	Rogers Robert P	S/Sgt	KIA	11/12/44	338780	222	11341
N	Rogers Edward J Jr.	2/Lt	KIA	25/06/43	230027	3	162
B	Rokosa Philip V	2/Lt	POW	08/10/43	230722	36	1398
P	Roling Hal E	2/Lt	KIA	22/02/44	239946	70	2936
B	Ronzio Frank	2/Lt	POW	25/07/43	229976	12	128

B	Roraback Douglas C	Lt	POW	17/08/43	230245	20	381
RW	Rose Marshall E	Sgt	POW	24/05/44	239890	116	5179
RO	Rose Russell M	T/Sgt	POW	20/03/44	231381	81	3415
TG	Ross Jack R	S/Sgt	POW	24/05/44	297174	116	5180
BT	Ruark William L	S/Sgt	POW	22/02/44	239946	70	2935
B	Rudisill William P	2/Lt	POW	25/09/44	231570	192	10203
RW	Rush Jacob	S/Sgt	POW	24/05/44	231391	116	5176
BT	Russo Rocco F	Sgt	POW	22/02/44	231696	70	2932
RO	Russolino L A	T/Sgt	KIA	22/03/45	48175	275	
RW	Rutigliano Gerald J	S/Sgt	POW	19/05/44	297454	112	4932
TG	Sabourin Eugene S	S/Sgt	KIA	19/08/43	23101	21	662
RO	Salzeider Herbert S	T/Sgt	POW	21/06/44	297174	140	5993
P	Sample Arthur M	Lt	KIA	08/10/43	229854	36	1395
	Samuelian George	Sgt	KIA	24/05/44		116	
TG	Sanford Loren L	S/Sgt	KIA	30/01/44	231047	62	2243
TT	Sango Nicholas A	S/Sgt	POW	25/ 04/44	23511	98	4286
LW	Sanzone Paul B	Sgt	POW	24/03/44	231490	84	3538
P	Saur Robert V	2/Lt	KIA	11/01/44	237986	59	1876
CP	Scal Richard C	2/Lt	POW	04.03/44	230151	75	2910
TG	Schaaf Carl	S/Sgt	KIA	24/05/44	238010	116	5178
BT	Scharff Robert B	S/Sgt	KIA	22/06/44	297084	141	5918
TG	Schenck Peter	S/Sgt	KIA	29/01/44	238045	61	2242
P	Scherman Paul J	2/Lt	KIA	09/03/45	339012	265	12960
BT	Schiek Earl B	S/Sgt	KIA	22/02/44	231533	70	2931
TG	Schilling Dale E	S/Sgt	KIA	25/02/44	237786	72	2933
CP	Schlintz Paul A	2/Lt	POW	08/03/44	238029	77	3002
RW	Schmidt Theodore E	Sgt	POW	20/06/44	337612	139	5991
LW	Schnalzer John J	S/Sgt	POW	08/10/43	230722	36	1398
N	Schneider Lester W	2/Lt	POW	12/08/43	229954	17	383
TT	Schoepf Jarrett	T/Sgt	POW	19/05/44	297454	112	4932
P	Schomberg Wayne G	Lt	KIS	31/03/44	229751		
P	Schrader Robert K	Lt	KIA	25/06/43	230027	3	162
N	Schuit Richard R	2/Lt	POW	06/03/44	231553	76	3241
LW	Schuitema Edward	S/Sgt	POW	11/01/44	231417	59	1879
TG	Schultz Louis C	Sgt	POW	06/03/44	23215	76	3000
BT	Schulz Elmo R	Sgt	POW	20/12 43	23563	51	1721
BT	Scoggins Grover L	Sgt	KIA	24/06/44	2102585	143	6534
TG	Scollon James B	S/Sgt	KIA	14/07/43	230011	9	133
RW	Scott Wallace K	Sgt	KIA	30/01/44	231047	62	2243
TT	Seabaugh Albert C Jnr.	S/Sgt	POW	06/03/44	23215	76	3000
TT	Sedoryk Harry C	S/Sgt	POW	18/04/44	237733	93	4051
CP	Segman Bernard	2/Lt	POW	21/06/44	231980	140	5990
TG	Sell Edward H	S/Sgt	KIA	28/04/44	238061	101	4241
G	Senk Edward C	T/Sgt	KIA	20/02/44		68	
CP	Settle James R	2/Lt	POW	30/01/44	229761	62	2244
RO	Sexton Frank C	S/Sgt	POW	11/04/44	231497	91	3821
RW	Sexton Mack Jr	S/Sgt	POW	11/01/44	229999	59	1880
TT	Shapiro Morris A	S/Sgt	KIA	21/01/45	297511	241	
P	Sharp Earl	Lt	POW	19/05/44	297454	112	4392
RO	Shattuck Chester E	S/Sgt	POW	17/08/43	23227	20	661
BT	Shaw Allen E	S/Sgt	POW	24/05/44	231291	116	5176
TT	Shelly William D Jr.	S/Sgt	POW	10/09/44	46095	185	8906
CP	Sherwood T Paxton	Lt	POW	13/04/44	231357	92	3865
TT	Shipe Paul F	S/Sgt	POW	17/08/43	23227	20	661
RW	Shorten Christopher J	S/Sgt	POW	06/03/44	231448	76	3001
G	Shott Richard L	S/Sgt	KIA	14/01/45		238	
P	Schultz Eugene	Lt	POW	02/03/44	239891	73	2738
TG	Siders Harry	Sgt	KIA	10/09/44	46095	185	8906
TG	Sieber Arthur J Jr	S/Sgt	POW	08/10/43	229765	36	883

RO	Siedeich John C	S/Sgt	POW	10/09/44	46095	185	8906
RO	Silverberg Charles G	T/Sgt	KIA	09/10/43	229958	37	886
TT	Simmons Murl F	S/Sgt	KIA	22/06/44	297084	141	5918
BT	Simone Theodore R	Sgt	POW	04/03/44	230151	75	2910
B	Simons Ralph R	2/Lt	POW	19/04/44	238004	94	4052
P	Simpson Weldon L	Lt	KIA	17/08/43	230245	20	381
TT	Sinquefield John W	S/Sgt	POW	05/01/44	230676	57	1962
RW	Skrinski Anthony Jr	S/Sgt	POW	06/11/44	297330	211	10154
RO	Slator Roy L	T/Sgt	POW	25/07/43	229976	12	128
TG	Slayton Lowell E	S/Sgt	POW	22/02/44	297474	70	2934
TT	Slomczenski Chester M	T/Sgt	KIA	30/03/45	2102590	281	13542*
TG	Smith Charles F	S/Sgt	POW	02/03/44	239891	73	2738
N	Smith Charles H	2/Lt	KIA	09/10/43	23180	37	888
CP	Smith Charles L	2/Lt	EVD	01/12 43	23540	46	1660
RO	Smith Fred M	S/Sgt	KIA	12/08/43	229954	17	383
P	Smith Harry M	Lt	POW	17/08/43	23220	20	384
BT	Smith Irwin W	S/Sgt	KIA	08/10/43	230009	36	1397
P	Smith James E	Lt	KIA	21/01/45	297511	241	
P	Smith Kyle S	2/Lt	KIA	26/11/44	2106994	217	11205
P	Smith Lee W	Lt	KIA	22/02/44	239895	70	2935
N	Smith Marvin L	Lt	POW	08/10/43	229941	36	884
RO	Smith Peter W	S/Sgt	KIA	06/03/44	23215	76	3000
RW	Smith Richard W	S/Sgt	KIA	08/10/43	230864	36	885
	Smulowitz Louis	Sgt	KIS	23/06/43			
BT	Snyder John S	Sgt	POW	06/03/44	231448	76	3001
B	Snyder Theodore F	2/Lt	POW	08/10/43	230009	36	1397
TG	Snyder Thomas E	S/Sgt	KIA	04/07/44	238117	147	6779
N	Sobole Seymour L	F/O	KIA	21/01/45	297511	241	
TT	Soderstrom Melvin A	T/Sgt	POW	11/01/44	231417	59	1879
P	Soeder Harlan D	Lt	POW	18/04/44	237733	93	4051
RO	Soell George W	S/Sgt	POW	20/12/43	23563	51	1721
B	Soled Milton	2/Lt	KIA	22/02/44	239946	70	2936
N	Soltwedel Edward B	2/Lt	POW	24/05/44	231291	116	5176
RW	Solway Reginald C	Sgt	KIA	22/02/44	239895	70	2935
N	Soper Charles F	2/Lt	KIA	21/01/45	240011	241	
TG	Sorbino Joseph G	S/Sgt	KIA	22/02/44	231533	70	2931
RO	Sornberger Archie W	2/Lt	POW	24/05/44	231291	116	5176
BT	Souder David W	Sgt	EVD	25/04/44	23511	98	4286
RO	Sowell Walter F	S/Sgt	POW	17/08/43	230028	20	380
B	Spaniol Edward J	2/Lt	POW	10/09/44	46095	185	8906
RW	Sparrow Louis F	S/Sgt	POW	13/04/44	231357	92	3865
RO	Spatz Kenneth L	S/Sgt	KIA	13/07/44	46148	153	
N	Spivey Leonard L	Lt	POW	19/08/43	23101	21	662
	Sproha Joseph F	Sgt	KIS	23/06/43			
TG	St Michael Wilfred	S/Sgt	POW	17/08/43	230028	20	380
B	Stahlecker Harry J	2/Lt	KIA	24/03/44	238102	84	
TT	Stahlke Edward A	T/Sgt	POW	13/04/44	231357	92	3865
LW	Starkey Harold G	Sgt	POW	01/12/43	229506	46	1578
BT	Stease Ralph E	S/Sgt	POW	17/08/43	23227	20	661
RW	Stecher Harry L	S/Sgt	POW	17/08/43	229731	20	663
P	Steele Henry D	Lt	POW	30/01/44	229761	62	2244
RW	Stephens T J	Sgt	KIA	24/05/44	231698	116	5319
N	Stern Milton W	2/Lt	POW	08/03/44	238029	77	3002
RW	Stinsman James	S/Sgt	KIA	08/10/43	23123	36	1396
RO	Stoll William M	S/Sgt	KIA	20/06/44	337612	139	5991
B	Stone George J	Capt	KIA	22/03/45	48175	275	13605
BT	Stonich Paul W	S/Sgt	KIA	11/01/44	237719	59	1881
RO	Stowe Minor H	S/Sgt	POW	25/09/44	231570	192	10203
B	Stracotenko John M	2/Lt	POW	17/08/43	230028	20	380

TG	Streich Walter A	Sgt	KIA	21/01/45	240011	241	
BT	Streicher Richard L	Sgt	KIA	04/01/44	231278	56	
P	Stuart Andrew H	2/Lt	POW	27/05/44	2107023	118	5182
RW	Stuart George A	S/Sgt	POW	08/10/43	230722	36	1398
RW	Stubblefield Guy Jr	Sgt	POW	30/03/45	2102590	281	13542
	Stull Paul H Jn	Capt	KIS	31/03/44	229751		
RO	Suchy William K	T/Sgt	POW	19/05/44	297454	112	4932
RW	Suggs Durward V	S/Sgt	POW	11/12/44	338780	222	11341
N	Sullivan Gerald J	2/Lt	KIA	13/07/44	46148	153	
RW	Sussek Walter H	S/Sgt	POW	07/01/44	23078	58	1873
RW	Swackhaner Edward A	S/Sgt	POW	08/10/43	229765	36	883
TG	Swarts Milton S	Sgt	KIA	21/01/45	297511	241	
RO	Sylvester Tony A	S/Sgt	POW	17/08/43	23220	20	384
BT	Tarcynski Thaddeus J	S/Sgt	POW	13/04/44	231357	92	3865
P	Tauro Nicholas F	F/O	KIA	21/01/45	240011	341	
WG	Taylor Allen	Sgt	KIA	21/01/45	297511	241	
	Taylor Fred A	S/Sgt	KIA	14/06/44			
B	Taylor Harold E	2/Lt	POW	03/03/44	237986	74	2737
TG	Taylor Warren G	Sgt	POW	03/03/44	237986	74	2737
TT	Teil Arthur R	Sgt	POW	22/02/44	231696	70	2932
TG	Telzerow Harry R	S/Gt	KIA	24/05/44	297214	116	5181
BT	Terry Floyd H	S/Sgt	EVD	03/09/43	229789	25	473
LW	Thomas Donald H	Sgt	KIA	24/05/44	231989	116	5177
P	Thomas Ralph A	F/O	KIA	04/04/45		283	
TT	Thomas Vivian M	S/Sgt	KIA	14/07/43	23223	9	
LW	Thompson Harry M	S/Sgt	KIA	01/12/43	231111	46	1659
BT	Thompson Jack L	T/Sgt	POW	19/05/44	232088	112	5030
BT	Thompson Logan A	Sgt	KIA	19/06/44	2107088	138	5994
TT	Thompson Asbury M Jr	S/Sgt	KIA	22/02/44	239946	70	2936
BT	Thompson John E Jr	S/Sgt	KIA	01/12/43	231111	46	1659
P	Thomson Thomas P	Lt	KIA	24/03/44	240008	84	3539
BT	Thomson Robert H Jr	Sgt	KIA	24/05/44	231989	116	5177
LW	Thueson Ford W	S/Sgt	POW	17/08/43	23092	20	399
WG	Tieman Ivan J	Sgt	KIA	25/06/43	23221	3	
B	Tietze Lionel N	2/Lt	RTD	16/03/44	297454	79	4878
WG	Toler Richard	S/Sgt	KIA	28/03/44	237754	87	
N	Tomlin Frank E	2/Lt	KIA	08/03/34	23123	36	1396
TT	Trainer Walter R	T/Sgt	KIA	04/01/44	231278	56	
BT	Trapell Robert M	S/Sgt	POW	02/03/44	239891	73	2738
N	Treanor Francis J	2/Lt	INT	18/07/44	2102663	155	7552
TG	Troxler Frank G	S/Sgt	POW	13/04/44	231357	92	3865
RW	True Robert G	S/Sgt	KIA	05/11/43	230854	42	1399
B	Tsialas William G	2/Lt	POW	30/07/43	23100	16	129
BT	Tucker Arthur L	S/Sgt	KIA	08/10/43	229941	36	884
B	Tull Paul E	2/Lt	KIS	23/06/43	229992	2	
LW	Tully John T	Sgt	KIA	30/01/44	230029	62	2495
B	Tully O D	2/Lt	POW	01/12/32	231097	46	1661
RW	Turk Walter H	Sgt	KIA	11/01/44	25878	59	1874
N	Turner William T Jr	Capt	KIA	09/10/43	230012	37	887
N	Tyler Marshall E	2/Lt	POW	05/11/43	230852	42	1399
	Ullman Edward C	Sgt	KIS	23/04/45	338856		
B	Ullom Harry H	2/Lt	POW	07/01/44	23078	58	1873
RO	Unger Maynard W	T/Sgt	POW	17/08/43	229978	20	382
RO	Urban Frank O	S/Sgt	POW	20/02/44	23562	68	2929
RO	Usher Edward W	T/Sgt	POW	25/07/43	230013	12	130
B	Utley Walter A	2/Lt	KIA	01/12/43	231111	46	1659
RO	Valinski John R	S/Sgt	POW	30/05/44	232188	121	5234
N	Van Hise Malcolm J	Lt	KIA	30/01/44	230029	62	2495
TT	Van Voorhis Charles C	Sgt	POW	04/03/44	230151	75	2910

B	Van Buskirk Robert	2/Lt	POW	30/05/44	46025	121	5235
CP	Van Ness Sidney B	2/Lt	POW	11/01/44	237730	59	1877
TT	Vaughn Edward R	T/Sgt	POW	17/08/43	23092	20	399
CP	Vaughn Glenn C	2/Lt	KIA	11/12/44	338780	222	11341
BT	Vaughn John M	S/Sgt	POW	17/08/43	23092	20	399
RO	Vaughn Leland N	S/Sgt	KIA	05/08/44	297771	167	7884
B	Vincent Edward L	Lt	POW	17/08/43	23227	20	661
TG	Vitkus Raymond D	Sgt	EVD	25/04/44	23511	98	4286
TT	Vogelbaugh Robert R	T/Sgt	KIA	30/01/44	230029	62	2495
RO	Vollbrecht Robert F	S/Sgt	POW	11/01/44	23514	59	1978
BT	Wackerman Albert G	S/Sgt	KIA	04/07/43	229928	7	161
TT	Wade Vinal L	T/Sgt	KIA	01/12/43	229506	46	1578
P	Wainwright Clarence D	Lt	KIA	24/05/44	231696	116	5319
RW	Wakefield James E	S/Sgt	POW	17/08/43	23092	20	399
N	Waldman Ralph J	Lt	KIA	04/01/44	231278	56	
TG	Waldow Ernest L	S/Sgt	POW	21/06/44	2102585	143	6534
N	Walker Laurence D	2/Lt	POW	11/01/44	23514	59	1978
B	Walker William G	2/Lt	KIA	05/01/44	230676	57	1962
LW	Walker Ira J Jr	Sgt	KIA	20/12/43	23563	51	1721
CP	Wall Leonard A	2/Lt	POW	03/02/45	2102873	245	12096
RW	Wall Morris A	Sgt	POW	01/12/43	229506	46	1578
RW	Wallace Curtis P	Sgt	POW	03/02/45	2102873	245	12096
CP	Waller David E	2/Lt	KIA	22/02/44	297474	70	2934
BT	Walters Joseph J	S/Sgt	EVD	17/08/43	23225	20	378
B	Ward Joseph C	S/Sgt	POW	06/11/44	297330	211	10154
P	Wardencki John A	Lt	KIA	24/05/44	297214	116	5181
B	Warren Douglas N	2/Lt	KIA	11/01/44	237962	59	1876
RW	Warren James W	S/Sgt	POW	08/03/44	238029	77	3002
TT	Warwick Russell L	T/Sgt	POW	17/08/43	230245	20	381
BT	Waters John F	Sgt	POW	06/11/44	238114	211	10153
B	Watkins Clarence A	2/Lt	POW	12/08/43	229950	17	385
TG	Watkins John M Jr	Sgt	KIA	25/07/43	230013	12	130
CP	Watson William L	2/Lt	KIA	24/05/44	239890	116	5179
TT	Way Clarence N	T/Sgt	POW	03/02/45	338989	245	12295
B	Wear Byron F	S/Sgt	POW	26/11/44	2106994	217	11205
N	Weaver Robert N	2/Lt	KIA	11/01/44	25878	59	1874
P	Webb Allen W	Lt	POW	06/08/44	46020	168	7882
TT	Webb William E	T/Sgt	POW	30/05/44	46025	121	5235
TG	Welch Paul O	Sgt	POW	30/01/44	227961	62	2244
RO	Welke Frank E	S/Sgt	KIA	22/06/44	297084	141	5918
B	Welmsley James A	2/Lt	KIA	13/07/44	46148	153	
N	Wemmer Jack W	2/Lt	POW	25/07/43	230153	12	131
N	Wendell Roy E Jr	2/Lt	POW	29/01/44	237884	61	2241
TG	Weniger Robert L Jr	Lt	POW	08/10/43	230864	36	885
LW	Wheeler John L	Sgt	POW	12/08/43	25847	17	660
LW	Whitman Norman G	S/Sgt	POW	17/08/43	230140	20	379
CP	Widosh Othmer G	2/Lt	POW	30/05/44	46025	121	5235
CP	Wierman John B	2/Lt	POW	06/03/44	23215	76	3000
TT	Wilbur Gerald B	Sgt	POW	24/03/44	231490	84	3538
B	Wilczek Simon J	Sgt	EVD	15/06/44	238009	136	5799
RO	Willdridge John M	T/Sgt	KIA	09/10/43	230012	37	887
TG	Williams Alex	S/Sgt	POW	11/01/44	23118	59	1943
RW	Williams Clarence T	S/Sgt	KIA	28/04/44	238061	101	4241
RO	Williams Durward I	Sgt	POW	24/03/44	231490	84	3538
BT	Williams Paul M	Cpl	POW	24/05/44	239890	116	5179
CP	Williams Robert P	2/Lt	POW	30/01/44	231047	62	2243
RO	Williams Walter R	S/Sgt	EVD	25/04/44	23511	98	4286
CP	Willis John W Jr	2/Lt	POW	03/09/43	229789	25	473
P	Wilson Arden D	2/Lt	POW	07/01/44	23078	58	1873

RO	Wilson Carroll W	T/Sgt	RTD	16/03/44	297454	79	4878
CP	Wilson Donald M	2/Lt	EVD	24/03/44	231490	84	3538
CP	Wilson Francis E	2/Lt	POW	11/01/44	23118	59	1943
BT	Wilson James E	S/Sgt	POW	30/05/44	46025	121	5235
BT	Wilson Joseph S	S/Sgt	POW	21/06/44	297174	140	5993
B	Wilson William O	2/Lt	POW	24/05/44	238010	116	5178
	Wilton Charles H	S/Sgt	KIS	23/06/43			
BT	Winn Charles K	S/Sgt	POW	25/07/43	229976	12	128
TT	Wise Gordon W	S/Sgt	KIA	19/06/44	2107088	138	5994
CP	Withers Robert L	Capt	KIA	09/10/43	230012	37	887
BT	Wittmer Weldon E	Sgt	POW	11/01/44	229999	59	1880
N	Wonning Earl H	2/Lt	KIA	25/02/44	237786	72	2933
TG	Wood Howard F	Sgt	POW	12/08/43	25847	17	660
TG	Woodyatt Richard E	S/Sgt	KIA	05/11/43	230852	42	1399
BT	Workman Ralph J	Sgt	EVD	15/06/44	238009	136	5799
P	Wright Neil H	2/Lt	POW	17/08/43	230028	20	380
TT	Wright Oscar S	S/Sgt	KIA	24/05/44	239890	116	5179
N	Wright Phelom T	2/Lt	EVD	11/02/44	231099	67	2431
BT	Wright Stanley A	S/Sgt	KIA	11/01/44	231417	59	1879
P	Wroblicka William	Lt	POW	12/08/43	229954	17	383
TT	Wydra Carl S	Sgt	POW	11/01/44	23514	59	1978
N	Yake William J	2/Lt	KIA	29/01/44	238045	61	2242
LW	Yanzek William J	T/Sgt	RTD	16/03/44	297454	79	4878
RO	Yarnell William W	T/Sgt	KIA	25/06/43	230027	3	162
CP	Yarnes Harry M	F/O	POW	03/02/45	338898	245	12295
TT	Yates Howard R	T/Sgt	RTD	30/05/4	240017	121	5385
P	Yorba Bernarde M Jr	2/Lt	POW	14/10/43	229803	39	1037
WG	York John P	Sgt	KIA	21/01/45	297511	241	
BT	Zahn Edgerton P	S/Sgt	POW	25/07/43	230013	12	130
P	Zapinski Leonard P	Lt	POW	30/05/44	46025	121	5235
RO	Zappala John W	T/Sgt	KIA	22/02/44	239895	70	2935
B	Zickterman A E	S/Sgt	POW	03/02/45	338898	245	12295
P	Zum Benjamin J	2/Lt	POW	03/09/43	229789	25	473

Appendix D:

381 BG MISSION LIST (Credited Sorties)

1943

Date	Briefed Target	Target-Category	Remarks
22 June	Antwerp, Belgium	Aviation Industry	
23 June	St.Martin-Bernay, France	Airfield	Mission recalled
25 June	Hamburg, Germany	Aircraft Factory	Target of Opportunity bombed
26 June	Villacoubley, France	Airfield	Mission aborted (weather)
28 June	St. Nazaire, France	Harbour Installations	
29 June	Triqueville, France	Airfield	Mission aborted (weather)
4 July	Le Mans, France	Airfield	-
10 July	Villacoubley France	Airfield	-
14 July	Amiens-Glissey, France	Airfield	-
17 July	Hannover, Germany	Railroad Installations	Mission recalled (weather)
24 July	Heroya, Norway	Aluminum Plant	-
25 July	Hamburg	U-Boat Construction Yards	Target of Opportunity struck
26 July	Hamburg, Germany	U-Boat Construction Yards	-
28 July	Kassel, Germany	Aircraft Plant	Mission aborted (weather)
29 July	Kiel	Ship Construction Yards	-
30 July	Kassel, Germany	Aircraft Plant	-
12 August	Gelsenkirchen, Germany	Oil Production Plant	-
15 August	Brussels, Belgium	Airfield	-
16 August	Le Bourget, Franc	Airfield	-
17 August	Schweinfurt, Germany	Ball-bearing Plant	-
19 August	Gilze-Rijen, the Netherlands	Airfield	-
24 August	Villacoubley, France	Airfield	-
27 August	Watton, France	V-weapons Site	-
31 August	Amiens-Glissey, France	Airfield	-
3 September	Romilly-sur-Seine, France	Airfield	-
6 September	Stuttgart, Germany	Ball-bearing Production Plant	-
7 September	Brussels/Evere	Airfield	-
9 September	Lille, France	Airfield (Lille/Nord)	-
15 September	Romilly-sur-Seine,France	Airfield	-
16 September	Nantes, France	Airfield (Chateau/ Bougon)	-
23 September	Nantes, France	Port Area for Shipping	
26 September	Paris, France	Industrial Plant	Mission aborted (weather)
27 September	Emden, Germany	Industrial Areas	-
2 October	Emden, Germany	Industrial Areas	-
4 October	Frankfurt, Germany	Industrial Areas	-
8 October	Bremen, Germany	Ship-construction Yards	-
9 October	Anklam, Germany	Aircraft Plant	-

10 October	Münster, Germany	Railroad Facilities	-
14 October	Schweinfurt, Germany	Ball-bearing Plant	-
20 October	Düren, Germany	Industrial Areas	Target of Opportunity struck
3 November	Wilhelmshaven, Germany	Port Areas for Shipping	-
5 November	Gelsenkirchen, Germany	Oil Refinery	-
7 November	Wesel, Germany	Industrial Areas	Mission aborted (weather)
16 November	Knaben, Norway	Molybedum Mines	-
26 November	Bremen, Germany	Industrial Areas	-
1 December	Leverkusen, Germany	Industrial Areas	-
5 December	Paris, France	Airfield	
11 December	Emden, Germany	Industrial Areas	-
13 December	Bremen, Germany	Port Area for Shipping	-
16 December	Bremen, Germany	Port Area for Shipping	-
20 December	Bremen, Germany	Port Area for Shipping	-
22 December	Osnabrück, Germany	Communications Centres	
24 December	Cocove, France	V-weapon Sites	-
30 December	Ludwigshafen, Germany	Oil Refinery	-
31 December	Bordeaux/Merignac, France Airfield	Chateaubernard A/F (S) hit	

1944

4 January	Kiel, Germany	Port Area for Shipping	-
5 January	Tours, France	Airfield	-
7 January	Ludwigshafen, Germany	Industrial Areas	-
11 January	Oschersleben, Germany	Aircraft Plant	-
21 January	Belleville-en-Caux, France	V-weapons Site	-
29 January	Frankfurt, Germany	Industrial Areas	-
30 January	Brunswick, Germany	Aircraft Plant	City Centre (S) bombed
3 February	Wilhelmshaven, Germany	Port Areas for Shipping	
4 February	Frankfurt, Germany	Marshalling- Yards	Target of Opportunity hit
5 February	St. Avord, France	Airfield	-
6 February	Nancy/Essay, France	Airfield	-
11 February	Frankfurt, Germany	Industrial Areas	Ludwigshafen (S) hit
20 February	Leipzig and Oschersleben, Germany	Aircraft Plants	-
21 February	Gutersloh, Germany	Airfield	Secondary (Achmer Airfield) hit
22 February	Oscherswleben, Germany	Aircraft Plant	Target of Opp. (Bunde) hit
24 February	Schweinfurt, Germany	Ball-bearing Plant	-
25 February	Augsburg, Germany	Aircraft Plant	-
2 March	Frankfurt, Germany	Marshalling-Yards	-
3 March	Berlin, Germany	Industrial Areas	Wilhelmshaven (O) hit
4 March	Berlin, Germany	Industrial Areas	Target of Opportunity (Rühr) hit
6 March	Berlin, Germany	Ball-bearing Plant	Target of Opportunity hit
8 March	Berlin, Germany	Ball-bearing Plant	-
9 March	Berlin, Germany	Industrial Areas	Secondary hit
16 March	Augsburg, Germany	Industrial Areas	-
18 March	Oberpfaffenhofen, Germany	Airfield	-
20 March	Mannheim, Germany	Industrial Areas	-
22 March	Berlin, Germany	Aircraft Plant	Secondary hit
23 March	Hamm, Germany	Industrial Areas	Ahlen (O) hit
24 March	Schweinfurt, Germany	Ball-bearing Plant	Frankfurt (S) hit
26 March	Marquise/Mimoyecques, France	V-weapons Site	
27 March	St Jean D'Angely, France	Airfield	-
28 March	Rheims/Champagne, France	Airfield	-
29 March	Waggum, Germany	Industrial Plant	Brunswick (S) hit
8 April	Oldenburg, Germany	Airfield	
10 April	Brussels and Woensdrecht, Belgium	Airfields	-
11 April	Cottbus and Sorau, Germany	Aircraft Plants	-
13 April	Schweinfurt, Germany	Ball-bearing Plant	-
18 April	Oranienburg, Germany	Aircraft Plant	-
19 April	Eschwege, Germany	Airfield	-

20 April	Croisette and LePlauy Ferme, France	V-weapons Sites	
22 April	Hamm, Germany	Marshalling-Yards	
24 April	Erding, Germany	Air depot	-
25 April	Metz/Frescaty, France	Airfield	-
26 April	Brunswick, Germany	Aircraft Plant	-
27 April	LaGlacerie, France	V-weapons Site	-
28 April	St. Avord, France	Airfield	-
29 April	Berlin, Germany	Industrial Areas	-
30 April	Lyon/Bron, France	Airfield	-
1 May	Troyes, France	Marshalling-Yards	-
6 May	LaGlacerie, France	V-weapons-Site -	
7 May	Berlin, Germany	Industrial Areas	-
8 May	Berlin, Germany	Industrial Areas	-
8 May	St Dizier,France	Airfield	-
11 May	Saarbrucken,Germany	Marshalling-Yard	Bettembourg (O), Thionville (S) hit
12 May	Lutzkendorf, Germany	Oil Refinery	-
13 May	Western Poland	Oil refineries	Stettin (O) and Stralsund (O) hit
19 May	Berlin, Germany	Industrial Areas	-
20 May	Villacoubley, France	Airfield	-
22 May	Kiel, Germany	Port Areas for Shipping	-
23 May	Saarbrüken, Germany	Target of Opportunity (Homberg) hit	
24 May	Berlin, Germany	Industrial Areas	-
25 May	Nancy/Essey, France	Airfield	-
27 May	Ludwigshafen, Germany	Marshalling-Yard	-
28 May	Central Germany	Oil refinery	Frankfurt (O) and Brandis/Polenz (O) hit
29 May	Posen, Poland	Aircraft Plant	-
30 May	Dessau, Germany	Aircraft Plant	-
31 May	Mulhouse, France	Railroads	Florennes Airfield (O) hit
2 June	Massy-Palaiseau, France	Railroads	-
3 June	Pas de Calais, France	V-weapons Site	-
4 June	Pas de Calais, France	Coastal Defences	-
5 June	Pas de Calais, France	Coastal defences	-
6 June	Vers-sur-Mer, France	Coastal Defences	-
6 June	Courselles, France	Coastal defences	-
7 June	Kerlin/Bastard, France	Airfield	-
8 June	La Frilliere, France	V-weapons Site	-
10 June	Hardelot, France	Military Installations	-
11 June	Beaumont-le-Roger, France	Airfield	-
12 June	Lille, France	Airfield (Lille/Nord)	-
14 June	Melun, Belgium	Airfield (Melun/Villaroche)	-
15 June	Bordeaux, France	Airfield (Bordeaux/Merignac)	-
18 June	Hamburg, Germany	Oil Refinery	-
19 June	Bordeaux, France	Airfield (Bordeaux/Merignac)	-
20 June	Hamburg, Germany	Oil Refinery	-
21 June	Berlin, Germany	Industrial Areas	-
22 June	Pas de Calais, France	V-weapons Site	-
23 June	Bachimont, France	V-weapons Site	-
24 June	Tours, France	Airfield (Tours/La Riche)	-
25 June	Toulouse, France	Airfield (Toulouse/Francazal)	-
28 June	Fismes, France	Bridge	-
4 July	Tactical Targets, France	Tours/La Riche Airfield (O) hit	-
6 July	Rely (Pas de Calais), France	V-weapons Site	-
7 July	Leipzig, Germany	Leipzig/Mockau Oil Refinery	-
8 July	Couvronne/Rely (Pas de Calais), France	V-weapons sites	-
9 July	Tactical Targets, France	St Omer Airfield (O) hit	-
11 July	Munich, Germany	Marshalling-Yard	-
12 July	Munich, Germany	Industrial Areas	-
13 July	Munich, Germany	Industrial Areas	Factory Complex (O) hit
16 July	Munich, Germany	Aircraft-engine Plant	-

16 July	Augsburg, Germany	Aircraft Plant	-
18 July	Peenemunde, Germany	Luftwaffe Research Establishment	-
19 July	Lechfeld, Germany	Airfield	-
20 July	Dessau, Germany	Aircraft-engine Plant	-
21 July	Schweinfurt, Germany	Ball-bearings Plant	-
24 July	St. Lo, France	Support for 1st. US Army Advance	-
25 July	St. Lo, France	Support for 1st. US Army Advance	-
28 July	Merseburg/Leuna, Germany	Oil Refinery	-
29 July	Merseburg/Leuna, Germany	Oil refinery	-
31 July	Munich, Germany	Industrial Areas	-
1 August	Melun, France	Airfield (Melun/Villaroche)	-
	Etampas, France	Etampes/Mondesir Airfield (O) hit	-
3 August	Mulhouse, France	Marshalling-Yard	-
4 August	Peenemunde, Germany	Luftwaffe Research Establishment	-
5 August	Nienburg, Germany	Oil-storage Depot	-
6 August	Brandenburg, Germany	Aircraft Plant	-
7 August	St. Florentin and Marlotte, France	Oil-storage Depots	-
8 August	Cauvincourt, France	German Troop Concentrations	-
9 August	Saarbrücken, Germany	Marshalling-Yard	-
11 August	Brest, France	German Troop Concentrations	-
13 August	Ruoen, France	Road Junctions	-
14 August	Metz, France	Airfield (Metz/Frescaty)	-
15 August	Ostheim, Germany	Airfield	-
16 August	Halle, Germany	Aircraft Plant	-
24 August	Weimar, Germany	Armament Plant	-
25 August	Neubrandenburg	Aircraft-assembly Plant	-
26 August	Gelsenkirchen, Germany	Oil refinery	-
27 August	Berlin, Germany	Industrial Areas	Marshalling-Yards at Emden (O) hit
30 August	Kiel, Germany	Port Areas for Shipping	-
3 September	Ludwigshafen, Germany	Opau Oil Refinery	-
8 September	Ludwigshafen, Germany	Opau Oil Refinery	-
9 September	Mannheim, Germany	Marshalling-Yard	-
10 September	Gaggenau, Germany	Motor Transport Plant	-
11 September	Merseburg, Germany	Oil Refinery	-
12 September	Brux, Czechoslovakia	Oil refinery	-
17 September	Eindhoven, the Netherlands	German Ground Defences	-
19 September	Hamm, Germany	Marshalling-Yard	-
21 September	Mainz, Germany	Marshalling-Yard	
22 September	Kassel, Germany	Armoured Vehicle Plant	-
25 September	Frankfurt, Germany	Marshalling-Yard	Industrial Areas (S) hit
26 September	Osnabrück, Germany	Marshalling-Yard	-
27 September	Cologne, Germany	Railroad Facilities	-
28 September	Magdeburg, Germany	Oil Refinery	Industrial Areas (O) hit
2 October	Kassel, Germany	Ordnance Plant	-
5 October	Cologne, Germany	Industrial Areas	-
6 October	Pölitz, Germany	Oil refinery	Stralsund (O) hit
7 October	Pölitz/Ruhland, Germany	Oil Refineries	Zwickau (O) hit
9 October	Schweinfurt, Germany	Ball-bearings Plant	-
14 October	Cologne, Germany	Marshalling-Yard (Cologne/Gereon)	-
15 October	Cologne, Germany	Marshalling-Yard (Cologne/Nippes)	-
17 October	Cologne, Germany	Marshalling-Yard (Cologne/Gremburg)	-
19 October	Mannheim, Germany	Industrial Areas	-
25 October	Hamburg, Germany	Oil Refinery (Hamburg/Rhenania)	-
26 October	Bielefeld, Germany	Road/Rail Communications	-
28 October	Münster, Germany	Marshalling-Yard	-
30 October	Gelsenkirchen, Germany	Oil Refinery	Hamm M/Y (S) hit 4 November
Hamburg, Germany	Oil Refinery (Hamburg/Harburg)	-	
5 November	Frankfurt, Germany	Marshalling-Yard	-
6 November	Hamburg, Germany	Oil Refinery (Hamburg/Harburg)	-

9 November	Metz, France	Transportation Targets	-
10 November	Cologne, Germany	Airfield (Butzweilerhof)	-
16 November	Eschweiler, Germany	German Ground Defences	-
21 November	Merseburg, Germany	Oil Refinery	Friedburg (0) hit
25 November	Merseburg, Germany	Oil refinery (Merseburg/Leuna)	-
26 November	Altenbecken, Germany	Railroad Viaduct	-
29 November	Misburg, Germany	Oil Refinery	-
30 November	Zeitz, Germany	Oil refinery	-
4 December	Soest, Germany	Marshalling-Yard	-
9 December	Stuttgart, Germany	Marshalling-Yard	-
11 December	Mannheim, Germany	Bridges	-
12 December	Merseburg, Germany	Oil Refinery (Merseburg/Leuna)	-
15 December	Kassel, Germany	Marshalling-Yard	-
18 December	Cologne, Germany	Marshalling-Yard (Cologne/Kalk)	-
24 December	Ettinghausen and Kirchgons, Germany	Airfields	-
28 December	Remagen, Germany	Rhine Railroad Bridge	-
30 December	Mainz,Germany	Marshalling-Yard	-
31 December	Prum, Germany	Communications Center	-
1945			
1 January	Kassel, Germany	Marshalling-Yard	
	Koblenz, Germany	City (O) hit	
2 January	Gerolstein, Germany	Marshalling-Yard	-
3 January	Cologne, Germany	Marshalling-Yard	-
5 January	Heimbach, Germany	Railroad Center	-
6 January	Cologne, Germany	Railroad/Road Bridges	-
8 January	Alzey, Germany	Railroad/Road Bridges	-
10 January	Cologne, Germany	Airfield (Cologne/Ostheim)	-
13 January	Germersheim,Germany	Railroad Bridge	-
14 January	Rodenkirchen, Germany	Road Bridge	-
17 January	Paderborn, Germany	Marshalling-Yard	-
20 January	Mannheim, Germany	Railroad/Road bridges	-
21 January	Aschaffenburg, Germany	Marshalling-Yard	-
28 January	Cologne, Germany	Marshalling-Yards	Gutersloh Airfield (S) hit
29 January	Niederlahnstein, Germany	Railroad Center	-
1 February	Mannheim, Germany	Marshalling-Yard	-
3 February	Berlin, Germany	Marshalling-Yard (Berlin/Tempelhof)	-
6 February	Gotha, Germany	Aircraft Plant	Ohrdruf (O) hit
9 February	Arnsberg, Gremany	Railroad Viaduct	-
14 February	Dresden, Germany	Marshalling-Yard	Brux,Czechoslovakia (O) hit
15 February	Ruhland, Germany	Oil refinery	Dresden (O) hit
16 February	Gelsenkirchen, Germany	Oil refinery	Langendreer (O) hit
19 February	Dortmund, Germany	Oil Refinery (Dortmund/Hoesch)	-
20 February	Nüremburg, Germany	Marshalling-Yard	-
21 February	Nüremburg, Germany	Marshalling-Yard	-
22 February	Stendal, Germany	Railroad/RoadCommunications	Kobbelitz (O) hit
23 February	Plauen, Germany	Marshalling-Yard	Meiningen (O) hit
24 February	Hamburg, Germany	Oil refinery (Hamburg/Harburg)	
25 February	Munich, Germany	Railroad station/Marshalling-Yard	-
26 February	Berlin, Germany	Railroad station (Schlesischer)	-
27 February	Leipzig, Germany	Communictions Center	-
1 March	Neckarsulm, Germany	Marshalling-Yard	-
2 March	Ruhland Germany	Oil refinery	Chemnitz (S) hit
4 March	Ulm,Germany	Munitions Depot	-
5 March	Ruhland, Germany	Oil Refinery	Chemnitz (S) and Plauen (O) hit
8 March	Hüls, Germany	Oil Refinery (Hüls/ August Viktoria)	-
9 March	Kassel, Germany	Marshalling-Yard	-
10 March	Sinsen, Germany	Railroad Communications	-
11 March	Bremen, Germany	U-boat Yard (Bremen/Deschimag)	-

12 March	Dillenburg, Germany	Marshalling-Yard	-
14 March	Vlotho, Germany	Railroad/Road Bridges	-
15 March	Oranienburg, Germany	Marshalling-Yard	-
17 March	Böhlen, Germany	Oil Refinery	Jena Zeiss Plant (S) also hit
18 March	Berlin, Germany	Railroad Station (Schlesischer)	-
19 March	Unknown (Germany)	Unknown	Plauen (S) hit
21 March	Rheine, Gremany	Airfield	-
22 March	Dorsten and Feldhausen, Germany	Military Encampments	-
23 March	Coesfeld, Germany	Marshalling-Yard	-
24 March	Vechta, Germany	Airfield	-
24 March	Twente, Netherlands	Airfield (Twente/Enschede)	-
26 March	Zeitz, Germany	Oil Refinery	-
28 March	Berlin, Germany	Munitions Plant (Berlin/Spandau)	-
30 March	Bremen, Germany	U-boat Yard	-
31 March	Merseburg?, Germany	Oil Refinery	Halle Marshalling-Yard (S) hit
4 April	Fassberg, Germany	Airfield	Hoya Airfield (S) hit
5 April	Grafenwöhr, Germany	Munitions Dump	-
7 April	Kohlenbissen, Germany	Airfield	-
8 April	Derben, Germany	Oil Dump	Stendal Marshalling-Yard (S) hit
9 April	Oberpfaffenhofen, Germany	Airfield	-
10 April	Oranienburg, Germany	Oil Dump	-
11 April	Freihan, Germany	Oil Dump	-
13 April	Neumünster, Germany	Marshalling-Yard	-
15 April	Soulac-sur-Mer, France	Gun Batteries	-
16 April	Regensburg, Germany	Railroad Bridge	-
17 April	Dresden, Germany	Marshalling-Yard	-
19 April	Elsterwerda and Falkenburg, Germany	Marshalling-Yards	-
20 April	Brandenburg, Germany	Marshalling-Yard	-
21 April	Munich, Germany	Marshalling-Yard	-
25 April	Pilsen, Czechoslovakia	Munitions Plant	-

Appendix E:

ABBREVIATIONS

AA	Anti-aircraft/Flak
AF	Air Field
AFSC	Air Force Service Command
AI	B-17 added to Air Force Inventory
AOS	B-17 Arrived Overseas
BG	Bombardment Group
CAM	Camoflage
CCRC	Combat Crew Replacement Center
CF	Caught Fire
CL	Crash-landed, pilot (s) had control
CR	Crashed, little or no control by pilot (s)
CTO	Crashed on take-off
DIT	Ditched
E & E	Escape and Evasion Report, National Archives, Report Group 332
EVD	Evaded capture/escaped from prison
EX	Exploded
FTR	Failed to Return
FTRINT	Failed to Return, Aircraft and/or Crew interned in Neutral Country
FTRLOC	Failed to Return, Aircraft and/or crew Landed on Continent behind the Allied Lines
FUEL	Ran out of fuel
G	Gained
GF	German Fighter
GMU	Group Maintenance Unit
GSE	German Single-engined Fighter
INT	Interned
KIA	Killed in Action
KIS	Killed in Service – Non-combat
LAND	Landing accident at Ridgewell, unless otherwise stated
MACR	Missing Air Crew Report, National Archives, Report Group 92
MECH	Mechanical
MID	Mid-air Collision
MRU	Mobile Repair Unit
MTO	Mediterranean Theater of Operations
NASA	National Air and Space Museum, Black and White Photgraph Number.
NASB	National Air and space Museum, Color Photograph Number
NMF	Natural Metal Finish
POW	Prisoner of War
RAF	Royal Air Force
RG	Regained
RTB	Returned to Base
RTD	Returned to Duty
RZOI	Remained in Zone of the Interior (U.S.)
SAL	Salvaged
TAXI	Taxi accident at Ridgewell, unless otherwise stated

ZOI	Zone of the Interior (U.S.)
1SF	1st Scouting Force
2SAD	2nd Strategic Air depot, AF Little Staughton and AF Abbotts Ripton
BAD1	Base Air Depot #1, Burtonwood
8AF	Eighth Air Force
8FC	Eighth Fighter Command
15AF	Fifteenth Air Force
?	Information Unknown
(?)	Information cannot be confirmed